SIXTH EDITION

Business and Government in the Global Marketplace

Murray L. Weidenbaum

Chairman,
Center for the Study of American Business
Washington University
St. Louis, MO

Prentice Hall
Upper Saddle River, New Jersey

Acquisitions Editor: Rod Banister
Editorial Assistant: William Becher
Editorial Director: James C. Boyd
Marketing Manager: Patrick Lynch
Production Editor: Evyan Jengo
Managing Editor: Dee Josephson
Manufacturing Buyer: Diane Peirano
Manufacturing Supervisor: Arnold Vila
Manufacturing Manager: Vincent Scelta
Cover Design: Jayne Conte
Composition: Digitype

Copyright ©1999, 1995, 1990, 1986, 1981 by Prentice Hall, Inc.
Upper Saddle River, New Jersey 07458

Library of Congress Cataloging-in-Publication Data

Weidenbaum, Murray L.
   Business and government in the global marketplace / Murray L. Weidenbaum. — 6th ed.
      p.   cm.
   Includes bibliographical references and index.
   ISBN 0-13-080625-0
   1. Industrial policy — United States.   2. Trade regulation — United States.   I. Title.
HD3616.U47W368   1998   98-2993
338.973 — dc21   CIP

Prentice-Hall International (UK) Limited, London
Prentice-Hall of Australia Pty. Limited, Sydney
Prentice-Hall Canada, Inc., Toronto
Prentice-Hall Hispanoamericana, S.A., Mexico
Prentice-Hall of India Private Limited, New Delhi
Prentice-Hall of Japan, Inc., Tokyo
Prentice-Hall Asia Pte. Ltd., Singapore
Editora Prentice-Hall do Brasil, Ltda., Rio de Janeiro

Printed in the United States of America

10 9 8 7 6 5 4

Brief Contents

PART SIX: THE FUTURE OF THE CORPORATION

Contents

Preface

Public policy—especially as shaped by a host of government and interest group inter-actions—is a pervasive influence on the business firm. This book analyzes both sides of that relationship, covering the ways in which government policy affects the activi-ties of the modern corporation and the key responses on the part of business.

The purpose of this book is not to indoctrinate the student but to provide a bet-ter understanding of the intricate relationship between the public and private sec-tors—why and how government intervenes in the economy and how business can re-spond. Thus, quite deliberately, this book does not present an all-embracing theoretical framework to guide the student to the author's personal view of the opti-mum public policy and the appropriate private response. It is hoped that the tools for that search are provided here, and instructors are free to provide their preferred guid-ance to the student reader.

This sixth edition represents a special effort to meet the changing needs and de-sires of the two main sets of users: students and faculty in schools of business and de-partments of economics. As someone who teaches both MBA students and upper level undergraduate economic students, I have tried out preliminary versions on both groups of students and have benefited from their reaction. Thus, this edition simulta-neously adds some necessary economic and policy analysis and eliminates older mate-rial that has become less relevant.

Part One, the shortest section of the book, is an overview of the tools that gov-ernment has available to influence business decision making. Part Two covers the field of government regulation in both the social and economic areas. Changes have been made to reflect a host of recent developments in public policy.

Part Three begins with a revised chapter on business and government in the in-ternational economy. The following two chapters include a substantial amount of new material and draw heavily on the author's recent research in this area.

Part Four brings together three ways in which government can assist business: tax policy, credit policy, and providing a market for the products of business. The chapter on tax policy has a new section on the flat tax and other tax reform proposals. The chapter on government as a market has been substantially rewritten to reflect the reorientation of government programs to civilian needs.

Part Five deals with the key responses of business to government influence. Each chapter has been updated to cover recent developments.

Part Six contains a revised chapter on corporate governance. In the last chapter, which focuses on the future of the corporation, an effort is made to identify the coming changes in government policies affecting private business.

As in the previous editions, the focus of this book is on the future practitioner—the business executive who will be dealing with issues of public policy as a day-to-day aspect of the job. Also, it is hoped that this book will assist present and future government officials and members of interest groups to better appreciate the various consequences of their actions on the business system.

The preparation of this book was supported in part by the Center for the Study of American Business. The author is indebted to Dino Falaschetti, Chris Hollenbeak, Will Lauber, and Michael Orlando for extremely helpful research assistance. I would like to thank the reviewers who supplied productive feedback on the sixth edition: Claire Hammond, of Wake Forest University, and David Lehr, of Indiana University. As she has in the past, Christine Moseley carefully typed the various drafts and helped ready the manuscript for publication.

I am particularly grateful to my wife, Phyllis, for once again providing me with the extra time to work on this book by taking on an extraordinary share of our joint responsibilities.

Murray L. Weidenbaum
Washington University

About the Author

Murray L. Weidenbaum is one of America's most widely quoted academics. He holds the Mallinckrodt Distinguished University of Professorship at Washington University in St. Louis, where he also serves as chairman of the university's highly regarded Center for the Study of American Business. For 25 years, he has been teaching a popular course on business and government.

In 1981–1982, Dr. Weidenbaum served as President Reagan's first Chairman of the Council of Economic Advisers. In that capacity, he played a major role in formulating the economic policy of the Reagan Administration and was a major spokesman for the Administration on economic and business issues, both domestic and international.

Dr. Weidenbaum has held a variety of business, government, and academic positions. He was the first Assistant Secretary of the Treasury for Economic Policy and served earlier as Fiscal Economist in the U.S. Bureau of the Budget and as Corporate Economist at the Boeing Company. He is a member of the board of directors of the May Department Stores Company, Tesoro Petroleum, Harbour Group, and Macroeconomic Advisers.

Dr. Weidenbaum is known for his research on business–government issues, taxes, government spending, and regulation. He is the author of seven books and has written several hundred articles in publications ranging from the *American Economic Review* to the *New York Times*. He also regularly prepares a column for the *Christian Science Monitor*.

Dr. Weidenbaum received his Ph.D. from Princeton University. He has received the Distinguished Writers Award from the Center for Strategic and International Studies, the Alexander Hamilton Medal "in recognition of distinguished leadership in the Department of the Treasury," the Leavey Prize for excellence in private enterprise education from the Freedoms Foundation, and the Adam Smith Award from the Association of Private Enterprise Education. In 1992, the Association of American Publishers honored Dr. Weidenbaum as author of the economics book of the year. In 1997, he was a finalist in the global competition for business book of the year.

PART ONE

Setting the Framework

A central issue facing a contemporary society is how to deal constructively with the dynamic tension between the public and private sectors. This uneasy relationship is evidenced by the continuing interaction between government and business, where government, on occasion, is both the unwelcome regulator and the most welcome customer, and business is simultaneously the suspicious recipient of subsidy and the mechanism for carrying out important activities of the society.

With the end of the Cold War, the locus of economic decision-making power has shifted, literally, from superpowers to supermarkets. The foremost challenge now is how to harness the innovative power and motivating incentive of the business enterprise in order to achieve the well-being of the overall society of which it is a key part—without weakening those positive and unique characteristics of business.

Surely there is no invariant set of answers suitable for all circumstances. Grappling with these issues is the continuing responsibility of decision makers in both the public and private sectors. Meanwhile, it is helpful to raise the information level available and to improve the techniques for analyzing and evaluating these issues. That is the task that we now embark on.

The substantial arsenal of power that resides in the public sector of a modern society generates numerous changes in the complex relationships between business and government. Part I examines the instruments through which that power is exerted. Such basic knowledge is essential to understand the impacts of government on business and to evaluate the responses of business, which are the tasks of the later parts of this book.

CHAPTER I

The Powers of Government and Business

The chairman of the board of Globally Diversified Enterprises (GDE) has just summoned the board's secretary (a bright, young MBA fresh from a tour of duty with the International Chamber of Commerce). The purpose of the meeting is to review the agenda for the upcoming meeting of the company's board of directors.

PREPARING FOR THE BOARD MEETING OF GLOBALLY DIVERSIFIED ENTERPRISES

Aside from the usual committee reports—audit, finance, executive compensation, and governance—the GDE board meeting will focus on the chairman's quarterly review of operations. The current year is progressing better than the previous one but is falling substantially short of the objectives set at the board's summer planning meeting. A longer-than-usual list of problems has arisen that the chairman wants to discuss with the board.

- The Industrial Machinery Division is behind schedule on its new factory. The division president is flying in from his headquarters in Frankfurt to explain the unexpected changes in the European Union's approval procedures.
- The Consumer Products Division has been turned down again by U.S. government regulators on key new products it has developed. Two chemical compounds have failed to receive clearance by the Environmental Protection Agency, and the division's marketing subsidiary in Amsterdam is anxious to move ahead on them on its own.
- The Government Products Division is in decline. With the end of the Cold War, its military order backlog has dwindled. So far, the division has been unsuccessful in developing new civilian programs to offset the loss of its traditional market.
- The Farm Equipment Division has reported an unexpected growth in sales, resulting from the expansion of overseas markets, especially in Asia. The division's management and the general counsel are urging the company to take a more active role in the national debate on most-favored-nation treatment of China, the division's major foreign customer.
- The treasurer has deferred the bond issue scheduled for this month in view of the unexplained gyrations in foreign exchange markets. Renewed economic growth has fueled speculation about the Federal Reserve raising interest rates.

- The senior vice president for human resources has been spending most of her time in Washington, trying to settle a class action suit instituted by the Equal Employment Opportunity Commission. The company has been receiving unfavorable national publicity for its alleged reluctance to promote recovering alcoholics to supervisory positions.
- The vice president for labor relations has begun preliminary negotiations with the International Association of Machinists on the expiring labor contract. Because GDE is in a pace-setting industry, the Secretary of Labor has publicly urged the company to take an "enlightened" attitude in dealing with union demands for enhanced job security.
- The secretary of the board has been meeting with representatives of the New York State Employees' Pension Fund, a major holder of the company's stock, on the fund's proposal to appoint new members of the board of directors.
- The executive board of the National Association of Manufacturers has asked for a go-ahead to nominate GDE's CEO as the next chairman of that broad-based business association.

The list goes on, but the chairman is reluctant to raise more of these extraneous or nonbusiness issues with the board all in one meeting. He wonders out loud whether Globally Diversified Enterprises is properly staffed and organized to handle this variety of matters. The secretary suggests bringing in some high-powered consultants to advise the company. This, the chairman objects, would at best be a quick fix, a short-term solution; similar matters would likely come up the following year.

The secretary asks to what extent some of these oddball problems have arisen or at least worsened because GDE's managers are not sufficiently trained or experienced to deal with them. "Precisely," replies the chairman. At this point, the company's lead investment banker calls with an opportunity to enter into a strategic alliance with a Singapore-based conglomerate with major subsidiaries in Taiwan and mainland China.

This scenario, of course, is hypothetical and simplified. However, problems like these regularly arise in modern corporations. The need to train the current as well as the future generation of managers to meet such problems is widespread. This book is a response to that need.

The public sector influences private-sector decision making in a great variety of ways. Most analyses of the interaction between business and government focus on the pros and cons of public policy actions. This book turns the tables on that conventional approach. Rather than just attempting to play public policy maker, we will also examine the interactions between business and government from the vantage point of the private business firm and its management.

The contemporary corporation is undergoing a difficult and fundamental transition from a business serving the home market to a transnational enterprise. This transition is far from complete, and many companies have only begun the change. Even the smallest firm, however, is subject to powerful indirect influences of the global marketplace. In large measure, this development is driven by economic and market factors. In a considerable variety of cases, however, these changes in business decision making are the direct result of domestic and foreign governmental policies.

In other instances, government awards monopoly power to private companies, notably in the areas of transportation, communication, and utilities. As we will see in later chapters, curbing that use of the government's power to create private monopolies can reduce costs and result in a more efficient economic system.

Assessing the role of private enterprise in a democratic society is not a simple choice among polar alternatives. Friedrich Hayek explained that point clearly in his *Constitution of Liberty:*

> A functioning market economy presupposes certain activities on the part of the state; there are some other such activities by which its functioning will be assisted; and it can tolerate many more, provided that they are of the kind which are compatible with a functioning market. . . . The range and variety of government action that is, at least in principle, reconcilable with a free market system is thus considerable.[2]

In practice, the democratic capitalistic nations are not uniform in the relative size of the market economy. Each draws the line between the public and private sectors at a different point. Moreover, that point varies over time, as would be expected in a free society. It seems quite clear, however, that in the case of the more successful societies—successful in both economic production and personal liberty—the bulk of economic activity is performed in the market economy.

We will first examine the types of actions government takes that can affect the business firm. Then we will see how these actions influence business decision making.

THE POLICY TOOLS AVAILABLE TO GOVERNMENT

Government possesses many mechanisms that it can use directly or indirectly to influence actions in the private sector. Some impacts on the business firm are ancillary to achieving government objectives, or they may even be unintentional. Nevertheless, the typical business firm faces an impressive array of government powers.

Government Payrolls (Government as Paymaster)

The oldest policy tool available to government is to hire people and put them on the government's payroll. Government employees represent such diverse professions as teachers, foresters, and revenue agents. Payrolls provide a cadre of officials whose actions can then be controlled in terms of their influence on the rest of society. This is the tip of the proverbial iceberg because small proportions of government resources are devoted to compensation of government employees.

At first blush, direct government hiring seems to have little impact on business, but often government sets the standards. In the United States, the eight-hour day began in the federal government. Wage restraint in the private sector in recent years followed President Reagan's actions in 1981 in breaking the strike of the government's air traffic controllers. In specific personnel categories, such as secretaries and teachers, government hiring patterns influence the entire labor market. In 1996, federal, state, and local government combined had an aggregate payroll of $748 billion.

Government Purchases

Substantial portions of government budgets are devoted to ordering goods and services produced in the private sector. Products purchased range from high-tech nuclear submarines to standard off-the-shelf typing paper. The importance of the government market is obvious to key defense industries, such as aerospace, electronics, ordnance, and shipbuilding. In addition, public sector buyers—from national, state, county, and municipal agencies—purchase items from virtually every industry. Government procurement can be the difference between a good year and a mediocre year for many companies. Thus, many businesses have a strong incentive to influence government actions (a subject that chapters 16–18 cover in detail).

Although the size of the government market is very large ($660 billion in 1996), the magnitude is considerably smaller than the more frequently encountered measures of "government expenditures" or even "government purchases of goods and services." As shown in Table 1.1, government purchases from the private sector exclude several important categories of public sector outlay: compensation of government employees, transfer payments, interest, and subsidies.

At the national level, military contracts to private industry continue to be the major category of purchases from private business. State and local government agencies, in contrast, contract mainly for roads and school buildings and various categories of office supplies. As we will see in chapter 15, the government procurement process is an important way in which government influences private-sector actions. The public sector's methods of doing business are very different from standard commercial operations. Moreover, for the companies that produce primarily for military and space markets, the government is virtually a monopoly buyer. It exerts powerful control over the contractor's internal operations by forcing it to act like a government agency and to be "socially responsible." Requirements imposed by government on private industry range from hiring and training minority groups to adopting federally set wage and hour standards.

A trend toward privatization of some traditional government functions, begun in the 1980s, has increased the size of the public-sector market for which business firms can compete. One survey of municipalities revealed that 59 percent of the respondents are contracting out solid-waste collection or disposal, and 45 percent depend on private companies for towing and storing automobiles. However, only 11 percent contract out airport operations, and only 12 percent rely on the private sector for the delivery of services for the elderly and handicapped.

TABLE 1.1 Derivation of the Size of the Government Market in 1996

Derivation of Market Size	Billions of Dollars
Government expenditures[a]	$2,650
Less: Transfers, interest payments, and subsidies	1,242
Equals: Government purchases of goods and services	1,408
Less: Compensation of government employees	748
Equals: Government purchases from the private sector	660

[a]National income and product accounts basis.

Transfer Payments

A third policy tool available to government is to provide money to individuals—what economists call transfer payments and what the public at large may refer to less euphemistically as handouts. The key example is the monthly social security check sent to senior citizens. Here the impacts are more indirect than in the case of government procurement. Such expenditures strongly influence the amount of consumption by the recipients and thus affect the size and composition of consumer markets available to business.

Moreover, government spending for transfer payments, most of which are labeled *entitlements*, has become so massive in recent years that trends in that category can be a significant factor in the entire business outlook and especially the prospects for balancing government budgets. In 1996, government transfer payments in the United States totaled $1,073 billion, mainly for social security and medical care programs.

Government Subsidies

Government subsidizes private activity in many ways. By absorbing a portion of the cost of private production, subsidies raise the demand for the subsidized products in relation to other items. For example, subsidies to the mining industry can mean the difference between continuing to operate and closing down a titanium mine. Generous subsidies are provided to many sectors of the economy—and sometimes are referred to pejoratively as *business welfare:* agriculture (farm price supports), fishing (financing for new vessels), nuclear energy (government payments for developing new products), transportation (aid to urban mass transit), housing (low-rent public housing), and mining (special tax benefits). Subsidies are also received by a variety of special clienteles, such as minority enterprises.

Subsidies often contain a regulatory blend. For example, government subsidies to shipbuilders can be vital in decisions to build ships in domestic yards rather than overseas. But to qualify for federal subsidies, the ships must incorporate specific national-defense and safety features spelled out by the government. These added features raise both acquisition and operating costs.

Government can be foe as well as friend to private business. In many ways, government is a competitor for funds or influence. Thus, the Tennessee Valley Authority competes with private utilities, the Government Printing Office with commercial publishers (especially mapmakers such as Rand McNally), and the U.S. Post Office with private parcel delivery services (United Parcel Service and Federal Express, most notably). Government enterprises also vie for business with private enterprises in the large markets represented by the government's own purchases. This competition between the public and private sectors is more visible at state and local levels, in such areas as health, education, recreation, trash collection, and neighborhood and building security services.

Government Loans

The government also acts as a banker, lending money to private firms and individuals as well as to many other categories of borrowers. The gamut of federal lending extends to exporters (Export-Import Bank), farmers (Farmers Home Administration), real estate developers (Federal Housing Administration), and small businesses (Small Business Administration). Sometimes low interest rate government loans merely substitute for available private funds. But, more frequently, the government credit is provided for projects whose expected returns are so low that private markets will not finance them. As we will see in chapter 14, government loans are anything but the proverbial free lunch.

Government Credit Programs (Government as Underwriter)

Even without spending its own money or establishing rules on private conduct, government can strongly influence private economic activity. It does so by use of its credit power. The method used most frequently is the guarantee of private loans, as in the dramatic case of Chrysler and the less well-known but more frequent guarantees of new ship construction and exports. Because some of the risk is shifted from the private lender to the government, borrowers who are not considered creditworthy by normal commercial standards are given access to funds. Also, the government fosters the creation of quasi-government credit corporations, such as in the agricultural and housing credit areas (the farm credit banks and the federal home loan banks). As shown in chapter 14, the use of the government's credit alters the flow of funds in the economy and thus strongly influences which companies and which individuals gain access to the resources of the economy.

Because they do not seem to require (at least initially) the direct expenditure of government money, loan guarantees have been proliferating, as have other uses of the government's credit. In 1996, all of the non-Treasury borrowing under federal auspices came to $3,080 billion. As seen in the bailouts of insured but failed savings and loan associations, the government's contingent liability can be converted to direct expenditure—and in very substantial amounts.

Government Regulation

A growing area of government involvement in business involves the use of the regulatory power. The alphabet soup of regulatory agencies has become well known to many business executives and often to the public at large: EEOC, EPA, FDA, OSHA, CPSC, CFTC, FCC, FTC, FERC, FMC, FAA, FEC, NLRB, MSHA, ITC, NTSB, NRC, SEC, and on and on (see the glossary at the end of this chapter). Regulations range from broad-gauged requirements for pollution control to rules on the sales of lemons in a given month, from wide-ranging rules on worker health and safety to specialized restrictions on transactions in futures markets. Aside from the limited use of government personnel to design and enforce regulations, the bulk of the costs generated is "off budget" because the costs are mainly for compliance by private companies and individuals being regulated. Because such expenses do not show up in the government's budget, regulation has become especially popular during periods of budgetary restraint. As we will see, the cumulative effects of regulation on business performance—and on consumers—are pervasive.

Attention in recent years has focused on efforts to reduce the burdens of government rule making by relying more heavily on economic incentives to achieve social objectives. Simultaneously, however, support continues for more extensive social regulation, especially in the area of the environment.

Taxation

The governmental tax collector does more than share profits with the owners of companies. Tax considerations are a major influence on business decision making. For example, the liberality of depreciation provisions and the level of marginal tax rates affect the threshold for making new investments. In contrast to these across-the-board provisions, many sections of the revenue code are aimed at very specific sectors of business.

Government regularly employs its tax power to provide incentives for designated private activities. Using the carrot of tax incentives, governments often foster what they consider to be greater social responsibility on the part of business. In the United States, specific internal revenue provisions include tax credits for hiring certain categories of people (minority groups) and tax deferrals for income from exports.

At times, there is a direct link between taxes and controls. For a company's retirement contributions to qualify as a federal tax deduction, a pension program must meet detailed requirements spelled out in regulations issued under the Employee Retirement Income Security Act. As shown in chapter 13, business has an important stake in the various proposals for comprehensive tax reform.

Government as Business Partner

In addition to affecting business practices through policy or legislative mandates, governments sometimes manipulate the private sector directly by entering into partnerships with business enterprises. The involvement of government in the ownership of business is common in less developed countries or in nations with a history of public control of business. As businesses become more global in their operations by expanding into foreign markets, they often establish joint ventures and other associations with their host governments.

For instance, McDonald's became the first U.S. firm to penetrate the Russian economy when it opened a restaurant in Moscow in 1990. The restaurant, located near the Kremlin, is a joint venture with the Moscow City Council.

Joint relationships between private and public enterprises are also common in Asia, particularly China, where the government owns a great variety of businesses. The close connection between the public and private sectors in China is illustrated by the Wuhan No. 2 Printing and Dyeing Company, which is jointly owned by Hongtex Development Company, a Hong Kong firm, and the city of Wuhan.

Monetary Policy (Government as Regulator of the Economy)

The conduct of monetary policy by central banks such as the Federal Reserve System is a prime example of government actions that profoundly affect business but are not normally considered an aspect of business–government relations. The Federal Reserve strongly influences interest rates, the flows of money and credit, inflation rates, and the overall level of business activity in the economy. The Fed is a creature of the Congress and, although technically independent of the executive branch, often responds to presidential leadership. The power of the Federal Reserve System via its purchases and sales of treasury securities and its setting of discount rates and bank reserve requirements greatly affects the economic and financial environment in which companies operate.

The cost and availability of credit can be key influences on the performance and at times the very existence of business firms. A company's board of directors may spend almost as much time discussing the outlook for the prime rate as the audit committee's report. During wartime and under other emergency conditions, governments often augment indirect monetary (and fiscal) instruments with direct controls over wages, prices, and the use of materials.

Moral Suasion (Government as Leader)

From time to time, leaders of every nation call on their people to take actions on a voluntary basis. Especially when an activist president occupies the White House, the U.S. government "jawbones" the private sector on specific issues. Several modern presidents have called on the private sector to do such "patriotic" things as limit wage and price increases or eliminate discrimination in the workplace. Such displays of presidential leadership can be compelling because of the vast array of government powers—the proverbial stick in the closet—available to reinforce the "request" for voluntary action.

Thus, in the 1970s, President Jimmy Carter threatened to pull back government contracts from companies that did not voluntarily submit to the administration's request to follow its wage and price standards. In 1990, following the Iraqi invasion of Kuwait, President George Bush jawboned the oil companies not to raise prices too much. The large producers promptly complied. Ironically, the result was to squeeze the high-cost, smaller, "independent" dealers who found it more difficult to absorb the higher cost of crude oil as established in world markets.

In that same year, Health and Human Services Secretary Louis Sullivan criticized R.J. Reynolds for marketing a new brand of cigarettes aimed at African-American consumers. As an African-American physician, he possessed a great deal of moral authority. Within 24 hours, RJR canceled plans to test market the new product. A year later, some members of Congress objected vociferously to the plan of Japan's Fanuc Ltd. to buy 40 percent of a Connecticut machine tool builder that helps make nuclear weapons. Although the legal authority to reject foreign purchases of American companies on national security grounds had lapsed, Fanuc backed off.

In 1993, then-Senator Paul Simon (D-IL) warned producers of television programs and TV networks to take aggressive action to curb violence on television or face congressional intervention. In response to earlier Senate hearings, the networks had already agreed to issue warnings to audiences prior to showing programs with substantial amounts of violence. In late 1996, after further public criticism, the major television networks established a voluntary system of describing the content of various categories of programs.

In every administration, corporate leaders are very susceptible to presidential suasion, especially when they are called into the Oval Office in small groups. The toughest executives often melt like butter when the President personally smiles on them.

IMPACTS ON THE BUSINESS FIRM

If one side of the business–government coin is the proliferation of government power to accomplish a variety of public purposes, the other side is the extent to which government pervades internal business decision making. An examination of business–government relations from the business executive's viewpoint shows a considerable public presence in what historically have been private matters.

Government is a continuing presence and often one of increasing influence in business decision making. As pointed out in the literature on public choice, government officials are motivated by incentives that often may be closer to their own needs and desires than to broad principles of public interest. In this view, as expressed most forcefully by Nobel Prize winner James Buchanan, "Bureaucrats could no longer be labeled 'economic eunuchs.'"[3] The mythology of the faceless bureaucrat following orders from above is thus replaced by the notion of government employees who make policy choices as well as carry out the decisions of others (e.g., voters).

Government influences business decision making of all types: planning, research and development, production, marketing, personnel, finance, facilities, and so forth. The organizational chart of a hypothetical industrial firm, shown in Figure 1.1, conveys graphically the diverse nature of government involvement in many aspects of business. It is as though there were an overlay of regulatory agencies matching the formal positions on each company's organization chart. To compound the problem, in reality there is a multiplicity of such overlays, representing state and local governments and the corresponding array of governments in each of the nations in which the company does business. Additional overlays are needed for international governmental organizations, such as the United Nations and the European Union. In practice,

FIGURE 1.1 Hypothetical Industrial Corporation and U.S. Government Relations

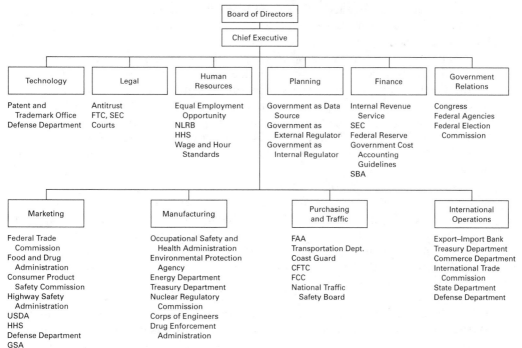

the precise nature of business–government relationships will vary by industry, size of firm, location, type of product, and markets served.

The modern array of government intervention affects management at all levels—from the board of directors to new hires on the production floor. The reach of government action extends to business managers with both line and staff responsibility, and it embraces the most senior executives, middle management, and first-line supervision.

No company, large or small, can operate without obeying myriad government rules and restrictions. Entrepreneurial decisions fundamental to the functioning of the enterprise are subject to government influence, review, and control. Decisions such as what lines of business to go into—in the case of utilities—are subject to approval by state public service commissions. The choice of products and services to produce, in the case of pharmaceuticals, is subject to the decision making of the Food and Drug Administration. Which investments can be financed is determined, especially for new enterprises, by the Small Business Administration. The Occupational Safety and Health Administration strongly influences how to produce goods and services. The costs to meet Environmental Protection Agency requirements have a major influence on where companies choose to make those products. Federal Trade Commission decisions on advertising affect marketing strategies. The Internal Revenue Service has a large say in what profits a firm can keep.

Virtually every major department of a typical company in today's economy has one or more counterparts in a government agency that controls or strongly influences its internal decision making. Much of the work of scientists in corporate research laboratories is aimed at ensuring that the products they develop are not rejected by lawyers in regulatory agencies. Engineers in manufacturing departments must make sure that the equipment they specify or design meets the standards promulgated by Labor Department authorities.

Marketing staffs must follow procedures set by government administrators in product safety agencies. The location of business facilities must conform with a host of environmental statutes. The activities of personnel staffs are geared to meet the standards for hiring, promotion, pay, and retirement set by the Department of Labor and the Equal Employment Opportunity Commission. Finance departments often bear the brunt of the paperwork burden imposed on business by government agencies. In short, few aspects of business activities escape some type of government review or influence.

Moreover, the scope of governmental involvement in business operations can multiply by several orders of magnitude if the enterprise has facilities in foreign markets. For a variety of political reasons—mainly to "protect" home industry owners, managers, and employees, but sometimes on ostensibly national security grounds—governments often erect barriers to international commerce that business enterprises must expend substantial resources to overcome. Businesses are often forced to choose second-best strategies when dealing with foreign governments. For instance, some host governments, such as Indonesia, restrict foreign ownership of local manufacturing facilities to minority shares only, forcing outside companies to enter into joint arrangements with native individuals, businesses, or governmental agencies.

ROLE OF CITIZEN GROUPS

A major expansion of government involvement in private industry in the United States has been underway for more than three decades (in other nations, nationalization of enterprises often took the place of regulation of private business activity). Continued impetus for this expanded government participation comes from a variety of consumer groups, labor unions, environmentalists, civil rights advocates, and other citizen organizations. Underlying support is provided by the belief that the private sector itself is responsible, at least in part, for many of the problems facing society. Concerns generating pressure for government involvement in business cover such social issues as pollution, discrimination in employment, unsafe products, unhealthy working environments, and misleading financial reporting.

Government looms large between business and its customers, its employees, its shareholders, and the public. Ralph Nader has noted on many occasions that business, too, has its power, and that is true. Actions by multibillion-dollar corporations can have strong positive or negative effects on a community or an entire region of a country. Money can be a very useful and also a corrupting influence in the political process. Yet the contrast between government and business power is striking. The largest company cannot tax you; the smallest unit of government can. The most profitable corporation cannot throw you in jail; the smallest municipality can.

Conclusions

Let us try to summarize the highlights of the relationship between business and government in a modern society. Government exercises a variety of important powers in dealing with the individual private enterprise, ranging from taxation to regulation. Business, in turn, relies on constitutional protections as well as on public support of its basic role in creating income, employment, and material standards of living. The business–government relationship in a dynamic society is constantly changing. The line between the public and private sectors frequently shifts.

In a global economy, the line is especially difficult to define. As we will see throughout this book, the strategies and issues discussed apply, with perhaps minor variations, to most governments and businesses around the world. Nevertheless, examples, illustrations, and discussions are taken in large measure from the experiences of firms headquartered in the United States—although increasingly they do business in many nations on several continents.

List of Acronyms—or the Bureaucrat's Alphabet Soup

ABC	American Business Conference
BLS	Bureau of Labor Statistics
BRAC	Business Research Advisory Council
CAB	Civil Aeronautics Board
CFA	Consumer Federation of America
CFTC	Commodity Futures Trading Commission

CPSC	Consumer Product Safety Commission
DOD	Department of Defense
DOT	Department of Transportation
ECOSOC	Economic and Social Council
EDF	Environmental Defense Fund
EEOC	Equal Employment Opportunity Commission
EPA	Environmental Protection Agency
ERISA	Employee Retirement Income Security Act
EU	European Union
FAA	Federal Aviation Administration
FACS	Foundation for American Communications
FAO	Food and Agricultural Organization
FCC	Federal Communications Commission
FDA	Food and Drug Administration
FDIC	Federal Deposit Insurance Corporation
FEC	Federal Election Commission
FERC	Federal Energy Regulatory Commission
FFB	Federal Financing Bank
FHA	Federal Housing Administration
FMC	Federal Maritime Commission
FTC	Federal Trade Commission
IAC	Industry Advisory Council
ILO	International Labor Organization
IOCU	International Organization of Consumers Unions
IRA	Independent Retirement Account
ITC	International Trade Commission
MNC	Multinational Corporation
NAAG	National Association of Attorneys General
NAD	National Advertising Division
NARB	National Advertising Review Board
NHTSA	National Highway Traffic Safety Administration
NIH	National Institutes of Health
NIOSH	National Institute of Occupational Safety and Health
NLRB	National Labor Relations Board
NRC	National Research Council
OECD	Organization for Economic Cooperation and Development
OFCC	Office of Federal Contract Compliance
OMA	Orderly Marketing Agreement
OMB	Office of Management and Budget
OSHA	Occupational Safety and Health Administration
PAC	Political Action Committee

PBGC	Pension Benefit Guaranty Corporation
RFC	Reconstruction Finance Corporation
SARA	Superfund Amendments and Reauthorization Act
SEC	Securities and Exchange Commission
TSCA	Toxic Substances Control Act
UNCTAD	United Nations Conference on Trade and Development
USDA	United States Department of Agriculture
VAT	Value-Added Tax
VER	Voluntary Export Restraint
WHO	World Health Organization
WTO	World Trade Organization

Notes

1. Arthur Schlesinger, Jr., "Has Democracy a Future?," *Foreign Affairs*, September/October 1997, p. 7.
2. F. A. Hayek, *The Constitution of Liberty* (Chicago: University of Chicago Press, 1960), pp. 224–225.
3. James M. Buchanan, "The Economic Theory of Politics Reborn," *Challenge,* March–April 1988, p. 5.

PART TWO

Government Regulation of Business

Of all the powers that government exerts on private business, regulation is the most pervasive—and often the least understood. Part II is devoted to a detailed examination of the many ways in which regulation takes place and the various impacts of government actions. The composition of regulation is changing rapidly—there is more environmental and other social regulation simultaneous with reforms and curtailments of economic regulation.

CHAPTER 2

The Rationale for Regulation

A basic way that government exerts its power over business is to issue regulations governing private-sector behavior. The use of regulatory power has grown in the United States, especially in recent decades. Many rationales have been put forth to justify this type of government intervention in the economy, notably the failure of private markets to work well.

Government regulation of private economic activity is as old as human history. In the Old Testament, the Book of Deuteronomy commands, "Thou shalt not lend upon usury to thy brother." The ancient Babylonian Code of Hammurabi established uniform weights and measures and limited the rate of interest. The prohibition of usury was included in medieval theology, along with the notion of a "just price." Modern regulation is often far more pervasive and requires an analysis of its theoretical underpinnings.

THEORIES OF REGULATION

Why do governments want to regulate private economic activity? The question is not easy to answer. Competitive markets, under the right circumstances, result in an efficient allocation of resources. At least in theory, the firms competing in such markets only produce those goods and services that consumers value most highly (in the quantities they are willing to purchase) and by methods that minimize the costs of production.

In practice, however, the economic system also produces many cases of *market failure*—a technical term referring to situations where competitive or market forces do not operate effectively. These market failures come in many forms, and government regulation is a frequent response. Let us examine the major justifications for such public-sector involvement in what are essentially private-sector activities.

Responding to Natural Monopoly Conditions

The classic case for regulation is natural monopoly. A natural monopoly can exist where economies associated with large-scale production make it inefficient for more than one firm to operate. In some industries characterized by large-scale production, cost per unit of output may become so low that the most efficient firm produces all or most of the industry's output. In technical terms, a natural monopoly exists when the production of a commodity is characterized by increasing returns to scale. That is, per-unit production costs decrease as the firm becomes larger. Consequently, the largest firm in the industry is also the most efficient; it has the lowest cost per unit of output.

Such a company has the ability to underprice competitors and drive them out of business. The smaller firms, as a practical matter, cannot compete and are forced to close down. In the absence of regulation, the monopolist company is free to charge higher prices than justified by cost.

Traditional policy toward natural monopoly has been to retain the single large firm but to use regulation to prevent monopolistic exploitation. The idea is that regulating a natural monopoly will allow society to reap the benefits of economics of large-scale production without the burden of monopolistic prices and without resorting to splitting the monopolist into smaller firms that would produce the same or less output at higher prices.

Local utilities are prime examples of such monopolies. State "public service" commissions regulating entry, prices, and profits are the most widely encountered governmental response. The fundamental rationale for this traditional style of economic regulation is that parallel and competing electric, gas, water, and telephone systems would entail wasteful duplication and higher costs to consumers. The main cases of natural-monopoly regulation at the federal level that are justified by the natural monopoly argument are oil and gas pipelines, and interstate transmission of electricity. State or local governments regulate local utilities as well as cable television.

Unregulated monopolies can cause social losses because they restrict production and raise prices. Such monopoly prices will enrich producers at the expense of consumers. Thus, decreasing cost industries present society with a dilemma. Competition in such industries is likely to be unstable and inefficient, but unregulated monopoly can result in high prices and discrimination among customers. The regulatory response typically involves setting rates (prices) for the monopoly firm and restricting or eliminating entry by competitors.

However, natural monopoly is only natural in a given technological or economic environment. With market growth or technological advances, competition may develop automatically. For example, when rail regulation began in 1887, competition possibilities were very limited in most markets. Natural monopoly in the railroad industry was one of the stated justifications for railroad regulation. Although the opportunities for competition in that industry are still limited, railroads face intense competition from trucks and inland waterway barges on most of the freight they haul. That competition insures that, on most routes and for most commodities, no monopoly of any significance can exist for the railroads today; consequently, Congress has abolished the Interstate Commerce Commission. Thus, yesterday's natural monopoly can become tomorrow's workably competitive industry.

Conversely, in the early 1900s, more than half the electric power used by industry was self-generated (or, in today's terminology, *cogenerated*) and regulation of electric utilities was far from universal. The term *cogeneration* describes the process in which useful thermal energy (usually steam) and electricity are produced in sequence from a single fuel source. However, as the availability of power supplied by the public utility companies increased, and the unit price declined, most of the early cogenerators abandoned their on-site power systems. Local electric utilities developed monopoly positions, and local or state governments became prone to regulate their prices and rates of return.

In this industry, the situation is turning again. Small but growing numbers of industrial firms have responded to the combined effects of a major run-up in energy prices and a more permissive regulatory environment by returning to cogeneration. Thus, the monopoly position of electric utilities may be weakened in those regions where industrial customers increasingly generate their own electrical energy. As this development continues, it will likely have a feedback effect on the regulatory decision-making process (see chapter 7 for a variety of recent developments affecting electric utilities).

Encouraging Sensible Use of Natural Resources

Regulation or other controls may be appropriate where a common resource must be allocated rationally or where there is no incentive to conserve natural resources. The electromagnetic spectrum is a good example of a resource owned by society as a whole. If everyone were allowed full use and access, chaos would result. Broadcasters using the same frequency would interfere with one another. Reception of signals would be poor or impossible. Some sort of government intervention is necessary.

When producers draw from a common pool of resources—such as a petroleum reservoir or a fish supply—no one will have sufficient economic incentive to conserve; if one person or organization holds back, the balance will simply be taken by others. Under American law, oil or gas belongs to whoever brings it to the surface on his or her own land. However, the oil or gas in a pool can flow underground, and the ownership of these pools is often fragmented. In the absence of regulation, property owners race to get the oil or gas out before the neighbors take it all. In responding to such a problem of the commons, government intervention in the form of regulation can avoid wasting such valuable nonreproducible resources.

Requiring Producers and Consumers to Take Account of External Costs

Regulation—or another form of governmental intervention—can be a means to compel individuals or organizations to take account of *external costs* or *spillover effects,* the costs they impose on other people. Environmental pollution and occupational risks, for example, cause substantial costs that—owing to the present system of property rights—may not be borne by the person or organization generating them. (See the box, "Private Property Rights.")

As shown in Figure 2.1, if some of the costs of producing a good or service are external to the firm, the firm's pricing actions will not reflect these costs. Thus, the private cost curve (C_{PR}) will understate society's true cost curve ($C_{PR} + C_{PU}$), which includes the externality of costs imposed on the public. As a result, the market price (P_1) will be lower than if it reflected the society's total costs (P_2). A larger amount of this good or service will be produced (Q_2) than would be the case if the firm's cost of production were to include the external effects (Q_1).

For example, a steel mill that produces smoke and soot imposes costs on its neighbors in the form of polluted air, bad health, and ugly surroundings. In the absence of controls, since these costs do not fall primarily on the mill, its management may choose to ignore them. On the other hand, if these "external" costs fell on the polluting firm, it would attempt to minimize them. Moreover, if these environmental costs were borne by the firm, they would be reflected in product prices. Consumers would be encouraged to avoid pollution-intensive products.

Private Property Rights

Understanding the role of property rights sets the stage for private action and public policy in a variety of regulatory areas, notably dealing with the environment. Within the framework of existing legislation, the courts determine private property rights, and executive branch agencies are responsible for enforcing those rights.

For example, a cigarette smoker and a nonsmoker are seated next to each other in a crowded subway car. Assuming an agreement could be reached, should the smoker compensate the nonsmoker for having to breathe the secondhand smoke, or should the nonsmoker compensate the smoker for not being able to enjoy a cigarette? It depends on who has what property rights: whether the smoker has the right to dissipate smoke into the environment or whether the nonsmoker has the right to breathe clean air. Different rulings on this issue have come from various state courts as well as from state legislatures.

For a real-life example, consider ASARCO, a copper-smelting plant located on Commencement Bay in Tacoma, Washington. In 1975, a high level of lead was discovered in the children of families who lived near the plant. In the smelting of copper, arsenic is produced and used in computer chip manufacturing. Also, lead is given off as a by-product and emitted into the air through the one huge smokestack at the plant. Is the air a common property resource, in which case ASARCO has the right to use it for waste disposal, or do the people living in the area have a right to a healthy environment free from such hazards as lead in the atmosphere? The case went to the courts to determine the property rights of the two parties.

In this case, the rights of the families prevailed. The courts determined that ASARCO must reduce the levels of lead emitted to be within federal standards. ASARCO deemed that the installation of smokestack scrubbers would not be cost effective and closed the plant down, putting a large number of men and women out of work. This action also decreased the amount of arsenic available to the producers of computer chips, perhaps increasing their costs and possibly reducing the availability of computer chips.

As seen in the ASARCO case, externalities can be internalized to the extent that private property rights are clearly defined and effectively enforced.

Of course, externalities can be produced by government agencies as well as by business firms. Upstream municipalities dumping inadequately treated sewage into a river can impose substantial cleanup costs (or polluted waters) on the people living downstream from them. Ironically, over a century ago, English common law rejected a potential private solution to the issue of externalities. When legal actions were brought against polluters, they were dismissed. General nuisances, such as factory smokestacks, were found to cause no *particular* harm to the plaintiffs—everybody was being polluted. Also, the courts reasoned that the polluters were operating within their statutory authority and that producing goods served a public interest. If the deci-

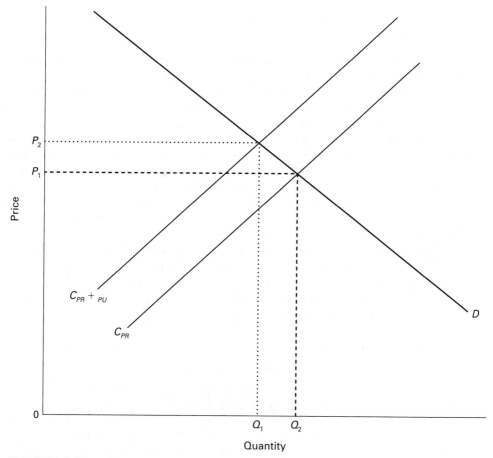

FIGURE 2.1 Effect of Externalities on Prices and Production

sions had gone the other way, we might now have class action suits instead of detailed government regulation of emissions into the environment.

In the absence of government intervention—and given the current regime of property rights—voluntary action to deal with environmental wastes places a firm under a competitive disadvantage. The specific company attempting to reduce the external costs imposed on the public would bear the full costs, while the benefits of the improvement would be widely dispersed in the society. "Free riders," or firms that do not make the expensive changes, nevertheless share in the benefit, and their prices may be lower. An example of this situation is provided by the regulation of pollution standards in the motor vehicle area. The basic justification given by government for setting such standards was clearly stated by a senior executive of a major automotive manufacturer:

> [A] large part of the public will not voluntarily spend extra money to install emission control systems which help clean the air. Any manufacturer who installs and charges for such equipment while his competition doesn't soon finds he is losing sales and

customers. In cases like this, a government standard requiring everyone to have such equipment is the only way to protect both the public and the manufacturer.[1]

Similarly, because market incentives for voluntary health and safety programs by employers may be insufficient in some instances, regulation can be used to force employers to "internalize" the costs associated with job hazards to their employees.

The economic justification for regulation of nuclear power is similar but a bit more complex. The external costs of nuclear power generation are not observable. They take the form of risk of bodily harm and property damage. The possibility of a nuclear mishap imposes a cost on all those it might injure. In technical terms, that cost is the expected value of the damage produced by a nuclear accident—the probability of an accident times the injury that would be inflicted. Well-designed government standards would reduce the hazard and, in the process, internalize in the firm some of these external costs. In the process, the price of nuclear power would rise to reflect those costs.

Federal law (the Price–Anderson Act) limits the total liability of the firms involved and provides that the government will indemnify them for some of the liabilities that do result from a nuclear accident. Such limitation of liability reduces the incentive to reduce risks, and it provides a justification for safety regulation by the Nuclear Regulatory Commission.

Inadequate Information

Another case of market failure arises where individuals are not sufficiently informed to make sensible decisions in the marketplace. Much product information is difficult or expensive to obtain. For example, in regulating the use of certain chemicals in the treatment of baby clothes, the Consumer Product Safety Commission has sought to mitigate any harm that might come to the children exposed to that hazard. The rationale for government action in such a situation is that consumers lack knowledge of either the chemicals with which the clothing is treated or the hazards that they give rise to. Correcting inadequacies in the information that producers provide about the products they sell is a justification underlying much health, safety, and consumer protection regulation.

Many companies have little incentive to make information on their products freely available. The marketplace may not provide enough information for the consumer to know which product contains cancer-causing additives, which device is defective, or what health hazards exist in a particular workplace. Some producers and employers may view it in their interests to provide incomplete or inaccurate information.

Regulation in this area can take two basic forms, depending largely on the knowledge of those affected. In areas where it is relatively easy or inexpensive for consumers to evaluate accurate information, the regulatory response may be to require accurate labeling and to prohibit misleading promotional statements. The Food and Drug Administration, for example, requires informational labeling telling consumers about the fat, protein, carbohydrate, and calorie content of certain foods.

However, the problem of imperfect knowledge is not solved in all cases simply by providing more information. Where it is very difficult for the people using the product to understand and act on the technical data involved, it may make more sense for the government to establish and enforce standards or even license producers. For example, consumers cannot generally be expected to acquire the expertise or resources needed to evaluate various prescription drugs. As a result, the Food and Drug Administration sets standards and approves specific products before they can be marketed to the general public. In the case of certain dangerous or highly addictive drugs, banning them may be the preferred solution to protect the public welfare.

As another example, it hardly would make sense for the passengers to have to inspect the qualifications of pilots or safety of the equipment on airplanes on which they fly. The Federal Aviation Administration exercises this responsibility, licensing pilots, prescribing aircraft standards, and specifying flight procedures. On the other hand, some governmental regulation reduces the amount of product information available to consumers. This is the case where government bans or restricts types of advertising, which is an underestimated form of information. For example, the FDA regulations at times discourage prescription drug ads from being shown on television, a major source of information for many consumers, because of the amount of technical material required to be included in the commercial.

The result is just the opposite of what the FDA wants to achieve. Due to the restraint on advertising, consumers may not be aware that a treatment exists for a certain condition, and so they will not consult a physician. In other circumstances, consumers may suffer some symptoms (e.g., thirst) without realizing that these are symptoms of a treatable disease (e.g., diabetes). Alternatively, a new remedy with reduced side effects may become available, but patients are not aware of it and do not visit their physicians to obtain a prescription.[2] Because consumers must obtain a prescription from a physician in order to acquire prescription drugs, there is less reason to fear deception in advertising in this market than in others.

Avoiding Phony Justifications

Given the power of the regulatory process, it is not surprising that many interests have cloaked their pleas for special treatment with a reference to some broader public purpose. One justification sometimes offered is that, in the absence of regulation, competition would be "destructive." That is, without controls, some industries might operate at a loss for long periods of time. In theory, this could occur in companies where large proportions of costs are fixed and where the resources employed are immobile. Agriculture and mining may at times provide pertinent examples.

Most studies of the subject, however, conclude that destructive competition is more a fear than a reality. In most of these cases, government intervention disrupts the normal movement of labor and other resources from industries with excess supply to expanding industries that could put those resources to more productive use. After all, not all losses and bankruptcies are bad. They weed out higher-cost producers and force companies to adopt more efficient techniques of production.

Outside the realm of market failures, it is often claimed that *distributive justice,* or concern with political and social equity, is a reason for government intervention. In other words, the government's involvement is seen primarily as a way of bringing about the transfer of income or wealth to a worthy segment of society. In practice, however, a small group (i.e., a special interest) usually benefits at the expense of the mass of consumers. Regulation has been used in this way to redistribute income among the regions of the nation, to promote one industry at the expense of others, to provide services for small communities, and to give special protection to those deemed particularly worthy (usually that means politically powerful).

Until deregulation, interstate trucking was a pertinent example of using government power to protect the "ins." Regulation of this industry merely insulated existing trucking firms and their employees from competition created by new trucking companies that had not received the approval of a regulatory agency (the Interstate Commerce Commission, or ICC) to enter the business. The redistribution of income in this case was from consumers in general to the owners, managers, and employees of the regulated industry. The elimination of ICC regulation has also resulted in substantial transfers of income and wealth, but this time it has been from the regulated portion of the industry to new entrants or what had been the unregulated part of the trucking industry (see chapter 8).

The "property rights" acquired by regulation—such as radio and television broadcasting licenses—are often valuable. Reducing regulation, therefore, can result in capital losses for some. When the Securities and Exchange Commission required negotiated brokerage rates, the value of seats on the New York Stock Exchange was drastically lowered. But the overall benefits to consumers-investors were far greater.

Assuring service to particular groups or communities is a frequent motivation for regulatory controls on rates, entry, and type of service. Of necessity, that entails cross-subsidies: transferring income from profitable business activities to less remunerative areas. The result is higher prices for some in order to support otherwise uneconomical service for others. The issue of cross-subsidization usually arises in the case of service to small or rural communities. The real and often obscured issues, however, are "service at what price?" or "who should pay?" Prior to the breakup of AT&T, higher charges for long-distance calls helped erase losses in providing household service, especially to sparsely populated areas. Under such circumstances, controls on entry of new competition are used to protect the profits necessary to finance the cross-subsidized service.

Once established, regulation spawns and then protects certain groups, which subsequently have a vested interest in its continuation. The "grandfather" clauses in many regulatory systems tend to confer "squatters' rights" on existing production facilities, compared to new ventures. For example, in "nonattainment" areas under the clean air statute, potential new sources not only need to meet more stringent standards, they also need to arrange for and finance offsets: actual reductions for the same pollutant in the same area from other sources.

Investment and modernization that could result in improved productivity are discouraged by pollution-abatement costs that are higher in newly built facilities than for older factories. Thus, existing facilities are given a degree of protection from competition by virtue of strict new source requirements. Older, less efficient, and more heavily polluting plants tend to be kept in operation longer and used more intensively, which can lead to pollution levels that are higher than if the regulatory hurdle for new investment were lower.

The application of more stringent requirements to new production processes or products than to those already in existence extends to water-pollution abatement, auto safety and fuel-economy rules, and controls over the safety and effectiveness of drugs. New investment and development of new products have accordingly been discouraged.[3] Thus, "protecting" existing firms from new competition via regulation generates pressures to continue the status quo. (See the box, "Taking Regulation for Granite.")

Taking Regulation for Granite

Vulcan Materials Co. dominates the unglamorous business of crushed stone. The company earns a profit of nearly 10 percent of sales, making it one of the more profitable industrial companies. Vulcan's president explained one of the reasons: "Back in the sixties you used to worry about who was going to open up a quarry right down the road, but now we never concern ourselves about that; problems with zoning and the EPA are so monumental. That gives us an ability to price our product that we didn't have before."

Source: Regulation, March–April 1982, p. 12.

Although regulation is often used by government as a means of correcting market failures, regulatory actions are not the only means available. Consumers can educate themselves and seek product information when they are making large purchases. Responding to normal economic stimuli, firms and their employees can be made more aware of on-the-job hazards. Workers can then bargain for improved working conditions or for higher pay as compensation for the risks. Alternatively, taxes can be levied on polluters and subsidies can be paid to those unfairly harmed by pollution to compensate them for the cleanup burden imposed on them. Regulations represent a halfway house between methods that involve more direct control (such as nationalization of an industry) and those that involve the use of indirect control mechanisms, such as taxes or subsidies.

Government Failure

Most of the discussions of the need for government regulation—especially to deal with the various types of market failure—are based on several very important but usually unstated assumptions. First of all, many proponents of regulation seem to believe that the process of government intervention is costless or, at least implicitly, that the benefits exceed the costs.

Of perhaps even greater importance, the typical advocate of regulation seems oblivious to what can be called *government failure,* the shortcomings in the operation of public-sector agencies.[4] Specifically, the incentives influencing individual government bureaus or officials may not lead them to take actions to attain socially desired results. Believing strongly in their mission, regulators may try to maximize the size of their efforts (and, indirectly, the size of their personal financial and psychic rewards) when the optimum amount of regulation might be substantially less. The economist's notion of diminishing returns often comes into conflict with the enthusiast's belief that, if something such as regulation is good, then more is always better than less.

Without forgetting the shortcomings of the marketplace (as described earlier), it is useful to recognize that regulation may also fall short of perfection. Like most government activities, regulation is generally not connected with any bottom line comparable to the profit-and-loss statement of business for evaluating performance. Moreover, experience shows that there is no reliable mechanism in the public sector for terminating governmental efforts if they are unsuccessful.[5]

Thus, the identification of inadequacies or "failure" in the marketplace may be a necessary but hardly a sufficient criterion for governmental intervention in private economic activity. The inadequacies or "failure" in the public-sector response may be even greater. Or, as the layperson might accurately say, the cure may be worse than the disease. The analyst can respond that there is no need to guess at or assume whether market failure is greater than government failure. Rather, under these circumstances, the need for analysis of the advantages and disadvantages of the proposed public-sector action is compelling. (Chapter 9 examines the methodologies used.)

THE GROWTH OF REGULATION

In the United States, regulatory activities began with the individual states. In the landmark decision *Munn v. Illinois* (1876), the Supreme Court ruled that the Illinois legislature could set a maximum charge for storing grain in warehouses. "When private property is devoted to a public use, it is subject to public regulation," the Court ruled.

In 1887, Congress established the Interstate Commerce Commission, the granddaddy of federal rule-making agencies, to regulate railroad rates and routes. In 1996, Congress acknowledged the substantial deregulation of surface transportation that has occurred by closing down the ICC and transferring its residual functions to the Department of Transportation.

In the first century of the Republic, the growth of federal regulatory activity was slow. The twentieth century has witnessed a series of rapid expansions. The Antitrust Division of the Justice Department was set up in 1903 to prosecute violators of the Sherman Antitrust Act. The Federal Reserve System was established in 1913 to oversee the commercial banking system. The Federal Trade Commission was created in 1914 to carry out the Clayton Act, designed to promote competitive behavior. The Federal Power Commission (now the Federal Energy Regulatory Commission) was established in 1920, covering the interstate transmission of electricity and other forms of energy.

The New Deal of the 1930s led to a burst of new government agencies, such as the Securities and Exchange Commission, the Federal Deposit Insurance Corporation, the Federal Home Loan Bank Board, the Federal Maritime Commission, the Federal Communications Commission, the National Labor Relations Board, and the Civil Aeronautics Board (which ceased functioning in 1985).

Government intervention in economic activity expanded rapidly in the 1960s and 1970s (see Figure 2.2). Examples of the newer regulatory agencies include the Environmental Protection Agency, the Consumer Product Safety Commission, the Occupational Safety and Health Administration, and the Equal Employment Opportunity Commission. A few small agencies were eliminated at the beginning of the Reagan administration, notably the Council on Wage and Price Stability, which had promulgated voluntary wage and price standards.

The direct costs of regulatory activities to the taxpayers are substantial. The operating expenses for the 53 major federal regulatory agencies came to more than $17 billion in fiscal year 1998—almost twice the amount spent a decade previously. In real terms (adjusted for inflation), federal regulatory budgets, after declining slightly from 1980 to 1985, have risen steadily since (see Table 2.1).

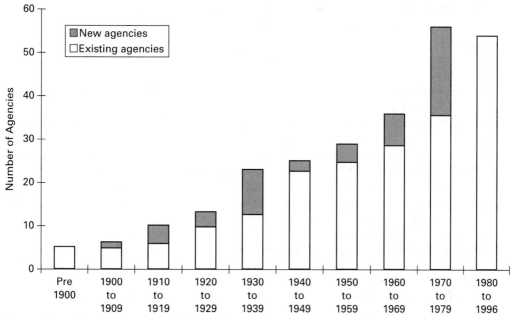

Source: Center for the Study of American Business, Washington University.

FIGURE 2.2 Growth of Federal Regulatory Agencies

TABLE 2.1 Administrative Costs of Federal Regulatory Activities (Fiscal Years, in Millions)							
Area of Regulation	*1970*	*1975*	*1980*	*1985*	*1990*	*1995*	*1998*
Social Regulation							
Consumer safety and health	$710	$1,491	$2,345	$2,686	$3,792	$5,193	$5,906
Job safety and other working conditions	128	359	753	862	1,002	1,201	1,314
Environment	214	841	1,651	2,495	4,164	5,175	5,979
Energy	64	275	550	481	462	582	505
Total Social Regulation	$1,116	$2,966	$5,299	$6,524	$9,420	$12,151	$13,704
Economic Regulation							
Finance and banking	$86	$151	$362	$624	$1,080	$1,384	$1,623
Industry-specific regulation	91	160	279	289	320	483	484
General business	115	206	355	507	743	1,235	1,364
Total Economic Regulation	$292	$517	$996	$1,420	$2,143	$3,102	$3,471
Grand total	$1,408	$3,483	$6,295	$7,944	$11,563	$15,253	$17,175
Percent increase		147%	81%	26%	46%	32%	13%
Total in 1992 dollars	$4,601	$8,254	$10,429	$10,111	$12,357	$14,176	$14,852
Percent real increase (decrease)		79%	26%	(3%)	22%	15%	5%

Source: Center for the Study of American Business, Washington University.

The biggest regulatory budgets are not those of the traditional economic regulatory agencies, such as the FCC and other industry-specific commissions. Rather, the largest proportion of the funds is devoted to the broader, social regulatory activities, such as environmental regulation by the EPA and consumer product regulation by the Department of Agriculture.

At first glance, government imposition of socially desirable requirements on business appears to be an inexpensive way of achieving national objectives. It seems to cost the government little (aside from the usually overlooked expenses of the regulatory agencies themselves) and therefore is not recognized as much of a burden on the taxpayer. There are obvious political attractions of such an activity whereby government can appear to do good without either levying taxes or increasing its debt.

But, on reflection, it can be seen that the public does not escape paying the full cost imposed by regulation. For example, when the Occupational Safety and Health Administration imposes on business a more expensive method of production, the cost of the resultant product necessarily will rise. Every time the Consumer Product Safety Commission imposes a standard that is more costly to attain, some product expenses will increase. The same holds true for the activities of the Environmental Protection Agency, the Food and Drug Administration, and so forth.

The point being made here should not be misunderstood. What is at issue is not the worthiness of the objectives of these agencies. Rather, the point is that the public does not get a "free lunch" by imposing public requirements on private industry. Although the costs of government regulation are not borne by taxpayers directly, in large measure they show up in higher prices of the goods and services that consumers buy. These higher prices represent the "hidden tax" of regulation, which is shifted from the taxpayer to the consumer. Moreover, to the extent that government-mandated requirements impose similar costs on all price categories of a given product (such as automobiles), this hidden tax will tend to be more regressive than the federal income tax. That is, the costs may place a heavier relative burden on lower-income groups than on higher-income groups.

Table 2.2 provides another way of looking at the trend of the federal government's regulatory activities, examining the changing size of the total workforce of the regulatory agencies. It shows the rapid growth in the decade of the 1970s (a 74 percent rise from 1970 to 1980) and the cresting of that regulatory wave in more recent years. The data show a 6 percent decline in the staffing of these activities from 1980 to 1990, reflecting the cutbacks during the initial burst of regulatory reform set in motion by President Reagan, and a modest upturn since. A regulatory head count of 126,147

TABLE 2.2   Personnel of Federal Regulatory Agencies (Fiscal Years, Full-Time Equivalent Employment)

Area of Regulation	1970	1980	1990	1998
Social regulation	52,500	95,448	87,303	97,529
Economic regulation	17,253	26,258	27,289	28,618
Total	69,753	121,706	114,592	126,147

Source: Center for the Study of American Business, Washington University.

in 1998, close to the all-time high, demonstrates a substantial continuing ability on the part of government to issue rules, conduct inspections, and otherwise impose requirements on private business.

THE CONDUCT OF REGULATION

Government agencies use two methods to carry out laws: *rule making* and *adjudication*. Through rule making, agencies issue general policy statements as well as detailed requirements. In contrast, through adjudication, the agencies formulate enforceable orders backed by civil or criminal penalties and settle specific factual disputes. Generally, rule making is described as the agencies' "legislative" function, and adjudication as their "judicial" function.

Rule Making

Rules, or regulations, are agency statements that implement, interpret, or prescribe a law or policy. Rules may be generated to carry out a new law or to modify rules under an older law. For example, after Congress passed the Clean Air Act Amendments of 1990, the Environmental Protection Agency (EPA) was required to issue a host of new rules as well as to issue other rules promulgated under the earlier laws that the new statute amended.

Often, legislation contains specific directions for agencies to follow while allowing them to maintain some discretion. Through the revised Clean Air Act, for example, Congress requires many service and industrial firms to obtain permits to continue operating. It leaves determining specific industry-by-industry standards for the reduction of toxic air pollutants to the EPA.

Uniform procedures for rule making allow the public to participate in the process. Under the Administrative Procedures Act at the federal level, an agency generally publishes a notice of proposed rule making in the Federal Register, announcing the rule it intends to put into effect and soliciting public comments. Comments may address a specific provision in the proposal or the entire proposed rule. To use the Clean Air Act example again, EPA has offered companies and others an opportunity to comment on each of the proposed standards.

Occasionally, agencies conduct public hearings and invite parties to present their views to the staff or heads of the agency. Rules are based on conclusions drawn from facts the agency gathers from its own research and from information provided by the public. For example, various company and trade-association executives have consulted with agency representatives to help them formulate specific environmental pollution rules.

An agency is required to consider all comments it receives and other data it has on an issue before promulgating a final rule. A final rule establishes a policy deemed to best serve the public interest and is enforceable as law. It usually becomes effective 30 days after it is printed in the *Federal Register*. This entire rule-making process can take from a few months to several years. In certain cases, if an agency's rule results only in minor changes to existing law, the final rule may be published without prior notice.

In most cases, publishing a final rule in the *Federal Register* is considered sufficient to alert the public of a change in law, with no other notification of affected parties being necessary. A final rule is incorporated into the *Code of Federal Regulations,* which contains the current regulations for all federal agencies. Implementing a single law may require many rules and involve more than one agency. Congress typically specifies deadlines for issuance of rules, with different dates for various provisions.

Adjudication

Adjudication is the regulatory agency's process for formulating an order. An *order* is any final disposition other than rule making. Adjudication can be formal or informal. Formal agency adjudication is known as a hearing, which is similar to a trial. If a company is charged with violating a law or regulation, it may defend itself before administrative law judges of the agency bringing the charges.

Informal procedures constitute the bulk of administrative adjudication. During informal adjudication, an agency determines the rights or liabilities of specific parties in a proceeding other than a formal hearing. Setting rates, awarding licenses or permits, and both civil and criminal law enforcement are all examples of adjudication. The owner or operator of a hazardous-waste storage facility seeking an operating permit would participate in adjudication.

THE CHANGING NATURE OF REGULATION

The industries subject to traditional economic regulation by federal and state agencies account for only one-tenth of the gross domestic product. Until the 1960s, most sectors—accounting for the great bulk of economic activity—remained relatively unregulated, except for certain general standards of business conduct, such as the antitrust laws and the exercise of state and local government "police powers" over public health. But that situation began to change fundamentally in the 1960s with the advent of social regulation, which now extends to virtually the entire American economy.

Social regulation is characterized by the use of agencies organized along functional or issue lines rather than industry categories. Many of the new-style regulatory agencies have power to regulate across all industries, although their jurisdiction is limited to one aspect of business activity. Examples include the Equal Employment Opportunity Commission (EEOC), the Environmental Protection Agency (EPA), and the Occupational Safety and Health Administration (OSHA). Others are more specialized, such as those charged with protecting consumers against unsafe products. The National Highway Traffic Safety Administration (NHTSA) covers automobiles and trucks. The jurisdiction of the Food and Drug Administration (FDA) extends to medical devices and cosmetics, in addition to food and drugs. The Consumer Product Safety Commission (CPSC) has a broad mandate, extending to most other consumer products with a few key exclusions—notably alcoholic beverages, motor vehicles, tobacco products, and firearms.

Social regulation did not suddenly emerge. One of the first major pieces of federal regulatory legislation was the Animal and Plant Health Inspection Act of 1884.[6] However, those early social statutes were usually limited to one specialized area of business activity.

The recent wave of social regulatory agencies (EPA, OSHA, EEOC, CPSC) has not been merely an intensification of traditional activities (see Appendix at the end of this chapter). In good measure, it has been a new departure. The standard theory of government regulation of business, which previously dominated thinking on the subject, is based on the model of the now defunct Interstate Commerce Commission (ICC). Under this approach, a federal commission is established to regulate a specific industry, with the related concern of promoting the well-being of that industry. Often, the public or consumer interest is viewed as subordinate, or is even ignored, since the agency focuses on the needs and concerns of the industry it is regulating.[7]

This specialized focus can acquire curious features. In some cases—because of the unique expertise possessed by the members of the industry or because of job enticements for regulators who leave government employment—the regulatory commission can become a "captive" of the industry it is supposed to regulate. This is still a widely held view of the development of the regulatory process.

But regulatory agencies now have rules that restrict the private employment of former employees. Federal law forbids former federal officials from participating in a matter in which they were involved while in government service for at least one year after leaving the government. Some agencies have even more stringent restrictions. The Federal Energy Regulatory Commission (FERC) will not permit a former employee ever to appear in a case before the commission if he or she participated in the case while working for the agency. The Federal Trade Commission (FTC) is even more strict; it bars any previous employee from participating in a proceeding pending while that person was employed by the FTC.

In any event, industries often become so accustomed to living with some types of government regulations that they fight efforts to reduce or eliminate them, even if they opposed the original imposition of the government intervention. For example, an attempt by the Treasury Department in 1982 to deregulate the alcoholic beverage industry was abandoned in the face of sustained opposition from the industry itself. Thus, the Bureau of Alcohol, Tobacco, and Firearms continues to administer such provisions of the Federal Alcohol Administration Act as the prohibition on suppliers from providing retailers with paid advertising, signs, fixtures, or other promotional aids.

Economists have developed a more general theory of the regulatory process. This theory pictures the process as the arena in which various interest groups invest their resources in order to effect an outcome more to their liking. The *capture theory* is seen in terms of the dominance of a small group with a relatively large stake in the affairs of the society as a whole, whose interests are more diffused.[8] For example, the major proponents of job safety regulation are labor unions; these unions have a strong desire to lock into, or capture, the regulatory activities of job safety agencies. The costs of the standards are borne by consumers, generally in the form of higher prices for manufactured goods. The benefits accrue almost exclusively to the special interest group itself.

A NEW MODEL OF GOVERNMENT REGULATION

Although the traditional type of federal regulation of business continues, the regulatory efforts established by Congress in recent years follow, in the main, a fundamentally different pattern. The new federal regulatory agencies have much broader jurisdiction than the ICC model. Simultaneously, however, in important aspects they are far more restricted. This paradox lies at the heart of this new style of rule making.

The changing nature of regulation can be seen in Figure 2.3. The vertical lines show the traditional relationship between the old style of government commission (FERC, FAA, FCC) and the specific industry it regulates. However, most sectors of the economy—manufacturing, trade, and services—are virtually exempt from that type of intervention.

In contrast, the horizontal lines show the newer breed of regulatory agency (EPA, EEOC, OSHA, CPSC). In the case of each of these relative newcomers to the federal bureaucracy, jurisdiction extends to the great bulk of the private sector, cutting through whole segments of the marketplace. This far-ranging characteristic makes it impractical for any single industry to dominate these regulatory activities in the manner of the traditional model. After all, what specific industry is in a position to capture the EEOC or OSHA, or would have the incentive to do so?

In comparison with the older agencies, however, the new regulators operate in a far narrower sphere in many important ways. They are not concerned with the totality of a company or industry but only with the one segment of operations that falls under their jurisdiction. The FCC, as an example of a traditional regulator, must pay attention to the basic mission of the telecommunications industry—to provide communications services to the public—as part of its supervision of rates and service in that business. The EPA, on the other hand, is interested almost exclusively in the effect of those operations on the environment. This limitation prevents the newer agency from developing too close a concern with the overall well-being of any company or industry. But it can also result in a lack of awareness or interest in the effects of its actions on a specific company or industry.

If there is any special interest that comes to dominate such an agency, it is not the industry being regulated but the group that is preoccupied with its specific task: ecologists in the case of environmental cleanup; civil rights, women's, and senior citi-

FIGURE 2.3 Variations in Federal Regulation of Business

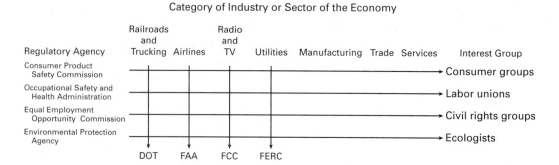

Category of Industry or Sector of the Economy

zens' organizations in the case of elimination of job discrimination; labor unions in the establishment of safer working conditions; and consumer groups in the reduction of product hazards.

Although important benefits may be gained by the newer form of social regulation, limited attention is given by the regulators to the basic mission of the industries they regulate: to provide goods and services to the public. Also ignored or downplayed are crosscutting concerns and matters broader than those dealt with in the specific charter of the regulating agency: productivity, economic growth, employment, cost to the consumer, and overall living standards.

Some important cases blend the old and new forms of regulation. The Securities and Exchange Commission (SEC) is a good example. In one aspect of its activities, it regulates a specific branch of the economy, the securities industry. Yet its rules also influence the way a great many companies prepare their financial statements and reports to shareholders. Economywide regulatory agencies (such as the SEC) are not entirely a recent creation; the FTC has existed since 1914.

Aside from these few hybrid exceptions, the traditional theory of regulation is geared to a world where the regulators, as well as the various private adversaries in the process, are primarily concerned with prices, entry, and profits. In contrast, the new breed of regulators, and the public interest groups supporting their efforts, are usually oblivious to those economic factors. Many of them condemn as callous or worse any consideration of cost or other business aspects in deliberations on product, personnel, or environmental safety. In this fundamental respect, the new wave of government regulation is a markedly different phenomenon than the traditional economic regulator.

The results of the new approach in government regulation of business can be the reverse of the traditional capture situation. Rather than being dominated by a given industry, the new type of federal regulatory activity is far more likely to use the resources of various industries, or to ignore their needs, in order to further the specific objectives of the regulatory agency and of its private-sector clientele. Detailed study of the activities of these newer agencies reveals many costs—for business, the economy, and the public—as well as the intended benefits.

Nevertheless, we must recognize that it is difficult to criticize the basic mission of these newer regulatory agencies. Only a Scrooge or a misanthrope would quarrel with the intent of the new wave of federal regulation: safer working conditions, better products for the consumer, elimination of discrimination, reduction of pollution, and so forth. And we must recognize that the programs were deliberately established by Congress in response to a surge of rising public expectations about corporate performance.

Each of these programs has yielded significant benefits to society. In the period 1986 to 1995, emissions of lead in the United States were down 32 percent. The pulp and paper mills of New Hampshire and Maine pour less than one-tenth of the particulates into the air than they did before 1970. Sulfur dioxide levels in Washington, DC, are down to less than half of their 1960 levels. Lake Erie, which once gained notoriety because some of the garbage floating on it caught fire, now attracts hundreds of thousands of fishermen each year.[9] Some companies have found new outlets for their products in the emerging market for pollution-control equipment, while society benefits from the social objectives that are achieved. For example, opening new employment opportunities for minority groups not only eliminates a basic social inequity, it also expands the effective labor force that can produce the goods and services desired by the society.

Even though the results of the new wave of regulation can be the reverse of the capture situation, we discover that strange and varying alliances arise in the process of promoting or attempting to reform a given type of regulatory activity. We find business firms and labor unions joining together to support the traditional, industry-oriented commission to which they have adapted. This often was the case when airline regulation was at its peak. In the area of occupational safety, however, labor unions and consumer groups form alliances to encourage the expansion of regulation, while business groups and economists often oppose such regulation because of excessive costs.

Hence, compatriots on one issue find themselves competitors on others. Specific safety regulations for automobiles may be opposed by both unions and companies in the motor vehicle industry, although the two groups differ strongly on job standards. Further, labor, management, and local governments may form a coalition when regulations, such as environmental standards, threaten the economy of their community, although some of these groups advocate general ecological advances.

Conclusions

There is little justification for either a general attack by business or other groups on all forms of government regulation or for a blanket endorsement of every instance of government intervention in the economy. Unless we are anarchists, we believe that government should set rules for society. But there is no need to jump to the conclusion that each regulation is effective in attaining its stated objective. As with most things in life, the sensible questions are not matters of either–or but of more or less, and how. Thus, we can enthusiastically advocate stringent controls to avoid infant crib deaths without simultaneously supporting a plethora of detailed federal rules and regulations dealing with the color of exit lights and the maintenance of spittoons. Simply put, there are serious questions as to what rules to set, how detailed they should be, and how they should be administered.

Proponents of regulation contend that many of the rules and directives have yielded numerous benefits to the public. The NHTSA claims that seat belts, head restraints, and other mandated safety devices save thousands of lives each year. The EPA notes that, because of its controls over industrial discharges, fish and marine life have returned to many rivers and lakes.

However, the regulatory process generates its own set of "externalities." Voters in one congressional district may achieve the bulk of the benefits from a federal regulation, but the costs are borne primarily by citizens in other parts of the nation. For example, regulations making it uneconomical to use low-sulfur (i.e., low-polluting) coal have been supported by those areas producing high-sulfur coal. Consumers generally have borne the costs that result from such special-interest regulation enacted in the guise of environmental improvement.

Because of the very substantial costs and other adverse side effects that government regulation gives rise to, society has begun to take a hard look at the full array of government controls over business. In several recent administrations, Democratic and Republican alike, efforts have been made to eliminate or reassess those rules that generate excessive costs. In theory, government regulation should be carried to the point where the incremental benefits equal the incremental costs. Overregulation (which can be defined as situations where the costs to society exceed the benefits) is thus avoided. In practice, it is difficult to obtain measurements with the necessary precision to make such determinations.

The expansion of regulation also has required a variety of changes in the way companies manage their operations. Complying with government requirements has had the overall effect of pushing companies toward a greater degree of centralization in the areas subject to regulation. The effect is most pronounced in dealing with equal-employment and environmental issues. More people are involved in the decision-making network. Prior consultation and multiple reviews are often the order of the day. Authority to take action often moves up the corporate ladder, and the decision-making process slows down.

Thus, productivity can suffer, especially as the costs of legal and other overhead activities rise. Within the company, a *counterbureaucracy* arises, a cadre of specialists whose knowledge, training, and narrow responsibilities are characteristic of the regulators themselves.[10] Corporate managers are becoming more sensitive to evolving social demands. Thus, they increasingly understand that responses to at least some of the public's expectations are a normal aspect of conducting business.

Notes

1. John J. Riccardo, "Regulation: A Threat to Prosperity," *New York Times,* July 20, 1975, p. F–12.
2. Murray Weidenbaum, *Restraining Medicine Prices: Controls vs. Competition* (St. Louis, Mo: Washington University, Center for the Study of American Business, 1993), p. 21.
3. Marvin H. Kosters, "Government Regulation: Recent Status and Need for Reform," in Michael L. Wachter and Susan M. Wachter, eds., *Toward a New Industrial Policy?* (Philadelphia: University of Pennsylvania Press, 1981), pp. 332–335.
4. See Charles Wolf, Jr., "A Theory of Nonmarket Failure," *Journal of Law and Economics,* April 1979, pp. 107–139.
5. Wolf, p. 114.
6. Bruce Yandle and Elizabeth Young, "Regulating the Function, Not the Industry," *Public Choice* 51, no. 1, 1986, pp. 59–70.
7. See George J. Stigler, *The Citizen and the State: Essays on Regulation* (Chicago: University of Chicago Press, 1975).
8. Sam Peltzman, "Toward a More General Theory of Regulation," *Journal of Law and Economics,* August 1976, pp. 211–240; George J. Stigler, "The Theory of Economic Regulation," in Thomas Ferguson and Joel Rogers, eds., *The Political Economy,* (Armonk, NY: M. E. Sharpe, 1984), pp. 67–81.
9. *National Air Quality and Emissions Trends Report, 1995* (Research Triangle Park, NC: U.S. Environmental Protection Agency, 1996).
10. Ronald Berenbeim, *Regulation: Its Impact on Decision Making* (New York: Conference Board, 1981), pp. v–vi.

APPENDIX

TABLE 2.3   Major Extensions of Regulation of Business, 1962–1996

Year of Enactment	Name of Law	Purpose and Function of Law
1962	Food, Drug, and Cosmetic Act Amendments	Requires pretesting of drugs for safety and effectiveness and labeling of drugs by generic names
1962	Air Pollution Control Act	Provides first modern ecology statute
1963	Equal Pay Act	Eliminates wage differentials based on sex
1964	Civil Rights Act	Creates Equal Employment Opportunity Commission (EEOC) to investigate charges of job discrimination
1965	Cigarette Labeling and Advertising Act	Requires labels on hazards of smoking
1966	Traffic Safety Act	Provides for a coordinated national safety program, including safety standards for motor vehicles
1966	Fair Packaging and Labeling Act	Requires producers to state what a package contains, how much it contains, and who made the product
1966	Child Protection Act	Bans sale of hazardous toys and articles
1966	Coal Mine Safety Amendments	Tightens controls on working conditions
1967	Flammable Fabrics Act	Broadens federal authority to set safety standards for flammable fabrics, including clothing and household products
1967	Age Discrimination in Employment Act	Prohibits job discrimination against individuals aged 40 to 65
1968	Consumer Credit Protection Act (Truth-in-Lending)	Requires full disclosure of terms and conditions of finance charges in credit transactions
1968	Interstate Land Sales Full Disclosure Act	Provides safeguards against unscrupulous practices in interstate land sales
1969	National Environmental Policy Act	Requires environmental impact statements for federal agencies and projects
1970	Clean Air Amendments	Provides for setting air-quality standards
1970	Occupational Safety and Health Act	Establishes safety and health standards that must be met by employers
1970	Amendments to Federal Deposit Insurance Act	Prohibits issuance of unsolicited credit cards. Limits customer's liability in case of loss or theft to $50. Regulates credit bureaus and provides consumers access to files
1970	Securities Investor Protection Act	Provides greater protection for customers of brokers and dealers and members of national securities exchanges. Establishes a Securities Investor Protection Corporation, financed by fees on brokerage houses

TABLE 2.3 *(cont.)*

Year of Enactment	Name of Law	Purpose and Function of Law
1970	Poison Prevention Packaging Act	Authorizes standards for child-resistant packaging of hazardous substances
1972	Consumer Product Safety Act	Establishes a commission to set safety standards for consumer products and bans products presenting undue risk of injury
1972	Federal Water Pollution Control Act	Declares an end to the discharge of pollutants into navigable waters by 1985 as a national goal
1972	Equal Employment Opportunity Act	Gives the EEOC the right to sue employers
1972	Noise Pollution and Control Act	Regulates noise limits of products and transportation vehicles
1973	Vocational Rehabilitation Act	Requires federal contractors to take affirmative action on hiring the handicapped
1973	Highway Speed Limit Reduction	Limits vehicles to speeds of 55 miles an hour
1973	Safe Drinking Water Act	Requires the EPA to set national drinking-water regulations
1974	Campaign Finance Amendments	Restricts amounts of political contributions
1974	Employee Retirement Income Security Act	Sets new federal standards for employee pension programs
1974	Hazard Materials Transportation Act	Requires standards for the transportation of hazardous materials
1974	Magnuson-Moss Warranty Improvement Act	Establishes federal standards for written consumer product warranties
1975	Energy Policy and Conservation Act	Authorizes greater controls over domestic energy supplies and demands
1976	Hart-Scott-Rodino Antitrust Amendments	Provides for class action suits by state attorneys general; requires large companies to notify the Department of Justice of planned mergers and acquisitions
1976	Toxic Substances Control Act	Requires advance testing and restrictions on use of chemical substances
1977	Business Payments Abroad Act	Provides for up to $1 million penalties for bribes of foreign officials
1977	Saccharin Study and Labeling Act	Requires warning labels on products containing saccharin
1977	Department of Energy Organization Act	Establishes a permanent department to regulate energy on a continuing basis
1977	Surface Mining Control and Reclamation Act	Regulates strip mining and reclamation of abandoned mines
1977	Fair Labor Standards Amendments	Increases the minimum wage in three steps
1977	Export Administration Act	Imposes restrictions on complying with the Arab boycott

continued

44 PART II Government Regulation of Business

TABLE 2.3 *(cont.)*

Year of Enactment	Name of Law	Purpose and Function of Law
1978	Fair Debt Collection Practices Act	Provides for the first nationwide control of collection agencies
1978	Age Discrimination in Employment Act Amendments	Raises the permissible mandatory retirement age from 65 to 70 for most employees
1980	Comprehensive Environmental Response, Compensation, and Liability Act	Creates superfund to pay for cleanup of hazardous chemical spills; taxes petroleum and chemicals
1980	Federal Trade Commission Improvements Act	Bars the FTC from enforcing antitrust laws against farm co-ops; prevents agency from issuing a regulation concerning funeral industry
1981	Cash Discount Act	Prevents merchants from imposing a surcharge on credit card sales
1984	Drug Price Competition and Patent Term Restoration Act	Gives generic drugs more market accessibility and restores some of the patent life lost during the development process
1984	Cigarette Safety Act	Requires a study of the feasibility of developing cigarettes with less tendency to set mattresses and upholstery on fire
1984	Insider Trading Sanctions Act	Increases sanctions against trading in securities while in possession of material "nonpublic" information
1986	Asbestos Hazard Emergency Response Act	Requires schools to inspect buildings for asbestos-containing materials and submit plans to states to deal with the problem
1986	Superfund Amendments and Reauthorization Act	Requires state and local governments to develop comprehensive emergency response plans; companies that make or use chemicals must report inventories and emissions to the public
1986	Age Discrimination in Employment Act	Abolishes mandatory retirement. Extends protections against discriminatory employment practices to workers over 70
1986	Single Employer Pension Plan Amendments Act	Restricts the circumstances under which an employer may terminate an employee pension plan. Increases employer's liability to participants when a terminating plan is underfunded
1988	Employee Polygraph Protection Act	Prohibits use of lie detectors by employers engaged in interstate commerce
1988	Clinical Laboratory Act	Regulates quality assurance standards and proficiency testing

TABLE 2.3 *(cont.)*

Year of Enactment	Name of Law	Purpose and Function of Law
1988	Worker Adjustment and Retraining Notification Act	Requires employers to provide 60 days advance notice of layoffs involving 50 or more workers
1989	Financial Institutions Reform, Recovery, and Enforcement Act	Restricts activities of savings and loan associations
1990	Clean Air Act Amendments	Requires many service and industrial firms to obtain permits to operate; sets industry-by-industry reduction standard for toxic air pollutants
1990	Americans with Disabilities Act	Gives civil rights protections to people with disabilities; requires employers to make "reasonable accommodations" for the disabled
1990	Nutritional Labeling and Education Act	Requires companies to use approved terms and to list specified information
1990	Oil Pollution Control Act	Includes new liability limits for various classes of vessels as well as double-hull requirements for oil tankers
1990	Pollution Prevention Act	Requires an annual report from each manufacturing facility that uses one or more of 300 listed chemicals
1991	Civil Rights Act	Reverses several Supreme Court decisions on what constitutes discrimination in employment
1991	Comprehensive Deposit Insurance Reform Act	Requires banking regulators to issue standards on "excessive" compensation and benefits for banking executives
1993	Family and Medical Leave Act	Gives employees a legal entitlement to take leave with job reinstatement rights
1995	Lobbying Disclosure Act	Extends disclosure requirements to include lobbying executive branch officials and providing more financial data by lobbyists
1995	Private Securities Litigation Reform Act	Limits court action by investors and caps damage awards against companies
1995	Telecommunications Competition and Deregulation Act	Opens telecommunications markets to competition
1996	Food Quality Protection Act	Replaces "zero risk" standard with "negligible risk" requirement
1996	Health Insurance Portability and Accountability Act	Helps maintain health insurance coverage for employees who switch or lose jobs
1996	National Securities Markets Improvement Act	Enables federal government to preempt states in regulation of financial markets
1996	Surface Transportation Board	Assumes residual functions of now-defunct Interstate Commerce Commission

CHAPTER 3

Government and the Consumer

Government regulation of consumer products takes many forms, ranging from outright bans to requirements for specific types of information on containers to changes in the products themselves. The regulations generate a variety of benefits as well as costs, which are ultimately borne by the consumer.

Consumer products are subject to regulation by a great variety of government agencies. In the United States, these public-sector review authorities include the Food and Drug Administration, the Department of Agriculture, the Federal Trade Commission, and the Department of Transportation. However, the Consumer Product Safety Commission (CPSC) has the broadest responsibility. The Consumer Product Safety Act of 1972 created an independent regulatory agency "to protect the public against unreasonable risks of injury associated with consumer products." A five-member commission sets safety standards for consumer products, bans products presenting undue risk of injury, and in general polices the consumer product marketing process from manufacture to final sale.

In establishing the commission, Congress adopted a no-fault view of accidental product injuries. Rather than stressing punitive action against the producers and distributors of unsafe products, the emphasis is on minimizing the likelihood that consumers will be subjected to product hazards. Under this approach, products are redesigned to guard against possible consumer misuse and ignorance of proper operation. In the words of E. Patrick McGuire of the Conference Board, "The most dangerous component is the consumer, and there's no way to recall him."

The CPSC truly has a broad mandate:

- To work with consumers and business to foster voluntary standards for product safety.
- To set and enforce mandatory standards.
- To ban unsafe products when a safety standard is not considered to adequately protect the public.
- To order firms to give public notice of substantial hazard associated with a product and to repair, replace, or refund the price of products that present a substantial hazard.
- To provide information to help consumers select and use products safely.

Consumers are assured the right to participate in the commission's activities. Any "interested person" can petition the commission to start a proceeding to issue, amend, or revoke a consumer product safety rule. Safety standards cover product performance and contents, as well as composition, design, construction, finish, packaging, and labeling. Any product representing an unreasonable risk of personal injury or death may, by court order, be seized and condemned. Under the Consumer Product

Safety Act, the commission's jurisdiction extends to more than 10,000 products. However, given its modest budget (one percent of that of the Environmental Protection Agency), the CPSC relies primarily on voluntary compliance. Table 3.1 shows the extensive array of such corporate cooperation in recent years.

Congress has excluded from the commission's authority several widely used products that are regulated by other federal agencies. These exclusions cover food, tobacco, drugs, and cosmetics (regulated by the Food and Drug Administration and the Department of Agriculture), pesticides (regulated by the Environmental Protection Agency), firearms and alcohol (subject to some supervision by the Treasury Department), and automobiles (regulated by the Department of Transportation). (See Appendix to this chapter, "Government and the Automobile.")

TABLE 3.1   Consumer Product Safety Commission Reports of Voluntary Corrective Actions

Product	Defect or Hazard	Action Taken
Notebook computer	Mounting can crack, short-circuiting the computer and causing fire	Refund of purchase price
Rayon skirt	Dangerously flammable	Product recalled
Infant coveralls	Buttons can detach and be swallowed	Refund of purchase price
Boat hoists	Electrocution hazard	Product redesigned; corrections made to units in distribution
Brass bench	Can collapse during use	Full refund
Chain saw	Sparks can cause fire	Free repair
Scuba regulator	Drowning can result from faulty mechanism	Product recalled and redesigned
Electric water heater	Fire hazard	Firm out of business; warning issued to consumers
Cigarette lighter	Could burn user	Company sent prepaid mailers and $5 check for returned product
Infant pillow	Potential asphyxiation	Full refund including mailing costs
Candle holder	Potential fire hazard	Full refund
Extension cord	Shock hazard	Full refund
Refrigerator compressor	Electric shock	Company replaced defective compressors in consumers' homes
Potpourri candles	Fire hazard	Recalled; consumers offered refund or replacement
Lawn mower	Can collapse	Dealers repaired defect
Liquid soap	Eye irritation	Product recalled for refund or exchange
Toaster	Fire hazard	Full refund or repair plus $25 gift certificate
Gasoline engine	Leaky shut-off valve	Replaced defective item
Halogen light	Fire hazard	Product recalled
Child's hamper	Child can get entrapped	Product recalled
Natural gas heater	Missing screw can cause injury	Retrofit kit provided
Hair dryer	Electrocution hazard	Manufacturer fixed and returned product

Source: U.S. Consumer Product Safety Commission.

THE IMPACT ON CONSUMERS—BENEFITS AND COSTS

Important benefits to the public can be expected from an agency designed to make consumers more aware of product hazards and to require that products likely to cause serious injuries be removed from the market. Simultaneously, it must be noted that such actions also generate substantial costs, which will be borne ultimately by the consumer in the form of higher prices or reduced variety of products. The consumer's total welfare is therefore enhanced by seeking out the most economical and efficient ways of achieving safety objectives. Thus, banning products can be viewed as the most direct way of responding to hazards, but that approach may not always be the most cost-effective one. Other alternatives range from relabeling a container (so that the consumer becomes aware of a previously hidden hazard) to recalling and modifying an existing line of products.

One way of looking at government-mandated product safety requirements is that they constitute a tie-in sale. All consumers, whether they want or need the new layer of protection, have to accept and pay for it. "What is made safe for the village idiot will cost the man of common sense more."[1] At times, higher prices to the consumer result from regulators forcing expensive complexity on the manufacturers of consumer products. Poor, and even middle-income, families may thus be priced out of many markets for consumer products. All this suggests that when a government agency decides to regulate a product and its use, it should consider a variety of relevant factors.

What Is an Acceptable Risk?

Many government regulations aim at eliminating all hazards. For example, the clean water law establishes an ultimate goal of zero discharge of pollutants into the nation's waterways. Prior to its replacement by the Food Quality Protection Act of 1996, the Delaney Amendment to the Food, Drug, and Cosmetic Act prohibited the use of any food additive if it contained the most minute trace of carcinogenic properties.[2]

Most people drink regular "tap" water, rather than buying more expensive—and purer—bottled water. In a similar attitude toward taking risks that they consider worthwhile, families drive on their vacations. They do so because often that is a cheaper and more convenient mode than air travel—even though airline safety records are superior to those of the average motorist. Likewise, individuals go skydiving, water skiing, or car racing because they willingly undertake the attendant risk in order to enjoy their leisure time. Similarly, some workers seek out employment in hazardous environments such as commercial deep sea diving because, in their view, the rewards are worth the danger involved.

The relevant questions involve which risks to take and how to sensibly minimize the dangers. It is useful to acknowledge that many people get hurt using the goods they buy. The questions that consumers regularly ask themselves, explicitly or implicitly, is which risks to take and how to minimize the dangers sensibly. Surely, that is how individuals tend to make their own decisions. However, as we will see later in this chapter, that is not how the world of government regulation works.

Surely not all hazards are equal. Some useful distinctions can be made among the different types of product hazards.

Types of Hazards

If the hazard is *hidden,* the unknowing consumer is denied the freedom of deciding whether to risk using the item. The risk in using a sharp knife is visible, and each individual may choose the degree of care in handling the instrument. Thus, there is no demand for regulation of that universal consumer product, which is associated with a variety of injuries. Hazards, however, may be unknown—such as the danger of cancer from exposure to asbestos, which was discovered only recently. Or the risk may be unexpected—such as the brake failure of a car while it is being driven. These hazards are not visible, and consumers have little or no choice in deciding whether or not they will expose themselves to them. So there may be a need for government intervention in the area of hidden risks. The precise nature of that intervention represents another category of decision making that we will take up later.

From the viewpoint of public policy, producers' or employers' provision of additional information to consumers or workers often constitutes an adequate response. When fully informed of the risks involved, some consumers, but not necessarily all, will reduce their purchases of hazardous products. Employees may insist on a "risk premium" in their pay to agree to work in the hazardous environment. On the other hand, product sales may fall so low, or the risk premium that workers insist on may be so high, that it pays the company to redesign the product or work process so as to reduce or eliminate the hazard. Often these voluntary responses are superior to government actions to ban products it deems hazardous. That arbitrary approach overlooks the possibility that, for some people, it is beneficial, or at least acceptable, to use the item (see Figure 3.1 for an example).

FIGURE 3.1 Taking a Chance

A Letter to the Editor
The Wall Street Journal, July 1, 1975

Your editorial "The Risks of Safety" (June 26) brings back memories.

In 1947 I was in our local sanitarium with service-connected TB. I had tuberculosis not only in the lungs but also in the throat, which was almost always fatal. I could hardly eat and guessed I had maybe two months to go, although I hadn't given up hope.

One day the medical director came to me and said, "Walter, there's a new drug, it may have side effects and it's so new the Vets won't pay for it. I'll let you have it for cost. Do you want to try it?" Of course I did. The drug was streptomycin; the cost was $1 a shot for 360 shots—one every six hours.

I'll never forget the throat specialist, who came up once a month, on his next visit. He looked in my mouth and said, "It's a miracle!" My throat was clear. Six months later I'd gained 70 pounds and was discharged with no side effects and have had no problems since.

If our present regulations concerning the release of new drugs were in effect then, I would have been dead for 28 years.

Walter A. Rothermel

Wyomissing, Pa.

A consumer's choice of a product will also depend on the *seriousness* of the potential harm (assuming the risk is known). Consumers have unequal tastes for safety as well as for other characteristics of product performance. Particularly where the safety hazard is minor (the occasional blister on a finger), large price increases to pay for eliminating the problem may merely deprive consumers of the use of many products. It is important to consider the cost of correcting safety hazards and to recognize that consumers regularly make trade-offs between safety and other criteria that are important to them.

For example, a power tool selling for $100 cannot be used for much more than an hour without overheating; the $800 piece of equipment can be safely used for a much longer period. Although the instructions on each tool may be very clear in this respect, some consumers will buy the cheaper model and knowingly take the chance of burning it out. A policy of complete safety would ban the cheaper item, thereby effectively depriving the low-income consumer (or the thrifty person) from buying a power tool or replacing an old, worn tool produced prior to the establishment of the new standard. If equity is a social goal, then this is an example of increasing safety at the expense of consumer welfare.

One trade-off between safety and other product characteristics can be seen in the following case. About one-fifth of the 16,000 injuries and 500 deaths a year due to burning clothing are caused by children's sleepwear catching fire. For this reason, the Consumer Product Safety Commission requires children's pajamas to possess a flame-resistant property. But when the National Cancer Institute found that Tris, the major chemical used, can cause cancer, the commission faced the dilemma of reducing the chance of cancer by increasing the chance of injury or death from fire. The commission chose to ban Tris, forcing manufacturers to seek a substitute.

Another example is that of the household ladder. The numerous accidents associated with that product have given rise to pressure for more detailed standards for its design and production. However, industry experts point out that if a ladder is made too difficult to use or too expensive to buy, many people will wind up climbing on a chair or a table instead—a far more dangerous procedure.

The CPSC mandate for childproof caps for medicines is another instance of the trade-offs involved in complying with regulations governing consumer products. Fewer children have been subjected to aspirin poisoning since the requirement was established. But other factors also occurred in the same time period, notably consumer shifts to nonaspirin forms of pain killers. In fact, almost half of all aspirin poisonings are reported to involve bottles that had been left open—an obvious but dangerous way of dealing with difficult-to-open childproof caps.[3] Children are not the only consumers who are affected. Shortly after a heart patient died with an unopened childproof bottle of nitroglycerin tablets, the commission sent a notice to doctors and pharmacists reminding them that childproof containers are not required for nitro tablets.

Personal behavior probably has the most pervasive influence on the risks individuals face. People learn to drive defensively and to lock their doors. The risks that people willingly face—and could choose to avoid—are often much larger than the risks that citizens worry about being obliged to endure. Of those who regularly drive or ride in automobiles, about 2 out of every 10,000 die in car accidents each year, for a total of about 45,000 deaths annually. By comparison, for those who live near municipal solid waste landfills, the mortality risk is substantially less than 1 in 1,000,000 and may be far lower—a minute fraction of the risk of automobile travel, and a risk that shows up (if at all) only decades later in life. Yet, public policy is much more severe on the latter, more remote type of risk.

The *probability of a hazard actually occurring* can be a prime consideration in the risks that we are willing to assume, although statutes limit the ability of regulators to exercise flexibility and judgment. For example, in testing whether TCE (trichlorethylene), a chemical used in decaffeinated coffee, might be a possible cause of cancer, the National Cancer Institute employed a generous dose of the chemical on its test animals—the equivalent of a person drinking 50 million cups of decaffeinated coffee every day for an entire lifetime. Despite the doubtful relevance of this test, the coffee industry quickly changed to the use of a different chemical, fearing another ban such as that imposed on cyclamates.[4]

From time to time, food poisoning scares upset the public, often needlessly. A dramatic example occurred in 1989 when the widely watched TV program *60 Minutes* publicized in dramatic fashion a charge by the Natural Resources Defense Council that spraying alar on apples posed a severe cancer risk. The resultant consumer panic subsided only after the issuance of a joint statement by the Food and Drug Administration, the Environmental Protection Agency, and the Department of Agriculture that it was safe to eat apples. It turned out that the alar residue on the apples was only one-fortieth of the EPA allowed limit.[5]

Also in 1989, a Chilean grape scare occurred because two grapes were found to contain three micrograms—one one-thousandth of one milligram—of cyanide (an ordinary lima bean normally contains 100 micrograms of cyanide). This succession of false alarms seems to have had a measurable effect on consumer attitudes. Back in 1984, the Food Marketing Institute reported that one out of every four shoppers was more concerned about chemicals in their food than other factors, such as sugar content. By 1991, two out of every five consumers were worried about fat and cholesterol. Chemicals showed up below salt and sugar concerns, being mentioned by less than one-tenth of the shoppers surveyed.

In practice, the public does not support every product ban that a government agency issues in an effort to reduce risk. In this regard, the consumer response to the Food and Drug Administration's attempt to ban saccharin (subsequently postponed by Congress) is instructive. It is readily summed up by a newspaper headline: "A Run on Saccharin Here to Beat Ban."

Also, government agencies do not adopt every proposal from the public to regulate consumer products. For example, the CPSC declined to act favorably on a petition to declare mistletoe hazardous. The commission's research did reveal that 132 "ingestions" of mistletoe were reported in a four-year period and that five of the people involved developed symptoms, two of whom required hospitalization. Although we are left to surmise the reasons for the commission's actions, it is reasonable to assume that the CPSC was wary of creating a field day for cartoonists. It is easy to conjure up illustrations of a couple kissing under a sprig of mistletoe and the accompanying caption reading, "The Federal Government Has Declared This Hazardous to Your Health." In any event, as good bureaucrats, the commission stated that denying the request should not "be construed as endorsement of the complete safety of these plants."[6]

On another occasion, the CPSC denied a petition to regulate pull-tab and pull-off lid containers even though they result in 5,600 emergency room cases a year. It turned out that injuries from conventional metal cans are responsible for over 60,000 emergency hospital visits annually. On yet another occasion, the CPSC promulgated a draft standard on matchbooks to make them more difficult to open. However, it quickly rescinded the standard when it realized, after many industry complaints, that the result often would be opened matchbooks left lying around.

Government experiences great difficulty in choosing the hazards it regulates. Take, for example, the problem of residential fires. The emphasis in public policy to date has been on wiring standards. How important a hazard is household wiring? According to the National Fire Protection Association, only 9 percent of fatal residential fires in the United States in recent years are caused by the electrical distribution system, a category that includes flaws in wiring. The other 91 percent comprises such more important causes as smoking (23 percent), arson (17 percent), heating equipment (14 percent), and children playing (10 percent). The dominant cause of residential fires, the carelessness of smokers, is beyond the CPSC's jurisdiction. Thus, the agency concentrates on a relatively minor cause that accounts for less than 8 percent of fatal fires.

A researcher at the University of Tokyo contends that "dangerousness is a continuum."[7] In that view, it is not possible to establish categories within which substances are uniformly dangerous or uniformly safe. Thus, whiskey will ignite, and large enough doses of sugar (or salt) can kill laboratory animals. Nevertheless, government officials are empowered to designate product hazards and to regulate or even ban specific products.

THE EFFECTS ON BUSINESS

Government regulation generates a wide variety of effects on the companies that produce and market to the consumer. The impact on one large industry—automobile manufacturing—is highlighted at the end of the chapter in the Appendix, "Government and the Automobile." For consumer goods generally, the Consumer Product Safety Commission has generated many specific requirements. The paperwork burden on business can be, at times, quite substantial. The CPSC has called on every manufacturer, distributor, and retailer—upon learning that an item sold "creates a substantial risk of injury"—to inform the commission and provide a wide array of information, including the following:

1. The number of products that present a hazard or potential hazard.
2. The number of units of each that are involved.
3. The number of units of each product in the hands of consumers.
4. Specific dates when the faulty units were manufactured and distributed.
5. An accounting of when and where such items (and the number of units of each) were distributed.
6. The model and serial numbers.
7. A list of names and addresses of every distributor, retailer, and producer, if known.

8. A description of the effort made to notify consumers of the defect.

9. Details of corrective tests, quality controls, and engineering changes made or contemplated.

The reporting requirement is not complete until the company submits a final report indicating that the potential hazard has been corrected. Thus, the commission shifts to the company the responsibility and costs of determining and remedying potential defects. Moreover, company decisions on whether or not to report a potentially hazardous product are influenced by the possibility of criminal sanctions should the commission disagree with a company's decision that a given item is not potentially hazardous.

Product Recalls

As a result of the expanded role of government regulation of product safety, corporate marketing departments have developed the capability to handle "reverse distribution"—product recalls. In addition to the highly publicized cases of motor vehicles and tires, various nonautomotive products are recalled from time to time, including adhesives, bicycles, computers, deodorants, drain cleaners, electric shavers, Epsom salts, gas ovens, heart monitors, lawn mowers, power drills, safety helmets, soup bowls, television sets, toys, and women's hygienic products.

Voluntary recalls predate the new wave of government regulation. In 1903, Packard recalled its Model K when it realized that the car's drive shaft had a habit of popping out of its housing. In the contemporary environment, companies at times have the option of initiating a voluntary recall of a product. This may obviate the need for formal government action and provide more flexibility in dealing with customers. Given the government's "stick in the closet," the voluntary approach provides the benefit of choosing the timing of the recall and minimizing the adverse publicity that may result.

Many companies, especially those catering to consumer markets, have introduced numerous modifications in their operating procedures to reduce the expense and anxiety associated with recalls. A system of coded identification numbers for each product or batch of products is often used to provide an expedited response to product recalls. Computerized information systems keep track of the products throughout the distribution chain. The identification includes the labeling of each shipping package and container with a code indicating item, batch or period, day, month, year, and plant. Warranty cards are a widely used method of providing the manufacturer with the names and addresses of purchasers of products as well as other details, some of which contribute to market research.

One large manufacturer of food products has issued an extensive management guide on product recalls, which includes the following steps:

- Establishing a procedure for evaluating customer complaints to detect potential problems as early as possible.
- Appointing a product recall coordinator to direct all activities involved in a recall.
- Developing a product code and monitoring system so that all products can be traced as far as possible through the distribution system.
- Setting up an emergency communication system to notify customers in the event of a recall.

- Conducting mock recalls of consumer products that have a potential for risk or injury to evaluate the effectiveness of the recall program.

- Assuming that all consumer products or components have a potential for risk of injury unless a determination has been made to the contrary by the law department and the quality control director.

Corporations are devoting considerable attention to preventive action, such as more carefully reviewing consumer complaints that cite specific product defects. Such an approach also can be used as evidence of the company's acting in good faith should a product subsequently be declared hazardous.

Responding to recalls can be burdensome. The expense varies with the number of products sold; the amount of time and effort required to track down purchasers; the percentage of products that require repair, replacement, or refund; and the cost per unit to remedy the problem. The cost of the recall can far exceed the price of the product itself. One company estimated that it cost, on the average, $5 to recall each defective 19-cent item. The costs in that case include notifying each user by return-receipt letter or personal call; locating, removing, and disposing of suspect items at various locations; redesigning the item; overtime manufacturing of new items; printing labels and instructions; packing, shipping installing, and testing new items; recording and reporting the actions taken; and medical and legal fees in connection with consumer complaints—all in addition to lost sales.

With product recalls a frequent experience and with high liability judgments, companies have added incentive to produce safer, albeit more expensive, products. The experience of Firestone Tire & Rubber Company with its "500" steel-belted radial tire surely illustrates the great stakes involved. After an acrimonious public battle with the National Highway Traffic Safety Administration, the company was forced to recall 13 million of its tires—the largest product recall in history. The damage to the company's sales and reputation was substantial, and for a while it operated in the red. Firestone eventually sold out to Bridgestone, a Japanese tire company. (For details of this case, see the section, "Firestone and the Highway Safety Agency" later in this chapter.)

Packaging and Labeling

Regulators' increasing attention to the role of information has resulted in some of the emphasis in consumer goods packaging being shifted from eye-catching decorative coverings to informational labeling (see Table 3.2). Greater amounts of information have been required on labels (especially for food products), as well as in supporting literature and catalogs. Under the Nutrition Labeling and Education Act of 1990, FDA and USDA have promulgated a set of nutrition-labeling rules that require food processing companies to adopt uniform labels for hundreds of thousands of products. The purpose is to give consumers more and better information about the nutritional content of food and to limit the health claims made by manufacturers. Companies now must provide information on cholesterol, sodium, carbohydrates, fiber, and fat. To be labeled "low fat," a product must contain no more than three grams of fat per serving. "Light" products must contain 50 percent less fat or one-third fewer calories than standard products.

TABLE 3.2 Authorized Nutrition and Health Claims on Food Packages

Label Claim	Definition (Per Serving)
Calorie free	Fewer than 5 calories
Low calorie	40 calories or less
Light or lite	⅓ fewer calories or 50% less fat
Fat free	Less than ½ gram fat
Low fat	3 grams or less fat
Cholesterol free	Less than 2 milligrams cholesterol and 2 grams or less saturated fat
Low cholesterol	20 milligrams or less cholesterol and 2 grams or less saturated fat
Sodium free	Less than 5 milligrams sodium
Low sodium	140 milligrams or less sodium

Source: Food and Drug Administration.

The Department of Health and Human Services estimated that the changeover cost industry approximately $2 billion but claimed that this one-shot expense would be more than offset by reduced health care costs resulting from improved nutrition.

The U.S. Department of Agriculture establishes specific requirements that must be met before an item can be labeled as poultry, hash, pizza, or other food products. At times, the amount of detail becomes humorous. For example, the department issued a regulatory change requiring that every frozen pizza have at least 12 percent cheese topping, with no less than half of that being real cheese topping. Not all consumers were pleased. One wrote in, urging the USDA to "leave the pizzas just the way they are. . . . My two-and-one-half-year-old son has asthma and allergies. He can't have any milk products. The pizza with fake cheese is a great treat for him."[8] Cartoonists had a field day. (See Figure 3.2 for an example.) To compound the problem, cheese pizza is regulated by the FDA because it contains 2 percent or less meat and poultry products. Sausage and pepperoni pizzas are covered by the USDA.

Enforcement of labeling rules can be arbitrary at times. In 1991, the FDA ordered manufacturers of vegetable cooking oils to remove the words "no cholesterol" from their labels. Did the products actually contain cholesterol? No, but the government agency considered the claim "misleading." Consumers, they feared, might mistakenly get the impression that no cholesterol means "no fat" or "no risk of heart disease." In 1997, however, the agency took a more sympathetic attitude. It allowed makers of oatmeal to claim that the product may reduce the risk of heart disease. However, the FDA added a proviso: The claim must also note that the beneficial effect is contingent on the oatmeal being part of a diet low in saturated fat and cholesterol.

Advertising

The government is a substantial influence both in terms of prescribing types of advertising and in restricting the claims that are made. Writers of copy are frequently instructed about the liabilities of a product—as well as its attributes. Advertisers and advertising agencies, spurred by federal action, often display awareness of consumer

Source: Washington Post, National Weekly Edition, December 26, 1983. Reprinted by permission of William T. Coulter.

FIGURE 3.2

safety in product advertising. Such advertising copy provides tangible benefits, notably enhancing product acceptability and reducing the possibility of unfavorable publicity and safety-related lawsuits.

Some heavy advertisers in consumer markets, or their agencies, have set up formal panels to review the approach to safety in their advertising. These panels include advertiser and agency personnel who have actual experience with the products involved—for example, parents of young children. The National Advertising Review Board, an industry self-regulatory organization, has developed the following checklist for reviewing company advertising to minimize the likelihood of violating federal product safety requirements:

- Is anything shown, described, or claimed in the advertisement that raises questions of consumer safety?
- Is everything known that should be known about the product's performance under both normal and misuse circumstances?
- Is there anything in the advertisement that might prove harmful to children who cannot comprehend the most familiar hazards in consumer products and tend to imitate what they see?
- Is allowance made in advertising for the susceptibility to suggestion of the elderly or the consumer predisposed toward risk taking?

Firestone and the Highway Safety Agency

A vivid example of the adverse effects on a business that can result from an inadequate response to governmental regulation of the company's product is the experience of the Firestone Tire & Rubber Company. In 1978, the National Highway Traffic Safety Administration urged Firestone to recall all 13 million of its Firestone 500 tire, then the company's top-of-the-line, steel-belted radial.

The case against the Firestone 500 rested on evidence that the tire's failure rate and likelihood of causing serious accidents were exceptionally high. Under its statute, the NHTSA is empowered to order recalls of motor vehicles and accessories that either fail to meet its specific standards for design and test performance or exhibit other evidence of a safety-related defect. The 500s did not violate any specific NHTSA standard. However, they had accident and adjustment rates far greater than those of other tires. By July 1978, NHTSA had gathered reports of 64 injury-producing accidents and 34 fatalities that involved the Firestone 500. Reports on steel-belted radials sold by Firestone's seven leading competitors showed only 21 fatalities for eight times the number of tires. Furthermore, between 1972 and March 1978, the overall adjustment rate for the 500s (the percentage of tires returned by customers and accepted for pro-rated credit toward new tires) was 17.5 percent, against only 1.7 to 5.3 percent reported by Firestone's leading competitors for their steel-belted radials.

In July, NHTSA announced an initial determination that the 500s contained a "safety-related defect" and might therefore be subject to recall. Firestone contended that the 500s were safe, dependable, and free of fundamental defects. It argued that the chief cause of failure had been the widespread and persistent tendency of drivers to keep their tires underinflated, thereby irreversibly damaging the tires and making them dangerously susceptible to failure. It discounted the adjustment-rate figures on the grounds that it had been unusually accommodating to customers. Firestone noted that no one had identified any specific defect in the tire and that the tire's reliability, rated in NHTSA's own test, was "far in excess" of the agency's requirements.

In August 1978, the House of Representatives Commerce Committee issued a report that rebutted many of Firestone's arguments. The report contended that manufacturers should make tires sufficiently durable to withstand, at least to a reasonable extent, such recognized common abuses as underinflation. For a company to do otherwise, the report suggested, is to produce tires with the expectation of having them fail.

Firestone's sales literature and ads had not, up to that time, warned consumers about the critical importance of keeping the 500s properly inflated, although underinflation of 4 pounds per square inch represented "the threshold of trouble" for the tire and 6 to 8 pounds underinflation meant "trouble for sure." More compelling to Firestone was that the steady barrage of unfavorable publicity about the safety of its key product was rapidly eroding its market share.

NHTSA was stymied in ordering a recall by Firestone's refusal to provide the information requested. Firestone insisted for many months that the overall adjustment rate of the 500s was 7.4 percent rather than the actual figure of 17.5 percent. Although the company claimed it had no indication of any safety problems with the 500 until NHTSA raised the matter, hundreds of internal company documents released after the signing of the recall show the opposite. A 1972 memo to a Firestone vice president warned that "we are in danger of being cut off by Chevrolet because of separation failures."

Without such evidence, NHTSA sought an agreement with Firestone for a voluntary recall. On November 29, 1978, Firestone signed an agreement with NHTSA agreeing to recall the Firestone 500. While less stringent than NHTSA would have liked, the agreement had the advantage of being immune to legal challenge. An estimated 7.5 million 500s sold after September 1, 1975, and manufactured before January 1, 1977, were eligible for free replacement. Although Firestone's legal counsel continued to urge the company to fight the regulatory agency, the top management saw that Firestone was rapidly losing its traditional position in its basic market. The steady public criticism of the safety of the 500 was devastating, and management reluctantly agreed to the recall. However, Firestone never recovered from the loss of consumer confidence in its tires; Bridgestone, the Japanese tire giant, soon after acquired the company.

REGULATION AND CONSUMERS

The regulation of pharmaceuticals by the Food and Drug Administration (FDA) provides cogent examples of the costs and benefits that flow to the consumer from governmental involvement. It is well known that patients in the United States have been spared such horrors as the deformities resulting from use of inadequately tested drugs such as thalidomide. What is not as widely recognized is the cost—both in dollars and lives—of the extra caution.

The direct expense of compliance with FDA procedures is substantial. Eli Lilly's application for a drug for arthritis came to 120,000 pages and weighed 2,038 pounds. But the full cost of delays in the lengthy approval process is far more than financial. A study of new drugs that were introduced in both the United States and the United Kingdom in the period 1977 to 1987 reported that far more—114—were first available in Great Britain, compared to only 41 that were first available in the United States.

For example, propranolol, an important advance in treating high blood pressure, was available more than seven years earlier in the United Kingdom. Sodium valproate, used to treat epilepsy, was available six years earlier in Switzerland. However, the people who died because the new and better pharmaceuticals were not available to them were not represented in the regulatory process.

We can understand why FDA reviewers ask for more studies and delay the introduction of new products. Consider the disparate impacts bluntly: If 16 people are harmed by side effects of an approved drug, that becomes front page news. On the other hand, if 10,000 people die prematurely because approval of a new drug was delayed, the public is unaware. That figure of 10,000 is the estimate of how many people died needlessly each year during the period 1967–1976 when FDA was slow in approving beta blockers for reducing the risk of heart attack. The United Kingdom had given the go-ahead several years earlier.[9]

PRODUCT LIABILITY AND THE COURTS

Even in the absence of regulatory requirements, the product liability system provides substantial incentives for companies to be concerned with the safety of the items they make. Under the U.S. legal system, the primary legal responsibility for product safety is borne by the manufacturer. To obtain financial compensation, injured consumers must bear the burden of instituting court action on their claims for compensation.

Alternative Approaches to Liability

A consumer harmed by a product may sue the manufacturer under one of three legal theories: negligence, breach of implied warranty, or strict liability.[10] Under the *negligence* theory, a manufacturer is liable for the harm caused by its product if the company knew or should have known of the defect that caused the injury. The issue that the court considers is whether a "reasonably prudent" producer under "similar circumstances" would have sold the product. The negligence theory recognizes that mistakes do happen and that the quality control system of a reasonably prudent company may not catch the defect. In such an event, the risk rests on the consumer.

Under the theory of *breach of implied warranty,* the manufacturer is responsible for damages if the product is not fit for the purpose for which it is intended or for other reasonably anticipated uses.

The theory of *strict liability* holds the manufacturer liable for injuries resulting from a defective product that is "unreasonably dangerous," whether or not the company acted unreasonably in setting limitations on implied warranties. The doctrine of strict liability is widely accepted today. The trend toward strict liability has been based on three lines of reasoning: (1) people who are injured by defective products should be compensated, notwithstanding legal niceties of negligence and warranty; (2) the cost of accidents should be spread among those who benefit from the product; and (3) the doctrine of strict liability fosters efficiency because the manufacturer is in the best position to reduce the cost and likelihood of accidents.

Even under strict liability, injured consumers must still meet several specific legal tests. Plaintiffs are required to prove three key facts:

- That the product was in a "defective condition"—that there was something wrong with it.
- That the defect rendered the product "unreasonably dangerous"—that the defect gave rise to dangers of which ordinary consumers were unaware.
- That the defect caused the injuries that gave rise to the suit.

In some cases, manufacturers have been successful in arguing that they should not be liable where a consumer used their product in ways that were unreasonable, negligent, or unforeseeable.[11] In 1988, the bellwether California Supreme Court, ruling in favor of a pharmaceutical company, used rather broad language:

> [I]n accord with almost all our sister states that have considered the issue, we hold that a manufacturer is not strictly liable for injuries caused by a prescription drug so long as the drug was properly prepared and accompanied by warnings of its dangerous propensities that were either known or reasonably scientifically knowable at the time of distribution.[12]

Nevertheless, the product liability process does play an important role in promoting product safety. A survey of 500 chief executive officers revealed that threatened or actual product liability suits caused 36 percent of the surveyed firms to discontinue making specific products. On the other hand, 35 percent of the companies reported that their liability experiences had resulted in improving the safety of their products, and 47 percent had improved their product warnings. Product liability costs also were a factor in deciding whether to introduce new products.[13]

High-performance automobiles provide a pertinent case in point. Although the Mercedes Benz SL roadster made its world debut late in 1988, it was not sold in the United States until the 1991 model year. The reason for the delay was that, if a new product has been in use in Europe for several years and has experienced few problems, it is easier to defend it against liability suits in the United States.

In the case of the drug bendectin, prescribed for morning sickness, a series of unsuccessful lawsuits against the manufacturer forced it to abandon production. The cost of insurance and legal defense almost equaled the profits earned on sales.[14] Unison Industries, Inc., withheld from the market a new and advanced electronic ignition system for light aircraft because of the liability risk that might result from its use. A producer of a pollution-abatement device withdrew that product after failing to obtain liability insurance.

As has been demonstrated in the case of producers of asbestos—such as the Manville Corporation, which declared bankruptcy—very large product risks can create claims far greater than a company's resources. In that case, it is unlikely that the full claims for the injuries suffered will be paid. The legal costs borne by the plaintiffs and the defendants exceed the compensation received by the injured parties. In other cases, court decisions have varied considerably, ranging from upholding consumer claims to denying redress. Here is a sample of how consumer product cases have been handled in recent years:

- A woman suffered a spontaneous abortion and nearly died while wearing a Dalkon shield. She argued that the device had been defectively designed and had caused an infection. The Colorado Supreme Court upheld a jury verdict of $600,000 in compensatory damages and $6.2 million in punitive damages.

- A child was lifted into a ceiling fan, suffering skull and brain lacerations. The plaintiff argued that the fan's design was defective and that the company should have warned of the danger. The jury found for the company.

- A 16-year-old boy lost an arm when a motorboat ran over the jet ski he was riding. The plaintiff argued that the ski was unstable and difficult to see in waves. The jury ruled that the company should pay $2 million. It then reduced the damages by one-third due to the boy's negligence.

Recent events demonstrate that the product liability process can play an important but limited role in promoting product safety. Legal costs can be awesome. The Rand Corporation, a nonprofit research institute, reports that three-fifths of the insurance-company payments, on average, go to the two sets of lawyers.

Conclusions

Despite some efforts in the early 1980s and again in the early 1990s to slow the pace of federal rule making, the existing body of product regulation continues in force. It is unlikely that government intervention in the design, production, and marketing of consumer products will greatly diminish.

As described earlier, the provision of adequate information can be a satisfying alternative to outright bans or detailed standards—providing the regulatory agency is aware of the problem of "overloading" consumers with more details than they can handle. The metal extension ladder now carries 37 warnings and instructions. But injuries associated with that product have risen since manufacturers adopted the warnings in 1982.[15]

The state of California has often set the pace of the information approach. Pursuant to a proposition passed by the voters in 1987, businesses must warn people of exposure to any of more than 200 chemicals if the level poses a significant risk of causing cancer or birth defects. Companies failing to do so are subject to a fine of up to $2,500 a day for each exposure. A "bounty hunter" provision allows any individual filing a successful suit under the new state law to collect 25 percent of the penalty imposed on a violator. Since the law puts the burden on business to prove the safety of its products or warn consumers, people are being bombarded by notices in gas stations, restaurants, hotels, stores, and newspapers.

The information route is the one that had been used primarily in the case of one of the most popular consumer products—cigarettes—until the late 1990s. The courts ruled in favor of the tobacco companies in almost every case claiming lung cancer resulted from smoking since the warning labels were required in 1966.[16] The courts said that the label required by the Surgeon General under the Cigarette Labeling and Advertising Act provided adequate warning to smokers.[17] Nevertheless, the Food and Drug Administration moved to declare nicotine a drug under its jurisdiction and thus cigarettes a "delivery system" subject to regulation.

The combination of the FDA's determination to regulate cigarettes and a host of suits by state governments seeking reimbursement for their payment of medical costs for smokers led the cigarette manufacturers in 1997 to agree to a comprehensive settlement. Subject to congressional and White House approval, the companies agreed to pay out over $368 billion over a period of years and to accept FDA regulation of nicotine as a drug as well as a ban on advertising cigarettes on billboards, on the Internet, or in sports promotions.

Providing pertinent product information can benefit consumers. Take the case of three-wheeled all-terrain vehicles (ATVs). One study showed that they are more dangerous than four-wheeled ATVs. When consumers learned that the four-wheeled version was safer, they ceased buying the three-wheeled models. The Consumer Product Safety Commission did negotiate a virtual ban on three-wheeled ATVs with the industry, but the ban had little effect. Consumers had already ceased buying the three-wheeled variety.[18]

Potentially, market competition can play a key role in reducing injuries from the products consumers use. Information on comparative product safety can provide one firm with a competitive advantage over another. In this way, the market itself would produce safer products.

But, ultimately, it may be more widespread knowledge of the many effects, and especially of the costs and benefits, of government intervention that alters the current reliance on government-mandated standards for private-sector production and consumption. This job of communication will not, however, be easily performed. The following lament of the Public Interest Economics Group is noteworthy:

> One of the most difficult problems faced in public interest lobbying is how to communicate basic economic principles without antagonizing consumer and other public interest groups who may not have taken them into consideration in formulating their position.[19]

In any event, despite the continuing concerns about product, workplace, and environmental hazards, it is heartening to note the steady increase in life expectancy in the United States, from 47 years for those born in 1900, to 68 years for "the class of 1950," and to 76 years for those born in 1996.[20]

Appendix: Government and the Automobile[21]

Federal regulation of passenger automobiles is the most extensive example of government influence on a consumer product. The individual regulations cover design, production, and operation of the vehicle. Government is directly involved in setting standards for such basic items as engines, bumpers, headrests, seat belts, door latches, brakes, fuel systems, and windshields, as well as the type of fuel that can be used.

However, there is no provision for coordinating among regulatory agencies and statutes. The law to control emissions also reduces fuel efficiency by 7.5 percent. The required side-door guard beams, the energy-absorbing steering column, and other safety features have added about 200 pounds to the weight of an automobile, lowering fuel economy and increasing pollution. In turn, fuel-economy standards have forced the manufacture of smaller, lighter cars that are inherently less safe than the cars that would otherwise be produced. When two cars of different size collide, the safety advantage lies with the occupants of the heavier vehicle. In fact, the chance of being involved in a fatal accident is about twice as great in a subcompact as it is in a larger automobile. The fuel-efficiency standards applied to cars made in the United States in 1990 are estimated to result in over 2,200 additional traffic deaths, even after taking into account the tendency of occupants of smaller cars to use their safety belts more frequently.

Between 1968 and 1991, safety and emissions requirements added approximately $2,000 to the price of the average new automobile (in 1990 dollars). This higher cost has meant that many people are driving their old cars longer and thus not getting the intended benefits of the host of safety-environmental-energy regulations that have been promulgated. Also, drivers are encouraged to use motorcycles and bicycles, which are often cheaper but less safe than conventional motor cars.

Automobile safety regulation in the United States is characterized by great reluctance to interfere directly with individual behavior. The major cause of automobile accidents is driver error, often on the part of drunken motorists. In addition, 40 percent of the pedestrians in fatal crashes could be considered legally intoxicated. Nevertheless, regulation concentrates on the companies that make the products that people use, rather than on the way people use them. This is evident when we compare softness in enforcing statutes on driving while intoxicated with the stringent requirements for safety-related components imposed on manufacturers of motor vehicles.

Because many automobile passengers do not use seat belts, the federal government, after considerable debate, requires the installation of more expensive passive-restraint systems. These systems can be activated without any action by the driver or passengers, notably air bags that inflate in a frontal collision. Yet, Table 3.3 shows the substantial benefit that results from simply requiring that all occupants of motor vehicles use their seat belts. In contrast, airbags have become controversial. Approximately 30 children and 20 adults were killed by airbags in the period 1981–1986. (A much larger number of people have been saved by the same equipment.) The prob-

TABLE 3.3 Impact of Seat-Belt Use Laws

| Nation | Seat Belt Usage | | Reduction in Fatalities |
	Before Law	*After Law*	
Australia	30%	80%	22%
Belgium	17	92	39
Canada	21	61	16
France	26	75	22
Great Britain	40	90	24
Sweden	36	79	46
Average	28%	80%	28%

Source: U.S. Department of Transportation.

lem arose because at first the government required the bags to have enough force to protect someone not wearing a seat belt. Public outrage forced a modification of this poorly-thought-through requirement.

Economists who have made such comparisons conclude that the costs of programs to regulate automobile safety, fuel economy, and emissions are greater than their benefits. As a result, less costly alternatives have been suggested. An incentive-based insurance policy could be developed with fees reflecting the driver's record and the actual "crashworthiness" of the car. Seat belts could greatly reduce fatalities at a low cost if a combination of education and enforcement increased their usage substantially. Stronger enforcement of laws against drunk driving would be much more effective than the status quo.

Another suggestion is to accelerate the replacement of old vehicles with high emissions rates and low fuel utilization through retirement bounties or high annual registration fees. At present, public policy operates in the reverse manner—owners of older cars tend to pay lower personal property taxes than the purchasers of newer, more fuel-efficient vehicles.

Notes

1. Walter Guzzardi, Jr., "The Mindless Pursuit of Safety," *Fortune,* April 9, 1979, p. 64.

2. The Delaney Cancer Amendment of 1958 provided that, "No additive shall be deemed to be safe if it is found to induce cancer when ingested by man or animal . . ." The 1996 law substitutes the more realistic standard of "reasonable certainty of no harm."

3. W. Kip Viscusi, "Consumer Behavior and the Safety Effects of Product Safety Regulation," *Journal of Law and Economics,* October 1985, pp. 527–553.

4. U.S. Food and Drug Administration, "Trichlorethylene (TCE) and Coffee," *FDS Talk Paper,* June 27, 1975.

5. Thomas H. Jukes, "Truth Is First Victim in Food Poisoning Scares," *Chief Executive,* July/August 1989, pp. 38–41.

6. *Briefing Paper on Poinsettia Plants and Mistletoe Sprigs* (Washington, DC: U.S. Consumer Product Safety Commission, December 17, 1975).

7. Kazuo Akita, "Handle With Care," *Look Japan,* October 1991, p. 30.

8. Ward Sinclair, "'Truth in Pizza' Rule Draws Crusty Responses," *Washington Post,* National Weekly Edition, December 26, 1983, p. 31.

9. Sam Kazman, "Deadly Overcaution: FDA's Drug Approval Process," *Journal of Regulation and Social Costs,* September 1990; Murray Weidenbaum, *Restraining Medicine Prices* (St. Louis: Washington University, Center for the Study of American Business, 1993).

10. W. Kip Viscusi, *Regulating Consumer Product Safety* (Washington, DC: American Enterprise Institute, 1984), p. 8.

11. Peter Asch, *Consumer Safety Regulation* (New York: Oxford University Press, 1988), p. 23.

12. *Brown* v. *Abbott,* Supreme Court of the State of California, March 31, 1988.

13. E. Patrick McGuire, *The Impact of Product Liability* (New York: Conference Board, 1988).

14. Peter W. Huber, "Biotechnology and the Regulation Hydra," *Technology Review,* November–December 1987, p. 64.

15. Michael de Courcy Hinds, "As Warning Labels Multiply, Messages Are Often Ignored," *New York Times,* March 5, 1988, p. 14.

16. In an unusual case, a plaintiff was awarded damages on behalf of his late wife who started smoking before warning labels were used. "Cracks Seen in Tobacco's Liability Dam," *Wall Street Journal,* June 15, 1988, p. 25.

17. W. Kip Viscusi, *Smoking: Making the Risk Decision* (New York: Oxford University Press, 1992).

18. Paul H. Rubin, "Why Regulate Consumer Product Safety," *Regulation,* Fall 1991, p. 60.

19. "PIE Lobbying," *Public Interest Economics,* December 15, 1976, p. 6.

20. *Life Insurance Fact Book* (Washington, DC: American Council of Life Insurance, 1997).

21. Robert Crandall, et al., *Regulating the Automobile* (Washington, DC: Brookings Institution, 1986); "David Among Goliaths: The Small Car Faces Reality," *Journal of American Insurance,* Spring 1981, p. 2; *Motor Vehicle Regulations* (Washington, DC: General Accounting Office, 1992).

CHAPTER 4

Protecting the Environment

E nvironmental protection programs are the most rapidly growing area of government regulation and the reason for a major extension of public-sector involvement in private decision making. This expansion has coincided with substantial improvement in the quality of the environment. Yet the relationship between the cost of environmental programs and their benefits has not been as straightforward as expected. Citizens enthusiastically support environmental activities but are reluctant to pay for them directly, preferring business and/or government to cover the cost.

This chapter undertakes the dual task of examining the gamut of government programs designed to protect the environment and the impact of these efforts on business and the economy. We begin with an economic overview.

THE ECONOMICS OF ENVIRONMENTAL REGULATION

Until fairly recently, air and water (and the environment generally) were viewed as common property, as "free goods." Individuals and organizations, both public and private, used the environment as a free dump—which, of course, is the act of polluters polluting. The polluters received private benefits, but social costs ("externalities") in the form of dirtier air and water resulted. Excessive pollution was encouraged, however, because although the social costs of polluting may have exceeded the social benefits, the private benefits usually exceeded the private costs. People tend to pollute more if they do not have to pay for the cost of cleaning up.

In 1994, the United States discarded 209 million tons of solid wastes, or 4.4 pounds per person a day. Only 49 million pounds, or one-fourth of this vast amount of discarded material, was recycled. Confronting a cleanup challenge of that magnitude is a formidable task. To an economist, the environmental pollution problem is essentially one of altering people's incentives. The basic assumption is that people pollute, not because they enjoy spoiling the environment, but because polluting is cheaper or easier than not polluting. Thus, from an economic standpoint, if prices of goods and services would reflect the costs imposed on the environment (perhaps as measured by cleanup costs), consumers would shift to those less expensive goods and services that embody lower environmental costs.

Figure 4.1 illustrates how the imposition of cleanup costs affects producers and consumers. In this simple example, raising the price of gadgets to cover cleanup costs (perhaps via a pollution tax) results in lower sales—and most likely less pollution.

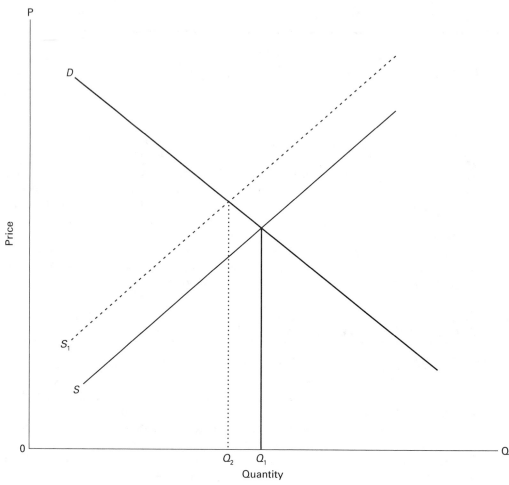

S = Supply of gadgets prior to imposing cleanup costs
S_1 = Supply of gadgets after imposing cleanup costs
Q_1 = Sales at old price schedule
Q_2 = Sales at new price schedule

FIGURE 4.1 Impact of Pollution Control on Market for Gadgets

Pollution taxes or effluent charges are tools to correct a serious source of market failure: the absence of a price needed to prevent the careless and excessive use of scarce environmental resources. Although most taxes create harmful side effects on the economy by distorting economic choices, taxes on pollution also have socially beneficial impacts.

There is considerable foreign experience with pollution fees. A cooperative association in Germany's heavily industrialized Ruhr Valley has used a "polluter pays" system since 1913. Fees are based on the amount and quality of the discharger's effluent. The funds generated by the charges help build and operate waste-treatment facilities in the basin. The effectiveness of this strategy in the Ruhr Valley led Germany to pass the Federal Water Act and Effluent Charge Law in 1976, establishing a nationwide fee system that took effect in 1981.[1] The German system delivers cleanup more efficiently than the command-and-control approach used in the United States. However, comparisons of water quality for the Mississippi River and the Ruhr suggest that Germany's fees may be set too low to achieve the water quality that Americans expect.

France has instituted a system of charges similar to the German program. Since 1969, fees have been used in conjunction with a permit system and primarily raise revenues for administrative costs and specific water-quality projects. Fees are a major, but not dominant, part of the French water-quality program.

Also since 1969, the Netherlands has administered a fee system that encourages dischargers to avoid polluting. Effluent fees in the Netherlands are higher than those in Germany or France. Fees are based on the volume and concentration of a discharger's effluent. Actual discharge levels are used to determine fees for large dischargers while small dischargers pay a fixed fee. As with Germany and France, revenues are used to finance projects to improve water quality. But, in contrast, the Netherlands' effluent fee system has a measurable impact on water quality. Increases in effluent charges are significantly correlated with declines in waterborne pollutants. Between 1976 and 1994, emissions of cadmium, copper, lead, mercury, and zinc plummeted 86 percent or more, primarily because of the charges.[2]

The idea behind pollution fees is not to punish polluters but to get them to change their ways as high-polluting products become more expensive than low-polluting products. Taxation (or an effluent fee) is a basic way of working through the price system. A tax or charge levied on high-polluting products alters relative prices in favor of low-polluting products. A low tax rate (similar to a revenue tariff) does not stop the act of polluting while it mildly discourages the taxed activity, but it does raise the revenue needed to pay for cleaning up. A high enough tax rate (comparable to a protective tariff) would stop the pollution by totally discouraging the purchase of the high-polluting product, although it would not raise revenue.

In practice, we would expect an intermediate result. The pollution tax or effluent fee would shift some, but not all, demand to the lower-priced (and less polluting) alternatives. Some, but not all, producers would have sufficient incentive to reduce the external costs they impose on society by changing to less polluting methods of production and distribution. Thus, producers would have more incentive than they do now to "economize" on pollution—an incentive similar to those for developing methods to reduce labor and material costs. The basic idea is that the price of a product should reflect its costs to, or burden on, the environment.

As an illustration of this proposal, a study of the Delaware estuary shows that effluent fees, set at a high enough level to achieve the desired level of water purity, would cost approximately one-half as much as a conventional regulatory program requiring an equal percentage reduction by all polluters. To achieve the standard of two parts of dissolved oxygen per million, the estimated annual cost comes to $2.4 million via an effluent charge, compared with $5.0 million for treatment of the pollution under a uniform regulation.[3]

Some indication of the practical problems that arise in shifting to an effluent fee system can be obtained from examining Table 4.1. Clearly, it would be less costly to use an effluent fee system to achieve the same amount of pollution cleanup in a 30-mile stretch of the Black Warrior River in Alabama—$1,224 a day compared to

TABLE 4.1 Estimated Cost of Cleanup in a 30-Mile Section of Black Warrior River under Alternative Approaches

Pollution Source	Daily Cost of Meeting Existing Standards	Daily Cost of Effluent Fees	Gain (+) or Loss (−)
Empire Coke	$ 116.00	$ 0	$116.00
B. F. Goodrich	72.90	0	72.90
Gulf State Paper	94.40	350.80	−256.40
Hunt Oil	30.40	5.60	24.80
Reichhold Chemicals	147.30	228.50	−81.20
Warrior Asphalt	15.90	3.20	12.70
City of Northport	122.20	145.20	−23.00
City of Tuscaloosa	1,240.40	491.10	749.30
Total	$1,839.50	$1,224.40	$615.10

Source: Albert H. Link and Frank A. Scott, "Effluent Fees, an Alternative System for Achieving Water Quality: A Case Study," *Water Resources Bulletin,* June 1981.

$1,839 a day under the existing pollution standards approach. However, three of the seven major polluters—Gulf State Paper, Reichhold Chemicals, and the city of Northport—would wind up paying more in pollution fees than their current costs of meeting the standards. Thus, support for a shift to effluent fees would not be universal. This pattern of variation would likely be the case in many other regions.

The customary approach that consists of government issuing uniform standards is defended on the grounds of equity: All polluters are treated equally; for example, all cars must meet the same air-pollution rules. However, as a consequence, much of EPA's staff resources have gone into defending the agency against thousands of lawsuits, brought both by environmentalists urging sterner enforcement and by companies seeking relief from what they regard as arbitrary interpretations.

Uniform standards are an expensive regulatory approach. It may cost a great deal to reduce the pollutants from one type of activity and very little from another. For example, it may be cheaper to redesign a new building still on the drafting boards than to totally revamp one that already is standing. Congress has taken an important step in accommodating the economic approach by authorizing "emissions trading" in the acid rain provisions of the Clean Air Act Amendments of 1990, discussed below.

THE DEVELOPMENT OF ENVIRONMENTAL POLICIES

Protecting the environment covers a great variety of concerns—air pollution, water pollution, pesticides, toxic substances, hazardous wastes, unsafe drinking water, ocean dumping, noise emissions, and other adverse impacts on human health and ecological systems. In the United States, the Environmental Protection Agency (EPA) is the main federal organization operating in this area, and it focuses on issuing rules, approving permits, and enforcing its regulations.

Because ecological influences do not always respect national boundaries, these issues increasingly involve the interaction of the public and private sectors of many countries. At times, an agency of the United Nations may provide the forum for intergovernmental actions in this area of policy. As we will see, this is especially so in dealing with the issue of global climate change.

The notion that environmental protection is a proper function of government did not originate in the twentieth century. Nor did a get-tough attitude toward polluters first arise in the United States. More than 600 years before the National Environmental Policy Act of 1969, the king of England proclaimed a no-nonsense pollution-control law, complete with penalties for offenders. As with most congressional action today, the king in 1308 did not consider it necessary to weigh the effectiveness of various deterrents such as fines or emissions fees. Instead, he tried the simple and more straightforward strategy of executing the polluters.

Even in the United States, protection of the environment is no newcomer to the realm of government activities. Prior to independence, the Massachusetts Bay Colony enacted regulations to prevent pollution in Boston Harbor. Following the Revolution, most coastal states took some action to ensure that no large floating debris would obstruct navigation of the waterways within their borders.

Throughout the eighteenth and nineteenth centuries and well into the twentieth, local governments bore primary responsibility for the regulation of water and air pollution. Unfortunately, localities found themselves quite helpless to control water pollution coming from upstream, and a shift in the prevailing winds was apt to make a sleepy hamlet the unwilling recipient of smoky particles from a more industrialized town.

By the end of the nineteenth century, the connections between dirty water and contagious diseases had stimulated most states to enact water-pollution laws. These early statutes were concerned with the human health aspects of dirty water rather than with abating pollution that affected ecological systems or that had aesthetic consequences. The result was a tendency for the pollution issues to be buried in public health agencies that largely ignored the problem once a disease had been eradicated.

Federal involvement in the environment during the first half of the twentieth century was piecemeal. Antipollution legislation was aimed primarily at keeping interstate and coastal waterways free from debris so as to maintain the flow of navigation. The Refuse Act of 1899 forbade dumping into navigable waters without a permit from the Corps of Engineers. The Oil Pollution Act of 1924 banned oil discharges into coastal waters. Otherwise, protecting health and safety was viewed as a function of the states under their police power.

The first breakthrough in federal pollution legislation was the Water Pollution Control Act of 1948. The law did little more than provide technical and research assistance to the states, but it demonstrated a national responsibility. The Air Pollution Control Act of 1955 very much resembled the 1948 water pollution legislation. Thus, as recently as 1955, a report of a congressional committee stated:

> [I]t is primarily the responsibility of state and local government to prevent air pollution. The bill does not propose any exercise of police power by the federal government and no provision in it invades the sovereignty of states, counties or cities. There is no attempt to impose standards of purity.[4]

During the 1970s, legislation progressively enlarged the role of the federal government in regulating the environment and committing the nation to ambitious goals. The EPA was established in 1970 to pull together a variety of scattered activities and provide a unified ecological policy at the national level. EPA now administers programs dealing with air pollution, water pollution, toxic substances, waste disposal, pesticides, and environmental radiation. The agency possesses an impressive arsenal of powers and duties buttressed by strong public support. When asked whether they would be willing to protect the environment even if it meant losing jobs in their community, 57 percent of a sample queried by the *New York Times* replied in the affirmative, and only 32 percent replied in the negative (the remaining 11 percent answered "don't know").[5]

THE RANGE OF NATIONAL ENVIRONMENTAL REGULATION

After Congress enacts environmental legislation, the focus of attention shifts to the executive branch agencies enforcing the statutes. Activities of the EPA center around setting and enforcing standards relating to environmental concerns. EPA has several means of enforcement. Upon finding a violation, it may seek voluntary compliance. If that fails, it can order compliance and take violators to court.

Air Pollution Controls

Table 4.2 shows the substantial amount of pollutants discharged into the air of the United States during 1995—approximately 92 million tons of carbon monoxide, over 18 million tons of sulfur oxides, and almost 22 million tons of nitrogen oxides.

Most air pollution results from economic activity. Transportation services and industrial processes are mainly responsible for emissions of hydrocarbons, nontoxic organic gases not dangerous by themselves. However, hydrocarbons combine with nitrogen oxides from fuel combustion and vehicular traffic to produce ozone—commonly

TABLE 4.2   Air-Pollutant Emissions, 1995, by Type and Source (in millions of short tons)

Source	Carbon Monoxide	Sulfur Oxides	Particulates	Nitrogen Oxides	Volatile Organic Compounds
Transportation	74.2	0.6	0.7	10.6	8.4
Fuel combustion	4.0	15.7	0.9	10.1	0.7
Industrial processes	7.4	2.1	0.9	0.9	13.4
Miscellaneous	6.5	0.0	40.1*	0.2	0.4
Total	92.1	18.4	42.6	21.8	22.9
Change 1986–1995	−16%	−18%	−17%	−3%	−9%

*Mainly fugitive dust.

Source: Office of Air Quality Planning and Standards, *National Air Quality Emissions Trends Report, 1995* (Research Triangle Park, NC: U.S. Environmental Protection Agency, 1996).

referred to as smog. While many other pollutants make up smog, ozone is the substance most closely monitored. The rationale is that ozone produces harmful, albeit transitory, health effects and is a reasonable proxy for the other, unmonitored pollutants.

Another group of major pollutants is sulfur oxides, which combine with water to create sulfuric acid and generate acid rain. A major source of sulfur oxide is electric power plants that burn coal. Carbon monoxide, a colorless and odorless gas that can pose serious health problems in high concentrations, is formed as a result of inefficient combustion of fossil fuels. (The rising concern about the role of carbon dioxide (CO_2) in global climate change is dealt with later in this chapter.)

The Clean Air Act of 1970 (including the substantial amendments enacted in 1990) is the primary legislation dealing with air pollution. Its basic mission is seemingly straightforward: to establish and enforce air quality standards that protect public health with an adequate margin of safety. The complex regulations issued under the act require four volumes in the *Code of Federal Regulations*. Attorneys specializing in this field have described the Clean Air Act as the environmental equivalent of the Internal Revenue Code—and that is not meant as a compliment.[6]

EPA has established National Ambient Air Quality Standards for six common air pollutants: carbon monoxide, lead, nitrogen dioxide, ground level ozone, sulfur dioxide, and particulate matter with a diameter of 10 microns or less. The agency also has set two types of standards: primary and secondary. Primary standards are designed to protect human health. Secondary standards are intended to protect vegetation and physical structures.

In establishing national air quality standards, the law divides the nation into several hundred air quality control regions, with the state government being responsible for attaining the standards within its jurisdiction. Each state is required to submit to EPA a state implementation plan specifying how the standards are to be achieved.

By 1989 it had become apparent that, despite significant gains in air quality, many regions of the country had not and would not meet the standards established in the original legislation. Moreover, heightened public concern over issues, such as stratosphere ozone depletion and acid rain, problems not widely recognized when the law was first written, led to increased criticism of existing air pollution standards. As a result, President George Bush proposed sweeping revisions of the Clean Air Act. After a year and a half of heated debate, Congress passed one of the most comprehensive environmental laws to date, the Clean Air Act Amendments of 1990.

Among the provisions included in the statute's more than 700 pages are a phasing out of ozone-depleting gases such as chlorofluorocarbons and carbon tetrachloride, as well as a significant reduction in sulfur dioxide and nitrogen oxide emissions. In addition, oil companies are required to offer new, cleaner-burning fuels to be used in urban areas plagued by ozone and carbon monoxide problems. While innovative approaches such as performance-based standards and emissions trading provide some flexibility in enforcement, the regulatory burden of the Clean Air Amendments ultimately affects virtually every industry in the United States, from local dry cleaners to giant corporations. A new requirement for obtaining 5-year operating permits involves smaller firms such as auto-body painting and repair companies, print shops, and gasoline service stations. (See Figure 4.2 for the complexity of business compliance activities.)

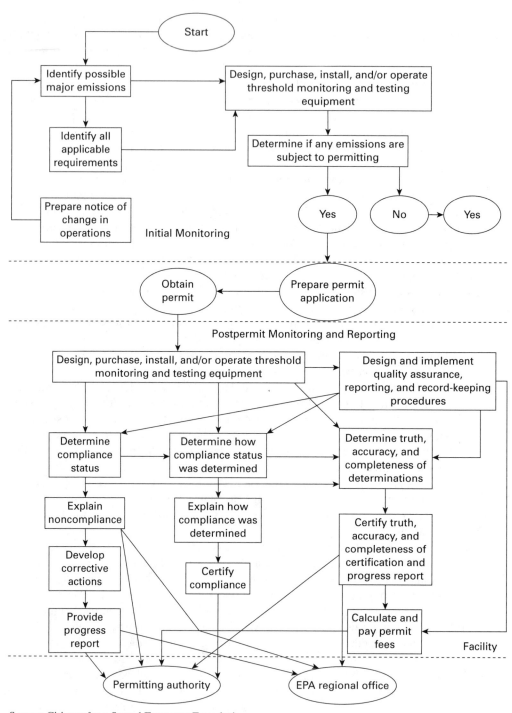

Source: Citizens for a Sound Economy Foundation.

FIGURE 4.2 Company Compliance with the Clean Air Act

Emissions trading is the major concession to economics in the revised Clean Air Act. The basic idea is that, given the opportunity, companies can often devise less costly ways of reducing the amount of pollution they generate than government regulators can. The Clean Air Act's emissions trading policy for sulfur dioxide emissions is an attempt to take advantage of this fact by creating markets in de facto rights to pollute. The economic benefits of this approach are basic: Trading of emissions rights can increase efficiency by concentrating air pollution control efforts on those emissions sources that are least costly to control. If one company can reduce emissions more cheaply than another, both can benefit by arranging a trade.

Emissions trading can result in substantial economic gains, in the form of reduced compliance costs for business, with no net effect on the environment. The basic unit of currency for emissions trading is the one ton emission reduction credit. Credits are created when pollution sources, such as public utilities, reduce their emissions below the levels allowed by their permits. These reductions can be achieved in a variety of ways: burning cleaner fuel, installing new control equipment, or shutting down a polluting facility altogether. Emissions allowances may be bought, sold, or banked like any other commodity. If a utility holds surplus allowances, it may sell them to units whose emissions levels exceed their allowance supply, or it may save them for use in future years.

The market for pollution credits has been developing. The volume peaked at 16.7 million credits traded in 1995 and has generally been in the range of 8 to 10 million a year. The typical price per ton-credit has declined substantially, from $600 in 1990 to $110 in 1997. Overall, the usefulness of this approach has been demonstrated quite clearly.

Illinois Power saved $91 million by purchasing allowances instead of installing scrubbers, and Wisconsin Electric Power saved almost $90 million by avoiding the need for scrubbers. This positive trend is continuing. Duke Power has projected savings of $300 million. Clearly, the new flexibility in the air pollution control law has eased the burden of complying with EPA standards.[7] In 1997, the New York State government found an interesting use for the pollution credits it possessed: It offered them as an attraction to a glass manufacturer who wanted to build a new factory in the state.

Water Pollution Controls

The Clean Water Act is the basis for the nation's water cleanup program. The act sets two specific national goals. The interim goal, commonly referred to as the "swimmable–fishable" goal, is to restore polluted waters, wherever possible, to a quality that allows for the protection and propagation of fish, shellfish, and wildlife and for recreational use. The final goal—which in practice is more in the nature of a wish—is to eliminate all discharges of pollutants into the nation's navigable waters. Two very different basic control strategies are employed: (1) tough compulsory controls at the point of discharge for municipal and industrial polluters and (2) largely voluntary efforts for other sources of water pollution, such as runoffs from city streets and farms.[8]

Not too surprisingly, some of the major pollution sources are the nonpoint discharges from streets and rural areas. Recent storm water regulations are beginning to reduce nonpoint source pollution from urban areas.

Specific provisions of the Clean Water Act have strong teeth. EPA can enter and inspect any polluting facility to check its records and monitoring equipment and to test its discharges. Failure to report the discharge of oil or other hazardous substances into the water can result in large fines. Dumping hazardous substances from a vessel can be punished with a fine of up to $5 million; also, heavy cleanup costs can be assessed to the polluter. Both the Clean Air and Clean Water laws empower citizens to bring suit against anyone violating these statutes. Citizens can also take court action against EPA itself if it fails to perform any duty required by the two laws.

Hazardous and Toxic Substances Controls

Four major environmental statutes cover hazardous and toxic substances; they are usually referred to by acronyms: TSCA, RCRA, FIFRA, and CERCLA or Superfund.

The Toxic Substances Control Act (TSCA) gives EPA substantial power over the chemical industry, including the following:

- Authority to require testing of new and existing chemical compounds.
- Mandates for premanufacturing notices 90 days prior to the production of any new chemical or significant new use of an existing chemical.
- Power to control the manufacturing, processing, distribution, use, and disposal of any chemical substance.
- Required reporting, which covers each chemical produced by every chemical manufacturer.

Because of the detailed authority EPA possesses under other statutes, much of the power granted by TSCA remains latent (the proverbial stick in the closet). Under the *Resource Conservation and Recovery Act* (RCRA), EPA regulates the current disposal of hazardous wastes. The law requires generators of wastes to create a record-keeping system to track the material from the point of generation to ultimate disposal. Large producers of hazardous wastes are required to furnish information on the waste to transporters and to designate a permitted disposal or treatment facility to which the residues must be taken. Under RCRA, EPA regulates the construction and operation of landfills, encourages the use of recycled products through government procurement programs, and oversees the development of state solid waste management plans.

Critics of RCRA charge that the legislation is intrusive and needlessly costly to comply with.[9] One example of this unnecessary financial burden concerns RCRA's administrative requirements. Under the Clean Water Act, waste treatment facilities are required to file a simple form with the EPA verifying that a fence is in place at the facility to restrict public access. RCRA, however, requires an additional 25 pages documenting the fence's design and location, the type of wire mesh used, the number of fence posts and gates, as well as other minor technical details. An Eastman Kodak factory found that its application for a Clean Water Act permit was 17 pages long, while its RCRA application formed a stack seven feet tall.[10]

Under the *Federal Insecticide, Fungicide, and Rodenticide Act* (FIFRA), products to eliminate agricultural pests and diseases are controlled to keep hazardous chemicals off the market and to prevent "unreasonable" adverse effects on humans or on the environment. Manufacturers of new products must register with the agency. In 1996, Congress amended the law to protect consumers against serious, albeit non-cancerous, risks in raw and processed fruits and vegetables. In what may become a valuable precedent for other environmental programs, the Congress requires EPA to publish, "in a format understandable to a lay person," a discussion of risks and benefits posed by chemicals in pesticides.

In 1980, Congress established a "superfund" to finance the cleanup of abandoned or inactive hazardous waste dump sites. The superfund law—the *Comprehensive Environmental Response, Compensation, and Liability Act* (or CERCLA)—attempts to assign the costs of cleanup to "potentially responsible parties." The statute requires the collection of a fee levied on the feedstocks for the chemical and oil industries to cover the cleanup costs where those responsible for the problem cannot be found. When it renewed the superfund statute in 1986, Congress increased the funds available for cleanups.

Remedial actions under CERCLA have been slow and costly. The program also has been controversial, especially since the reach of the law is retroactive to times when dumping was legal. Moreover, major shares of the costs incurred are for legal and court activity rather than actually cleaning up the dump sites.

One part of the 1986 law, known as the Emergency Planning and Community Right-to-Know Act, requires nearly every facility that produces or uses any of 329 designated hazardous substances to make two sets of reports. First, it must file detailed inventories of those hazardous substances with the local fire department. Second, it must report to EPA and designated state officials on the emissions of designated substances into the air, land, water, and waste treatment facilities—the toxic release inventory or TRI report. Thousands of companies are affected by this reporting requirement, ranging from major chemical manufacturing facilities to local dry-cleaning establishments.

The availability of information concerning the volume of discharges into the environment has had an important feedback effect on business decision makers. One chemical company responded by announcing that it would voluntarily reduce emissions of the listed chemicals by 90 percent by 1992. Monsanto achieved that goal by a variety of means, including changing production processes and closing down some high-polluting facilities.[11]

BENEFITS AND COSTS OF A CLEANER ENVIRONMENT

Compliance with pollution standards is neither easy nor cheap. Public and private expenditures for pollution abatement in 1994 totaled $122 billion or 2 percent of gross domestic product (see Table 4.3).[12] EPA estimates that, by the year 2000, these environmental cleanup costs could reach $215 billion a year (in 1996 dollars). The lion's share of these expenditures are made by the private sector, with the petroleum, chemical, primary metals, food, and paper industries making the largest outlays. Ultimately, people, as consumers and taxpayers, pay the costs of cleaning up the environment—and also receive the benefits that ensue.

TABLE 4.3 Expenditures for Pollution Abatement in the United States, 1994 (in billions of dollars)

Category	Air	Water	Solid Waste	Total
Consumers	9.8	—	—	9.8
Business				
Capital investment	17.6	6.9	3.9	28.4
Operating costs	7.7	8.0	22.4	38.1
Government	2.6	27.5	15.5	45.6
Total	37.7	42.4	41.8	121.9

Source: U.S. Department of Commerce.

The Benefits of Environmental Regulation

The benefits achieved by environmental regulation are substantial. Before examining the dry statistics on environmental improvement, it is helpful to recall the ecological condition of the United States when EPA was first established in 1970. In Cleveland, the Cuyahoga River exploded into flames. Vast areas of the Atlantic Coast and the Great Lakes shoreline were closed to swimming and fishing. The shores of the Potomac River near Washington, DC, were marked by signs warning citizens not to touch the water.

As measured by traditional indexes, such as the amount of pollutants in surface water and air, the overall quality of the environment in the United States has improved substantially since the EPA became active. The number of days when air quality has not met national standards is declining. Numerous streams and rivers have once more become fishable and swimmable. A dramatic instance is the cleanup of the Willamette River in Oregon that has permitted the salmon to run again.

America's air continues to get cleaner. Almost all of the pollutants for which the EPA has set national standards show substantial declines in emissions from 1982 to 1994. Carbon monoxide levels in the air decreased 16 percent, lead levels 94 percent, particulate emissions 20 percent, and sulfur dioxide 20 percent. Emissions of nitrogen oxide, the exception, rose 1 percent.[13] As shown in Figure 4.3, the number of areas in the United States not attaining air pollution standards declined significantly from 1978 to 1996.

The quality of the nation's water likewise has shown a marked improvement. By 1990, 70 percent of the rivers and 60 percent of the lakes in the United States met the Clean Water Act's interim goal of "fishable and swimmable" water quality. In addition, advances in sewage and industrial waste treatment technology since the mid-1970s have led to significant improvements in water quality, offsetting the adverse effects of population growth and industrial expansion. Agricultural and urban runoffs remain serious problems, especially because environmental legislation and regulation focus on "point" discharges of pollution, legislation that mainly covers specific facilities such as factories and public treatment works. On balance, it appears that the pollution control measures enacted in recent years have had a positive effect on the nation's environment.

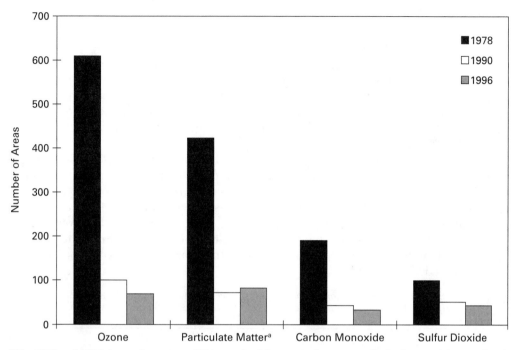

^aThe 1990 and 1996 data reflect a new EPA standard for particulate matter limited to particles smaller than 10 micrometers in diameter.

Source: Office of Air Quality Planning and Standards, *National Air Quality Emissions Trends Report, 1995.*

FIGURE 4.3 Number of Areas in the United States Not Attaining Air-Pollution Standards

Determining the benefits to human health from this cleaner environment, however, is complex and fraught with uncertainty. One complication centers on the limited reliability of conventional risk assessments. In order to quantify the human benefits from pollution abatement, the health risks posed by a given pollutant must be known. Obtaining such information often requires relying on studies in which human health effects are extrapolated from animal studies. Unfortunately, demonstrating that animals react in a given way when exposed to *very high doses* of a toxin does not imply that *much lower* levels of exposure in humans will produce the same result. Rather than portraying the risk a pollutant poses to the average person, the government's risk assessments tend to be worst-case, or upper-bound estimates. Current regulations, based on these exaggerated estimates, therefore overvalue the benefits of pollution abatement. As one FDA official observed, "Linear extrapolation of rodent . . . data embodies the regulator's credo ('It's better to be safe than sorry') far more than it does the scientist's ('It's better to be right than wrong')."[14]

In some instances, it may be possible to more fully achieve the public's regulatory desires while avoiding cost increases or even reducing the burden of compliance. As shown in the accompanying box ("The Second Battle of Yorktown"), that may take some statutory changes.

The Second Battle of Yorktown

A landmark undertaking in 1989–91 by EPA and a private company—a joint study of Amoco's Yorktown, Virginia refinery—showed the benefits of focusing on overall environmental performance rather than following the customary regulatory standards. Approximately 97 percent of the required hydrocarbon emission reductions could be achieved for about 25 percent of the cost that Amoco was incurring.

For example, complying with the controls on sewers required by Clean Air Act regulations cost $31 million and captured less than 10 percent of the benzene emitted from the refinery. Controls on a different source—barge loading operations—would have resulted in capturing 55 percent of the plant's benzene emissions, at a cost of only $6 million. Thus, Amoco could have achieved over five times the emission reductions at one-fifth the cost. Unfortunately, the statute prohibits the company from substituting marine facility controls for the required sewer controls.

Source: Robert W. Hahn, *Reforming the Clean Air Act,* Testimony Before the Subcommittee on Oversight and Investigation, U.S. House of Representatives, June 29, 1995, p. 4.

The Costs of Environmental Regulation

The costs of complying with environmental regulations are substantial. For a great many American companies, a considerable portion of the funds available for modernization and expansion is diverted to meet the EPA standards—or state environmental agency requirements. It has been estimated that for each $1 increase in environmental compliance costs, total factor productivity is reduced by $3 to $4.[15] That is a large loss of potential efficiency and competitiveness.

Opening up new production facilities literally involves surmounting a host of regulatory obstacles. William D. Ruckelshaus, former administer of EPA, has described the process vividly:

> Think of what it now takes to site a major industrial facility. A firm often must obtain agreement from perhaps dozens of agencies and authorities at each of three levels of government, not to mention the courts. And it doesn't help to satisfy . . . a majority of interests involved; a single "no" anywhere along the line at any time in the process can halt years of planning, effort and investment.[16]

By increasing investment and operating costs, many environmental regulations work like a tax on capital equipment. This reduces total investment and capacity and thus leads to higher prices at lower levels of production. On the other hand, creative solutions can at times convert a cost into a benefit. For example, an Allied-Signal Corporation plant in Metropolis, Illinois, created a veritable sea of calcium fluoride sludge as a by-product of its manufacture of fluorine-based chemicals. It was generating the sludge at the rate of 1,000 cubic yards a month. Analysis showed that the sludge could be mixed with another waste stream to produce a reaction. The result: neutralization of the waste and production of synthetic fluorspar that Allied uses as a raw material at another location. The $4.3 million facility to accomplish these results saves the company about $1 million a year, an attractive return on an investment that also eliminates the problem of disposal of a growing stream of sludge.

Compliance with environmental laws places a proportionately greater burden on small plants. Small facilities find it more difficult to survive, given the economies of scale involved in regulatory compliance. Although pollution controls increase prices because they raise costs, compliance expenses vary greatly among competitors because of differences in production methods, economies of scale, and product mixes. The lack of uniformity of compliance costs has been demonstrated by studies of petroleum refining, pulp and paper, textiles, aluminum, and metal finishing. Those firms whose compliance costs are below average operate at a competitive advantage, increasing market shares or attaining higher profitability. In contrast, companies whose costs are greater suffer reduced profits, lower sales, or both.

New producers are usually subject to more stringent controls than existing producers, but they may also be able to employ the latest cost-reducing technology. Where new capacity has higher abatement costs than existing capacity, environmental controls can confer a competitive advantage on existing firms. To some extent, therefore, regulation protects the "ins" against the "outs," or potential new competitors. New investment and development of new products are discouraged by treating existing pollution sources more leniently. Simultaneously, strict "new source performance standards" increase the value of existing plant and equipment and discourage their replacement by more economically efficient facilities.

Optimizing firms may choose to risk penalties for noncompliance or to gain waivers or exemptions from regulations rather than comply. These may be lower-cost alternatives for the firm, and they may produce lower than expected regulatory benefits to society. On the other hand, companies can go beyond merely adding the required abatement devices to existing production processes. They may shift to advanced production technologies that are less polluting. In such cases, regulation hastens the development and adoption of new technology.

Environmental requirements can become an important factor in the operation of existing manufacturing facilities. The regulatory experience of Dow Chemical Company's plant in Pittsburg, California, is instructive. The company must file 563 separate permit applications each year to cover its direct emissions into the air. In addition, Dow must obtain 370 permits for the sources that produce the materials that escape through the emissions point.

Under the National Environmental Policy Act, environmental impact statements are required by federal agencies on various actions that affect the environment. The coverage of the law is very broad. Detailed statements are usually triggered in the case of any private development requiring a federal permit. As shown in Table 4.4, environmental impact statements are very detailed analyses—in part to guard against court challenges. The process also provides for greater community participation in determining whether the project should be built at a given location. Currently, it often takes 18 to 24 months merely to obtain the permits before beginning a major construction project. In contrast, the construction of the Empire State Building in Manhattan in the 1930s took less than two years from start to finish, including demolishing the earlier building on the site.

TABLE 4.4 Environmental Impact Analysis Required for a Residential Construction Project

Condition to be Examined	Characteritics Required to be Analyzed	Example of an Analysis
Land and climate	Soil: general characteristics, load-bearing capacity, existing and potential erosion, permeability	No special climatic, subsurface, or unusual conditions
	Topography: general characteristics, slope grade of site	Soil: permeable, clayey Topography: average, 3% slope
	Subsurface conditions: geological characteristics, geologic faults	
	Special conditions: flood plain; potential for mudslide or earthquake	
	Unusual climatic conditions: subject to flash floods, hurricanes, or tornadoes, extremes of temperature	
Vegetation, wildlife, and natural areas	Extent and type of vegetation and wildlife; existence of on-site or proximity to wildlife breeding area, parks	Site 50% covered with beech, oak, sassafras, and dogwood trees
		Adjacent to 20-acre urban park
Surrounding land uses and physical character of area	Type of development: family or high-rise residential, industrial commercial, open space	Mixed: single-family, high-rise, and open-space area
		Density: about 60 dwelling units per acre in immediate site area
Infrastructure	Water supply, sanitary sewage and solid-waste disposal, storm sewers and drainage, energy and transportation	Site controlled by waste system and sanitary and sewer system; there is ample capacity
		Site on bus line
		All-electric project
Air-pollution levels	Extent of pollution: smog, dust, odors, smoke, hazardous emissions	No obvious dust, odors or smoke in site area
		Community has smog alerts in summer
Noise levels	Source: nearby airport, railway, highway	Project is on major arterial road, but noise exposure is minimal
Water-pollution levels	Ground and surface water: source of water supply, water bodies with implications for health and recreation uses	No streams are on project site; there are no bodies of water nearby

TABLE 4.4 (cont.)

Condition to be Examined	Characteritics Required to be Analyzed	Example of an Analysis
Community facilities and services	Description: location; relation of capacity to existing demand of schools, parks, recreational, and cultural facilities; police and fire, and health facilities	Complete community facilities within walking distance of site (i.e., 200-bed hospital, library, museum, police, and fire station)
Employment centers and commercial facilities	Employment centers and commercial facilities servicing site	Site is ¼ mile from shopping center, 1 ½ miles from central business district
Character of community	Socioeconomic and racial characteristics	Mainly white, 30% African American, 4% Hispanic, and 10% elderly
Existing aesthetic community	Aesthetic characteristics; proximity to historic, archaeological, or architectural site or property	The Historic Society is across the street from the site

Source: U.S. Department of Housing and Urban Development.

In addition to examining the direct physical and economic impacts, environmental analyses deal with the indirect effects, including the implications of the planned facility for regional development patterns, the effects on demand for housing and public utilities, and the possibility of further technological development that may have subsequent impacts.

One unappreciated limitation on the construction of new manufacturing facilities is the diminished availability of sites for disposing of the hazardous wastes that may be produced. The key limit on the availability of these sites is neither economic nor technological; it is the political pressures that have to be faced (the NIMBY or "not-in-my-backyard" syndrome). The Minnesota experience is indicative. EPA granted the state pollution control agency $3.7 million to establish a model chemical landfill that fully met all of the federal agency's safety requirements. All 12 of the locations initially proposed by the agency were rejected because of public opposition. An additional four locations were dropped after vocal objections. Three years after receiving the grant, the state returned the federal money to the EPA.[17]

GLOBAL ENVIRONMENTAL PERSPECTIVE

The United States is by no means the only country in the world to devote considerable resources to addressing environmental issues. Nations in Europe and the Pacific Rim have likewise responded to public interest in curbing pollution and protecting endangered resources. Moreover, recent attention to global concerns, such as ozone depletion, greenhouse warming, and the loss of biodiversity, has led to a variety of international agreements to deal with these issues. As a result, environmental factors are coming to play a significant role in defining how businesses and governments function on an international scale.

Environmental Policies of Other Industrialized Nations

As was the case in the United States, the amount of environmental legislation enacted in Europe grew at an unprecedented rate during the 1980s and early 1990s. Between 1989 and 1991 alone, the European Union (EU) issued more ordinances concerning the environment than in the previous 20 years combined. Businesses must now follow over 450 environmental regulations or directives, with 100 new rules being added yearly. By establishing communitywide standards, EU ministers hope to prevent individual national governments from using environmental regulations as obstacles to trade. Without uniform guidelines, nations with more stringent pollution controls would find their goods at a competitive disadvantage. They would face such unpleasant choices as reducing their environmental standards or violating EU agreements by excluding goods manufactured in countries with lower requirements.[18]

While the uniformity of standards has furthered the cause of economic integration, it has also made establishing environmental policy for Western Europe a laborious and complex process. Relatively affluent members of the EU, most notably Germany, Denmark, and the Netherlands, usually urge tough pollution control measures, while Great Britain, Italy, and Greece are less enthusiastic about stringent requirements. As a result, finding common ground on pollution regulations is often arduous and time-consuming.

In many ways, Western Europe lags behind the United States in environmental protection. The EU did not require catalytic converters on cars until 1992, a move this country made in 1975. Lead-free gasoline is not widely available in Europe, while 99 percent of American autos burn only unleaded fuel. Whereas the United States debates how tough wetlands protection should be, the EU has no law to protect wetlands—or to deal with the underground storage of hazardous wastes.[19]

Nevertheless, some European nations have used "green" taxes in novel, if not necessarily effective, ways. Sweden taxes batteries, while Belgium has a special levy on disposable razors. Denmark, Finland, the Netherlands, Norway, and Sweden tax emissions of carbon dioxide, a major greenhouse gas—which helps to explain why the EU outpaces the United States in supporting firm targets for reducing carbon dioxide emissions.[20]

In Japan, the pace of environmental regulation has been somewhat different. During the late 1960s and early 1970s, a major expansion occurred in environmental regulation. Some slowdown occurred during the 1980s. Compared to Europe and the United States, the Japanese environmental movement remains largely unorganized, poorly funded, and commands little political influence. Nevertheless, domestic concern about uncontrolled pollution along with foreign criticism of Japanese environmental policy has forced government officials to take a more active stance. Legislative attention is focused on wetlands preservation, ozone depletion, and global warming.

Ironically, in 1991 Peru took more seriously than did the United States the classification of chlorine as carcinogenic. In trying to reduce the risk of cancer association with chlorination of water, it ceased treating its drinking water with chlorine. Peru subjected its people to the more immediate risks from water-borne diseases. The subsequent outbreak of cholera in that country killed nearly 7,000 people and affected over 800,000.[21]

The UN as a Regulator

In addition to enacting significant pollution legislation domestically, Europe, Japan, and the United States have come to play an important role in pushing for international environmental accords. Although nations have traditionally been reluctant to restrict their use of domestic resources, the success of the United Nations-sponsored Montreal Protocol (1987) and the London Conference (1989) in curtailing global reliance on certain ozone-depleting gasses has led to a number of other international accords. In total, over 200 multilateral agreements have been enacted since 1960, covering virtually the entire gamut of environmental issues.

The international community has also begun working toward environmental goals through organizations with financial resources such as the World Bank and the United Nations Development Program. Bolivia, Ecuador, and Costa Rica have all benefited from "debt for nature" swaps in which developing countries are relieved of debt or other obligations in return for conservation programs.

The most ambitious international agreements concerning environmental issues resulted from the 1992 Earth Summit in Rio de Janeiro. One such accord, Agenda 21 — presumably covering the twenty-first century — was described as a "blueprint for action in all major areas affecting the relationship between the environment and the economy." Among the extensive array of global goals outlined in Agenda 21 are the eradication of poverty, reversing the destruction of renewable resources, and changing the system of incentives and penalties that motivate economic behavior. Other commitments made at Earth Summit include preserving biological diversity and ratifying the UN Framework Convention on Climate Change, designed to returning worldwide emissions of greenhouse gasses to the 1990 levels. To monitor compliance with all of these goals, the UN established a high-level Commission on Sustainable Development, but so far no agreement has been reached on a timetable for returning to the 1990 emissions levels or on a mechanism for enforcement.

Considerable dispute continues on the nature of global warming, the phenomenon that gives rise to the pressure for limiting emissions (especially of CO_2) into the atmosphere. In 1996, the UN's Intergovernmental Panel on Climate Change stated that "the balance of evidence suggests that there is a discernible human influence on global climate." However, some distinguished scientists have challenged the report. Simultaneously, several economic studies concluded that legislating the proposed 1990 emission cap would require governmental policies — such as a high tax on fossil fuels or total energy used — that would substantially reduce economic growth and employment in the United States. Nevertheless, considerable public concern over global warming is evident.[22]

Conclusions

The problems of environmental pollution and the need for developing more efficient and effective responses are likely to remain urgent public concerns. The great majority of citizens, especially of the developed nations, continue to want something done about toxic waste dumps, water quality, and air pollution.

There are sensible changes in environmental policies and priorities that can reduce costs or deliver greater benefits. For example, several thousand pounds of hazardous waste are generated for every person in the United States. Over 99 percent of federal and state environmental spending is devoted to controlling pollution after it is generated. Less than one percent is spent to reduce the generation of waste. In an era of continuing budgetary pressures, opportunities are likely to arise for sensible reallocation of the substantial amounts of resources now devoted to cleaning up the environment. As shown in Table 4.5, many foreign countries do a great deal to minimize the amount of waste created in the first place.

Pollution control policies typically aim at one medium at a time (air or water or land). The result often has been merely to shift pollution from one area to another. For example, in 1977 the Clean Air Act amendments required all coal-burning power plants to have scrubbers to remove sulfur dioxide from their smokestacks. This resulted in generating tons of sulfur sludge that fouled substantial land surfaces. Moreover, by reducing energy efficiency, the introduction of the scrubbers increases emissions of other pollutants such as CO_2, a chemical implicated in the global warming controversy.

TABLE 4.5 Waste Minimization Encouragement in Other Countries

Type	Japan	Canada	Germany	Sweden	Netherlands	Denmark
Tax Incentives						
Waste end taxes			X		X	X
Tax incentives			X			
Economics						
Price supports for recycling			X		X	
Government grants and subsidies	X	X	X	X	X	X
Low-interest loans	X		X			
Technical Assistance						
Information service	X	X	X		X	X
Site consultation	X	X				
Training seminars		X	X			X
R&D						
Technical development labs				X	X	X
Demonstration projects	X	X	X	X		
Industrial research			X	X	X	
Reduction Plans						
National waste management plans					X	
Waste reduction agreements	X					
Waste reduction as a part of permits				X		
Waste Exchange						
Regional waste exchanges	X	X	X		X	X

Source: U.S. Environmental Protection Agency.

From these and many other examples, it would seem necessary to perform comprehensive benefit/risk analyses of the various environmental policies before embarking on ambitious new or expanded programs (see chapter 9).

Notes

1. Gardner M. Brown and Ralph W. Johnson, "Pollution Control by Effluent Charges: It Works in the Federal Republic of Germany Why Not in the U.S.?," *Natural Resource Journal,* October 1984, p. 935.
2. Robert W. Hahn, "Economic Prescription for Environmental Problems: How the Patient Followed the Doctor's Orders," *Journal of Economic Perspectives,* Spring 1989, pp. 104–106; David Roodman, *Getting the Signals Right* (Washington, DC: Worldwatch Institute, 1997), pp. 10–11.
3. Allen Kneese et al., eds., *Managing the Environment* (New York: Praeger, 1971), Appendix E.
4. Quoted in Frank P. Grad et al., *Environmental Control* (New York: Columbia University Press, 1971), p. 49.
5. "Environment and White House Policy," *New York Times,* July 31, 1996, p. A-12.
6. See Frederick R. Anderson, Daniel R. Mandelker, and A. Dan Tarlock, *Environmental Protection: Law and Policy* (Boston: Little, Brown, 1984), pp. 135–143.
7. Dallas Burtraw, "Trading Emissions to Clean the Air," *Resources,* Winter 1996, pp. 3–6; Robert F. Guerrero, *Air Pollution* (Washington, DC: U.S. General Accounting Office, 1997).
8. See James Lis and Kenneth Chilton, *Clean Water—Murky Policy* (St. Louis: Washington University, Center for the Study of American Business, 1992), pp. 40–44.
9. The 1976 RCRA law contains an interesting finding: One of the causes of the rising amount of solid wastes is "sludge and other pollution treatment resolves" generated "as a result of the Clean Air Act . . . and other Federal and State laws respecting public health and the environment."
10. James Bovard, "RCRA: Origin of an Environmental Debacle," cited in *A Plain Man's Guide to Garbage: The Reauthorization of the Resource Conservation and Recovery Act* (Washington, DC: Heritage Foundation, March 30, 1992), p. 5.
11. The public focus on pollution by business firms results, at least in part, from a strange omission in the Community Right-to-Know provisions: Government installations are exempt from the reporting requirements even though some of the biggest polluters are federal agencies, such as the Departments of Defense and Energy.
12. Christine Vogan, "Pollution Abatement and Control Expenditures, 1972–94," *Survey of Current Business,* September 1996, pp. 48–67.
13. *See Environmental Quality,* 25th anniversary report of the Council on Environmental Quality (Washington, DC: U.S. Government Printing Office, 1997), pp. 433–439.
14. Robert J. Scheuplein, "Uncertainty and the Flavors of Risk," *AIHC Journal* 1, no. 2, Summer 1993, p. 16.
15. Wayne B. Gray and Ronald J. Shadbegian, *Environmental Regulation and Manufacturing Productivity Growth* (Cambridge, MA: National Bureau of Economic Research, 1993).
16. William D. Ruckelshaus, "'Not in My Backyard!' Institutional Problems in Environmental Protection," speech to the Economic Club of Detroit, April 15, 1984, p. 8.
17. Comptroller General, *How to Dispose of Hazardous Waste* (Washington, DC: U.S. General Accounting Office, 1975), pp. 5, 6, 13; Comptroller General, *Hazardous Waste* (Washington, DC: U.S. General Accounting Office, 1988), p. 15.

18. See David Vogel, "Environmental Protection and the Creation of a Single European Market," *Business & the Contemporary World,* Winter, 1993, pp. 48–66.

19. Linda G. Stuntz, *Debunking the Myth of the Environmentally Ugly American,* a presentation at the M.I.T. Center for Energy and Environmental Policy Research, Cambridge, MA, April 30, 1992, p. 2.

20. "Taxes for a Cleaner Planet," *The Economist,* June 28, 1997, p. 84.

21. John D. Graham and Jonathan B. Wiener, "Confronting Risk Tradeoffs," in John D. Graham and Jonathan B. Wiener, eds., *Risk versus Risk* (Cambridge, MA: Harvard University Press, 1995), pp. 13–15.

22. Gary W. Yohe, *Climate Change Policies, the Distribution of Income, and U.S. Living Standards* (Washington, DC: American Council for Capital Formation, 1996); S. Fred Singer, "Dirty Climate," *National Review,* November 25, 1996, pp. 62–63.

CHAPTER 5

Achieving Equal Employment Opportunity

In a great variety of ways, government regulations influence hiring and firing, pay and working conditions, training and retirement plans, relations with unions, and many other personnel practices of private industry. These regulations affect a wide spectrum of economic activity, covering most of the public and private sectors. Equal employment opportunity and related affirmative-action programs are among the most conspicuous and controversial of these government influences on personnel policies. (Chapter 6 covers other government regulation of the workplace.)

ADMINISTERING EQUAL EMPLOYMENT OPPORTUNITY

Government responsibility for ending job discrimination in the United States rests primarily with two federal agencies: the Equal Employment Opportunity Commission (EEOC) and the Office of Federal Contract Compliance (OFCC) in the Labor Department.

The Agencies and Their Mandates

The EEOC was created by Title VII of the Civil Rights Act of 1964 to prohibit job discrimination on the basis of race, color, religion, sex, or national origin in all employment practices, including hiring, firing, layoffs, privileges, conditions, or benefits of employment. Those covered by the act are firms and labor unions with 15 or more members, joint labor–management committees for apprenticeship and training, employment agencies, educational institutions, and state and local governments.

The EEOC conducts its enforcement through the following procedure. People who believe they have been discriminated against file charges of discrimination (see Figure 5.1). After receipt of each charge, the EEOC investigates it to determine if sufficient evidence of discrimination exists. If so, the commission tries to persuade the employer to remedy the situation voluntarily. If the conciliation attempts fail, EEOC files suit in federal court. Court-ordered compliance with Title VII often results in large expenses to the employer, usually exceeding the cost of voluntary affirmative action. Expensive settlements are at least partly a result of the retroactive liability of the employer. Companies are held liable for back pay for two years prior to the filing of

(PLEASE PRINT OR TYPE)

CHARGE OF DISCRIMINATION	EEOC CHARGE NO.	FORM APPROVED OMB. NO. 124-R0001

INSTRUCTIONS

If you have a complaint, fill in this form and mail it to the Equal Employment Opportunity Commission's District Office in your area. In most cases, a charge must be filed with the EEOC within a specified time after the discriminatory act took place. IT IS THEREFORE IMPORTANT TO FILE YOUR CHARGE AS SOON AS POSSIBLE. *(Attach extra sheets of paper if necessary.)*

CAUSE OF DISCRIMINATION

☐ RACE OR COLOR   ☐ SEX

☐ RELIGIOUS CREED

☐ NATIONAL ORIGIN

NAME *(Indicate Mr. or Ms.)*	DATE OF BIRTH
STREET ADDRESS	SOCIAL SECURITY NO.
CITY, STATE, AND ZIP CODE	TELEPHONE NO. *(Include area code)*

THE FOLLOWING PERSON ALWAYS KNOWS WHERE TO CONTACT ME

NAME *(Indicate Mr. or Ms.)*	TELEPHONE NO. *(Include area code)*
STREET ADDRESS	CITY, STATE, AND ZIP CODE

LIST THE EMPLOYER, LABOR ORGANIZATION, EMPLOYMENT AGENCY, APPRENTICESHIP COMMITTEE, STATE OR LOCAL GOVERNMENT WHO DISCRIMINATED AGAINST YOU *(If more than one, list all)*

NAME	TELEPHONE NO. *(Include area code)*
STREET ADDRESS	CITY, STATE, AND ZIP CODE

OTHERS WHO DISCRIMINATED AGAINST YOU *(If any)*	

CHARGE FILED WITH STATE/LOCAL GOV'T. AGENCY ☐ Yes ☐ No	DATE FILED	AGENCY CHARGE FILED WITH *(Name and address)*

APPROXIMATE NO. OF EMPLOYEES/MEMBERS OF COMPANY OR UNION THIS CHARGE IS FILED AGAINST	DATE MOST RECENT OR CONTINUING DISCRIMINATION TOOK PLACE *(Month, day, and year)*

Explain what unfair thing was done to you and how other persons were treated differently. Understanding that this statement is for the use of the United States Equal Opportunity Commission, I hereby certify:

I swear or affirm that I have read the above charge and that it is true to the best of my knowledge, information and belief.		N O T A R Y P U B L I C	SUBSCRIBED AND SWORN TO BEFORE ME THIS DATE *(Day, month, and year)*
DATE	CHARGING PARTY *(Signature)*		
Subscribed and sworn to before this EEOC representative.			SIGNATURE *(If it is difficult for you to get a Notary Public to sign this, sign your own name and mail to the District Office. The Commission will notarize the charge for you at a later date.)*
DATE	SIGNATURE AND TITLE		

EEOC FORM JUN 72 **5**	Previous editions of this form may be used.	U.S. GOVERNMENT PRINTING OFFICE: 1973-728-451/1250 G P O 821.188

Source: U.S. Equal Employment Opportunity Commission.

FIGURE 5.1

the charge and, if two additional years were required to settle the case, the employer would be liable for four years' back pay.

The Labor Department's Office of Federal Contract Compliance examines the antidiscrimination programs of companies with federal government contracts or subcontracts of $50,000 or more and 50 or more employees. These companies must have affirmative-action plans listing the specific goals and timetables for the hiring of women and minorities. Even if only one division of a company has a government contract of $50,000 or more, the entire firm must participate in the required affirmative-action program.

The statutes governing antidiscrimination guidelines are numerous and complex. Individual or class action suits can be filed against a firm under any one, or any combination, of the following laws and directives:

- The Fifth and Fourteenth Amendments to the Constitution.
- The Civil Rights Acts of 1866, 1870, and 1871.
- The Equal Pay Act of 1963.
- Titles VII and IX of the 1964 Civil Rights Act.
- The Civil Rights Act of 1991.
- The Age Discrimination in Employment Act of 1967, as amended by the Older Worker Benefit Protection Act of 1990.
- Executive Order 11246, as amended by E.O. 11375.
- Executive Order 11478, Equal Employment Opportunity in the Federal Government.
- The Equal Employment Opportunity Act of 1972.
- The Comprehensive Employment and Training Act of 1973.
- 1973 Amendments to the Omnibus Crime Control and Safe Streets Act.
- The Vocational Rehabilitation Act of 1973.
- The Vietnam Era Veterans Readjustment Assistance Act of 1974.
- The Pregnancy Discrimination Act of 1978.
- The Americans With Disabilities Act of 1990.

These regulations in the aggregate cover a majority of the population (although with varying degrees of stringency): Women and African Americans; those of Spanish, Asian, Pacific Island, American Indian, or Eskimo ancestry; Vietnam-era veterans and the handicapped; workers between the ages of 40 and 64 (and most of those 65 and over); and members of religious and ethnic groups, such as Jews, Catholics, Italians, Greeks, and Slavs.

These categories overlap significantly. To complicate the matter, affirmative-action programs cover many, but not all, of the aforementioned categories. Government contractors must maintain special efforts to recruit, train, and promote members of the following designated groups: African Americans, women, Spanish-surnamed Americans, those with disabilities, and Vietnam War veterans. Other companies have been required to set up affirmative-action programs when the courts have found them to have discriminated, and still others have established affirmative-action programs voluntarily.

Federal contractors and subcontractors with 100 or more employees and a contract in excess of $100,000 must develop written affirmative-action plans for the increased utilization of women and minorities. The requirements for an acceptable affirmative-action plan are quite detailed:

1. An analysis of all major job categories at each facility, with explanations if minority-group members are being "underutilized."

2. Specific goals, timetables, and affirmative-action commitments designed to correct the deficiencies.

3. Compilation and maintenance of support data and analysis.

4. Special attention to six categories that the government has identified as most likely to show underutilization of minorities: officials and managers, professionals, technicians, sales workers, office and clerical workers, and skilled craft workers.

Litigation in Practice

Practitioners of EEOC litigation often report that employers usually attempt to settle such cases out of court, whether or not they believe the complaint is justified. The costs involved are a powerful incentive to do so, aside from the unfavorable publicity that is attached to the very institution of the suit. The interrogatories, motions, depositions, and hearings that precede trial of an EEO case can be expensive. In addition, there is the risk that an individual charge of discrimination will escalate into an extremely costly class action suit. (See Table 5.1 for some large recent settlements.)

In 1997, Texaco formed a high-level, independent Task Force on Equality and Fairness to evaluate its progress in hiring and promoting minorities and to examine potential improvements in its human resource programs. The Task Force was part of a settlement reached the previous year with African-American employees who had sued the company on grounds of racial bias.

The cost to shareholders in terms of the adverse consequences of news of an EEOC case on the price of a company's stock can exceed the amount that firms are required to spend to settle the case. A study of 241 EEO cases between 1964 and 1985 estimated the average loss of equity value on the day a suit, decision, or settlement was announced at $28.8 million. The drop in the corporation's share value may arise from many causes, such as the expected costs of changing employment practices and

TABLE 5.1 High Cost of Discrimination

Company	Settlement or Jury Award (in millions)
Texaco	$176
Shoney's	105
Publix	85
Denny's	46
Southern California Edison	18
Illinois Central	13
Pitney Bowes	11

Note: Amounts cover settlements or jury awards against companies in the 1990s covering racial or gender bias in hiring, promotions, or layoffs.

the information revealed about the firm's management.[1] Offsetting factors include the concern that an out-of-court settlement will encourage other employees to bring groundless suits and the belief that it is wrong to pay off employees who make such complaints.

James Ledvinka and Vida Scarpello of the University of Georgia describe a case that borders on a no-win situation for a small company faced with a charge of racial discrimination by an African-American employee who was passed over for a pay raise. The firm successfully opposed the charge, but only after incurring the cost of preparing a four-part statistical study that included the following:

1. A thorough analysis of all jobs performed at the company for the period of time covered by the lawsuit.

2. Classification of all employees during that time by race and job.

3. Determination of the labor–market group having the requisite qualifications for each job.

4. Statistical comparison of African-American percentages in each job between the firm's employees and the relevant labor market.

The resultant analysis showed that the portion of the firm's workforce that was African-American consistently exceeded the African-American percentage of the relevant labor market, that the firm paid African-Americans, on average, slightly more than whites, and that its highest-paid employee was African-American. Moreover, the employee bringing the charge was shown to be chronically absent from his job and often late to work—and was paid an above-average wage. Considering the expense of responding to this by a company whose total payroll is about 175 persons, Ledvinka and Scarpello cynically conclude that an employer may be helped more in preventing EEO lawsuits and defending against them by a good set of employee statistics than by an aggressive affirmative-action plan.[2]

Seeking Voluntary Responses

The EEOC itself presses business firms to agree to sex and minority hiring goals "voluntarily," or, in other words, without resorting to federal court suits or the cancellation of federal funds or contracts. Employers are asked to make what are viewed as good-faith efforts. They are not asked to treat their minority hiring goals as mandatory quotas, yet the commission expects companies to take the kinds of actions that will enable them to reach the goals. The accompanying box, "EEOC Affirmative Action Program Guidelines" lists the many specific actions urged by the commission. It is taken from the EEOC's employer guidebook, *Affirmative Action and Equal Employment.*

The spirit of quotas, if not the letter, often does persist, however. According to the EEOC's long-range goals, a company can completely satisfy the commission only if its workforce reflects the minority–group situation in the area in which it is located. A plant in Alaska, for example, should employ a high percentage of Inuit; a plant in Oklahoma should have a high proportion of Native Americans. This strategy can backfire: An employer can avoid the problem by locating its new facilities in largely white communities, making it more difficult for applicants from minority groups to obtain jobs.

TABLE 5.2 Employment Interviews and Antidiscrimination Rules

Subject	What Employers Can Ask	What Employers Cannot Ask
Age	Are you between 18 and 65? If not, state your age.	How old are you? What is your date of birth?
Religion	Nothing	Which church do you belong to? What religious holidays do you observe?
Race	Nothing	What is your skin color or complexion?
Sex	Nothing (unless directly job related)	Do you have a picture you can send us?
Disability	Can you perform the job?	Do you have a disability?
Name	Have you ever worked for this company under a different name?	State other names under which you have worked.
Citizenship	Are you a citizen of the United States?	Of what country are you a citizen?
Character	Have you been convicted of a crime?	Have you ever been arrested?
National origin	Nothing	What nationality are you or your parents?
Education	Where did you go to school?	
Experience	What kind of jobs have you held?	
Relatives	Do you have any relatives working for the company?	Are you married? Do you have children?
Organization memberships	Are you a member of any organization (exclude those indicating race, creed, color or national origin)?	List all societies to which you belong.

The influence of EEOC has permeated the personnel function in many ways, including the very nature of personnel selection via interviews and testing. At the job interview, general questions such as "Do you have a disability?" are considered unlawful. Questions must be limited to those specific disabilities that relate to a particular job to be performed (see Table 5.2). Formal testing has been reduced or abandoned in many instances because of the time and expense of demonstrating the validity and bias-free nature of the tests. The informal oral interview, however, may present other, less measurable opportunities for bias.

Effectiveness

A comprehensive statistical analysis of corporate affirmative-action programs by the National Bureau of Economic Research concluded that the goals are inflated and are not being fulfilled with the rigidity that might be expected of quotas. Nevertheless, establishments that promise to employ more minorities and women actually do so. Yet the author concluded that the specific enforcement tools of the compliance review program are of doubtful utility.[3]

Some personnel experts point out that the employee database generated to meet EEOC and affirmative action requirements can also be used for the company's own human-resource management efforts. Texas Instruments, for example, originally set up such a database, including five-year employment histories and job performance ratings, solely for EEO work. But company managers have found other uses for the information. Some analyze the characteristics of successful production supervisors

EEOC Affirmative Action Program Guidelines
and Affirmative Action Results

The most important measure of an Affirmative Action Program is its RE-SULTS.

Extensive efforts to develop procedures, analyses, data collection systems, report forms and fine written policy statements are meaningless unless the end product *will be measurable, yearly improvement in hiring, training and promotion of minorities and females in all parts of your organization.*

Just as the success of a company program to increase sales is evaluated in terms of actual increases in sales, the only realistic basis for evaluating a program to increase opportunity for minorities and females is its actual impact upon these persons.

The essence of your Affirmative Action Program should be:

- Establish strong company policy and commitment.
- Assigning responsibility and authority for program to top company official.
- Analyze present workforce to identify jobs, departments and units where minorities and females are underutilized.
- Set specific, measurable, attainable hiring and promotion goals, with target dates, in each area of underutilization.
- Make every manager and supervisor responsible and accountable for helping to meet these goals.
- Re-evaluate job descriptions and hiring criteria to assure that they reflect job needs.
- Find minorities and females who qualify or can become qualified to fill goals.
- Review and revise all employment procedures to assure that they do not have discriminatory effect and that they help attain goals.
- Focus on getting minorities and females into upward mobility and relevant training pipelines where they have not had previous access.
- Develop systems to monitor and measure progress regularly. If results are not satisfactory to meet goals, find out why, and make necessary changes.

Source: U.S. Equal Employment Opportunity Commission.

and use that profile in making appointments. Others examine turnover factors. Compensation specialists study the company's merit pay system to see if it is undercut by automatically rewarding seniority. Some managers try—rules permitting—to target poor performers for layoffs during a business downturn instead of arbitrarily discharging some of their best people.

All in all, despite its imperfections, the EEO process has succeeded in alerting company management to the special problems that must be faced in successfully developing and maintaining a diverse workforce containing persons of both sexes and of various races and ethnic backgrounds.

GUIDANCE FROM SUPREME COURT DECISIONS

Heated controversy about the legality and wisdom of affirmative action as social policy characterized much of the 1970s and 1980s. The newness of such efforts meant that a definitive body of law and judicial decisions was not available. The resulting uncertainty about what was constitutionally permitted intensified conflict over specifics. During the 1980s, the U.S. Supreme Court rendered decisions in several key cases. However, each decision came from a divided Court and left many important questions unanswered. In 1991, Congress passed a new Civil Rights Act that modified or superseded many of the later court rulings. The 1991 law provides a sharper emphasis on protection of minority concerns in employment.

Although both Congress and the courts continue to wrestle with many difficult questions, two fundamental points are clear. First of all, overt discrimination is wrong and illegal. There is no question about that. The continuing controversy deals with what actions or inactions constitute discrimination. Second, there is a continuing role for affirmative action because discrimination and its legacy in the workplace have not been fully eliminated. The specific content of the role for that preferential treatment is still being developed, often on a case-by-case basis.

Justice Sandra O'Connor wrote in a Supreme Court case of "the tension between the Fourteenth Amendment's guarantee of equal treatment to all citizens, and the use of race-based measures to ameliorate the effects of past discrimination. . . ." Under the circumstances, it is useful to review the key cases and statutes that constitute today's policy legacy.

The first contemporary landmark case was *California* v. *Bakke*. Bakke appealed being denied admission to the University of California Medical School, claiming reverse discrimination. In 1978, the Court held it permissible under both the equal protection clause of the Fourteenth Amendment and Title VII of the Civil Rights Act of 1964 for a state medical school to include race as a factor in competitive admissions. Four of the justices, composing a bare majority, advanced a broad constitutional justification of government-adopted compensatory racial preferences intended to offset current effects of past discrimination on the part of society as a whole. However, Bakke was granted admission to the state medical school by a five-to-four vote with six written opinions.

In *Steelworkers* v. *Weber* (1979), a white employee at Kaiser Aluminum's Gramercy, Louisiana, plant filed a complaint that challenged the selection of African-American employees with less job seniority for an apprenticeship training program. A collective bargaining agreement had set aside half the craft openings for African Americans until the percentage of minority craft workers reflected that of African Americans in the area's workforce. The white employee charged that this practice constituted a racial preference forbidden by Title VII of the 1964 Civil Rights Act. The Court rejected that reasoning, holding that the Civil Rights Act permitted the private sector voluntarily to apply a compensatory racial preference in employment. African Americans thus were given preference for admission to the company training program by a five-to-two vote with four opinions.

In *Fullilove* v. *Klutznick* (1980), a 10 percent set-aside of federal funds for minority businesses, provided for in the Public Works Employment Act of 1977, was held constitutional by a vote of six to three with five opinions.

These three cases make clear that the adverse effects of racial preferences under affirmative action programs experienced by the rest of the workforce—often referred to as reverse discrimination—are not by themselves sufficient grounds for invalidating such preferences as long as the intent of such practices is to make up for past discrimination. But limits to affirmative action were set, at least for a while. In a 1984 decision (*Memphis Firefighters Local Union No. 1784* v. *Stotts*), the Supreme Court narrowed the scope of affirmative action. It ruled that Title VII of the Civil Rights Act "protects bona fide seniority systems" even if that means minorities are laid off. The court also held that it is inappropriate to deny innocent employees the benefits of their seniority in order to provide a remedy in a "pattern of practice" equal-employment-opportunity suit. Thus layoffs of workers must follow seniority as specified in a union agreement—unless there are African-American employees that can prove they are victims of race bias. Here the vote was six to two with four opinions.

The Stotts case was followed by a series of even closer votes on the part of the Supreme Court justices. In *Wygant* v. *Jackson Board of Education* (1986), the Court rejected the Michigan School Board policy of laying off white teachers before minority teachers with less seniority by a vote of five to four. However, the Court held that government might be allowed to give preference in hiring if the plans were narrowly tailored to redress past discrimination. This case, restricting the scope of affirmative action, was soon followed by another that went the other way.

In *Local 93* v. *City of Cleveland* (1986), the Court returned to upholding affirmative action. It held that lower courts have broad discretion to approve decrees in which employers settle discrimination suits by agreeing to preferential hiring or promotion. The vote was six to three.

In *Local 28* v. *EEOC* (1986), the Court again endorsed affirmative action. It approved a lower court order requiring a local of the Sheet Metal Workers union to meet a goal for minority membership of 29 percent. It also made the union pay for training new minority members. By a vote of five to four, the Court also held that judges may order racial preferences in union membership if necessary to rectify especially "egregious" discrimination.

The Supreme Court also upheld affirmative action in two 1987 cases. In *U.S.* v. *Paradise,* it affirmed a district court order to Alabama requiring the promotion of one African-American state trooper for every white promoted. The justification was to make up for severe past discrimination. The vote was a close five to four. Another strengthening of the legal foundations of affirmative action occurred in *Johnson* v. *Transportation Agency.* In a six-to-three vote, the Court ruled that public employers may voluntarily implement affirmative action that favors women over men in hiring even if the purpose is merely to change the balance of employment between men and women. No instance of overt discrimination need be involved.

However, in 1989, the Supreme Court demonstrated that the role of affirmative action had not been clearly delineated by the courts. In four cases, the Court further reduced the scope of affirmative action. The decisions also triggered a backlash that resulted in the passage of the Civil Rights Act of 1991 (discussed later).

In *City of Richmond* v. *Croson,* the Court disallowed the city's set-aside plans that required that 30 percent of the subcontracts awarded for a public project go to minority-owned firms. In a six-to-three ruling, the Court noted that the city's plans were unacceptable because they did not require a clear history of discrimination. *Martin* v. *Wilks* made it easier to challenge labor agreements establishing affirmative action plans. The Court ruled that employees of the Birmingham, Alabama, fire department could challenge a settlement on the grounds that they were not part of the original agreement. Thus, claims of reverse discrimination could be made. (This ruling was reversed by the 1991 law. The statute provides that individuals can be bound by consent degrees if they had a chance to object at the time or if their interests were represented by an earlier party.)

Wards Cove Packing Co. v. *Antonio* was a key case reversed by the 1991 law. This ruling, by a five-to-four vote, imposed tougher standards on employees trying to prove discrimination via statistics alone. By requiring signs of overt discrimination, the Court reduced the grounds for class action discrimination suits. *Patterson* v. *McLean Credit Union* affirmed an earlier ruling prohibiting discrimination in the private sector. However, the Supreme Court also held that an 1866 civil rights statute only banned racial harassment in hiring and in promotion, not in the workplace. (This decision was also reversed by the 1991 law.)

The Civil Rights Act of 1991 overturned the Wards Cove Packing case by returning the burden of proof to employers, forcing them to justify practices that are alleged to adversely affect women and minorities. The law describes the circumstances under which employers can impose a requirement on or test employees (and prospective hires) without being accused of discrimination: Once a plaintiff shows that an employment practice has a "disparate impact," the burden of proof shifts to the employer.

Thus, the employer must justify the questioned employment practice as "job-related for the position in question and consistent with business necessity." Plaintiffs in discrimination cases must now specify the hiring or promotion methods they consider to have a "disparate impact" on the workforce. Because the law avoids defining these terms, the courts are having to decide, for example, what constitutes "business necessity." Not surprisingly, the workload of the Equal Employment Opportunity Commission has been rising rapidly since the 1991 law went into force.

In a close five-to-four decision in 1995, however, the Supreme Court held that programs that award benefits on the basis of race, even for ostensibly benign purposes, can only survive if they are "narrowly tailored" to accomplish a "compelling government interest" (*Adarund Constructors* v. *Pena*). The Court went on to state that, because of racial discrimination, government is "not disqualified" from responding to that situation. The specific way in which these key terms will be interpreted by the courts is likely to involve extended future litigation. This is especially so in view of the changing composition of the Supreme Court.

DEVELOPMENTS IN EQUAL EMPLOYMENT OPPORTUNITY

The scope of equal employment opportunity legislation has been expanding over the years. The Pregnancy Discrimination Act of 1978 makes clear that discrimination in employment based on pregnancy, childbirth, or related medical conditions constitutes unlawful sex discrimination under Title VII of the Civil Rights Act. Thus, benefits from health insurance plans for sickness or temporary disability must be given to women disabled by pregnancy, miscarriage, or childbirth.

Also in 1978 and again in 1986, the Age Discrimination in Employment Act was amended to restrict and ultimately ban mandatory retirement (with a few exceptions, such as workers in high-risk jobs and highly paid executives). The typical age-discrimination case is filed by a white male in his fifties who held a managerial or professional position. In the words of one attorney, "It's very hard to convince a jury that a nice, white-haired man who lost his job after 20 years doesn't deserve something against the big, bad corporation."[4] Even casual asides—such as a supervisor referring to an employee as "the old man"—can be evidence of discrimination.

Age-discrimination cases are increasingly linked with "wrongful discharge" of employees. The traditional "employment at will" (or "fire at will") doctrine has rapidly eroded. It has become much more difficult for a company to fire a worker without demonstrating just cause, proper procedure, and so on—especially in the case of an older employee. The incentive to file suit is substantial, and the 1986 legislation banning mandatory retirement in most cases furnished added impetus. In a case involving 530 laid-off employees, Equitable Life Insurance Company paid out $12.5 million. Three terminated employees at an I. Magnin store received $1.9 million. One former worker at a Sears Roebuck store in Colorado received $20 million—but lost the case on appeal.

Sexual harassment on the job goes back to Old Testament days; Joseph was cast into prison when he would not lie with his master's wife (Genesis 39:6–13). In 1980, the Equal Employment Opportunity Commission issued guidelines forbidding sexual harassment of employees by their supervisors. (Key excerpts from the ruling are contained in the box, "EEOC Rules on Sexual Harassment.")

In 1990, Congress passed landmark legislation to give disabled people increased access to services and jobs. *The Americans With Disabilities Act* (ADA) was widely hailed as an important protection of the civil rights of a disadvantaged minority. The new law bars employment discrimination against people with physical or mental disabilities. It also requires access to public buildings, mass transportation, and government services for people who have disabilities covered by ADA.

Critics of the legislation focus on the vague wording. What is a "reasonable accommodation"? What is an "undue burden"? What is an "essential" job function? On the other hand, many employers also worry about the expansive definition of "disability." For example, the protections of ADA extend to recovering drug users who are participating in a supervised drug rehabilitation program and are no longer using drugs.[5]

Many of the regulations issued under ADA are quite specific. Five percent of the rooms in a hotel, and about half of the drinking fountains on each floor of an office building must be fully accessible to disabled people, including those in wheelchairs. The rules also prescribe how many parking spaces must be reserved for disabled people and specify the maximum slope of ramps and the maximum pile height for carpet—one-half inch. (A steep slope or a plush carpet cannot be navigated easily in a wheelchair.) Violators of the rules may be punished by a fine up to $50,000 for a first offense and $100,000 for any subsequent offense.

EEOC Rules on Sexual Harassment

Harassment on the basis of sex is a violation of Section 703 of Title VII of the Civil Rights Act of 1964. The Equal Employment Opportunity Commission (EEOC) has provided specific definitions of what constitutes sexual harassment: unwelcome sexual advances, requests for sexual favors, and other verbal or physical conduct of a sexual nature when (1) submission to such conduct is made, either explicitly or implicitly, a term or condition of an individual's employment, (2) submission to or rejection of such conduct by an individual is used as the basis for employment decisions affecting such individual, or (3) such conduct has the purpose or effect of substantially interfering with an individual's work performance or creating an intimidating, hostile, or offensive working environment.

In determining whether alleged conduct constitutes sexual harassment, the commission looks at the record as a whole and at the totality of the circumstances, such as the nature of the sexual advances and the context in which the alleged incidents occurred. The determination of the legality of a particular action is made from the facts, on a case-by-case basis.

Applying general Title VII principles, EEOC states that an employer, employment agency, joint apprenticeship committee, or labor organization is responsible for its acts and those of its agents and supervisory employees with respect to sexual harassment regardless of whether the specific acts complained of were authorized or even forbidden by the employer and regardless of whether the employer knew or should have known of their occurrence.

Source: Equal Employment Opportunity Commission.

Many companies have tried to adopt a compliance mode that avoids generating ADA complaints (see Table 5.3). Since the enactment of ADA in 1990, "hidden" impairments such as mental illness and back injury, as well as more exotic disabilities such as "multiple chemical sensitivity," have become the most cited impairments in charges filed against employers. Those "hidden" disabilities now far exceed in frequency of charges the more familiar and apparent disabilities such as those involving sight, hearing, and mobility.[6]

To critics and supporters alike, it is useful to note that ADA is an antidiscrimination statute, not an affirmative action program. In a 1996 decision, a federal circuit court held that "It prohibits employment discrimination against qualified individuals with disabilities, no more and no less."[7]

The Family and Medical Leave Act of 1993 requires employers with at least 50 workers to provide up to 12 weeks of unpaid leave a year to employees who are dealing with births, adoptions, or family medical problems. During the leave, the employer must continue to provide any health care coverage the employee had been receiving. After the leave, the employee must be taken back with no loss of job responsibility or seniority.

TABLE 5.3 Corporate Efforts to Improve Treatment of Disabled Persons

Company	Action
Ford Motor Company	Tests managers' knowledge of ADA
Intermagnetics	Schedules meetings on ground floors
Nike	Adopted hiring policies to highlight contributions by the disabled
Mycogen	Eliminated requirement for lab workers to be able to stand for several hours a day
AT&T	Employs specialists to help disabled employees get necessary equipment
U.S. West	Provides special headsets for blind customer service representatives
Pioneer Hi-Bred	Reviews job descriptions to conform with ADA
Pacific Telesis	Adapts tools for use by disabled employees
Sears, Roebuck	Lowers work platforms for wheelchair users

The proponents of the various employer mandates downplay the costs, which are primarily borne by the employer. However, a study at the National Bureau of Economic Research found significant results when examining state laws passed in the 1970s requiring employers to provide female workers with health insurance including full maternity coverage. For every dollar of cost associated with the maternity mandates, the wage rates of the targeted women's group fell by a dollar. Thus, women workers who did not plan to have children wound up subsidizing, by way of reduced wages, a free benefit for women workers who were having children.[8]

An indication of things to come in the years ahead is contained in a report on employee leave issued by the National Research Council, an agency of the National Academy of Sciences.[9] The study by this prestigious organization concluded that U.S. employers have not kept pace with the needs of a diverse workforce. The Council's report offered the following specific recommendations:

- Paid family leave to care for infants and ill family members.
- Paid sick leave, including leave for disabilities related to pregnancy and childbirth.
- More opportunities for flexible schedules, part-time work, and alternative work locations.
- Resource and referral programs, employee assistance programs, and other forms of direct and indirect help.

The panel writing the report came up with an intriguing conclusion: Employers should be expected to share the responsibility of making it possible for workers to do justice to both their jobs and their families.

Equal Pay for Comparable Work

Women in the labor force in the United States, on average, earn only two-thirds as much as men. A widely held belief is that much of the difference results from discrimination. In partial response, Title VII of the Civil Rights Act of 1964 requires employers to pay equal wages to men and women working in the same jobs. That law was designed to end the practice of lower wage scales for women.

The Wage Gender Gap   The overall wage differences between men and women remain substantial, but the gap has been narrowing. In 1980, working women earned an average of 60 percent of the wages earned by men. By 1995, the U.S. Department of Labor reported that the ratio of women's median weekly earnings to men's had risen to 76 percent (see Figure 5.2). Although that still sounds quite discriminatory, those numbers are just the beginning of any serious analysis.[10]

The greatest gains are being recorded by the youngest female age groups, a good indication of future progress. Controlling for education, union status, and other measurable variables, the earnings of women in the age group 16 to 29 rose to 92 percent of the male average by 1993.[11] Women increasingly are making the same kind of schooling and occupational choices as men. Nevertheless, the analysis still leaves an 8 percent gap, an unexplained residual that likely includes discrimination—as well as other factors not subject to direct measurement.

While the debate continues about the presence of a glass ceiling to promotion of women to top management positions in large companies, it is useful to note the progress in small business. The number of women-owned businesses increased 43 percent from 1987 to 1992. In 1993, women started new businesses at twice the rate of men. By 1995, 7.7 million women-owned companies in the United States employed 15.5 million people and generated sales of $1.4 trillion.[12]

A new response to the continued difference in earnings is the doctrine of *equal pay for comparable work.* The doctrine rests on the observation that certain occupations are filled predominantly by women and others mainly by men. For example,

FIGURE 5.2 Female/Male Pay Ratio from 1969 to 1996

Female/male earnings ratio based on median weekly earnings of full-time workers ages 16 and over.

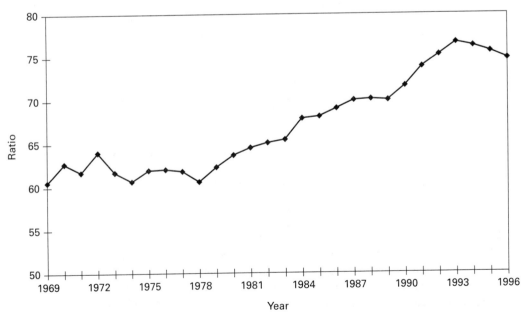

Source: U.S. Department of Labor, Bureau of Labor Statistics.

TABLE 5.4   Male- and Female-Dominated Occupations, 1996

Female-Dominated Occupations	Percent Women	Median Income	Male-Dominated Occupations	Percent Men	Median Income
Registered nurse	92%	$36,100	Aerospace engineer	96%	$57,100
Speech therapist	94	36,000	Mechanical engineer	93	50,400
Licensed practical nurse	95	24,200	Electrical equipment repairer	100	37,100
Secretary	99	21,100	Firefighter	98	34,400
Dental assistant	98	18,700	Plumber	98	30,500
Kindergarten teacher	98	18,700	Crane and tower operator	97	29,000
Receptionist	97	17,300			
Pre-school teachers' assistant	98	12,000	Driver-sales worker	95	26,800
			Truck driver	97	25,200
Maid	93	11,500	Auto mechanic	99	25,000
Child care worker	99	10,300	Carpenter	99	24,700

Source: U.S. Department of Labor, Bureau of Labor Statistics.

lawyers, physicians, and the building trades have been traditional male occupations, whereas women have typically obtained jobs as schoolteachers, nurses, and secretaries.

Table 5.4 shows average earnings in 1996 for occupations with the largest concentration of men and women. It can be seen that, on average, the male-dominated occupations pay more than the female-dominated jobs. Yet variations within and between the categories are substantial. Thus, the highest paid female-dominated occupation (registered nurses) is paid more than any of the five most male-dominated occupations (such as carpenters) and four times the lowest paid female-dominated occupation (child care workers). Clearly, many factors are involved in the determination of pay scales, including the differential pattern of unionization. For example, highly paid, male-dominated, blue-collar categories are heavily unionized, while low-paid, female-dominated occupations tend to be unorganized. The unions, perhaps not surprisingly, are in the forefront of support for comparable worth.

Advocates of equal pay for comparable work believe that wage differences between male- and female-dominant occupations mainly reflect bias against women. Accordingly, they suggest reinterpreting Title VII to prohibit a lower rate of pay for employees of one race or sex for jobs that require an equivalent amount of skill, effort, and responsibility.

Opponents of the new approach maintain that relative wages result from the interplay of many other forces, especially "supply side" factors. Even in the absence of prejudice and when performed under conditions of equal skill, effort, and responsibility, the real market value of dissimilar work can differ markedly. Studies restricted to white males have yielded such results.[13]

Market Effects of Wage Differentials   Economists point out that wage differences play a constructive role: They serve to guide labor into those occupations and locations where it is in short supply and discourage people from entering those in which an excessive supply is already available. For example, the wages of petroleum geologists and petroleum engineers increased dramatically following the OPEC oil embargo of 1973. This led to large increases in the supply of these specialists, which made possible a rapid expansion in exploration and drilling for oil and gas.[14] Artificially forcing wage increases in occupations now filled mainly by women will increase the number of individuals preparing for careers in these "higher-paying" occupations; however, employers will simultaneously tend to reduce their demands for these more expensive jobs.

The experience of public schools underscores the concerns of the critics of the comparable-worth doctrine. Historically, teachers are paid on the basis of years of service and level of education, ignoring the market forces that affect different specialties. The outcome can be predicted by any student of Economics 101: chronic shortages of math and science instructors and continuing surpluses of gym teachers. If colleges were to adopt the comparable-worth approach—and equalized pay across the various schools and departments—they would go bankrupt if they raised liberal arts faculty to the pay scales of medicine. Conversely, any attempt to bring down the salaries of medical faculty would cause an exodus of the teaching staffs.

Practical Problems   Washington State was the first government unit to make the concept of *comparable worth* operational. Its experience provides the precedent for at least 19 other states studying or applying comparable-worth pay adjustments. Many of those states are in earlier stages, such as commissioning studies of their current pay structures. Several county and city governments also have adopted variations of the comparable-pay approach (or pay equity, as it is often called).

In 1974, the Washington State government hired Willis and Associates, a job-evaluation firm, to "examine and identify salary differences that may pertain to job classes predominantly filled by men compared to job classes predominantly filled by women, based on job worth." At that time, pay rates had been based on prevailing market rates.

The firm worked with an evaluation committee, composed primarily of Washington State employees, to rate jobs based on four factors: knowledge and skills, mental demands, accountability, and working conditions. For each job, points were assigned to each of the four factors and were aggregated to determine total job value.

The Willis job-evaluation technique differed sharply from the market in its judgment of job "worth" throughout the range of occupations studied.

- A level IV registered nurse was worth 573 points, more than any other job studied, while a computer systems analyst received only 426 points. In the market, on the other hand, computer systems analysts are among the most sought-after and highest-paid workers. They earn about one-half more than registered nurses.
- A clerical supervisor was assigned points equal to a chemist in knowledge and skills and was granted more points overall—whereas the market would pay the chemist about two-fifths more than the clerical supervisor.
- Truck drivers were placed at the bottom of the new ranking system. They were given fewer points in knowledge and skills, mental demands, and accountability than the lowest ranked telephone operators or retail clerks. The market—or at least union contracts—judged otherwise, paying the drivers 30 percent more than retail clerks.[15]

On average, the Willis job-evaluation system determined that Washington State underpaid women-dominated occupations by 20 percent. In 1983, however, when Washington State sought the expertise of a second job-evaluation firm, it discovered that job-evaluation studies varied substantially. The second firm, Jeanneret and Associates, examined the same set of positions and found that no disparity in compensation existed on the basis of "job worth." Not too surprisingly, the second firm criticized the work of the first for:

> . . . the failure to use expert job evaluators in the conduct of the study, the limited number of factors used in studying such a large, diverse employer, and the lack of objectivity in the scoring of job worth.[16]

These differences are symptomatic of the problems that arise when comparisons are made across states, even adjacent ones. As shown in Figure 5.3, a secretary is ranked first among the three jobs shown in Washington State and Iowa, but last in Minnesota and Vermont. A data entry operator places first in Minnesota but third in Iowa, while Vermont and Washington rank the job second.[17]

The political response to comparable worth in the public sector has been positive but limited. Increasing the pay of women-dominated occupations without reducing that of men-dominated groups seems to create winners but no losers. The losers, of course, are the taxpayers, who wind up paying for more expensive government. The adoption of proposals to extend comparable worth to the private sector would generate much greater repercussions. Arbitrarily raising labor costs would be inflationary in domestic markets and reduce the competitiveness of American products in overseas markets.

Alternative Approaches   Alternatives to "comparable worth" have been suggested for bridging the pay gap between men and women. One approach is to let existing policy work. An indication of the progress being made is the narrower wage gap for younger people. As noted previously, in 1993, women aged 16 to 29 earned 92 percent of men's earnings. In contrast, women in the age group 30 to 40 received 78 percent of the male average, and women aged 45 and older received only 67 percent of the average for men in the same age group.[18]

FIGURE 5.3 Comparable-Worth Job Rankings Across States[a]

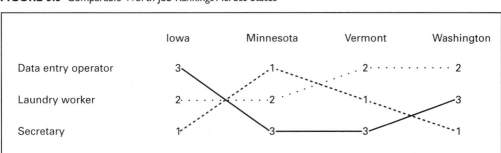

[a]Rankings are from 1 to 3, with 1 being the highest rated of the three jobs and 3 being the lowest.
Source: Center for the Study of American Business, Washington University.

Moreover, change appears to be greatest in the professions requiring higher education—and slowest in the occupations with heavy craft union membership. For example, between 1970 and 1995, the percentage of women accountants more than doubled (from 25 percent to 52 percent) and the ratio of women to men lawyers jumped from 5 percent to 26 percent. During the same period, the proportion of women automobile mechanics and plumbers stayed at 1 percent.[19]

Notes

1. Joni Hersch, *EEO Law and Firm Profitability,* Working Paper No. 87/7 (Eugene, OR: University of Oregon, Department of Economics, 1987).
2. James Ledvinka and Vida Scarpello, "Surviving an EEO Lawsuit," *SAM Advanced Management Journal,* Summer 1982, p. 23.
3. Jonathan S. Leonard, *The Impact of Affirmative Action Goals* (Cambridge, MA: National Bureau of Economic Research, 1984).
4. Sydney P. Freedberg, "Forced Exits? Companies Confront Wave of Age-Discrimination Suits," *Wall Street Journal,* October 13, 1987, p. 7.
5. Robin Andrews, "The Americans With Disabilities Act of 1990," *Cumberland Law Review* 21, no. 3, 1991, pp. 629–646.
6. Jack Faris, *The Americans With Disabilities Act* (Washington, DC: National Legal Center for the Public Interest, 1996), pp. 7–9.
7. Cited in Faris, p. 25.
8. Richard B. McKenzie, *The Mandated-Benefit Mirage* (St. Louis: Washington University, Center for the Study of American Business, 1991).
9. National Research Council, *Work and Family: Policies for a Changing Work Force* (Washington, DC: National Academy Press, 1991).
10. In biblical times, for purposes of tithing, women of working age were valued at 30 silver shekels, while men were valued at 50 (Leviticus 27:3–4), eerily close to the 1980 level.
11. Diana Furchtgott-Roth and Christine Stalba, *Women's Figures: The Economic Progress of Women in America* (Arlington, VA: Independent Women's Forum, 1996), p. 8.
12. Furchtgott-Roth and Stalba, p. 27.
13. Jacob Mincer, "The Distribution of Labor Incomes: A Survey with Special Reference to the Human Capital Approach," *Journal of Economic Literature,* March 1970, pp. 1–26.
14. *Comparable Worth: "Women's Issue" or Wage Controls?* (Washington, DC: American Legislative Exchange Council, 1984), pp. 9–10.
15. June O'Neill, "The Trend in the Male-Female Wage Gap in the United States," *Journal of Labor Economics* 3, no. 1, 1985.
16. Quoted in U.S. Office of Personnel Management, *Comparable Worth for Federal Jobs* (Washington, DC: U.S. Government Printing Office, 1987), p. 41.
17. Richard E. Burr, *Are Comparable Worth Systems Truly Comparable?* (St. Louis: Washington University, Center for the Study of American Business, 1986).
18. Furchtgott-Roth and Stalba, *Women's Figures,* p. 9.
19. Jane Katz, "Occupational Divide," *Federal Reserve Bank of Boston Regional Review,* Spring 1996, p. 17.

CHAPTER 6

Government and the Workplace

The rising role of government in the workplace is a key example of the public's unwillingness to accept the impacts on society that result from the unregulated workings of the free market. Equal-employment-opportunity regulations and affirmative-action programs by no means constitute the entire catalog of the federal government's involvement in personnel matters.

The Occupational Safety and Health Administration in the U.S. Department of Labor also takes important actions affecting the workplace. In addition, many other agencies, ranging from the National Labor Relations Board to the Pension Benefit Guaranty Corporation, play significant roles in setting and enforcing workforce regulations. Many of these government actions generate intense feelings, and the need for analysis is great.

JOB SAFETY REGULATION

The Occupational Safety and Health Administration (OSHA) was created in 1970 "to assure so far as possible every working man and woman in the nation safe and healthful working conditions and to preserve our human resources."[1] Congress provides several means—both voluntary and compulsory—for OSHA to use in fulfilling this mandate:

1. Encouraging employers and employees to reduce hazards in the workplace and to institute health and safety programs.
2. Establishing responsibilities and rights for employers and employees (mainly responsibilities for employers and rights for employees).
3. Authorizing OSHA to set mandatory job safety and health standards.
4. Providing an enforcement program.
5. Encouraging the states to take responsibility for administering their own job safety and health programs, which must be at least as effective as the federal program.
6. Setting up reporting procedures for job injuries, illnesses, and fatalities.

Compliance with OSHA regulations is enforced through inspections. These inspections may be triggered by serious accidents or employee complaints. Inspections can be aimed at "target industries" or "target health hazards," or they may be randomly selected workplaces. Target industries—those with injury rates more than double the national average—include longshoring, meat and meat products, roofing and sheet metal, lumber and wood products, and miscellaneous transportation equipment. Target health hazards are associated with the five most hazardous and most commonly used toxic substances: asbestos, carbon monoxide, cotton dust, lead, and silica.

If, upon inspection, an employer is found in violation of an OSHA regulation, the violation is placed in one of the following four categories:

- *De minimis.* A very minor condition having no direct or immediate relation to job health and safety (e.g., lack of toilet partitions).
- *Nonserious violations.* A condition directly related to job safety and health but unlikely to cause death or serious physical harm (e.g., tripping hazard). A penalty of up to $7,000 is optional. Such a penalty may be reduced by as much as 50 percent, depending on the severity of the hazard, the employer's good faith, the history of previous violations, and the size of the business. Another 50 percent reduction occurs if the employer corrects the violation within the prescribed time.
- *Serious violation.* A condition in which substantial probability of death or serious physical harm exists, and in which the employer knew or should have known of the hazard (e.g., absence of guards on punch presses or saws). A penalty of up to $7,000 is mandatory. This penalty also may be reduced up to 50 percent for good faith. The law requires a minimum penalty of $5,000 for willful violations.
- *Imminent danger.* Where there is reasonable certainty that the hazard can be expected to cause death or serious physical injury immediately or before the hazard can be eliminated through regular procedures. If the employer fails to deal with the violation immediately, OSHA can go directly to a federal district court for legal action.

Although the OSHA program is designed primarily to benefit employees, its efforts are aimed at employers. It is the employer's responsibility to assure that safe and healthful conditions exist in the workplace and to purchase equipment necessary to correct unsafe or unhealthy conditions. It is the employers who must make sure that the employees adhere to safety rules and safe practices. For example, if an employee is instructed to wear a particular piece of personal protection equipment, such as safety-toe footwear, but the employee fails to do so and sustains an injury as a result of this failure, the OSHA law requires that any penalty be levied against the employer. Contributory negligence by the employee is not a defense for the employer, nor is the worker cited. (The influence of the labor unions in the writing of the OSHA statute is quite clear.)

Reactions to OSHA

The Occupational Safety and Health Act was passed by an overwhelming vote in the Congress—83 to 3 in the Senate and 383 to 5 in the House of Representatives—clearly indicating strong support on the part of the public's congressional representatives. But, despite the obvious worthiness of the agency's objectives (who is opposed to safer workplaces?), much of the public reaction to OSHA has been negative. From its inception, the agency has been subject to a constant barrage of criticism from almost every quarter: business, labor, academic researchers, the media, and government itself. Corporate and trade-association executives claim that the agency's standards are needlessly burdensome and costly. Union representatives complain that OSHA is spread too thin and is not tough enough. Government analysts and university econo-mists criticize the agency for not being cost-effective.

Unintentionally, OSHA has been the target of an array of jokes about govern-ment incompetence. "Did you hear the one about the OSHA inspector who required separate 'his' and 'hers' employee toilets for a two-person business where the employ-ees were married to each other?" "Did you see the OSHA regulation requiring that spittoons be cleaned daily?" "Did OSHA really require a company to print its signs in both English and Spanish because it had an employee of Spanish descent (who only spoke English)?" Other continuing criticisms, however, have been far more substan-tive.

Economists contend that the agency is not effective in achieving its basic objec-tive. The conclusions of a study by Thomas J. Kniesner and John D. Leeth are typical of academic reactions: Large percentages of workplace accidents (as many as 75 per-cent) result from workers' carelessness or momentary physical hazards such as wet floors. If every firm in the country were to comply fully with OSHA's standards, total injuries would be reduced by only 10 to 20 percent.[2]

Labor-union representatives have criticized OSHA for administrative ineptness and extended delays. Except for a few large and highly publicized cases, the average OSHA fine is only a few hundred dollars. Moreover, inspections are infrequent. The average employer faces a visit from OSHA once in 66 years.

The inspection–fine approach ignores the extent of market incentives for safer workplaces. In a competitive market economy, the riskier the job, the higher the pay, other things being equal. W. Kip Viscusi estimates that, in one recent year, the "risk premium" paid to workers in the private sector of the United States totaled $69 bil-lion, or $925 a worker. Such large pay premiums provide a strong incentive for em-ployers to make workplaces safer. Any expected OSHA fines come to a small fraction of the amount.[3]

Nevertheless, a study at the National Bureau of Economic Research reveals that OSHA inspections do significantly reduce injuries. This effect comes exclusively from inspections that impose penalties. Factories that are inspected—and penalized—in a given year experience a 22 percent decline in their injuries in the following several years. Inspections that do not impose penalties appear to have no effect on injuries.[4] In 1990, Congress increased maximum OSHA fines sevenfold: to $70,000 for willful violations, to $7,000 for serious as well as "nonserious" violations; and to $7,000 a day for failure to abate violations.

A more powerful, albeit indirect, incentive to curb on-the-job accidents comes from the workers' compensation program. Surging medical costs have pushed outlays for workers' compensation to over $50 billion a year. The state laws typically require employers to pay 100 percent of the medical costs resulting from on-the-job injuries.

Impacts on Business

OSHA has had a significant impact on company capital investments. Business firms in the United States devote more than $5 billion in plant and equipment outlays annu-ally to meet OSHA requirements. Many manufacturing departments have revised their procedures to conform with the agency's regulations pertaining to air, noise, and heat. Although the cost of compliance rises, on the average, with the size of the com-pany, the increases are not proportional. The smaller firms bear a disproportionately large share of the expenses that arise from employee safety and health regulation. Larger employers benefit from the economies of scale involved in complying with OSHA rules (and many other types of government regulation). They can afford to maintain professional safety departments that have the capability to keep abreast of the government's mandates and to learn the OSHA lingo.

We can recall the experience of the small business owner testifying at a congressional hearing on the paperwork burden imposed by government agencies. A committee member stated that the executive did not have to bother personally with the forms. The company staff could fill them out. The response was a classic, "My staff, sir, is me."

The OSHA approach to safety regulation is based on the notion that employers can best prevent workplace accidents and disease. In a series of cases, the Occupational Safety and Health Review Commission ruled that the employers should do more than merely make protective equipment available. Employers must establish an effective policy to ensure that the equipment is used and must continually monitor its enforcement to make certain that their employees are complying with it.

There are limits, however, to a company's responsibility for lack of safety consciousness by its employees. In one case (*Secretary of Labor* v. *Standard Glass, Inc.*) where the evidence demonstrated that the employer had done all that could reasonably be required to ensure that employees used their protective equipment, the commission ruled that their isolated failures to use it were not a violation by the employer. The commission held that the employer could not be expected to guarantee that all employees would observe good safety practices at all times.

An extensive study of successful private-industry safety programs concluded that the participating employers place great emphasis on training, education, and awareness programs. About three-fourths schedule safety meetings for workers. Half of the companies have ongoing safety training programs for supervisors and new hires. Several firms offer specialized training in jobs where accident data reveal specific hazards. When unsafe conditions or procedures are discovered at specific job sites, some firms issue safety alerts, warning managers of other divisions with similar working conditions. In job safety, as in other areas, information thus seems to be a more widely used tool in voluntary private safety programs than in government regulatory efforts.[5]

Benefits of Job Safety Controls

Although it is useful to be aware of the problems encountered in the regulation of job safety and health, the potential benefits from a less hazardous work environment should also be recognized. Many of the most important results of occupational safety and health are substantial but not readily quantifiable—at least not without making numerous assumptions about the value of an arm, of hearing loss, or of life itself. Nevertheless, we can identify the various types of benefits that can be expected. The advantages of a safer workplace also constitute an incentive to business to minimize job-related hazards, even in the absence of government regulation. The following are the major benefits that accrue from enhanced workplace safety:

1. Greater productivity of those who would have sustained a job-related injury or illness in the absence of government regulation.

2. Greater enjoyment of life by those who thus avoided work-related disabilities.

3. Savings of resources that would have had to be used in the treatment and rehabilitation of victims in work-related injuries or illnesses that were avoided.

4. Saving of resources that would have had to be used to administer workers' compensation and insurance and to train those who would have been needed to replace the sick or disabled.

5. Decrease in damage to buildings and equipment.

6. Savings that result from less disruption of work routines caused by accidents, plus potential improvements in the morale and productivity of the workforce.

OSHA Effectiveness

How effective is OSHA? We can answer that question indirectly by examining the trend of workplace injuries and illnesses in the United States since the agency was created. Figure 6.1 shows that the rate of job-related illnesses and accidents declined from 11 per 100 workers in 1973 to 8 percent in 1995. However, a total of 6.6 million injuries were reported that year.[6] The main point of these statistics is that, despite substantial progress, the problem of workplace safety has not been solved. Thus, analysis of the underlying question of job hazards is in order.

Researchers who have focused on workplace safety and health regulation almost uniformly conclude that the fundamental flaw in the OSHA approach is the decision by Congress at the outset to rely primarily on government-promulgated standards. In theory, such a decision would be made only after an analysis of the causes of job injuries and illnesses and an evaluation of the alternative methods to reduce

FIGURE 6.1 Occupational Injury Incidence Rates in the U.S. Private Sector, 1973–1995

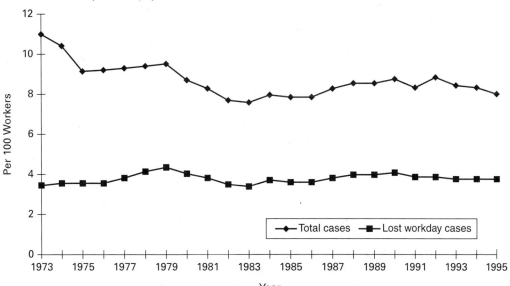

Source: U.S. Department of Labor, Bureau of Labor Statistics.

them. In practice, Congress followed the more traditional procedure, not unlike that in the old comic routine, where the straight man reads off an answer and the comic is asked to infer what the question is. No attempt was made to analyze the causes and cures of occupational safety and health. In drafting the OSHA statute, no serious consideration was given to any approach other than regulation via the promulgation of standards.

Many safety professionals believe that OSHA's reliance on standards and its inevitable emphasis on capital equipment clashes with their knowledge that the worker's behavior is the prime determinant of accidents. One study estimated that only about 10 percent of injuries are preventable by enforcement of OSHA standards.[7] According to a report in the *British Journal of Industrial Medicine,* exposures to lead of employees working at almost identical jobs differed by ratios of up to 4 to 1. This was attributed totally to personal differences in working habits.[8] Hence, the role for training would seem to merit more attention than it receives under the OSHA approach of "benign neglect."

The data are clear—even if full compliance with OSHA rules were achieved—large numbers of job-related accidents would still occur. An analysis of offshore drilling rigs concludes that the rule of management is crucial in achieving good safety records. "There's no point in taking the companies with good safety records and beating them over the heads with nitpicking regulations. . . . If you're going to change safety offshore, you have to change the attitude of management in the companies where the safety record is poor."[9] (See the box "How One Company Responded to Workplace Injuries.")

Two investigators attempted to determine if states with stiffer regulations and tighter enforcement had lower injury rates. Neither was able to show any significant effects. Moreover, other studies show that inexperienced workers have high accident rates. At lower production rates, there is more time for training and repair of equipment. Statistically, the turnover rate among workers is the most important single factor in determining injury rates.[10] During rapid expansions in production characterized by new hires, there is more pressure on workers to produce and less time for educational efforts and maintenance of machinery. Moreover, new employees tend to be less experienced, or their skills are rusty if they have been out of work for some time.

The Scripps Clinic reports that people are especially likely to make errors if they have not slept seven to eight hours within the previous 24 hours. Also, people are most likely to make mistakes between midnight and 6 A.M., even when they have slept seven to eight hours during the day.[11] Under the circumstances, there seems to be an important role in workplace safety for both training and for changes in work procedures.

The way in which a safe and healthful work environment is achieved is a managerial matter. Some companies reduce job hazards by buying new equipment; others initiate new work procedures. Still others do it by better training of workers and supervisors. Yet other employers might provide financial incentives to their employees—for example, paying them to wear earmuffs instead of spending much larger sums on so-called engineering noise containment.

In this vein, a U.S. district court barred OSHA from preventing a company's use of "personal protection devices" instead of the more expensive engineering controls.

How One Company Responded to Workplace Injuries

In the first few years following the establishment of OSHA, Deere & Company, a large manufacturer of agricultural equipment, experienced a continuation of an earlier rise in accident rates. However, in 1974, the company shifted away from what it termed the "OSHA approach" to workplace safety, which focuses on compliance with standards. By 1987, the incidence of injuries and illnesses was reduced by 90 percent and it has remained very low (see Figure 6.2). Deere's injury and illness rates are now one-fourth the national average. This improvement in employee welfare was accomplished by means of the following four-point program:

1. Create an accurate information base by which to identify and control hazards. An extensive computerized data-collection program was developed that identified where injuries and illnesses were occurring by job classification, the nature of the injury or illness, the body part affected, the accident type, and the object that caused the accident.

2. Focus available resources on the most serious and most numerous injuries and illnesses. Deere emphasized preventing those injuries and illnesses that were contributing most substantially to its safety problem. It discovered that about 85 percent of its job accidents were due to actions, often unintentional, of individual workers—an aspect of the safety problem that it believed must be overcome by motivation and education.

3. Recognize safety as a joint employee–employer responsibility. Both supervisory and hourly employees pointed out practices that made jobs safer, and their suggestions were taken seriously.

4. Recognize that safety is a sensible corporate investment. Apart from moral or regulatory considerations, the economic rewards to the company from a safer work environment were considered to justify the safety program.

FIGURE 6.2 Deere & Company Injury and Illness Incidence Rate[a]

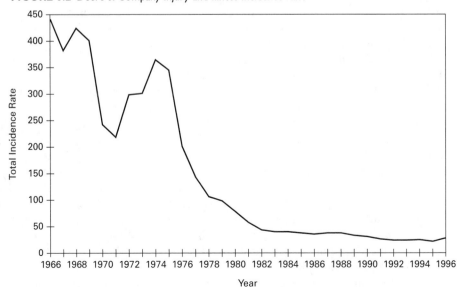

[a]Number of first aid and OSHA recordable cases per 200,000 hours worked.

The judge noted that the company's current program of earplugs and earmuffs was more effective than OSHA's preferred alternative. The judge's order stated:

> Defendants [OSHA and the Secretary of Labor] must leave plaintiff alone in this issue, unless or until the Secretary can specify and prove the feasibility of some engineering or administrative controls . . . which will do as effective a job of employee protection as the present personal protection devices at comparable cost.[12]

The Attractions of Private Action

Drawing on the material in earlier chapters, we can note that more information about hidden hazards on the job can result in greater attention to safe practices on the part of employees. Likewise, tougher enforcement of existing liability laws provides greater incentive to management. Some state courts have held that companies can be charged with criminal action in connection with industrial hazards. In 1984, California's highest court affirmed a decision on a construction accident that declared for the first time that corporations can be charged with manslaughter.[13] The following year, a Cook County, Illinois, circuit judge found three top officials of Film Recovery Systems, Inc., guilty of murder for willfully working their employees under conditions that were literally deadly.[14] These cases have gained the attention of many other companies.

Two sets of statistics help to understand OSHA's role as well as its limited effectiveness. For many industries, the lost time due to illnesses and injuries off the job far exceeds that due to on-the-job hazards. Exxon, for example, states that nonoccupational diseases and injuries account for about 96 percent of the time lost due to disability. The OSHA-mandated efforts are thus limited only to the remaining 4 percent of the disability-caused absenteeism in that large company. Along the same lines, B.F. Goodrich reported in one year that its employees experienced almost eight times as many injuries off the job as on and missed work more than four times as often from off-the-job injuries as from those that occurred at work. For the nation as a whole, the National Safety Council reports that workers are four times as likely to suffer a fatal accident off the job than at work.

Table 6.1 contains some comparisons along these lines. The data demonstrate that recreational activities are often far more hazardous than employment. For example, whereas eight deaths are anticipated each year for every 100,000 workers in manufacturing industries, the figure for power boating is 17 and for canoeing 40—even though the duration of exposure is much greater for factory work.

Thus, attention is warranted to the possibility of less costly job safety and health standards. Such an approach was presented in the case of OSHA's benzene standard. In that instance, the U.S. court of Appeals set aside major portions of the regulation that would have required employers to assure that no employee is exposed to airborne concentrations of benzene in excess of one part per million over an eight-hour day. The court stated that it took such action because OSHA had not shown that the costs being imposed bore a "reasonable relationship" to the benefits to be obtained. However, the Supreme Court subsequently ruled that the OSHA statute forbade even this simple form of benefit–cost analysis.[15]

Substantial improvement in OSHA regulation may come only when Congress shifts the agency's mandate to analyzing actual causes of job-related injuries and then evaluating and choosing the most appropriate methods to eliminate them.

TABLE 6.1 Variations in Hazards

Activity	Annual Projected Deaths Per 100,000 Participants
Motorcycle racing	180
Horse racing	130
Automobile racing	100
Rock climbing	100
Canoeing	40
Power boating	17
Typical manufacturing job	8

Source: American Industrial Health Council.

It seems likely that the optimum mix of safety methods varies by industry, location, and over time. Elements of successful safety programs focus on private, rather than governmental, responsibilities. These include getting top management to recognize safety as an important business concern, involving workers as well as management, finding out more about the nature and causes of on-the-job injuries and health hazards, and focusing on the truly serious safety problems. (Recall Deere's favorable experiences.)

REGULATION OF PRIVATE PENSIONS

The regulation of employee pensions is another important area of government influence on personnel practices. There is a close connection between changes in federal law and the attractiveness of company retirement plans. During World War II, many firms set up pension plans as a way to recruit workers with needed skills without violating wartime wage controls (fringe benefits were not subject to those controls). The extension of the income tax to labor incomes also made nontaxable fringe benefits more important. As a result, private pensions grew rapidly during and after the war, with millions of workers being enrolled. Table 6.2 shows that pensions, life insurance, and health insurance are now provided by most large and medium-size companies and by a significant but lesser proportion of smaller firms.

ERISA Requirements

Beginning in the 1960s, a series of business failures and the collapse of a number of pension plans began to cause public concern. After much debate, in 1974 Congress passed the Employee Retirement Income Security Act (ERISA). The main purpose of that law is to protect the rights of participants in retirement plans so that workers receive the benefits they have been promised.

ERISA is one of the most complicated laws ever enacted, with enforcement powers assigned to both the Department of Labor and the Internal Revenue Service. After the law's enactment, over 10 percent of existing pension plans were terminated to avoid the expense of ERISA compliance, and most of the remaining plans were revised to comply with the new requirements. Since then, many other companies have

TABLE 6.2 Percentage of Full-Time Employees Participating in Employee Benefit Programs, 1995

Employee Benefit Program	All Employees	Professional and Technical Employees	Sales and Clerical Employees	Service and Production Employees
Holidays	89	88	93	88
Paid vacations	96	97	99	94
Paid personal leave	22	24	34	15
Funeral leave	80	83	85	75
Jury duty leave	85	91	89	79
Military leave	44	59	46	35
Sick leave	58	74	78	39
Short-term disability	53	48	52	57
Long-term disability	42	60	53	26
Life insurance	87	93	89	83
Defined benefit pension	52	53	55	50
Defined contribution plan	55	67	64	45
Paid family leave	2	3	2	1
Unpaid family leave	84	89	86	80
Medical care	77	80	76	75
Dental care	57	66	57	51

Note: Covers medium and large private establishments.

Source: U.S. Department of Labor, Bureau of Labor Statistics.

abandoned their traditional pension plans because of the onerous paperwork and reporting requirements. About 10,000 notices of voluntary plan termination are filed each year, mainly by small employers.

The government's power to compel compliance with ERISA is overwhelming. A company's contributions to its pension plan are tax deductible only if the Internal Revenue Service has approved the plan. Seven categories of requirements must be met:

1. *Eligibility.* An employee must be eligible to participate in the retirement plan when he or she is 25 years old and has worked for one year.

2. *Vesting.* Explicit regulations are established on the time it takes for an employee to earn the right to a pension. Once vested, the employee has a right to a pension at retirement even if he or she is not working at the company at the time.

3. *Surviving-spouse benefit.* In the event of the retired employee's death, the surviving spouse must receive at least 50 percent of the pension benefit.

4. *Funding.* Employers must fully fund their annual cost of the retirement program. They must also contribute an additional amount to amortize existing liabilities over a designated period of time.

5. *Fiduciaries.* Those who manage or administer a pension plan or those who give investment advice for a fee are placed under strict rules of conduct. They must act as a "prudent" person would in similar circumstances.

6. *Plan termination insurance.* The U.S. Pension Benefit Guaranty Corporation (PBGC) was chartered to guarantee the payment of pension benefits should a plan be eliminated with

insufficient assets to pay pension liabilities. Firms are liable for up to 30 percent of their assets if they drop a pension plan that is not fully funded. The assets of PBGC arise from annual assessments on the companies covered by ERISA.

7. *Reporting and disclosure requirements.* Extensive reports on benefits are required of all employers, including a detailed plan description, a summary plan description understandable to the layperson, and an annual report.

The Labor Department is responsible for enforcing the law with regard to disclosure and fiduciary standards. Civil penalties may apply to disclosure violations. The Internal Revenue Service enforces the provisions regarding vesting, funding, and participation.

The paperwork requirements of the new pension law hit small businesses hardest. Plans must be communicated in nontechnical language, but the plan summary has to include many technical items. Some employers solve the problem through duplicate communications. One publication explains the program in layperson's language and another in technical, legal language that will satisfy the law.

Many employers are shifting from the standard defined benefit approach (where the employer is committed to paying a given level of benefits) to a defined contribution plan, where the employer only makes a stipulated payment to the employee's retirement savings plan. The latter are often called 401[k] plans, referring to the pertinent section of the Internal Revenue Code. More workers and retirees are now participating in the new form of retirement savings plans (approximately 50 million in 1995) than are enrolled in traditional pension plans (about 40 million).

In addition to avoiding coverage by the Pension Benefit Guaranty Corporation, defined contribution plans shift the risk of loss from investments from the employer to the individual participant—who also receives the benefit of unexpected appreciation of the assets in which the individual's funds are invested.

Underfunded Plans

Since the enactment of ERISA, concern has focused on companies that lack the financial resources to meet their pension-fund liabilities. That problem plagues many labor-intensive companies in declining industries, many of which have gone through bankruptcy so that they can dump their pension liabilities on the government. The burdens on the Pension Benefit Guaranty Corporation have required large increases in the annual fees paid by the covered employers.[16]

The enactment of amendments to ERISA in 1987 and 1994 changed the basis of company premium payments from flat-rate to a variable premium that increases with the underfunding of a pension plan. As a result, the Pension Benefit Guaranty Corporation (PBGC) reported a modest $869 million surplus of assets over liabilities in fiscal year 1996. PBGC believes that the vast majority of companies are now maintaining well-funded plans. However, as of September 30, 1996, 15 million workers and retirees were covered by underfinanced pension plans.

Overfunded Plans

Since the early 1980s, a very different development has also surfaced. Large layoffs plus stock-market gains have left many corporate pension funds with more assets than are needed to meet ERISA requirements. Despite the poor position of some corporate retirement plans, since 1982 the total amount of overfunding in registered plans has exceeded the aggregate of the underfunding.

As a result, some companies discovered that they held far more in pension-fund assets than needed to pay their anticipated obligations. This type of situation generates potential risks as well as benefits. The risk is that the excess cash will invite attempts by other firms to take over the company. Also, companies pressed for cash can siphon off the excess pension fund assets (or at least what are so determined by an actuarial report under specific assumptions) and use them for other corporate purposes. That can be done by terminating the present pension plan, purchasing annuities to cover the benefits accrued under the plan, and pocketing the difference.

MINIMUM-WAGE LAWS AND UNEMPLOYMENT

Raising the statutory minimum wage is generally popular because low-income people seem to be getting more generous incomes as a result. (See Table 6.3 for data on the historical growth of this government requirement.) However, this conclusion is very controversial, especially among economists. Most—but not all—studies of the minimum wage laws conclude that often the increase in labor costs is inflationary and also raises the country's unemployment rate, especially in the case of minority teenagers.

The basic economic problem arises because Congress can legislate what employers must pay if they hire workers, but it cannot legislate worker productivity. Therefore, people who cannot produce enough to justify the minimum wage are denied jobs. A compulsory minimum wage effectively outlaws some job opportunities, leaving a larger number of workers competing for a smaller pool of jobs. A study at the National Bureau of Economic Research estimates that a 10 percent increase in the minimum wage causes a 1- to 2-percent decline in the number of employed teenagers and smaller declines in employment for young adults.[17] An analysis of the restaurant industry concluded that between one-quarter and one-half million jobs have been lost in that sector due to the minimum wage law.[18]

The impacts are compounded over time. By being denied the chance to work at low wages, young people are prevented from acquiring the skills, experience, and work habits that increase their value to employers. The real solution is to improve the work skills of minimum-wage workers so they can qualify for higher-paid jobs.

Much of the pressure for increasing the compulsory minimum wage comes from labor unions whose members are paid far more than the minimum wage. This may be a variation of the infatuation on the part of many business firms with government regulation—as a means of protecting the "ins" from the "outs." In the case of the minimum wage, each raise means that some category of currently working employees will face less competition from unemployed people who are willing to accept a lower wage. Nevertheless, some highly regarded studies show that, at least under some circumstances, raising the statutory minimum wage does not reduce employment. This would be the case if the major effect was to increase the supply of labor via a more attractive entering wage.

TABLE 6.3   Minimum-Wage Rates ($/hour)

	Non-Farm Workers		
By Year End	*Covered*	*Newly Covered*	*Farm Workers*
1938	$0.25	$ —	$ —
1939	0.30	—	—
1945	0.40	—	—
1950	0.75	—	—
1956	1.00	—	—
1961	1.15	1.00[a]	—
1963	1.25	1.00	—
1964	1.25	1.15	—
1965	1.25	1.25	—
1967	1.40	1.40	1.00[b]
1968	1.60	1.60	1.15
1969	1.60	1.60	1.30
1974	2.00	2.00	1.60
1975	2.10	2.10	1.80
1976	2.30	2.30	2.00
1977	2.30	2.30	2.20
1978	2.65	2.65	2.65
1979	2.90	2.90	2.90
1980	3.10	3.10	3.10
1981	3.35	3.35	3.35
1990	3.80	3.80	3.80
1991	4.25	4.25	4.25
1996[c]	4.75	4.75	4.75
1997[c]	5.15	5.15	5.15

[a]Beginning in 1961, coverage extended to large retail and service enterprises as well as local transit, construction, and gasoline service stations.

[b]Beginning in 1967, farm workers (and some other occupational categories) were covered by the federal minimum wage law.

[c]A subminimum wage of $4.25 an hour is established for employees under 20 years of age during their first three months of employment.

Source: U.S. Department of Labor.

LABOR–MANAGEMENT RELATIONS

Union Representation

In most industrialized nations, unions represent large numbers of employees in bargaining with management over wages and working conditions. In the United States, however, before the Clayton Act of 1914, there were numerous, successful prosecutions of labor unions under the Sherman Antitrust Act and earlier under the common law. Back then, any combination of workers was generally viewed as a monopoly. Not until the passage of the Norris–LaGuardia Act of 1932 did labor unions gain effective immunity from antitrust prosecution. That act removed the courts' power to intervene in labor disputes unless violence and property damage were involved. Union immunity from the antitrust laws never has been total. Joint actions by a union and a company aimed at another company, even though the activity is something the union itself can undertake, have been held to be violations of the Sherman Act.

The substantial, albeit far from complete, unionization in the United States that has occurred since the 1930s makes it difficult to think about an economic environment in this country without a large number of powerful labor unions. Nevertheless, only a minority of the workforce is currently unionized (14 percent in 1996, down from over 30 percent in the 1950s). We can theorize, of course, about the economic effects of the union movement that now exists. Large, nationwide labor organizations, especially those operating under union-shop agreements, do limit employer access to other workers, thus reducing competition for labor.

The elementary economics of unionized labor markets is straightforward: (1) the lessened competition among workers increases wage rates of workers in unionized plants, (2) the higher production costs that result lessen the demand for the products produced by unionized labor, and hence (3) the demand for unionized labor will be lower than in the absence of the labor organization.

The actual measurement of the gains to the employed union members and the losses suffered by unemployed union members and nonunion workers involves intricate theoretical and empirical questions. Inevitably, business firms make adjustments to the initial effects of unionization. Within the recruiting restraints that may be imposed, firms try to hire higher quality workers and increase their capital–labor ratio. The lower turnover that results among unionized workers (encouraged by nonportable pension funds, special seniority provisions, and so on) and the resulting incentives for job-specific training increase the productivity of the unionized firm.

However, union work rules and union resistance to technological change reduce productivity gains: limits on the load handled by workers, restrictions of the tasks performed by employees in given occupations, requirements that unnecessary work be done, requirements for unneeded standby crews or crews of excessive size, and enforcement of limits on the pace of work. The consuming public bears the burden of the higher prices and lower output of goods and services that can result from monopolization of labor markets by labor unions.

The effects in any industry in any given time period may deviate from the general expectation. Labor unions have incentives to develop innovative institutional arrangements that inhibit the operation of the market forces, which yields the results described above. For example, unions use an output tax in coal mining that reduces the effect of unionization on employment but intensifies the impact on product prices.

Other impacts of union activity are noticeable, such as the changes in the geographic distribution of production. The desire for more competitive labor markets has been a factor in the shift of industry from highly unionized urban locations to less unionized suburban and rural areas. In a broader sense, the same motivation exists in the shift of low-skilled labor production from high cost areas such as the United States and Western Europe to much lower cost locations in East Asia and Latin America.

The union movement also has attempted to use the powers of government to achieve its various objectives. Some of these relate fairly directly to wages. For example, the Davis-Bacon Act in effect ensures that union wage rates are used on most federal construction projects.[19] The compulsory minimum-wage law helps to insulate higher union wage rates from competition from lower-paid nonunion workers. Other government activities that have been fostered by unions include various income-maintenance transfer payments and benefit programs. Examples range from social security and unemployment insurance to workers' compensation and the establishment of the Occupational Safety and Health Administration.

Almost paradoxically, as the unionized portion of the nation's workforce has declined, union attempts to influence government policy has risen. Part of the void left by the decline in union representation has been filled by the growing number of laws regulating employment practices. The number of such regulatory statutes grew from approximately 40 in the 1960s to over 150 by the 1990s. An accompanying development has been an increase in litigation before administrative agencies and the courts.[20]

The legislative wish list of the AFL-CIO has supplemented, if not replaced, much of the traditional collective bargaining agenda. These legislative desires range from OSHA reform to mandated health benefits to paid family leave. In any event, labor unions in the past half century have become an established feature of the American economy. This is one aspect of labor–management relations that has become institutionalized, especially under the spur of government regulation.

The National Labor Relations Act and the major agency it established, the National Labor Relations Board (NLRB), govern many aspects of management dealings with employees and their unions. The board conducts representation elections at which employees decide whether they want a union to represent them in dealing with management. In an effort to protect the rights of union members, the law prohibits the following types of "unfair labor practices":

- Management interference with employee rights to join and participate in unions.
- Company domination of unions or interference with their administration.
- Discrimination against employees for union activity.
- Discrimination for filing charges or giving testimony to the NLRB.
- Refusing to bargain collectively with an authorized representative of labor.

Considerable controversy has arisen over many specific provisions of the National Labor Relations Act and the NLRB's interpretations. In order to avoid setting limits on employers' free speech, an amendment to the act declares that "the expressing of any views, arguments, or opinions shall not constitute or be evidence of an unfair labor practice . . . if such expression contains no threat or reprisal or force or promise of benefit."[21]

Efforts to Expand Mandated Social Benefits

Since the issue of reducing federal budget deficits became a serious public policy problem, unions and other interest groups have favored off-budget devices for achieving social objectives. Specifically, pressures have risen for Congress to require business

TABLE 6.4 Compulsory Employer-Financed Benefits and Private Payrolls ($ in billions)								
Cost to Business	*1960*	*1965*	*1970*	*1975*	*1980*	*1985*	*1990*	*1995*
Social security	$6	$8	$17	$31	$56	$92	$140	$171
Medicare	—	—	2	6	12	23	34	47
Unemployment compensation	3	3	4	14	18	18	22	29
Workers' compensation	1	2	3	7	14	22	37	39
Total	$10	$13	$26	$58	$100	$155	$233	$286
Private wages and salaries	$277	$290	$427	$639	$1,112	$1,594	$2,229	$2,822
Compulsory fringe benefits as percent of wages and salaries	4%	4%	6%	9%	9%	10%	10%	10%

Source: U.S. Department of Commerce.

to finance various employee benefit programs, ranging from child care to universal health insurance. As noted in the previous chapter, Congress has enacted mandated but unpaid family leave for several types of employee concerns.

The impacts of social mandates are controversial. Many employers and economists argue that benefit packages are a zero-sum game, that mandating one benefit reduces flexibility in setting up a full array of fringe (nonwage) benefits. For example, a study of retail establishments in New York City found that, in response to a minimum-wage increase, many stores reduced commission payments, eliminated year-end bonuses, and decreased paid vacation and sick leave. A report on the restaurant industry revealed that, for every 1 percent rise in the minimum wage, restaurants reduced shift premiums by 4 percent, severance pay by 7 percent, and sick leave by 3 percent.[22]

Proponents of mandated social benefits believe that they are necessary to help reconcile a competitive market economy with a compassionate democratic society. They also consider such mandates to be comparable to the conservatives' privatization efforts to contract out government activities. In both cases, the performance of social functions would theoretically benefit from the greater efficiency of the private sector. Moreover, many companies that make liberal health and other benefits available to their employees favor the government's imposing comparable costs on their competitors—albeit via additional regulation. Compulsory fringe benefits rose more rapidly than business payrolls during the period 1960–1985. Since then, the portions of employee compensation devoted to fringe benefits has been fairly constant at 10 percent (see Table 6.4).

IMPACTS ON PERSONNEL DEPARTMENTS

The growth in government regulation of the workplace has resulted in a comparable expansion in the size and role of corporate personnel departments. The change is symbolized by the upgrading of the traditional personnel director to a vice president for human resources. In effect, a constituency for regulation has been created within the business firm.

In many companies, the business response to family issues has resulted in full-time positions to deal with the various problems that arise. The new jobs bear such titles as director of workforce partnering, family issues coordinator, program manager of work–life balancing, and manager of work–family issues. These new executives write rules for employee concerns such as leaves from work, flexible work schedules, child care, and family benefits planning.

For many companies, government regulation has forced them to focus more attention on how they manage their workforces and specifically on why they fire one person and promote another. Frequently, the success of these expanded staff offices is judged by their ability to learn to live with the rules issued by the EEOC, OSHA, and other such government bodies and to keep their employers out of trouble with the regulators and the courts.

Regulatory agencies affect most aspects of company personnel policies and practices: hiring, promoting, and training activities; employee testing; compensation, including fringe benefits; the composition and funding of pension plans; the physical work environment; and basic work relationships, such as discipline, job termination, union negotiation, and communicating with employees. In some cases, a government agency has effective authority to approve or disapprove company actions (e.g., to decide whether company pension contributions qualify as a tax deduction). In numerous other situations involving requirements, which range from equal employment opportunity to the health and safety aspects of the job, federal agencies can file legal charges against companies—and do so with considerable frequency.

Training and Recruitment

The widening array of government regulatory legislation has required corporate human relations departments to expand their orientation and training programs. Supervisors, for example, need to be highly trained in many aspects of safety and health. Skills that are taught vary from the ability to administer first aid to the leadership capability necessary to convince employees always to use personal protective equipment.

In response to regulatory requirements, companies have been hiring people with a widening array of specialized capabilities: safety directors and engineers, industrial hygienists, in-house medical staff, and material buyers with special knowledge of protective clothing and nonhazardous equipment. Moreover, required reports and applications, such as hazardous-waste disposal records, necessitate inputs from many disciplines. As a result, companies find that they must either retain an array of experts on their own staffs or obtain expert opinions via consulting arrangements. These specialists are involved in such fields as chemistry, ecology, economics, sociology, geology, climate, engineering, mining, forestry, and aquatic life, as well as public communications. Businesses also use specialized consulting services both to provide advice on meeting Consumer Product Safety Commission and Occupational Safety and Health Administration standards and to provide more health services to employees (e.g., periodic examinations and return-to-work checkups).

FUTURE TRENDS

An important trend in regulation of personnel practices is a rising sense of expectation among workers, professionals, and executives for more participation in decision making and greater protection of individual rights in the workplace.

Labor unions focus attention on the economic aspects of the workplace, especially pay, fringe benefits, and working conditions. Generally they are less interested in such nontraditional or social matters as the secrecy of employee records or other aspects of worker civil liberties on the job. Company managements tend to be ambivalent on employee rights issues, supporting the general notion but also concerned about the inherent reduction of loyalty and attachment to the company.[23]

One aspect of personnel management that overlaps the standard economic concerns and the newer social concerns is the area of company freedom to terminate employees, the so-called "employment at will" doctrine. Every other developed nation requires employers to have a "just cause" for firing an employee. However, in recent years, American judges have been reducing the traditional employer's right to fire workers. This has led a rising number of companies to introduce voluntary systems to review dismissals. The need for such procedures is underscored by the tendency of state courts to allow employees to sue their employers if they were fired for pursuing an action that was in the interest of public policy ("whistleblowers") or if their employer broke an implicit agreement.

Public policy in this area, as in many others, is driven by extreme situations. *Petermann* v. *International Brotherhood of Teamsters,* a 1959 case, set the precedent for the "at will" cases that followed. That landmark suit was initiated by an employee who was fired because he refused to perjure himself for his employer before an investigative body of the state legislature. The California Court of Appeals ruled that it would be contrary to public policy to allow an employer to discharge any employee "on the grounds that the employee declined to commit perjury." In subsequent cases, courts have ruled in favor of employees fired for serving on a jury or for refusing to participate in an illegal price-fixing scheme.

In order to maintain the basic authority to fire employees, some companies are explicitly stating their right to terminate at will in the application forms that prospective employees must sign. A balance needs to be struck between a company's right to fire incompetent people and the need to cultivate a sense of loyalty and fairness in personnel relations.[24]

Notes

1. Occupational Safety and Health Act, Public Law 91-596.
2. Thomas J. Kniesner and John D. Leeth, "Improving Workplace Safety," *Regulation,* Fall 1991, pp. 65–66.
3. W. Kip Viscusi, *Risk by Choice: Regulating Health and Safety in the Workplace* (Cambridge, MA: Harvard University Press, 1983).
4. Wayne B. Gray and John T. Scholz, *Do OSHA Inspections Reduce Injuries?* (Cambridge, MA: National Bureau of Economic Research, 1991).

5. U.S. Comptroller General, *How Can Workplace Injuries Be Prevented? The Answers May be in OSHA Files* (Washington, DC: U.S. General Accounting Office, 1979), pp. 33–35.

6. U.S. Department of Labor, Bureau of Labor Statistics, *Workplace Injuries and Illnesses in 1995* (Washington, DC: U.S. Department of Labor, 1997), pp. 1–13.

7. John Mendeloff, "The Hazards of Rating Workplace Safety," *Wall Street Journal,* February 11, 1988, p. 22.

8. M. K. Williams, et al., "An Investigation of Lead Absorption in an Electric Accumulator Factory with the Use of Personal Samples," *British Journal of Industrial Medicine* 26 (1969), pp. 202–216.

9. David Jarmil, "Maintaining Safety on Offshore Drilling Rigs," *National Academy of Sciences News Report,* May 1984, p. 8.

10. Ann P. Bartel and Lacy G. Thomas, "Direct and Indirect Effects of Regulation: A New Look at OSHA's Impact," *Journal of Law and Economics* 28, April 1985, pp. 1–25; Wayne B. Gray and Carol A. Jones, "Are OSHA Health Inspections Effective?" *Review of Economics and Statistics* 23, no. 3, August 1991, pp. 504–508.

11. Merrill M. Mitler, "Punch the Clock, Hit the Hay," *New York Times,* January 11, 1992, p. 13.

12. "Judge Issues OSHA Noise Decision," *Insight,* August–October 1978, p. 10.

13. "Why More Corporations May Be Charged with Manslaughter," *Business Week,* February 27, 1984, p. 62.

14. Barry Siegel, "Murder Case a Corporate Landmark," *Panorama,* 2nd quarter 1986, pp. 55–65.

15. *American Petroleum Institute* v. *OSHA,* no. 78-1253 (5th Cir., 10-5-78).

16. Pension Benefit Guaranty Corporation, *Annual Report 1996* (Washington, DC: U.S. Government Printing Office, 1997).

17. David Neumark and William Wascher, *Evidence on Employment Effects of Minimum Wages and Subminimum Wage Provisions* (Cambridge, MA: National Bureau of Economic Research, 1992). But also see David Card and Alan B. Krueger, "Minimum Wages and Employment," *American Economic Review,* September 1994.

18. William T. Alpert, *The Minimum Wage in the Restaurant Industry* (New York: Praeger, 1986), p. 101.

19. In one year, 302 of 530 area prevailing wage determinations were simply union rates rather than the result of wage surveys. See Morgan O. Reynolds, *Power and Privilege: Labor Unions in America* (New York: Universe Books, 1984), p. 136.

20. Thomas Kochan, "The American Corporation as an Employer," in Carl Kaysen, ed., *The American Corporation Today* (New York: Oxford University Press, 1996), p. 251.

21. David P. Twomey, *Labor Law and Legislation* (Cincinnati: South-Western Publishing Co., 1980), p. 152.

22. Alpert, *The Minimum Wage in the Restaurant Industry.*

23. Archie B. Carroll, *Business and Society: Managing Corporate Social Performance* (Boston: Little, Brown, 1981), pp. 217–218.

24. Thomas R. Horton, "If Right to Fire Is Abused, Uncle Sam May Step In," *Wall Street Journal,* June 11, 1984, p. 18.

CHAPTER 7

Traditional Economic Regulation

Economic regulation—traditionally exemplified by that now defunct industry regulatory body, the Interstate Commerce Commission—was considered virtually the entire field of regulation 30 years ago. This form of regulation is characterized by the use of independent, politically balanced agencies organized more or less along industry lines. These agencies attempt to regulate the behavior of the companies subject to their jurisdiction through the control of economic variables, such as maximum and minimum prices, the markets that a firm can enter and leave, and the type of service that it is permitted to offer. As we will see in chapter 8, this type of regulation is being cut back as the public learns that competition is often a more effective guardian of consumer welfare.

Simultaneously, antitrust enforcement—a mainstay of traditional economic regulation—is undergoing a major reevaluation on the part of both practitioners and analysts.

INTRODUCTION

The most widespread use of economic regulation is at the state level, where public utility commissions continue to have jurisdiction over electric, gas, and telephone utility companies. An example of economic regulation at the municipal level is the franchising of local cable television systems. There has been little outright deregulation by state or local governments, although several public utility regulatory commissions are experimenting with loosening the controls over prices and profits, especially in the case of electric utilities.

Examples of economic regulation at the federal level include control by the Federal Aviation Administration over interstate air transportation when it involves the use of aircraft above a certain size and passenger capacity; control by the FCC over interstate telephone rates and broadcasting licenses; control by the Federal Reserve System and the Comptroller of the Currency over the establishment and operation of certain types of banks; and the establishment of rules for issuing securities by the SEC.

As of the late 1960s, the industries subject to economic regulation by federal and state agencies accounted for about one-tenth of the gross national product. Thus, the great bulk of economic activity remained relatively unregulated, except for general standards of business conduct, such as the antitrust laws and the exercise of "police powers" by state and local governments over public health and similar matters. But that situation began to fundamentally change in the 1960s with the advent of the kind of social regulation described in earlier chapters.

ELECTRIC UTILITY REGULATION

Let us examine the area of state economic regulation that is most widespread and visible to the public: regulation of the electric utility industry. It will be seen that, even in this most staid area of economic regulation, the combination of technological advance and economic incentives is forcing a modernization aimed at replacing regulation with marketplace competition in important segments of the industry.

Nature of the Industry

The electric utility industry in the United States began in the late 1870s as a street lighting and electric railway business, principally by private electric companies. Many small electric companies were formed, and an inefficient duplication of facilities resulted. In 1907, for example, 45 companies were serving Chicago while in rural areas there was a lack of facilities.

Some municipally owned electric systems were established to provide street lights and to replace arc lighting systems during a depression period, when electric companies were unable to secure funds for expansion. State regulatory bodies began to establish service territories and to grant exclusive rights to sell electricity within these territories, along with the obligation to provide service for all who applied. Through the years, electric utilities have grown to become one of the nation's largest group of business enterprises.

Electricity service is customarily viewed as consisting of three parts: production of power, transmission of the energy over high-voltage lines, and local distribution for short distances over low-voltage lines to final consumers. Until very recently, most private firms in the industry have been vertically integrated, providing generation, transmission, and distribution services as a single firm or through separate companies controlled by the same holding company. As we will see, significant structural changes are occurring in the generation and transmission segments.

The federal government entered the commercial power industry only incidentally; electric power was produced as a by-product of irrigation and flood-control projects. Power not needed in the operation of the projects was sold commercially, with preference to municipalities. Later the preference was changed to "public bodies and cooperatives."

Numerous federal multipurpose projects, including power, were undertaken in the 1930s. The Tennessee Valley Authority and the Bonneville Power Administration were formed and became major commercial power enterprises. The federal government provided loans and grants for the formation of new state and district power agencies and municipal electric systems. Rural electric cooperatives were formed with financing provided by the federal government's Rural Electrification Administration.

Currently, private electric companies provide about three-fourths of the electric power generated in the United States. The federal government's share is only one-tenth. The remainder consists of municipalities, state and district agencies, and cooperatives.

The Nature of Utility Regulation

The movement to regulate electric power resulted from two basic factors. First, consolidation in the early 1900s of competing utilities often produced price fixing. Second, most students of the subject assume that utilities are natural monopolies and that attempts to introduce competition would increase unit costs by forcing duplication of costly transmission and distribution networks. (See chapter 2 for analysis of natural monopoly.)

The principal solution to these problems, which evolved over a considerable number of years, is to permit franchised monopolies to operate under government rule making. Regulation is designed to serve as a substitute for competition so that the economies resulting from using a single supplier are passed on to the customers.

The primary emphasis of state regulatory commissions has been on regulation of rates, although their activities extend into many phases of company operations: granting the basic franchise, approving financing, establishing uniform accounting systems, auditing, validating costs, reviewing depreciation policies, and oversight with reference to safety, adequacy of service, and impact on the environment.

On the federal level, the Securities and Exchange Commission has limited regulatory authority over utility holding companies. The Federal Energy Regulatory Commission (FERC) regulates wholesale rates of all companies operating in interstate commerce—typically a utility in one state selling power to a utility in another. As a practical matter, this includes about 95 percent of the companies. The Federal Energy Regulatory Commission also approves issuance of securities for some of the companies, prescribes accounting systems, requires extensive and detailed reporting, and reviews applications for development of hydroelectric projects on navigable rivers.

Current Rate Regulation

An important function of regulatory commissions—perhaps the most crucial one—is to determine the proper level of return on investment, or profit, that can be allowed. This in turn requires that the commission validate the expenses of the utility and arrive at conclusions concerning the "cost of capital." Without this validation process, firms have little incentive to keep costs down. If their costs increase, the regulatory commission may simply allow prices to rise to insure a given rate of return.

To these tasks are also added the difficult job of verifying that prices charged to different classes of customers are just and reasonable and based on an equitable distribution of cost. The end results, the maximum allowable rates to be charged, are fundamentally based on two key objectives:

1. To protect consumers against exorbitant charges that might otherwise result from the monopoly aspect of public utility franchises.
2. To set rates for service at levels that will afford the companies an opportunity to earn a fair and reasonable rate of return.

In carrying out their functions, regulatory commissions are concerned that their current decisions maintain the capability of the regulated companies to fulfill their obligations to serve customers in the future. Thus, regulatory decisions attempt to take into account the future needs of the customers to be served and the capital required to provide the facilities to meet these needs. The long lead times that characterize electric utility plant construction mean that new facilities must be planned and financing arranged many years before the facilities enter into service.

Although differences on specifics eventually emerge, there is virtually universal agreement on the general objectives of rate regulation. Indeed, the courts have consistently upheld the general principles of a reasonable rate of return on investment. In the landmark *Hope* case, the U.S. Supreme Court laid down guidelines for utility regulation:

> [I]t is important that there be enough revenues not only for operating expenses but also for the capital costs of the business. These include service on the debt and dividends on the stock. . . . By that standard the return to the equity owner should be commensurate with risks on investments in other enterprises having corresponding risks. That return, moreover, should be sufficient to assure confidence in the financial integrity of the enterprise, so as to maintain its credit and to attract capital.[1]

This sounds as though a substantial measure of financial protection is assured by law. However, public utilities are not guaranteed any specific rate of profit or level of earnings. This has been clearly stated by the Supreme Court in the *Natural Gas Pipeline* case (1942), when the Court said:

> [T]he utility gets its return . . . by rates sufficient, having in view the character of the business, to secure a fair return upon the rate base, provided the business is capable of earning it. But regulation does not insure that the business shall produce net revenues, nor does the Constitution require that the losses of the business in one year shall be restored from future earnings . . . the hazard that the property will not earn a profit remains on the company in the case of a regulated, as well as an unregulated business.[2]

In spite of the multiplicity of regulatory agencies, rate-of-return-on-investment regulation continues to be the dominant feature of electric utility regulation. This is due primarily to the influence of the U.S. Supreme Court. The historic case of *Munn* v. *Illinois* (94 U.S. 113-1877) suggested the concept of a public utility. *Smyth* v. *Ames* (169 U.S. 466-1898) introduced the concept of fair value in the regulation of rates and, as mentioned previously, *FPC* v. *Hope Natural Gas* further developed the notion of an adequate rate of return. However, several state commissions are using more flexible approaches to utility regulation, such as permitting utilities to vary rates within a stated price "cap."[3]

From time to time, some observers have expressed concern over the hardships imposed on poor people by rising energy prices. One instinctive response is to lower the price for low-income customers. On reflection, such an action increases demand for energy resources without helping to attract additional supplies.

The answer that present public policy provides is not a hard-hearted one. It is to provide an adequate income to help low-income groups buy the goods and services they require, without distorting relative prices or exempting the beneficiaries from the price pressures necessary to conserve relatively scarce and hence relatively expensive resources. The generosity of existing policy can be seen in the substantial array of unemployment compensation, welfare, social security, and similar entitlement programs maintained by federal, state, and local governments.

Utility Pricing Strategies

Block Discounts   Pricing of utility service presents difficulties to both the companies and the regulatory agencies. Efficiencies are involved in delivering energy to heavy users, such as the savings achieved by using high-voltage lines to deliver electric service to large customers. In contrast, residential customers require expensive and complex distribution networks. One recurring suggestion for change is to replace the present system of declining rates for greater use with a structure that more nearly approximates marginal-cost pricing. In other words, the user is charged according to how much it costs to deliver the last unit of electricity consumed in a given period of time. Such a structure would include peak-load rate differentials for both time of day and season of the year.

The current practice is defended on the basis of the underlying economics. The total cost per kilowatt-hour tends to decline with volume, as many items of fixed cost are spread over a larger number of units. In this approach, price is related to cost of service.

Peak Pricing   Another approach to promote the more efficient use of energy resources is to use electricity pricing to even out usage and thus reduce the need to build expensive new power plants. There is precedence in other industries for discouraging usage in peak periods, when production is more costly, and to encourage off-peak use, when the cost of production is very low. Movie houses, parking lots, and other kinds of businesses set their prices according to the time of day in order to spread the use of their facilities in the most efficient pattern. Telephone companies do this by charging higher rates for long-distance calls in the daytime and thereby encouraging nighttime, off-peak use of their facilities. Similarly, many airlines offer lower "night-owl" and Saturday rates. Utilities have taken limited steps in this direction, such as charging lower rates for dusk-to-dawn lighting. Also, some utilities promote electric heating in winter months by offering bargain rates in an effort to offset the summer air-conditioning peaks. Ironically, summer air conditioning was originally encouraged by the utilities when their peaks resulted from winter heating demands.

Inverted Prices   Another suggestion for changing the structure of utility charges is to invert the rates, eliminating the discounts now given to large users and, to foster conservation, increasing a customer's unit charges as demand rises. Such a change would constitute a fundamental departure from the principle that prices should reflect marginal costs. It costs a utility more to bring power to small separate residences or retail stores than to one large industrial plant, but it is not inevitable that existing rate differentials exactly match these cost differences.

Long-run marginal costs of producing electric power have been rising. The cost of producing power from new facilities is greater than the cost of using older sources.

But there are reasons for state public service commissions not to respond to sharp changes in long-run marginal cost by abandoning rate levels based on average costs and quickly adopting levels based entirely on the new incremental costs. If they did so, many utilities would reap windfall returns (economic rents) on their present investments. Existing customers would be required to pay more than the actual costs of service.

There is a theoretical solution to the problem: charging higher rates based on long-run incremental costs for new customers and for any new additional loads of existing customers. Such a proposal, however, is likely to encounter great public and political resistance because of the apparent discrimination among individuals. Substantial energy conservation might require significant modifications in living and working habits. We can only speculate as to the extent that price incentives will encourage people to put off electricity-consuming chores during the daytime and wait until the evening to use household appliances and office machines, or to get them to turn off the air-conditioning when they leave the buildings in which they reside or work.

Restructuring Electric Utilities

Meanwhile, the entire electric utility industry is being restructured by means of a series of regulatory and organizational changes. In general, these developments are motivated by the notion that technological progress is obviating the need for much of the traditional regulation of this sector of the economy.

Specifically, improvements in the technology of transmission have made spatial location of power generation less important, allowing producers at different locations to compete effectively in the same markets. The impetus for promoting this form of deregulation also comes from concern about the future adequacy of supplies of electricity. Many utilities have canceled or postponed new construction for a variety of reasons: uncertainty about demand and operating costs arising from gyrations in fuel prices; adverse rulings by state public service commissions on charges for new capital costs; large cost overruns on nuclear power plants; and unwillingness of state and local government officials to develop the safety procedures required to operate nuclear facilities.[4]

Under these circumstances, at times other firms can be in a better position to both build and operate power plants, selling the electricity to traditional utilities. This relieves the regulated firms of the current risks of building plants only to find that they cannot recover the full costs from their own consumers. The new competitors have the opportunity to earn more on their investments than utilities because they are not subject to the same state regulations governing prices charged and allowable rates of return.

Moreover, the utilities' monopoly on power generation has been broken by several thousand small power plants that have been built as a result of the Public Utility Regulatory Policies Act of 1978. That law requires regulated utilities to buy the power produced by "alternative" generators of electricity, such as solar energy, even if the costs are higher than the power traditionally available to them. By 1990, the independent power producers sanctioned by the 1978 law were bringing more new generating capacity into commercial service than were the traditional construction programs of the regulated utilities.[5]

More recently, the Comprehensive National Energy Policy Act of 1992 has encouraged the entry of a new class of power producers—so-called exempt wholesale generators (EWGs)—to generate and sell electricity wholesale. That law also requires utilities to share their transmission lines. Thus, a utility in a high-rate state like New Hampshire can buy much cheaper electricity from West Virginia and have it delivered for a fee across regional transmission lines. In the state of California, beginning in 1998, all electricity users will have the right to choose their own suppliers. New Energy Ventures, Inc., of Los Angeles quickly signed up more than 60 clients, ranging from department stores to private colleges, to receive hydroelectric power from the Bonneville Power Administration at lower rates than those they had been paying.

The initial benefits of competition in terms of lower prices, however, are proving to be quite moderate due to a variety of transition regulations. Medium-size customers, such as stores and office buildings, anticipate savings in the neighborhood of 7 percent, less than the mandatory 10 percent rate cut that homeowners and small businesses were scheduled to receive. After the year 2002, with a more complete transition to the more competitive electricity market, much larger savings are anticipated.[6]

The success of the alternative or independent producers of electricity has inspired some utilities to set up subsidiaries to sell power to other utilities and to compete for contracts with large industrial customers. These subsidiaries are usually structured as joint ventures with independent producers of electricity. They tend to operate outside of the power utility's jurisdiction and, therefore, are exempt from traditional utility regulation.[7]

Important advances have occurred in the technology of power transmission. Line losses, which increase with distance, have been sharply reduced by more efficient transformers. Major transfers of bulk power now occur over long distances. Utilities in Southern California obtain power from Oregon and Washington, where low-cost hydroelectricity is available. Local utilities in different states are increasingly interconnected through regional power grids. In a real geographic stretch, in 1997 the Southern Company, a major southeastern utility, acquired Consolidated Electric Power Asia, making it the largest independent power producer in Asia.

In turn, these organizational and technological innovations have spurred a variety of economic responses (see the box, "Scenario for Deregulation of Electric Utilities—Present and Future"). Proposals for change vary from splitting apart the generation, transmission, and distribution segments to provide more competition in meeting consumer needs (which has begun to take place) to outright deregulation of electric utilities, which is only at the discussion stage now.

A major argument for moving to sole reliance on marketplace competition is that a deregulated market would allow a more rational incorporation of risk into decision-making processes. Risks from shifts in public policy would be reduced if the price of power were based on market pricing rather than on a regulated rate of return. In such eventuality, the changing scenes in the following hypothetical drama might well approach reality:

Scene I (1988): "Wow, Marge, our electric bills this winter have been out of sight! We're going to go broke if it doesn't warm up soon so we can quit running the furnace."

Scene II (2008): "Wow, Marge, look at all this junk mail! First it was the credit card companies, then the long-distance carriers, and now the power brokers hitting us up with special deals. Seems like every day we get offered some new plan for buying electricity at a discount. How can we keep them all straight?"[8]

Scenario for Deregulation of Electric Utilities — Present and Future

PHASE I

1. Spin off generation from existing electric utilities, which now perform generation, transmission, and distribution.
2. Remove territorial restrictions on sales to distributors and large industrial customers.
3. Eliminate price and entry regulations in the generation of electric power.

PHASE II

1. Separate transmission from existing electric utilities, which continue to operate as franchised monopolies in the distribution of energy to end users.
2. Continue regulation of retail rates at the state level and of interstate power pooling and wheeling agreements at the federal level.
3. Terminate preferential access to federal power and preferential tax and capital-cost treatment for municipalities and cooperatives.

PHASE III

1. Eliminate all federal and state price and entry regulation.
2. Encourage mergers among small wholesale power producers to foster more coordination and pooling.
3. Scrutinize under the antitrust laws all major mergers as well as memberships in power pools and joint ventures.
4. Require separation of electric and gas utilities.

REGULATION VIA THE ANTITRUST LAWS

Competition is fundamental to a market system and to the private enterprise activity that characterizes economies such as that of the United States. Economists' suspicion of efforts by business to restrain trade dates back at least to Adam Smith's often-quoted statement, "People of the same trade seldom meet together, even for merriment and diversion, but the conversation ends in a conspiracy against the public, or in some contrivance to raise prices." Without vigorous competition, the private enterprise system probably would not attract and maintain sufficient public support for its continuance. In order to promote that objective, over the years, Congress has enacted three key antitrust statutes that outlaw attempts at monopoly and agreements in restraint of trade on the part of private firms.

The Development of Antitrust Laws

The term *antitrust* derives from a form of business organization (the trust) that was popular around the turn of the century. The trust was a device for pyramiding control over several operating companies. Key examples included the sugar trust, the tobacco trust, and—by far the best known—the oil trust (Standard Oil).

The Sherman Antitrust Act   The grandfather of antitrust law in the United States is the Sherman Act, passed in 1890. Its ringing language is noteworthy. Section 1 declares that "Every contract . . . in restraint of trade or commerce . . . is illegal." Section 2 states, "Every person who shall monopolize or attempt to monopolize any part of . . . trade or commerce . . . shall be . . . guilty."

The Sherman Act is primarily enforceable by the Department of Justice, which initiates lawsuits against alleged violators. Such litigation may be either "criminal," aimed at establishing guilt and assessing fines or other penalties, or "civil," designed to secure court decrees requiring cessation of illegal practices or remedial changes in illegal situations. The trigger is a "contract," "combination," or "conspiracy." In the absence of some cooperative conduct or joint action involving at least two separate companies, the act does not apply.

The real contribution of the Sherman Act has been to turn restraint of trade and monopolization into offenses against the federal government and to require enforcement by federal officials. Initially, the act was used mainly as a means to break strikes. In 1897, it was employed to convict a price-fixing ring. In 1904, President Theodore Roosevelt used it to justify trust busting. Since then, the act has been the mainstay of U.S. policy on competition.

A variety of specific business practices—many of which are legal in other western nations—may be found illegal under the Sherman Act:

- Agreements to fix or stabilize the prices or terms at which products or services are sold. In some industries, at times, there has been a widespread understanding that "gentlemen do not chisel on price."
- Group boycotts or concerted refusals by two or more companies to deal with a third company.
- Agreements to divide markets geographically or to limit the total volume of production or sales.
- Tie-in sales, where the seller has a dominant position in one product and requires the buyer also to purchase other products as a condition of sale.
- Reciprocal dealing, where sellers use their buying power to induce their suppliers to buy from them also. (But it is apparently legal for the federal government to require some of its suppliers to purchase special equipment from government facilities.)

Clayton Act   The second major antitrust law is the Clayton Act, passed in 1914 and amended on various occasions since. The Clayton Act names as illegal several important types of business policies or conduct that might be conducive to monopolization or the restraint of competition. These prohibited actions include price discrimination, exclusive and tying contracts, and interlocking directorates—where the effects of the practices "may be to substantially lessen competition or tend to create a monopoly." The Clayton Act is generally enforceable either by the Department of Justice through direct court litigation or by the Federal Trade Commission through its investigative and hearing procedures.

Federal Trade Commission Act   In 1913, Congress also passed the Federal Trade Commission Act, which has been amended since. This act proscribes unfair methods of competition and, since 1938, unfair or deceptive acts or practices in commerce. The substantive prohibitions of the act against unfair competition are enforceable by the commission, a quasi-administrative and quasi-judicial body empowered to make investigations, hold hearings, and issue orders requiring violators to "cease and desist" from their illegal practices.

Many unfair methods of competition or deceptive practices are illegal under the Federal Trade Commission Act. They include deceptive advertising, bait-and-switch selling techniques, harassment and untruths about competitors' products, inherently coercive marketing systems, deceptive guarantees, inducing breach of contract, intimidation, and commercial bribery.

However, several types of monopolies are legal in the United States. The federal government grants inventors patent monopolies for a period of 17 years. State governments, as noted earlier, grant monopoly franchises to regulated public utilities such as telephone, gas, and electricity suppliers. Local governments franchise noncompeting cable television stations.

Moreover, all levels of government operate commercial enterprises while prohibiting private firms from competing with them. The U.S. Post Office is the largest example. The federal government's express mail statutes prohibit private carriers from offering first-class mail delivery service. Many states operate retail liquor stores on a monopoly basis. Quite a few localities own and run their own electric or gas utilities, again with no competition.

It is interesting to note that the original justification for antitrust laws was not to protect consumers but to help weak competitors. During the congressional debate on the Sherman Act, the following argument was made by a leading proponent:

> [T]rusts have made products cheaper, have reduced prices; but if the price of oil were reduced to one cent a barrel, it would not right the wrong done by the trusts which have destroyed legitimate competition and driven honest men from legitimate business enterprises.[9]

Goals of Antitrust

Two conflicting viewpoints dominate current economic theorizing on antitrust. One (often called the *efficiency approach*) claims that the only legitimate goal of antitrust is consumer welfare, which is equivalent to economic efficiency.[10] Because some consumers benefit from the economies stemming from a merger, society as a whole also benefits. Mergers eliminate duplication and generate cost savings difficult to obtain from internal growth. The savings can be passed on in the form of reduced prices, resources saved, and stockholder gains. Adherents of the efficiency approach believe that antitrust policy should not favor one group of consumers (buyers) over another group (stockholders). Thus, the correct goal is economic efficiency, under which society can maximize the size of the pie without regard to considerations of income distribution or redistribution.

An alternative view is the *competitive approach*. Its proponents believe that the intent of the Sherman Act is to establish the right for buyers to pay no more than the competitive price. Thus, any merger that raises prices transfers money from buyers to stockholders.

In general, improved economic efficiency resulting from a merger will result in either (a) lower prices and increased profits or (b) if market power is enhanced in the process, higher prices and small cost savings. In the case of higher prices and cost savings, profits could increase more than the increase in price (expenditure) to the buyers. The efficiency approach would allow such a merger because shareholder gains are greater than buyer losses. In contrast, the competitive approach would oppose such a merger, favoring buyers over stockholders. Such action may benefit buyers, but it lowers aggregate consumer wealth by preventing the economy from operating more efficiently.

There are practical difficulties to be faced by antitrust enforcers. Mergers create efficiencies as well as transfer income. A merger that does not create market power will still transfer wealth. The question remains, should this type of merger-created transfer be ignored if it does not create market power but be considered if it does increase market power and hence raises price?

Market Versus Structural Approaches

Antitrust policy is more than a series of statutes and judicial decisions. It represents a political and social philosophy, and interpretations of the support for that philosophy vary considerably. Practitioners and analysts who adhere to a *market* or competitive view of the antitrust process generally believe that current laws should be enforced to allow the economic system to operate closely to the free market norm.

In this view, antitrust is the antithesis of regulation. Its objective is to maintain markets sufficiently competitive that they will regulate themselves. Proponents of the market approach view laws prohibiting price fixing as merely requiring firms to conform with the model of a competitive market economy. With varying degrees of enthusiasm, they support the laws controlling mergers and attempts to monopolize, although increasingly they question their need and effectiveness. This approach does not regard large enterprises as inherently bad so long as they have evolved as a result of the operation of natural economic forces.

Market Enthusiasts   A small but growing minority holding the market viewpoint have grown totally disenchanted with the notion of antitrust laws. They note a part of Adam Smith's *Wealth of Nations* that is rarely quoted: "It is impossible indeed to prevent such meeting [of 'people of the same trade'], by any law which either could be executed, or would be consistent with liberty and justice." Thus, the most adamant holders of the market position believe that the most dangerous sort of market power is that which emerges from government-granted protection. In contrast with the traditional market or competitive view of the antitrust laws, these critics from the right would allow liberal amounts of price discrimination and tying agreements and would not impede conglomerate mergers or vertical integration in most markets. They generally defend internal growth even if it results in a more concentrated market structure.[11]

Most holders of the market or competitive approach believe that corporate expansion is the reward for outperforming competitors and that such growth benefits consumers. Many large enterprises, they contend, benefit from economies of scale and greater innovation through investments in research and development, which raise productivity and keep prices down.

Some studies do tend to show that profits are related more closely to market share than to degree of concentration of the market.[12] Thus, it seems that higher profits associated with higher market share are correlated with lower costs, rather than with higher prices. Profits of oligopolists may be more likely attributed to efficiency than to collusion. High concentration ratios may be more an indication of virtue than a sign of vice. In this view, to use the antitrust laws to break up such companies would destroy the benefits that competition itself has produced.

To summarize the market viewpoint, large companies have gotten big because they are effective at meeting customers' desires, not because they are successful at ripping off consumers. The top 100 corporations in the United States now hold a smaller percentage of business assets than was the case in 1970. So do the top 200.

Structuralists   On the other hand, those who take a *structural* view of the antitrust process believe that these laws should be used to reorganize the economy. Many structuralists believe that if companies grow too large, they are no longer subject to the discipline of competition. Like the proponents of the market or competitive approach, the structuralists have a range of viewpoints. Some believe that bigness by itself is bad and that the power of large corporations should be curtailed drastically. When then FTC Chairman Michael Pertschuk was asked by a congressional committee if he thought "bigness is necessarily bad" he replied, "Actually, I do." Pertschuk defended this view of antitrust by contending that antitrust does not merely deal with the allocation of resources, "but of power."[13]

The structuralists contend that large companies not only produce adverse economic consequences but also exercise excessive social and political power. Other structuralists advocate reorganization of certain important segments of the economy. They are not necessarily opposed to bigness as such, but only to very large corporations that control a dominant share of a given market. They point, for instance, to several major industries (such as aluminum and automobile production) where the sales of three or fewer companies comprise a major share of the domestic market, ranging from 50 percent upward.

It is claimed that such industry leaders have discretion to set prices and target profit margins where they wish and have the power to drive new competitors out of the market or at least keep them small. However, there is considerable dispute among economists over the patterns of profits, prices, and innovation in concentrated industries. Some of the structuralist economists find that the large firms in concentrated industries earn higher rates of return on investment. More market-oriented economists tend to find no evidence of this relationship and also note the increasingly global nature of the markets in which large U.S. corporations compete.

From the structuralist viewpoint, antitrust enforcement is not controlling the adverse effects of concentrated industries. Those who hold this view condemn the fact that many industry leaders are increasing their market shares through internal growth as well as through mergers and acquisitions. One proposal considered but not adopted by Congress would compel divestiture in any case in which four or fewer companies account for 50 percent or more of the sales in "any line of commerce."

Antitrust Policy in the Reagan and Bush Administrations

The Reagan Administration followed the market or competitive approach. In 1982, the Antitrust Division of the Justice Department replaced a simple standard established in 1968 that generally held that a merger was suspect if it resulted in an industry in which four or fewer companies held 60 percent of the market. The new rules apply a formula (the Herfindahl Index) that measures competition by taking account of both the total number of firms serving a market and the relative power they wield, giving proportionately greater weight to the larger companies (see Table 7.1).[14]

A merger likely would be permitted if it created an industry in which four equally sized competitors controlled 60 percent of the market while an additional 40 firms controlled 1 percent each. If, on the other hand, a merger created one firm with 57 percent of the market, it might be challenged immediately, even though the dominant firm still had 43 competitors. This approach focuses the administration of the antitrust laws on those company actions that directly inhibit price competition.

In 1984, the Justice Department revised its merger guidelines to give greater consideration to various judgmental factors, such as efficiency claims, imports, barriers to new entrants, and the problems of declining industries. Under the revised merger guidelines, the Justice Department is not expected to try to stop or reverse a merger if entry into a market is easy, regardless of the degree of market concentration in the industry or the market shares of the merging partners. Since the mid-1980s, the federal government has refrained from blocking a variety of mergers of unparalleled size.

In 1992, the Department of Justice and the FTC, for the first time, jointly issued revised Horizontal Merger Guidelines, which were a modest modification of the 1984 version. The major innovation is to substantially reduce the possibility that either agency will challenge a proposed merger that is unlikely to injure competition.

TABLE 7.1 Alternate Measures of Market Concentration

Company Rank	Traditional Method (Market Share)	Herfindahl Index (Market Share Squared)
1	18%	324
2	16	256
3	10	100
4	9	81
5	7	49
6	6	36
7	5	25
8	4	16
9	4	16
10	4	16
Total	83%	919
	Four-firm concentration ratio = 53%	Herfindahl Index = 919

Antitrust enforcement officials are expected to look beyond the raw concentration data and attempt to ascertain the practical impact of the merger on competition.

Under the 1992 revised antitrust guidelines, FTC and antitrust division reviewers must seek answers to the following five questions:

1. Will the merger significantly increase market concentration and give rise to a concentrated market as properly defined and measured?
2. Will it give rise to adverse competitive effects?
3. Would new entry be timely, likely, and sufficiently effective to counteract the probable adverse competitive effects of the merger?
4. What efficiency gains—which could not reasonably be achieved through other means—would flow from the merger?
5. If the merger does not occur, would either party be likely to fail, causing its assets to be withdrawn from the market?[15]

A number of large horizontal combinations, including several oil-industry mergers, did go through (albeit with some restrictions) during the Reagan and Bush presidencies. Such agreements would undoubtedly have met stiffer challenges under previous administrations. Production joint ventures, such as that undertaken by GM and Toyota New United Motor Manufacturing, Inc. [NUMMI]) are important vehicles for the spread of "systems" innovations in management and manufacturing as well as technology transfers in production. The fact that recent joint ventures have been permitted by antitrust officials bodes well for such innovations.

The approval of the joint venture between two major rivals, General Motors and Toyota, while easily accepted given the current realities of the global marketplace, would have been unthinkable a decade earlier. The two companies agreed to a Toyota-designed automobile from parts supplied by both companies, with Toyota supplying top management and GM furnishing the production site.

The "New" Federal Trade Commission   Since the 1980s, the Federal Trade Commission has attempted to promote competition in the marketplace in novel ways, at least for the FTC. Thus, the commission has launched numerous investigations of state regulatory boards that use their occupational licensing power to restrict entry into the market and prohibit advertising by professionals. The new FTC thrust covers activities of accountants, lawyers, surveyors, funeral directors, and optometrists—representing a substantial shift from the previous leadership of the agency.[16]

The commission has played a major role in advocating fewer restrictions on attorney advertising. Allowing lawyers to advertise opens up the possibility of deceptive advertising, but it enhances information flows that encourage competition. There is a large range of permissible contact between competitors that traditionally elicits little if any antitrust concern. Trade association memberships, social contacts, and industry-wide lobbying for favorable legislation and regulation usually escape challenge.

Antitrust Policy in the Clinton Administration

The activities of the antitrust agencies during the Clinton Administration raise considerable uncertainty as to the future direction of antitrust enforcement. The heads of the FTC and the Antitrust Division, in their public speeches and testimony, tend to sound far more activist than their counterparts in the Reagan and Bush presidencies.

Indeed, they have challenged several mergers that, in the earlier period, likely would have been allowed to proceed without federal intervention. For example, in 1996, the Commission objected to the proposed merger of two large area drugstore chains: Rite-Aid and Revco. The following year, the Commission rejected the planned merger of two large office supply discounters: Staples, Inc., and Office Depot, Inc. In both cases, the FTC claimed that the combination would lead to higher prices for the consumer (even though each of the proposed mergers would have represented a small fraction of national sales in the respective markets).

On the other hand, the number and size of mergers have hit record highs since President Clinton took office (see Figure 7.1). Moreover, many of these combinations have involved large companies operating in the same sector of the economy. In 1995, Walt Disney acquired Capital Cities/ABC in an $18.8 billion transaction. The following year, Bell Atlantic paid $21.3 billion for NYNEX and SBC Communications combined with Pacific Telesis ($16.5 billion). During the same period, an extended series of mergers has occurred among major defense companies (see chapter 15).

Contestable Markets

A recent intellectual innovation in the antitrust field is the development of the concept of "contestable markets." This approach relies heavily on the idea that competition is fostered by the knowledge that potential new entrants can contest the positions of entrenched companies. Thus, where entry is unimpeded, measures of market concentration lose their significance as predictors of business behavior.

FIGURE 7.1 Pace of Merger Activity

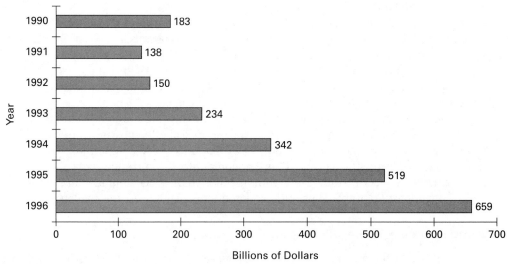

Source: Mergers & Acquisitions, various issues.

Conceptually, a contestable market is one into which entry is free and exit is costless. Freedom of entry does not necessarily signify that entry is costless or easy but that an entrant will suffer no disadvantages in terms of production techniques or perceived product quality. In a contestable market, firms need not be small or numerous, nor need they produce homogeneous products. The crucial feature is the market's vulnerability to hit-and-run entry and its hospitality to painless exit.[17]

However, large sunk costs can create barriers to entry. Not many new firms are anxious to invest the large sums required to build automobiles or airplanes. On the other hand, many types of assets are mobile. Jet airliners, for example, have been called "capital on wings." In the modern high-tech economy, information is a key asset and readily mobile.

The question naturally arises, "Why should antitrust lawyers challenge mergers in industries with easy entry? The answer, it turns out, is not as simple as it may appear. William Baumol, the leading figure in the contestable-market literature, warns that no industry in reality is perfectly contestable or is ever likely to be. He also adds that many are not even approximately so.[18]

In Baumol's view, where markets are characterized neither by a large number of incumbents nor by ease of entry, public-sector intervention may be required to prevent the exercise of monopoly power. In such cases, there is a strong presumption that the regulatory or antitrust agencies serve the public interest best if their intervention secures the sort of behavior on the part of incumbent firms that effective market pressures might otherwise enforce.

In any event, there is still a strong consensus that horizontal price fixing is anticompetitive and also that horizontal mergers in concentrated industries, protected by barriers to entry or to expansion by fringe competitors, should be viewed with suspicion.

An example of the real-world difficulty with the contestable-market notion is the airline market. Since the advent of deregulation, it would seem that the carriers could readily shift their equipment from one airport to another. However, landing slots are restricted and it is necessary for a newcomer to go through the difficult process of buying a slot from an existing holder. In practice, this typically means a firm can enter a given air-travel market only by acquiring a company already in that market.

Antitrust and the Global Marketplace

Whatever its proclivities, every recent presidential administration finds itself strongly influenced and perhaps inhibited by the pervasive and growing scope of the global marketplace. The competitive reality has frequently become a situation characterized by the larger U.S. firms increasingly competing against overseas giants as well as against smaller domestic companies.

In recent years, antitrust authorities have been grappling with the challenge of reshaping a government policy that was developed when the largest markets were primarily national or smaller. Between 1992 and 1997, the proportion of the Justice Department's Antitrust Division work that had an international dimension rose from 2 percent to almost 30 percent.[19] As the pressures of increasing world competition grow, the efficiency of a firm's operations takes on new weight as a reason for mergers and other actions that are likely to result in demonstrated savings in cost. The critical antitrust task of defining the relevant market includes locating the appropriate geographic boundaries in which the competitive battle occurs.[20]

Foreign competition can no longer be factored into the antitrust equation simply by counting imports as the totality of foreign firms' share of the U.S. market. In many domestic industries, which are relatively concentrated according to conventional measures, American firms are competing directly with foreign enterprises that may be much larger. Moreover, increasingly the relevant market may be virtually the entire global marketplace. The reach of government antitrust agencies is being undercut by three key factors: the internationalization of production; the increased cross-border flows of information, money, and technology; and the resultant rise of the transnational enterprise (see chapter 10).

In the case of key industries such as automobiles, steel, and chemicals, this global view means that what seems to be a rather concentrated U.S. industry is really part of an unconcentrated and larger group of worldwide competitors. For example, Table 7.2 shows only three U.S. firms on the list of the top 20 global automobile manufacturers, and they only account for 39 percent of total sales. Even more striking relationships hold in other large, important markets. For example, 9 of the world's 10 largest banking corporations are headquartered overseas, as are 9 of the 10 largest electrical and electronics companies, 8 of the 10 biggest insurance enterprises, and 8 of the 10 largest chemical firms. All 10 of the largest construction and engineering companies are domiciled outside the United States, as are all 10 of the biggest electric and gas utilities.

TABLE 7.2   The Global Automobile Industry, 1996

Rank	Company	Country	Sales (billions)
1	General Motors	USA	$168
2	Ford	USA	147
3	Toyota	Japan	109
4	Daimler-Benz	Germany	72
5	Volkswagen	Germany	67
6	Daewoo	Korea	65
7	Chrysler	USA	61
8	Nissan	Japan	59
9	Fiat	Italy	51
10	Honda	Japan	47
11	Renault	France	36
12	BMW	Germany	35
13	Peugeot	France	34
14	Mitsubishi	Japan	33
15	Volvo	Sweden	23
16	Isuzu	Japan	17
17	Mazda	Japan	17
18	Hyundai	Korea	14
19	Suzuki	Japan	13
20	Man	Germany	13
Total			$1,081

In 1994, Congress passed the International Antitrust Enforcement Assistance Act, enhancing the Antitrust Division's ability to prosecute international antitrust cases involving foreign defendants and overseas violations of the antitrust laws. However, foreign governments regard such cases as unjustified extraterritorial enforcement of the domestic laws of the United States. The United States is one of the few countries in which antitrust violations are a criminal offense.[21]

Many new factors are involved in broadening the traditional U.S. antitrust approach. The range of foreign government intervention in international trade must be taken into account, including public-sector subsidies to home industries and restrictions of foreign competitors. As we will see in later chapters, however, American hands are not as clean in this regard as we may think.

Conclusions

The influence of federal economic regulatory agencies on the transportation, banking, and communications industries has greatly declined in the past decade. The most pervasive example of industry-specific regulation is now state-level regulation of utilities. However, because of improved technology and updated approaches to the role of government, the standard natural-monopoly justifications for utility regulation are now being questioned. Meanwhile, innovative approaches to pricing policies are also being instituted.

Antitrust regulation has also changed significantly during the past decade. The criteria for judging harmful levels of industry concentration have been altered. Market proponents who challenge the need for continued strict enforcement of the Sherman and Clayton Acts are squaring off with the more traditional "structuralists," who are concerned with the power—economic and political—of large firms. Meanwhile, the increasingly important international economy looms ever larger in hitherto domestic decision making.

Notes

1. *F.P.C.* v. *Hope Natural Gas Co.*, 320 U.S. 591, 603 (1944).
2. Cited in Charles Tatham, *Measures of Public Utility Bond Quality* (New York: Bache and Co., 1970), p. 19.
3. In 1990, the California Public Utilities Commission adopted an incentive-based regulatory system for telephone service whereby the utility could earn up to a 30 percent higher rate of return if it kept its costs low in relation to expected productivity increases.
4. An example of the latter situation was the inability of the Long Island Lighting Company to operate its $5 billion Shoreham nuclear power plant because the governor of New York State would not prepare an emergency evacuation plan.
5. Don D. Jordan, "The Deregulation Dilemma," *Chief Executive*, January–February 1997, pp. 46–51.
6. "Electricity Deregulation and the Consumer," *Resources*, Winter 1997, pp. 8–11; Benjamin Holden, "Electricity Savings to Be Short-Circuited," *Wall Street Journal*, September 24, 1997, p. A2.

7. Jeannie Mandelker, "The Change in Power," *Infrastructure Finance,* October 1996, pp. 11–16.
8. Adapted from Jonathan Marshall, "Competition Comes to the Electron Superhighway," *The American Enterprise,* May–June 1995, p. 83.
9. Cited in Thomas J. DiLorenzo, "The Origins of Antitrust: An Interest Group Perspective," *International Review of Law and Economics,* 1985, no. 5, pp. 80–81.
10. Robert H. Bork, *The Antitrust Paradox* (New York: Basic Books, 1978). See also E. Thomas Sullivan, ed., *The Political Economy of the Sherman Act* (New York: Oxford University Press, 1991).
11. Fred L. Smith, Jr., "Why Not Abolish Antitrust," *Regulation,* January–February 1983, pp. 23–24.
12. See P. Pautler, "A Review of the Economic Basis for a Broad-Based Horizontal-Merger Policy," *Antitrust Bulletin,* Fall 1983, pp. 571–651.
13. Quoted in "New Wave in Antitrust," *Perspectives on National Issues* (Washington, DC: National Association of Manufacturers, 1979), p. 2.
14. James A. Langenfeld, "The Merger Guidelines As Applied," in Malcolm Coate and Andrew Kleit, eds., *The Economics of the Antitrust Process* (Boston: Kluwer Academic Publishers, 1996), pp. 41–47.
15. James F. Rill, "An Antitrust Screen for Merger Masters of the 1990s," *Mergers & Acquisitions,* September/October 1992, pp. 52–57.
16. James Langenfeld and David T. Scheffman, "The FTC in the 1980s," *Review of Industrial Organization,* Summer 1990, pp. 87–88.
17. William J. Baumol, John C. Panzar, and Robert D. Willig, *Contestable Markets and the Theory of Industry Structure* (New York: Harcourt Brace Jovanovich, 1982); William J. Baumol, "Contestable Markets, An Uprising in the Theory of Industry Structure," *American Economic Review,* March 1982, pp. 1–15.
18. William J. Baumol, "On Contestable Market Analysis," in *Antitrust and New Views of Microeconomics* (New York: Conference Board, 1986), pp. 13–14.
19. Joel I. Klein, "International Antitrust Enforcement," in George C. Landrith III, ed., *A Day With the Department of Justice* (Washington, DC: National Legal Center, 1997), p. 1.
20. John H. Shenefield and Irwin N. Stelzer, *The Antitrust Laws: A Primer* (Lanham, MD: AEI Press, 1993).
21. Janusz A. Ordover, "Bingaman's Antitrust Era," *Regulation,* Spring 1997, pp. 21–26.

CHAPTER 8

Economic Deregulation

T he substantial deregulation of American transportation, telecommunications, energy, and financial markets that has been underway since the late 1970s represents a fundamental change from the experience of the previous 90 years. From the establishment of the Interstate Commerce Commission in 1886 to the passage of the Toxic Substances Control Act in 1976, government regulation of economic activity in the United States steadily expanded, creating in its wake powerful constituencies who benefited from the regulation. Despite the inevitable gaps between the ideal and the reality, on balance deregulation has strengthened the economy and benefited the consumer.

The unprecedented reduction of economic regulation that has occurred in the United States was not caused by a realignment of political forces. The most significant developments were supported by a bipartisan coalition in both the legislative and executive branches of the federal government. Consumer activists such as Ralph Nader offered support at vital points, as did leaders of both political parties, including Presidents Ford, Carter, and Reagan. But the most important role was played by a very unusual set of actors in the public policy arena: economists, political scientists, legal scholars, and similar purveyors of ideas.

ORIGINS OF DEREGULATION

Three streams of economic research and policy analysis dealing with different aspects of regulation reached a confluence in the 1970s. The first, and most substantial, focused on the fact that the widely distributed burdens imposed by economic regulation, especially in the field of transportation, were much larger than the far more concentrated benefits. The second stream dealt with the fundamental nature of the regulatory process, especially the relationships between regulators and those regulated. The third focused on the general costs of regulation, especially to the consumer.

It is difficult to pinpoint the exact start of the influential research that led to transportation deregulation. *The Economics of Competition in the Transportation Industries,* written by John R. Meyer and his associates in 1959, was a landmark study.[1] Important work followed on each of the major modes of transportation, notably George W. Douglas and James C. Miller III, on airlines, and Thomas Gale Moore on trucking.[2]

The airline industry provided the clearest examples of the heavy cost of regulation, particularly the differential prices charged by regulated and nonregulated airlines. Interstate travel was under the jurisdiction of the Civil Aeronautics Board (CAB); intrastate travel was beyond the CAB's purview. Research found that a traveler could fly 500 miles from San Diego to San Francisco in the unregulated California market and pay less than someone flying 300 miles from Portland, Oregon, to Seattle, Washington, under the CAB's control. During the 1970s, most economists writing in this field also concluded that Interstate Commerce Commission (ICC) regulation was protecting the carriers (railroads and truckers) and their unions while increasing costs to shippers by billions of dollars a year.

A consensus gradually emerged. Transportation regulation in the United States did not protect its purported beneficiaries—consumers—but instead was benefiting the employees, executives, and shareholders of the companies being regulated. Government rule making shielded entrenched firms from potential new competitors and kept a high price umbrella over the regulated industries.

The second, and related, stream of research focused on the political efforts of interest groups that benefited from regulation.[3] In 1955, political scientist Marver Bernstein presented a "capture" theory of regulation. As the only political force in a regulatory agency's environment with any stability, the industry would eventually force an agency to accommodate its needs. Economists George Stigler and Sam Peltzman generalized this theory, contending that regulatory policy reflects the interests and the power of the concerned groups, not necessarily the consumer's.[4] In 1982, Stigler was awarded the Nobel Prize in Economics for his seminal research on the theory of regulation and his empirical studies of the effect of regulation on specific industries.

The third line of research—focusing on costs to consumers—saw the topic move from the business pages and academic journals to the front pages and the nightly news. The American Enterprise Institute led the way in the mid-1970s with several widely cited reports on the high cost of regulation, among them my own on government-mandated price increases via regulation, Sam Peltzman's on pharmaceutical regulation, John P. Gould's on the Davis-Bacon Act, and Rita Ricardo-Campbell's on food safety regulation.[5] The issue hit a responsive chord with the media, influential policy groups, and finally the Congress.

Deregulation was politically attractive because it presented policy makers with an opportunity to curb inflation in a way that did not involve a trade-off with jobs. Indeed, reduced regulation would cut both costs and barriers to production and employment.

The burdens of regulation were characterized as a hidden tax on the consumer. Carefully researched examples of regulatory silliness also helped bring these concepts to the public's attention. Perhaps the first example was the dead haul—requiring that trucks return empty from delivery even though there was ample opportunity to fill them with cargo. The public needed no great expertise in industrial organization to resent the waste that resulted.

This unusual form of applied research (horror-story telling) concentrated increasingly on the Occupational Safety and Health Administration (OSHA). Jokes about OSHA, based on that research, became a staple of business conversation. Is it true that OSHA made one company build separate his and her toilets even though the only two employees of the firm were married to each other? Did OSHA really issue a bulletin to farmers telling them to be careful around cows and not to step into manure pits? Both of those questions could, quite accurately, be answered in the affirmative.

By the late 1970s, support for regulatory reform had become widespread. It included business executives who found themselves inundated with a flood of rules to follow and reports to file, lawyers and political scientists who thought that the regulatory agencies often were captured by the regulated industries, and economists who believed that regulation reduced competition and increased costs. Congressional hearings on the subject yielded support for less regulation from such disparate groups—and surprising allies—as the American Conservative Union and the Consumer Federation of America.

PROGRESS TOWARD DEREGULATION

Progress on deregulation built up slowly but gathered strong momentum in the mid and late 1970s. In 1968, a Supreme Court decision permitted non-AT&T equipment to be hooked to the Bell telephone system. The following year, the Federal Communications Commission (FCC) allowed a non-Bell company to connect its long-distance network with local phone systems. Although these two actions attracted little attention at the time, they triggered the forces that led to the breakup of the Bell system.

In the 1970s, interest rates on deposits of $100,000 and over were deregulated. Again, one move toward deregulation ultimately led to another. As securities firms took advantage of this loophole, banks responded. A process was set in motion that has resulted in eliminating interest-rate ceilings, paying interest on consumer demand deposits, and greater competition among financial institutions.

Two important regulatory changes took place in 1975. The Securities and Exchange Commission (SEC) ordered an end to fixed brokerage fees for stock market transactions, and the ICC prohibited rate bureaus for either trucking firms or railroads from protesting independent rate filings by members. Clearly, the regulatory ice was breaking.

In 1977, the Civil Aeronautics Board (CAB), led by two economists, chairman Alfred Kahn and member Elizabeth Bailey, instituted several changes that ultimately led to airline deregulation. The CAB gave airlines increased freedom in pricing and easier access to routes not previously served. The results were spectacular. Coach fares fell sharply, planes filled, and airline profits soared. The CAB experience provided a striking example of how regulation had been hurting the traveling public. In response, a bipartisan coalition in Congress passed legislation in 1978 that phased out the CAB and its authority to control entry and prices.

The year 1980 was an eventful one for deregulation. The FCC eliminated most federal regulation of cable television. Economist Darius Gaskins became chairman of the ICC and economist Marcus Alexis was appointed a member of the commission. That, in turn, encouraged the trucking industry to support congressional leadership of reform in this field, in the expectation that the changes would be less drastic than those pursued by the new leadership of the ICC. Later in the year, a trucking law provided much more pricing freedom to individual carriers, made entry into the market much easier, and eliminated many costly ICC restrictions—but the ICC presence was retained. Also passed in 1980, the Staggers Rail Act gave the railroads new pricing freedom.

In 1981, the FCC eliminated much regulation of the radio industry. President Reagan decontrolled crude-oil prices and petroleum allocation and terminated the Council on Wage and Price Stability and its wage-price guidelines. But the pace of deregulation slowed significantly after 1981. Although regulatory reform was one of the four original pillars of Reaganomics (along with tax reduction, budget cutting, and anti-inflationary monetary policy), it never received as high a priority as the other three. A backlash in the environmental area, fueled in part by the controversial personalities of some of the administration's appointees, put the entire regulatory reform movement on the defensive.

Nevertheless, changes continued to be made. Banking legislation enacted in 1982 allowed savings and loan associations to make more commercial and consumer loans. The interest-rate differentials between banks and thrift institutions also were removed. (As we will see, that incomplete deregulation was as much bane as blessing.)

The Bus Regulatory Reform Act of 1982 permitted bus companies to change routes and fares. In 1984, the Shipping Act enabled individual ocean shipping companies to offer lower rates and better service than so-called "shipping conferences" (really cartels). Also in that year, AT&T agreed to divest local operating companies as part of its historic antitrust settlement with the Justice Department.

AIRLINE DEREGULATION

The greatest progress to date toward deregulation has occurred in the transportation area, especially the commercial aviation industry. Until the late 1970s, the Civil Aeronautics Board (CAB) regulated the airline industry extensively. It allocated interstate routes among the airlines and controlled airline fares on those routes. Through its power over air routes, the CAB restrained entry into the industry. From its inception in 1938 until the late 1970s, the CAB did not allow any new airline to enter the interstate markets that served major population centers.

In 1977, the CAB began to ease restrictions on fares and entry. In 1978, Congress affirmed and extended the agency's actions by passing the Airline Deregulation Act, which provided for the gradual deregulation of the airlines. CAB's domestic route authority was ended in 1981, and its domestic pricing authority was terminated in 1983. The CAB itself went out of business in 1985.

A host of other factors always makes it difficult to analyze the effects of a fundamental change such as airline deregulation. Nevertheless, it is clear that since 1977, air traffic has grown faster and air fares have fallen more rapidly than they did while the industry was regulated. Simultaneously, employment has risen and labor productivity increased. Despite several highly publicized crashes, the safety record of U.S. airlines since deregulation is superior to that for the earlier period. According to the General Accounting Office, "Airline deregulation has led to lower fares and better service for most air travelers. . . ."[6]

The experience since 1978 has not been without negatives. Contrary to expectations, an unprecedented wave of mergers has led to a more concentrated industry structure. The failure of government—which owns most of the airports and manages the air navigation system—to keep pace with rising demand has led to congestion in airports and in the sky and to delays and other service problems. As a result, some small- and medium-size communities in the East and Upper Midwest have experienced higher fares and worse service since deregulation.[7]

Let us examine the pluses and the minuses of airline deregulation.

Positive Effects Since Deregulation

On a case-by-case basis, more communities have fared better under deregulation, but some are worse off. For instance, cities located within an hour's drive of major airports have tended to lose air service because travelers from those cities now drive to the major hubs where they can get discounts and more flight choices. Those smaller cities lack enough passengers for the airlines to stop there. In contrast, locations with a good population base that were not well served by the major carriers have attracted more regional and commuter airlines.

One clear benefit of airline deregulation has been an increase in service in terms of number of flights and number of routes (or "city-pair" markets) served. Following the relaxation of entry restrictions in airline markets, airlines developed "hub and spoke" networks. These hub and spoke systems have led to increased flights to medium-size and smaller cities, by aggregating smaller city traffic toward single destinations and thereby raising to profitable levels the number of passengers per flight.

Hub and spoke systems allow airlines to use their aircraft more efficiently, carrying more passengers per flight and operating aircraft more hours per day. Average load factors on many flights have increased substantially. Moreover, the proportion of trips involving a change in plane has declined. Competition has forced the carriers to pass on these savings to their customers.

Overall, a larger proportion of the American public is flying today than ever before. That welcome development has been fostered by a more competitive fare structure for air travel. Fares in 1996 were 22 percent lower than they would have been under regulation. The savings to air travelers have been estimated at over $12 billion a year (in 1993 dollars).[8]

Clearly, average air fares are substantially lower than they would have been in the absence of deregulation. Although that would seem to be a fairly straightforward statement, it is too subtle for the typical passenger to appreciate. After all, who can make a mental adjustment for general inflation? The more usual approach is simply to conclude that fares are higher today than yesterday or, in any event, that fare schedules are far more confusing than they used to be.

That is so because, prior to deregulation in 1976, only 15 percent of all airline passengers received discount fares; most paid standard fares. Presently, the great majority of airline passengers travel on discount tickets (which are often more complicated in terms of special provisions such as difficulty in changing flight plans).

Airline Safety

Although the Airline Deregulation Act of 1978 did not change the authority of the Federal Aviation Administration to regulate the safety of air travel, public concern about safety has risen since deregulation. A striking result of deregulation has been an enormous increase in passenger volume. A decade ago, only 1 American in 10 had ever flown in an airplane. Today, more than one-third of the population flies each year.

The combination of increased flights and more passengers has resulted in greater congestion in airports and airways. Despite the public furor, however, the airline accident rate has declined since deregulation. In the prederegulation period of 1975–78, an average of 11 accidents occurred per million departures; in the post-deregulation decade of 1979 to 1989, the average was fewer than 6 accidents per million departures. During the same period, the number of fatal accidents declined from two per million departures to one per million. The overall airline accident rate in the United States was lower in 1990–1995 than in 1978.[9]

Economists have suggested methods of reducing air congestion by encouraging the users of the airways to avoid bunching their takeoffs and landings in the most popular times. As in the case of telephone services, higher prices would be charged during periods of peak usage and lower fees at times when demand is low (e.g., fewer planes are flying).

Also, avoidable congestion arises because landing fees for executive, personal, and other small aircraft are lower than the costs such planes impose on the transportation system. Raising the fees charged these light (private) airplanes for using the major airports would encourage their operators to shift to smaller, less frequently used facilities. Most aircraft accidents involve at least one light (private) airplane. When the Massachusetts Port Authority proposed raising landing fees at Logan Airport in Boston, the pressures from the owners and operators of light planes was so intense that the matter was tabled.

Negative Effects Since Deregulation

After the initial burst of new entries following deregulation, a handful of large airline companies has gained very large market shares. Overall, the number of major carriers has declined from 11 prior to deregulation to 8 in 1996. This net change came about from an initial expansion of the number of carriers followed by a series of mergers and bankruptcies.

Most proponents of airline deregulation did not expect the market concentration that has occurred. The three major U.S. airlines hold a 55 percent share of the domestic market, compared to only 37 percent in 1981 (see Table 8.1). In good measure, that situation has resulted from Congress's giving the Department of Transportation (DOT) authority (which lapsed in 1989) to review the antitrust aspect of airline mergers. DOT approved every prospective airline merger, many over the strenuous objections of the Justice Department's Antitrust Division. Several studies have shown that airline mergers, on balance, do exert an upward force on the fares for the routes for which competition has been reduced. A study of airline mergers during 1985–88 reported that they increased air fares by an average of 9 percent relative to routes unaffected by the merger.[10]

In general, passengers flying from a hub city with substantial airline competition pay lower fares than those departing from a city with one or two dominant carriers. The General Accounting Office found, in 1992, that fares at "concentrated" airports (where one or two carriers dominate) were 22 percent higher than fares at less concentrated airports, even when differences in the distance flown were accounted for.[11]

TABLE 8.1	Share of U.S. Airline Traffic Held by Three Largest Carriers

Year	Combined Share
1981	37
1982	37
1983	38
1984	37
1985	35
1986	39
1987	41
1988	44
1989	47
1990	46
1991	52
1992	56
1993	57
1994	56
1995	55
1996	55

Source: Data from Air Transport Association.

PARTIAL DEREGULATION IN SURFACE TRANSPORTATION

Many new laws were enacted in the late 1970s and early 1980s to reduce the degree of regulation in surface transportation. The major ones were the Railroad Revitalization and Regulatory Reform Act of 1976, the Motor Carrier Act of 1980, the Staggers Rail Act of 1980, and the Bus Regulatory Reform Act of 1982. In 1994, Congress passed the Trucking Industry Regulatory Reform Act, eliminating much of the remaining trucking regulation and prohibiting states from regulating rates for in-state transportation of nonhousehold goods. In 1996, the ICC was eliminated and its residual functions shifted to the DOT.

Trucking Deregulation

The deregulation of trucking has been very beneficial. Estimates of annual savings from trucking deregulation—including lowered inventory needs—range up to $50 billion a year. Operating costs per mile are down about one-third since 1980.[12] Shippers in general appear to be satisfied with the rates, service options, and competition for their business. Service to small communities has not deteriorated, as was originally predicted by the opponents of deregulation.

The number of trucking firms has increased substantially, although the short-run adjustments in the industry were substantial. More than 300 truckers went out of business in the first three years following the passage of the 1980 legislation. During the same period and continuing to the present, however, thousands of new, nonunion, low-cost truckers entered the business, as the ICC dropped its barriers to entry. The number of carriers in operation mushroomed, from about 47,000 in 1982 to more than 300,000 in 1997.

Railroad Deregulation

The experience since the partial deregulation of railroads in 1980 is similar to that of trucking. Although not everyone has benefited, on balance the cost of transportation has been reduced. Railroads have increased their shipments of some commodities, such as fruits and vegetables, that were previously carried almost exclusively by trucks. Over 27,000 miles of their more unprofitable rail lines were abandoned by 1990. Following a difficult period of bankruptcies and liquidations, the remaining firms in the railroad industry are in stronger financial condition, and the future of this troubled industry has brightened. A substantial reduction in operating costs has occurred because, since the Staggers Act, the railroads can keep as much of their gains from greater efficiency as competition will allow.

Railroad rates dropped substantially following deregulation. Managerial innovations, such as intermodal operations and use of double-stack cars have helped. In the aggregate, railroad costs per ton mile of freight hauled dropped about 50 percent from 1980 to 1996, adjusted for general inflation. Moreover, the cost cutting that followed lessened regulation enabled the railroads to pay for upgrading equipment and long-deferred maintenance.[13]

Responding to the pressures of competition in a deregulated environment, major U.S. railroads are operating with 20 percent fewer locomotives than in 1980, 230,000 fewer employees, and thousands fewer freight cars. The implicit increase in productivity in varying degrees has been passed on to the using industries, enhancing their market positions at home and abroad.

DEREGULATION OF TELECOMMUNICATIONS

In 1982, the federal government and AT&T announced that they had settled an eight-year-old government antitrust suit with a consent agreement that required AT&T to spin off its local telephone operating companies. Since 1984, consumers no longer have been able to buy their basic local telephone service and long-distance services from the same company.

Splitting up the Bell System was expected to enhance competition and lower prices to the consumer. Competition certainly was enhanced. Prices followed a more complicated route. In comparison to the Bell System monopoly of long-distance telephone service in the United States prior to the breakup, approximately 95 percent of telephones now have access to at least three competitive long-distance companies. More densely populated areas are often served by five or more firms.

This competition has lowered prices substantially. The decline in long-distance rates, however, has been partially offset by a rise in the rates for local telephone service. In part, this reflected a deliberate attempt by the FCC to reduce subsidies for local telephone service that traditionally had been received from long-distance service. To fully understand the implications of the AT&T breakup, it is necessary to take into account the historical development of telecommunications regulation.

Historical Regulation of Telephone Rates

For decades, telephone service has been regulated at the federal and state levels by commissions whose concerns have been more with "fairness" than with economic efficiency. Until the 1970s, few users or policy makers objected if long distance subsidized local telephone service as long as AT&T, its local operating companies, and the other local operating companies that accounted for 10 to 15 percent of total telephone subscribers did not appear to earn an excessive rate of return. Local rates were priced on a flat monthly basis. Long-distance calls were priced at a flat rate per mile, even though this approach penalized callers on low-cost dense routes and subsidized those in rural areas.

While transmission costs declined in the 1960s and 1970s, state and federal regulators did not allow long-distance rates to fall proportionately. A larger share of local-service costs was allocated to long distance. But as long as the overall cost of telephone service kept dropping, few complained. Throughout that period, overall telephone rates fell substantially relative to inflation. Between 1960 and 1980, real telephone rates fell by more than 50 percent. In part, this decline was caused by rapid technological progress. Productivity rose much more rapidly in the telephone industry than elsewhere in the economy. In addition, rates were suppressed in the inflationary 1970s by a regulatory process that relied on histo....

The combination of distortions in telephone rates and changing technology began to invite new entrants in the 1960s. At first, this competition was limited to private lines used by large businesses and to simple devices attached to telephone lines. By the mid-1970s, alternatives were available for most terminal equipment—such as private branch exchanges (PBXs) and telephone handsets—and, more importantly, for long-distance service. Companies such as MCI and Sprint began to compete actively for long-distance customers.

The new marketplace forces in long-distance service began to exert downward pressure on rates during the late 1970s. AT&T responded by reducing its private-line rates and by trying to frustrate the new competitors' efforts to reach customers through AT&T-owned operating companies. These activities induced the Justice Department to file an antitrust suit, which was settled by the 1982 decree that forced AT&T to divest itself of its local operating companies.

Telephone Regulation Since the AT&T Breakup

The structure of telephone rates is undergoing a dramatic change as a direct result of government policy. Long-distance rates are falling in real terms while local rates have tended to rise. The price of local service is now more nearly based on the number of calls made and the length and duration of these calls. Telephone receivers and other terminal equipment are now rarely leased from the local phone company; most subscribers now own their equipment. Subscribers are much more likely to be charged substantial installation fees because local telephone companies are not able to capitalize these installation costs in their balance sheets.

These changes can be attributed to the emergence of competition that has followed deregulation in the telephone industry. The uneconomic pricing decisions that regulators promoted or sanctioned in the 1960s and 1970s have come unraveled. Competition can destroy cross-subsidies in a manner that makes life very difficult for legislators and regulators who are still held accountable by the erstwhile beneficiaries of such subsidies. To understand the current pressures on regulators in this more competitive era, however, one has to understand the uneasy equilibrium that has evolved.

Monopoly or Competition?

In its earliest form, the telephone industry may well have been a "natural" monopoly. Stringing paired copper wires between homes or businesses and telephone switching centers initially was more efficient when conducted by a single monopolist than by a number of competitors. But even during those early years, it was not clear that AT&T should also monopolize the manufacture and distribution of handsets and other terminal equipment. After all, local gas utilities have a natural monopoly in distributing gas, but they do not try to control the sales of water heaters, furnaces, and kitchen ranges. Thus, it was not surprising that a long-running debate occurred over AT&T's right to produce the telephone equipment used in the delivery of its services.

In the 1950s, technological changes occurred that greatly complicated the problem of regulating the telephone monopoly. Users began to demand the right to attach to their telephone lines equipment not provided by the telephone company. At first, these were simple devices. Eventually, however, subscribers began to demand the right to connect their own answering machines, computer modems, and PBXs to the lines. Users even wanted to own their handsets—perhaps even some that were unlike any offered by the local telephone company.

Technological change also altered the nature of telephone signal transmission. Long-distance calls began to be transmitted by microwave radio, a technology with modest economies of scale on dense routes. Large users could opt out of AT&T services altogether by using microwaves.

The Federal Communications Commission gradually responded to the demand for entry into long-distance communications and terminal equipment. In the late 1960s, the FCC began to allow competitive entry into private-line (point-to-point) services and installation of terminal equipment on the grounds that these services and products could be supplied most efficiently by a competitive market. AT&T's offering of these services and products, however, continued to be regulated. The commission refused to allow new entrants into the "network" that involve both local and long-distance services because it was unpersuaded that competition was a viable and efficient means for delivering these services. Local service, regulated by state public utilities, also remained under monopoly control.

The entire regulatory process came unglued in the mid-1970s when MCI (originally formed as Microwave Communications, Inc.) entered the switched long-distance market without FCC permission. The commission had authorized MCI to provide private-line service, but it had not contemplated that MCI would try to offer ordinary long-distance service. At first, the FCC tried to block MCI's expansion, but it was defeated in court proceedings because it failed to demonstrate that competition in long-distance markets was either infeasible or socially undesirable.

By the late 1970s, the FCC and the courts had transformed the telephone monopoly into a set of competitive long-distance carriers and equipment vendors, each connecting their services or equipment to the lines of franchised local monopolists. AT&T could operate in the long-distance market subject to regulatory restraints, and it did so with such aggressive effect that it became the target of a wave of antitrust suits. But the 1956 decree continued to prohibit AT&T from competing in the new world of mixed communications and computer services.

The FCC and the state commissions did not know how to set rates efficiently and to establish fair ground rules for the new world of competitive telecommunications markets. The FCC tried for nearly two decades to separate the various costs of telecommunications services from each other, but the nature of the services and the rapid pace of technological change in the industry made the commission's task difficult if not impossible.

The new competition in terminal equipment and long-distance service had predictable effects. The regulators could no longer attempt to subsidize basic monthly service from excess charges for long-distance service. As long as the FCC and the state commissions combined to keep long-distance rates artificially high, new competitors would eagerly enter this market. As MCI, Sprint, and others began to make inroads into AT&T's erstwhile long-distance monopoly, AT&T tried to fight back through competitive rate reductions and actions designed to frustrate its competitors' access to customers through AT&T's local operating companies.

The Divestiture

In 1982, AT&T agreed to its own dismemberment in settlement of the government's 1974 antitrust suit. In return, AT&T was given the right to retain Western Electric and its research arm, Bell Laboratories. The 1956 consent decree that barred AT&T from entering new computer-related businesses was set aside. The divested operating companies were prohibited from manufacturing equipment and offering long-distance or information services but were required to develop "equal access" technology for all long-distance carriers.

The decree was designed to separate the suppliers of access to local subscribers—the regional AT&T operating companies—from those offering long-distance and other information-age services. As a result, the divested operating companies were not allowed to compete with MCI, AT&T, Sprint, or other companies in the long-distance market. To preserve fair competition, the local operating companies were limited in much the same way that AT&T was under the now defunct 1956 decree.

AT&T was free to compete for any business except local exchange service. It remains a regulated carrier. At first, the divested telephone operating companies were owned by seven independent regional holding companies (NYNEX, Ameritech, Pacific Telesis, etc.). In the late 1990s, several of these holding companies merged, notably Southwestern Bell and Pacific Telesis.

Telecommunications Act of 1996[14]

Continued technological advance has generated opportunities for a greater degree of competition in telecommunications services—for the possibility of local telephone companies providing long-distance service, for long-distance carriers entering or reentering the local service market, and for telephone and cable companies competing directly with each other. In an effort to rationalize this process, Congress passed the Telecommunications Act of 1996. The ostensible purposes were to end the franchised monopolies that state regulatory commissions have granted local telephone companies, to permit local telephone companies to enter the long-distance market, and to allow telephone companies to offer cable television service.

The results have not been that straightforward. Rather, they are reminiscent of the loaded question on a final examination given by the author, Does the federal government deregulate as badly as it regulates? The answer, at least in this case, is "yes." The 1996 law, coupled with the way the FCC is administering it, seems destined to keep the entire matter of telephone deregulation tied up in the courts for years.

First of all, each state regulation commission is charged with developing guidelines for the entrance of new local carriers. To "help" them in that task, the FCC has provided a massive document of nearly 700 pages. Under the new rules, an existing local carrier must provide a competitor with access to its network at a price based on its most modern technology rather than its actual costs. Thus, the newcomer will be able to operate at a lower average cost than its existing competitor (who uses both old and new equipment) and will be able to do so without making a major investment. In July 1997, a federal appeals court threw out the FCC rules, but the Supreme Court has not yet passed judgment on this case.

To complicate matters, the existing local telephone companies are forced by state regulators to serve small towns and rural areas at prices substantially below their costs. This means having to charge business customers and residences in large cities rates substantially above costs. Clearly, this convoluted rate structure (what economists call "cross subsidies") cannot survive a competitive assault from new entrants who can lease capacity at low cost.

The new entrants are likely to focus on such potential customers as small businesses, urban residents, and heavy users of long distance, whose rates have been kept far above costs. The new competitors will happily cede to the existing local carriers the rest of the market where rates are generally below cost, particularly the residential markets in small cities. The average residential customer in 1996 paid about $20 a month for flat–rate local telephone service, while rural residents paid less (the full cost of providing service to rural areas has been estimated at $40 to $50 a month).

Compounding the problem, many state regulatory commissions are reluctant to let the below-cost rates rise. They prefer instead to finance these subsidies from a "universal service" tax on all telecommunications carriers. Furthermore, the FCC is adding on charges required by the 1996 law to pay for linking libraries, schools, and medical services to the Internet. This hidden tax likely will be levied mainly on business and residential customers who have more than one phone.

Complications abound in the supposed new "deregulated" environment. Before entering the long-distance market, the local carriers (the so-called Baby or, more accurately, Regional Bells) must meet a 14-point deregulatory checklist and the FCC must certify that a separate subsidiary will operate the long-distance service. The Regional Bells are also allowed to manufacture telecommunications equipment and provide cable TV service. Before doing so, however, they must receive FCC verification that their local exchanges are open to competition. Other provisions in the 1996 law relax foreign ownership restrictions on U.S. telephone and broadcast companies. Investment is allowed in U.S. broadcast companies by businesses from countries that also allow U.S. firms to invest in their broadcast properties.

In the aggregate, these rules have generated such uncertainty and controversy as to scare away most potential new entrants into the various sectors of the telecommunications market. Cable television, long-distance, and local telephone companies have scaled back the investment plans that they originally developed in the initial burst of enthusiastic response to the 1996 law.

If this stalemate endures, it is likely that Congress will reconsider the Telecommunications Act, especially to simplify the approach to liberalizing entry into the markets for telephone service. Decades of experience in the airlines, trucking, and railroad industries have demonstrated that even imperfect unregulated competition is better than regulated competition. Robert Crandall of the Brookings Institution estimates that opening up the entire telecommunications market to competition would add $30 billion a year to the gross domestic product of the United States, far more than the gains from trucking or airline deregulation.[15]

PARTIAL DEREGULATION OF FINANCIAL INSTITUTIONS

Although public discourse is filled with allusions to deregulation of financial institutions, a veritable maze of regulatory agencies continues to influence the operations of banks and other financial enterprises (see Figure 8.1). As will be covered in a subsequent chapter, many savings and loan associations and some banks have gotten into great financial difficulties and many have been closed down or otherwise "bailed out" by the federal government.

FIGURE 8.1 Regulation of Banks and Their Holding Companies

Regulatory Agencies ⟶

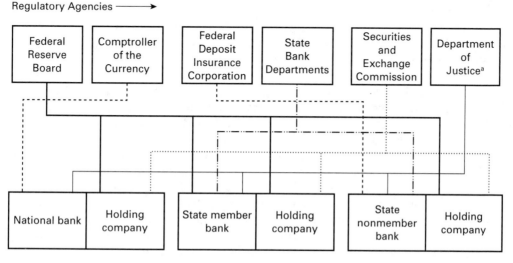

Types of Regulated Institutions ⟶

[a]Antitrust enforcement only.

Economic Deregulation Efforts

A substantial amount of regulation exists, although less than in earlier years. Until 1980, small savers were denied the benefits of market competition because of federal government ceilings on interest rates on savings deposits. Money-market funds with more competitive interest rates began taking business away from depository institutions. Since 1980, the combined influence of technological advancement and statutory revision has substantially increased the flexibility allowed to financial institutions and consumers, and the market for savings deposits has become extremely competitive.

In 1982, the Depository Institutions Act provided a wide variety of new and expanded powers for banks and other depository institutions. The act enabled banks to establish deposit accounts "directly equivalent to and competitive with money market and mutual funds." The new accounts carry no maximum interest rate and modest minimum-balance requirements. The changes had powerful and almost instantaneous effects. By early 1984, less than 20 percent of time and savings deposits were in accounts subject to fixed rate ceilings, compared to about 60 percent at the beginning of 1980. Also, the shift of deposits from money-market mutual funds to commercial banks and savings institutions has been massive. The new law enabled depository institutions to compete head-on with money-market mutual funds.

The 1982 law also accelerated the elimination of the higher interest rates allowed thrift institutions, thus helping achieve the "level playing field" that commercial banks have been advocating. For an initial three-year period, interstate acquisitions of troubled financial institutions were authorized, including banks with assets of $500 million or more.

The deregulation in the early 1980s is commonly cited as a contributing cause of the thrift crisis and the ensuing S&L bailout. According to the Congressional Budget Office, the problem was not necessarily deregulation itself but its poor timing. Eliminating interest rate ceilings and permitting thrifts to invest in a wider range of assets was an appropriate response to the interest rate risk that accompanied wide swings in inflation and interest rates.

Unfortunately, government decision makers waited until the S&Ls were locked into low-yield, long-term mortgages and only then permitted them to charge market rates of interest for their deposits. This combination of forces—lending long-term at low interest rates and borrowing short-term often at high rates—was a recipe for financial disaster.[16] The need for the federal government to bail out the many failed S&Ls resulted from the role of the federal government as insurer of the deposits of these institutions. With a generous insurance ceiling of $100,000 per account, it was less costly for the government to take over the failed institution rather than directly making good on the deposit liability. The knowledge that the federal government had underlying responsibility created opportunities for S&L managers who were willing to take on extraordinary risks ("heads" they would be heroes, "tails" the taxpayer would wind up holding the bag).

As part of the thrift bailout process, in 1989 Congress passed the Financial Institutions Reform, Recovery, and Enforcement Act (FIRREA). That law changed many aspects of U.S. statutes governing the operation and regulation of financial institutions. FIRREA restricts the type and extent of activities in which S&Ls can engage, such as purchases of junk bonds and investments in nonresidential real estate. Also, S&Ls must meet higher capital standards than in the past and have loan loss reserves similar to those of commercial banks.

The degree of competition among financial institutions is far greater today than it was in the 1960s or even 1970s (see Table 8.2). Some of that change results from legislation. The pace of change also results from technological advances and institutional innovation. But the enhanced scope for marketplace competition is occurring in a political and economic climate that is more conducive and encouraging than in the past. That marketplace, moreover, is increasingly global.

As shown in Table 8.3, the major industrialized nations of Western Europe give much wider latitude to their depository institutions, especially in the fields of insurance and investment banking. In contrast, Japan follows the American example.

In the 1990s, Congress effectively eliminated one of the two statutes that restrict competition in financial markets, and enlightened (or at least less active) regulators reduced the effectiveness of the other. The Interstate Banking and Branching Efficiency Act of 1994 made the McFadden Act, which inhibited interstate banking, virtually irrelevant. Under the 1994 law, a bank holding company can acquire a bank in any state—so long as the holding company does not control 30 percent of the deposits in the state and it is judged to be adequately capitalized and managed. Also, its CRA record (the Community Reinvestment Act is described later) must pass review by the Federal Reserve Board. Acquisition of a failing bank need not meet these requirements.[17]

The second restrictive law, the Glass–Steagall Act (which erected a wall of separation between commercial and investment banking) remains on the books. However, financial institutions have found innovative ways around those restrictions. Through purchase and operation of commercial banks in certain states, brokerage houses can offer their customers deposit and withdrawal services. In turn, bank holding companies can offer their customers a variety of services, including purchase and storage of government bonds.

TABLE 8.2 Expansion of the Financial Services Industry

Products	Commercial Banks 1960s	1990s	Thrifts 1960s	1990s	Insurance Companies 1960s	1990s	Securities Firms 1960s	1990s
Checking accounts	X	X		X				X
Savings accounts	X	X	X	X		X		X
Time deposits	X	X	X	X		X		X
Installment loans	X	X		X		X		X
Business loans	X	X	X	X		X		X
Mortgage loans	X	X	X	X		X		
Credit cards		X		X		X		X
Insurance					X	X		X
Brokerage/ underwriting		X		X		X	X	X
Mutual funds						X	X	X
Real estate				X		X		X

TABLE 8.3 Limits on Service of Commercial Banks

Are banks allowed to provide these services?	Belgium	Canada	France	West Germany	Italy	Japan	Luxembourg	Netherlands	Switzerland	United Kingdom	United States
Insurance											
Brokerage	Y	N	Y	Y	N*	N	Y	Y	N	Y	N*
Underwriting	Y	N	N*	Y*	N*	N	Y	N	N	Y*	N
Equities											
Brokerage	Y	Y*	Y	Y	Y	N	Y	Y	Y	Y	Y
Underwriting	Y	Y*	Y	Y	Y	N	Y	Y	Y	Y*	N
Investment	Y	Y	Y	Y	Y	Y	Y	Y	Y	Y*	N
Other underwriting											
Government debt	Y	Y	Y	Y	Y	N	Y	Y	Y	Y*	Y
Private debt	Y	Y*	Y	Y	Y	N	Y	Y	Y	Y*	N
Mutual funds											
Brokerage	Y	Y	Y	Y	Y	N	Y	Y	Y	Y	N
Management	Y	Y*	Y	Y	Y	N	Y	Y	Y	Y	N
Real estate											
Brokerage	Y*	N	Y	Y	N	N	Y	Y	Y	Y	N*
Investment	Y	Y	Y	Y	Y	N	Y	Y	Y	Y	N
Other brokerage											
Government debt	Y	Y	Y	Y	Y	Y	Y	Y	Y	Y	Y
Private debt	Y	Y	Y	Y	Y	Y	Y	Y	Y	Y	Y

Note: N = No; N* = No, with exceptions; Y = Yes; Y* = Yes but not directly by the bank.

Source: American Bankers Association.

In 1990, J.P. Morgan, through a loophole, received permission to underwrite bonds and then stocks as long as they did not exceed 10 percent of its securities revenues. In 1996, the Federal Reserve Board increased the amounts of revenue that banks generally could obtain from securities operations from 10 to 25 percent. In the following year, several major commercial banks acquired investment banks that underwrite new issues of securities.

Rising Social Regulation

Despite the reduction of economic regulation, Congress has not relented in imposing social regulation on financial institutions. The Equal Credit Opportunity Act prohibits financial institutions from discriminating in granting credit on the basis of sex, race, religion, or marital status. The Home Mortgage Disclosure Act requires depository institutions to disclose where their mortgage and home-improvement loans have been made so that depositors and others can judge whether they are meeting the housing-related credit "needs" in the local community.

Other social regulation of banking and finance includes the Truth-in-Lending Act, the Fair Credit Billing Act, the Fair Credit Reporting Act, the Consumer Leasing Act, the Real Estate Settlement Procedures Act, and the Electronic Fund Transfer Act. These regulations extend from home-purchase closing costs to information on the cost of credit.

The Community Reinvestment Act (CRA) encourages banks and other institutions to help meet the credit needs in their respective communities. It is a legislative response to the complaints of low-income housing advocates that many lenders "red line"—draw a figurative line around a low-income neighborhood and stop or restrict lending to its residents and businesses, regardless of the merits of their individual credit applications.

The law requires the regulatory agencies to rate the performance of individual lenders in meeting the mandate of CRA and to take this performance into account when reviewing the lender's applications for expansions, acquisitions, or mergers. This provision gives community activists opportunity to negotiate with a bank that wants to avoid the delay that occurs when a proposed acquisition is challenged on CRA grounds.

The Interstate Banking and Branching Efficiency Act requires the CRA reviews to be conducted on a state-by-state basis, even if a bank has branches in several states. That provision effectively eliminates the practice of using out-of-state branches primarily for generating deposits. It also runs counter to the trend toward national banking by perpetuating the notion that depositors want their deposits to stay in their locality.

The Outlook

Much of the motivation for continuing government involvement in banking regulation derives from the government's exposure to the risk of loss resulting from its role in deposit insurance and the Federal Reserve's discount window. Simultaneously, however, banks have responded to technological innovation and intensive competition by branching out in the bundle of products and services they deliver. The multiproduct bank of the future is evolving through a combination of competition, consolidation, and relaxation of restrictions on bank powers.

An open question remains about whether it is desirable public policy for banks to own industrial corporations and other nonfinancial institutions—and vice versa. In any event, the notion of *firewalls* separating commercial banking from less traditional but permissible activities remains a topic for discussion within financial institutions and among regulators.

OTHER ECONOMIC DEREGULATION

In 1981, President Ronald Reagan decontrolled the prices of crude oil and refined petroleum products and removed government allocations of energy use. Contrary to much contemporary criticism, the subsequent trend of energy prices in the United States has been clearly downward. The real price of gasoline (adjusted for general inflation) fell 46 percent from decontrol in 1981 to 1996.

A comparison of a regulated and a deregulated oil industry can be made by contrasting conditions during the Arab oil embargo of the 1970s with the Gulf War of 1990. In both cases, a major disruption in world oil supplies occurred, but the effect of the Gulf War period—characterized by an absence of regulation—was far less. Although the retail price of gasoline initially rose in both cases, it continued rising in the earlier period, and long gasoline lines accompanied stringent price and allocation controls. In the more recent, unregulated experience, even while the Gulf War was raging, gasoline prices quickly started declining and soon returned to approximately the prewar level. With the market free to adjust supply and demand, there were no gas lines or production disruptions, in marked contrast to the earlier period.

In 1984, the Federal Communications Commission abolished its guidelines requiring television stations to present a minimum amount of news and public affairs programs and limiting the number of commercials they can air each hour. The agency also eliminated rules that required TV stations to keep public records of the programs they air and to determine the programming needs of the communities in which they operate. These changes mainly resulted in less paperwork because most stations provide more news and public affairs than the FCC required and fewer than the maximum number of commercials previously allowed.

BASIC TRENDS IN DEREGULATION

Table 8.4 shows the highlights of the deregulation movement since the late 1960s. It is evident that a great deal of the traditional economic regulatory apparatus has been cut back. In general, reduced regulation—ranging from outright deregulation to simplification and streamlining of rule making—has enabled the competitive process to work better. More people are traveling by air at lower real costs. Depositors in financial institutions are receiving higher returns on their money, as a greater variety of companies compete for their business. Long-distance telephone users are finding that greater competition has resulted in lower rates, while subsidies to local services have been reduced.

TABLE 8.4 Milestones in Economic Deregulation

1968	Telecommunications: U.S. Supreme Court in Carterfone decision permits non-AT&T equipment to be hooked to AT&T's system.
1969	Telecommunications: FCC allows MCI to connect long-distance network with local phone systems.
1975	Energy: Energy Policy and Conservation Act provides for decontrol of gasoline and petroleum products by 1981.
1978	Financial institutions: Financial Institutions Regulatory and Interest Rate Control Act establishes uniform reporting systems for banks, S&Ls, and credit unions.
1978	Energy: Natural Gas Policy Act provides for partial decontrol of natural gas by 1987.
1978	Transportation: Airline Deregulation Act gives carriers freedom to decide fares and routes and phases out CAB.
1980	Financial institutions: Depository Institutions Deregulation and Monetary Control Act phases out interest rate ceilings and permits S&Ls to offer interest-bearing checking accounts.
1980	Transportation: Staggers Rail Act enables railroads to adjust rates without government approval and enter into contracts with shippers.
1980	Transportation: Motor Carrier Act removes barriers for new entries and lets operators establish fares and routes with little ICC interference.
1982	Financial institutions: Garn-St. Germain Depository Institutions Act creates federally insured money-market accounts, allows S&Ls to make more commercial and consumer loans, and removes interest rate differential between banks and S&Ls.
1982	Transportation: Bus Regulatory Reform Act allows intercity bus companies to change routes and fares.
1984	Telecommunications: AT&T agrees to divest local operating companies as part of antitrust settlement with Justice Department.
1984	Transportation: Shipping Act permits individual companies to offer lower rates and better service than shipping conferences.
1994	Banking: Interstate Banking and Branching Efficiency Act permits more interstate branching.
1996	Transportation: Interstate Commerce Commission is abolished. Residual functions are transferred to new Surface Transportation Board.

Inevitably, the wrenching changes brought about by deregulation have generated counterpressures from interest groups that have lost government protection. Managers and workers of many deregulated firms have seen their pay and fringe benefits decline to the competitive norm. Some companies have been unable to survive in the new competitive environment and have gone bankrupt or have been acquired by stronger firms. All economic change involves transitional costs, which at first may even seem to outweigh the benefits. But the economy as a whole has benefited from the reduction of governmental interference with the competitive process.

Although generalities are always difficult to make, several types of effects on the competitive structures of the deregulated industries have emerged to date. First of all, the range of variability of performance among the companies in the deregulated industry increases.

Second, the most profitable products come under substantial price pressure. Competition grows most rapidly in those markets. In the brokerage industry, commission rates in the lucrative institutional segment fell 26 percent in the four months following deregulation. In the less profitable area of brokerage sales to individuals, rates decreased only 2 percent.

Third, the resulting industrywide profit squeeze forces personnel reductions and other cost-cutting efforts. These economizing activities occur in both small and large firms, in the latter case primarily to meet competition from new entrants. The pressures on costs tend to be greatest in established firms with higher labor costs than in new entrants into the industry.

Financial institutions have responded to rate deregulation by closing branch offices and reducing payrolls. In contrast, when the government limited the interest they could pay on deposits, banks tended to compete by providing greater convenience and other services.

On the positive side, two types of winners emerge from deregulation. The first category consists of companies that tend to serve national markets with a full line of products and services. For example, the brokerage firm Merrill Lynch took innovative steps prior to the various deregulation steps affecting financial institutions to position itself to expand into segments of the industry that it now was free to enter. Its cash-management account, which combines conventional banking and investment banking features, is a successful example of the melding of new technology and new markets. Both Delta Airlines and the Burlington Northern Railroad took steps prior to deregulation to position themselves for rapid geographic expansion. Heavy capitalization with relatively low debt-to-equity ratios gave them the flexibility to weather the profit squeeze.

The second category of winners under deregulation is low-cost producers that focus on a highly price-sensitive segment of the market. Some of the new entrants turn out to be the successful, low-cost producers—notably Southwest Airlines—although many of the undercapitalized enterprises stay small and unprofitable. Many established old-line firms are burdened with heavy cost structures built up during regulation, and such outlays are difficult to reduce quickly.

The major winners under deregulation are the customers of the previously regulated industry. In the case of freight hauling, company traffic and distribution managers now have a far greater array of carriers to choose from. They have access to an abundance of rate and service package plans not previously permitted by the ICC. Further, they can enter into long-term agreements with railroads or truckers with few restrictions. Alternatively, the shippers can rely on their own trucking operations via various types of leasing arrangements, even in coordination with other carriers.

Notes

1. John R. Meyer, et al., *The Economics of Competition in the Transportation Industries* (Cambridge: Harvard University Press, 1959).
2. George W. Douglas and James C. Miller III, *Economic Regulation of Domestic Air Transport* (Washington, DC: Brookings Institution, 1974); Thomas Gale Moore, *Freight Transportation Regulation* (Washington, DC: American Enterprise Institute, 1972).

3. Marver Bernstein, *Regulating Business by Independent Commission* (Princeton: Princeton University Press, 1955).

4. George J. Stigler, "The Theory of Economic Regulation," *Bell Journal of Economics and Management Science,* Spring 1971, pp. 3–21; Sam Peltzman, "Towards a More General Theory of Regulation," *Journal of Law and Economics,* August 1976, pp. 211–240.

5. Murray L. Weidenbaum, *Government Mandated Price Increases* (Washington, DC: American Enterprise Institute, 1975); Sam Peltzman, *Regulation of Pharmaceutical Innovation* (Washington, DC: American Enterprise Institute, 1974); John P. Gould, *The Davis-Bacon Act* (Washington, DC: American Enterprise Institute, 1971); Rita Ricardo-Campbell, *Food Safety and Regulation* (Washington, DC: American Enterprise Institute, 1974).

6. John H. Anderson, Jr., *Airline Deregulation* (Washington, DC: U.S. General Accounting Office, 1997), p. 1.

7. Ibid. For a more optimistic view, see Steven A. Morrison and Clifford Winston, "The Fare Skies," *Brookings Review,* Fall 1997, p. 43.

8. Clifford Winston and Steven Morrison, *The Evolution of the Airline Industry* (Washington, DC: Brookings Institution, 1996).

9. See Richard B. Mckenzie, *Airline Deregulation and Air-Travel Safety* (St. Louis: Washington University, Center for the Study of American Business, 1991); *Airline Deregulation* (Washington, DC: U.S. General Accounting Office, 1996).

10. E. Han Kim and Vijay Singal, "Mergers and Market Power: Evidence from the Airline Industry," *American Economic Review,* June 1993, pp. 549–569.

11. *Airline Competition* (Washington, DC: U.S. General Accounting Office, 1993), p. 2.

12. Council on Competitiveness, *Legacy of Regulatory Reform* (Washington, DC: U.S. Government Printing Office, 1992), p. 19; *Economic Report of the President, 1997* (Washington, DC: U.S. Government Printing Office, 1997), p. 190.

13. *Railroad Regulation: Economic and Financial Impacts of the Staggers Rail Act of 1980* (Washington, DC: General Accounting Office, 1990); *Economic Report of the President, 1997,* p. 190.

14. This section draws on Robert W. Crandall, "Are We Deregulating Telephone Services?", *Brookings Institution Policy Brief,* March 1997, pp. 1–11.

15. Robert W. Crandall, "Waves of the Future," *Brookings Institution Review,* Winter 1996, p. 29.

16. *Resolving the Thrift Crisis* (Washington, DC: Congressional Budget Office, 1993), p. 9.

17. "The Nation's New Interstate Banking Law," *Federal Reserve Bank of Philadelphia Business Review,* November/December 1994, p. 21.

CHAPTER 9

Reforming Government Regulation

O ver the years, the many proposals that have been made to improve the process of government regulation of business tend to be variations on a common theme. Some of the changes would have required legislative enactments; they have been slow in coming. Many others could be carried out by executive-branch authority; substantial progress has occurred in that way. In the aggregate, most of the proposals share a common approach: Governmental decision makers should examine the various impacts of regulatory programs before they issue new regulations. Requiring benefit–cost analyses before rules can be promulgated is the most frequent and ambitious reform proposed.

The advent of a professional literature on the impacts of regulation of business[1] has fueled a concern about improving the effectiveness and reducing the burden of the vast network of rules, prohibitions, and requirements that government imposes on the private sector.

EXECUTIVE BRANCH REFORM INITIATIVES

Ford to Clinton

Growing public awareness of the high costs of regulation has provided the impetus for the executive branch of the federal government to undertake important changes during the last five presidential administrations. President Gerald Ford instituted a requirement whereby federal agencies had to prepare "inflation impact" statements prior to issuing new regulations.[2] With modifications, this requirement continues.[3] President Jimmy Carter created a Regulatory Analysis Review Group (RARG), headed by the chairman of the Council of Economic Advisers, to review the economic impact of 10 to 20 proposed major regulations each year.

The knowledge that a proposed regulation would be reviewed by the RARG increased the regulatory agencies' awareness of costs and other economic impacts. But the extent to which the review procedure actually resulted in less costly regulation was difficult to judge. The Carter administration stressed that its requirements for a regulatory analysis should not be interpreted as subjecting rules to a benefit–cost test. It believed that requiring agencies to demonstrate mathematically that benefits outweigh costs would act as a straitjacket to inhibit new regulations.

The Reagan administration took a major step by formally requiring benefit–cost analysis in the regulatory development process, and this approach was continued by President George Bush. By executive order, President Reagan required that regulatory impact analyses (RIAs) be made an integral part of the process in which regulations are developed, instead of being mere after-the-fact justifications. The new policy statement created stronger White House oversight of regulatory activity through the Office of Management and Budget (OMB). Regulatory agencies under the president's jurisdiction were required to make their regulatory decisions according to benefit–cost and cost-effectiveness criteria, to the extent permitted by law.

Under the executive order, all proposed and final regulations had to be submitted to OMB for review at least 60 days prior to publication in the *Federal Register.* On occasion, OMB asked for further information before a rule was published, but its concurrence was not required. Regulatory agencies determined which of their new regulations were major and submitted regulatory impact analyses to OMB along with their proposals. An economic impact of $100 million a year was the designated threshold for determining whether a regulation was "major," although there were many exceptions.

The incoming Clinton administration rescinded the Reagan executive orders on regulatory review in early 1993. Nevertheless, regulatory reform continues to have a place in President Clinton's agenda. By Executive Order 12866, President Clinton reaffirmed OMB as the central agency charged with review of proposed regulations. However, the regulatory agencies only have to find that the benefits of the intended regulation "justify" its costs. OMB retains no formal power to hold up rule making or to require a demonstration that the benefits generated by a regulation exceed the costs imposed.

Clinton's executive order tells the agencies to do many sensible things in the process of drafting rules, including identifying alternative ways of meeting governmental objectives, considering benefits and costs, and using market-based alternatives and performance standards. (See the box "Economic Analysis of Federal Regulations.")

Agency compliance with the presidential directives is not universal. In the case of EPA, the largest regulatory agency, from April to September 1994 only 6 of 45 rules labeled *significant* contained a determination that the benefits justified the costs. Of the other 177 rules issued by the EPA during that period (including those not considered significant), none were supported by the determination that the benefits justified the costs.

In the aggregate, the federal rule making list has grown. The April 1997 version of the semiannual regulatory plan is a 1,466 page document. It takes all that space merely to list very short summaries of the multitude of regulatory actions the federal departments and agencies are working on, including 225 entries by the EPA alone.

Shortcomings and Accomplishments

On balance, all of the formal systems of review from Ford through Clinton have tried to convince the often reluctant officials of the federal regulatory agencies to analyze the implications of their rules before issuing them. That approach has been somewhat successful in getting regulators and their supporting interest groups to think about the costs and the benefits they impose on society.

Economic Analysis of Federal Regulations

According to the Office of Management and Budget, an economic analysis of federal regulations should contain the following elements:

1. *The need for the proposed action*
   a. Does the problem to be dealt with constitute a significant market failure?
   b. If not, is there another compelling need for it, such as concerns relating to income distribution or improving governmental processes?
   c. Or is the proposal the result of a statutory or judicial directive?

2. *An examination of alternative approaches*
   The analysis should show that the government agency has considered the most important alternative approaches to the problem and should provide the agency's reasoning for selecting the proposed regulatory change over such alternatives. The agency should consider:
   a. More performance-oriented standards for health, safety, and environmental regulations.
   b. Different requirements for different segments of the regulated population.
   c. Alternative levels of stringency.
   d. Other methods of ensuring compliance and other effective data for compliance.
   e. More market-oriented approaches, including relying on improved information to those affected.

3. *Analysis of benefits and costs*
   a. *General considerations:* Where benefit or cost estimates are heavily dependent on certain assumptions, those assumptions should be made explicit, and the effects of using alternative assumptions should be analyzed. Where benefits and costs occur in different time periods, they should be discounted to present values, the discount rate approximating the opportunity cost of capital (the before-tax rate of return to incremental private investment, an average of 7 percent in real terms).

   In choosing among mutually exclusive alternatives, benefit–cost ratios should be used with care. Selecting the alternative with the highest benefit–cost ratio may not identify the best alternative since an alternative with a lower benefit–cost ratio may have higher net benefits (the absolute difference between the benefits and the costs).
   b. *Benefit estimates:* The analysis should state the beneficial effects of the proposed regulatory change and its principal alternatives. It should include estimates in monetary terms of the present value of all potential real incremental benefits to society to the maximum extent possible. Benefits estimated in monetary terms should be expressed in constant undiscounted dollars. Other favorable effects should be presented and explained.

   There should be an explanation of the mechanism by which the proposed action is expected to yield the anticipated benefits. A schedule of monetized benefits should be included, showing the type of benefit and to whom and when it would accrue. The principle of "willingness-to-pay" captures the notion of opportunity cost by providing an aggregate measure of what individuals are willing to forego to enjoy a particular benefit. In expressing the benefit of reducing fatality risks, the analysis may estimate the value of life-years extended by the proposed regulation.

c. *Cost estimates:* The analysis should include estimates in monetary terms of the present value of all potential real incremental costs to society of the proposed regulatory change and its principal alternatives. Other costs should be presented and explained. Estimates of costs should be based on credible changes in technology over time, such as a slowing in the rate of innovation because of delays in the regulatory approval process.

Transfer payments from one group to another, such as taxes and insurance premiums, should not be included in the calculation of costs, but they nevertheless should be identified.

4. *Choosing the proposed regulatory action*
When an agency determines that a regulation is the best available method of achieving the regulatory objective, it shall design its regulations in the most cost-effective manner to achieve the regulatory objective. In doing so, the agency shall consider incentives for innovation, consistency, predictability, the costs of enforcement and compliance (to the government, regulated entities, and the public), flexibility, distributive impacts, and equity.

Source: U.S. Office of Management and Budget.

Nevertheless, some shortcomings of the regulatory review process have become increasingly apparent, although some of them have existed from the outset. The most serious of these is the inherently limited scope of executive branch review. The most critical part of the regulatory process occurs when Congress writes and enacts the statutes under which the regulatory agencies operate. That crucial legislative stage is exempt from any requirement to examine the potential impact or effectiveness of the proposed law.

Compounding the problem, many regulatory statutes, especially in the area of environment and job safety, prohibit or severely restrict any use of economic analysis in the executive branch's rule-making process. For example, the Supreme Court, in two related decisions, *Industrial Union Department, AFL-CIO* v. *American Petroleum Institute* (1980) and *American Textile Manufacturers Institute* v. *Donovan* (1981), undercut the role of cost-effective analysis in the development of regulations under OSHA.

Thus, it is often futile for any president to direct a regulatory agency to choose "the most cost-effective approach." This is certainly the case, and frequently so, when the governing statute closely prescribes the specific actions to be taken, which may be far from the most cost-effective approach.[4]

Another shortcoming of the regulatory review process is that the various independent regulatory agencies are exempt from any presidentially mandated regulatory review process, although they may voluntarily choose to follow some of the procedures. This limitation means that large agencies of the regulatory establishment are beyond the purview of reform efforts, namely the Federal Communications Commission, the Federal Energy Regulatory Commission, the Federal Trade Commission, the International Trade Commission, the National Labor Relations Board, the Nuclear Regulatory Commission, the Securities and Exchange Commission, and the Federal Reserve Board.

Concern about the cost of regulation has resulted in the introduction in Congress of hundreds of bills on the subject. These proposed laws cover a wide variety of approaches, ranging from mandating economic impact statements for proposed regulations to giving Congress a veto over individual agency rulings. Several key alternatives, not necessarily mutually exclusive, have received the bulk of the attention in legislative hearings to date.

OPPORTUNITIES FOR REFORM

General Policy Guidelines

In taking up the task of statutory revision, Congress could consider some general guidelines for regulatory policy. The following 10 pointers are not a recipe for deregulation but rather an effort to attain more effective and efficient rule making by government in both the legislative and executive branches.

1. Regulations should be issued only on reasonable evidence that their potential benefits exceed their potential costs. Regulatory objectives, and the methods for achieving these objectives, should be chosen to maximize the net benefits to society.

2. Regulation of prices and production in competitive markets should be avoided. Entry into private markets should be regulated only where necessary to health or safety or to manage public resources efficiently.

3. Federal regulations should not prescribe uniform quality standards for private goods or services, except where these products are needlessly unsafe or product variations are wasteful and where voluntary private standards have failed to correct the problem.

4. Regulations that seek to reduce health or safety risk should be based on scientific risk-assessment procedures. They should address risks that are real and significant rather than hypothetical or remote.

5. Health, safety, and environmental regulations should address ends rather than means.

6. Licensing and permitting decisions and reviews of new products should be made swiftly and should be based on standards that are clearly defined in advance.

7. Qualifications for receiving government licenses should be the minimum necessary. Where there are more qualified applications than available licenses, the licenses should be allocated by auction or random lottery rather than by administrative procedures.

8. Where regulations create private rights or obligations, unrestricted exchange of these rights or obligations should be encouraged.

9. Federal regulations should not preempt state laws or regulations, except to guarantee rights of national citizenship or to avoid significant burden on interstate commerce.

10. Regulations establishing terms or conditions of federal grants, contracts, or financial assistance should be limited to the minimum necessary to achieve the purposes for which the funds were authorized and appropriated.

Economic Analysis

The most popular proposal to reform the process of issuing government regulations is to establish by statute a formal requirement for providing an economic analysis of the proposal. The institution by executive order of economic impact statements for new regulations is an important and useful innovation, but that approach has basic limitations. As noted earlier, the *independent* regulatory commissions, such as the FCC (in contrast to the cabinet departments and operating agencies), are not subject to presidential review on regulatory matters. Moreover, the courts have held that many regulatory agencies (FDA and OSHA, for example) are prohibited or limited by their legislative charters in weighing economic factors in their decision making. A general law passed by Congress requiring each government agency to perform economic analyses of its regulations before issuing them might overcome such objections. Several variations of this idea have been introduced, but none has been enacted.

Under some legislative proposals, the government official responsible for issuing a proposed rule also would be charged with preparing a statement analyzing many of its impacts, including (1) cost to consumers and business; (2) effects on employment, productivity, competition, and supplies of important products; and (3) alternatives, including an explanation of why they were rejected. Such requirements for merely analyzing the impacts of regulation constitute the mildest reform approach.

Specifying the weight given to economic factors in agency decision making presents another opportunity for reform. After all, a reluctant agency can merely go through the motions of studying the effects of its actions on the economy and proceed as it originally intended. To deal with this concern, proposals have been made to codify the formal benefit–cost analysis that has been required through executive order (which can be changed by any successor).

Formal benefit–cost tests with numerical measurements of the advantages and disadvantages represent a logical follow-through. Thus, regulation could be carried to the point where the added costs equaled the benefits, and no further. Overregulation (regulation for which the incremental costs exceed the benefits) would be avoided. But the actual implementation of this approach involves difficult conceptual and measurement questions. There is a natural tendency for a government agency, or any other organization, to be generous in estimating the good that it does (the benefits) and to deprecate the magnitude of the resources required to achieve those results (the costs).

In recent years, Congress has considered, but not enacted, legislation to require regulatory agencies to perform detailed assessments of costs and benefits. In 1995, the proposed Comprehensive Regulatory Reform Act was passed in the House of Representatives but failed in the Senate by one vote. This proposal would have required each regulatory agency to show a comprehensive benefit–cost analysis prior to issuing a new rule. Although the detailed requirements for demonstrating that benefits exceeded costs would have slowed down the issuance of new regulations, they also would have made it more difficult to simplify or eliminate existing ones.

By requiring detailed benefit–cost analyses to be prepared for any regulation imposing $25 million or more of annual costs, the proposed statutory could have swamped the regulatory review effort in paperwork. Moreover, it is not likely that the federal agencies possess sufficient analytical capacity to perform the multitude of analyses that would have to be undertaken. Some of the critics raised the issue: would all of the required benefit–cost analysis pass a benefit–cost test?

A Regulatory Budget

The appropriations for the regulatory agencies are relatively small portions of the government's budget; the totals for 53 federal regulatory agencies in fiscal year 1998 came to less than 1 percent of all federal outlays. As a result, limited attention is given to regulatory expenses during the budget preparation and review process. One reform approach is to give each regulatory agency a "budget" of private compliance costs that it can impose by its regulations. Not only would an agency be given $X million for operating costs, it would be given a ceiling of $Y billion of social costs that it could generate during the same year. Under the regulatory budget concept, Congress would be focusing on the *total* costs involved in the process of government regulation.

A regulatory budget can be viewed from three different perspectives: as an information mechanism, a policy-management device, or a method of expenditure control. As an information mechanism, a regulatory budget would require statistical reporting of regulatory outlays and the compilation of a regulatory database that would be similar to the existing national income and product accounts. This activity would be carried out independent of the policy process.

Alternatively, a regulatory budget could be a part of the policy-making process at the outset. Regulatory budget goals would be established as an important part of determining regulatory policy, but not as absolute ceilings.

A third approach would be to establish a regulatory budget process analogous to the existing fiscal budget process. This would involve preparation of the regulatory budget under the supervision of the president, review by Congress, and implementation by the Office of Management and Budget. Because regulatory budget ceilings would be enforced, the regulatory budget process would become a key control over policy.

Sunset Laws

Many government programs tend to prolong their existence far beyond their initial need and justification. Under the sunset approach, Congress would periodically review each regulatory agency to determine whether its continuation was worthwhile in light of present circumstances. This procedure would provide Congress with a formal opportunity to revise the underlying regulatory statutes or to determine that a given agency is no longer needed and that the "sun" should be allowed to "set" on it. Several states have enacted similar proposals, with uneven results to date. At the federal level, the sunset mechanism might be an effective way of pursuing a deregulation approach in the case of the older, one-industry regulatory agencies.

The sunset device is viewed by its proponents as an action-forcing mechanism because the prospect of termination of an agency's charter (in the absence of positive congressional action) would force needed reviews of existing regulatory programs. However, as some skeptics note, the impact of this reform may be less than intended. The reviews may be perfunctory, and the extension of popular regulatory legislation might even be the occasion for adding irrelevant or undesirable riders to the renewal statute.

Statutory Reform

The most significant legislative action in the regulatory reform area to date has been the Airline Deregulation Act of 1978, which provided for the Civil Aeronautics Board to go out of business. In contrast, none of the procedural reforms described earlier—economic analyses, regulatory budgets, or sunsetting—has been enacted by Congress.

The relative success of the CAB experience has drawn attention to the possibility of fundamentally revamping the statutory basis for individual regulatory agencies. Experience over the years confirms that the fundamental shortcomings of government regulation result more from statutory than from executive deficiencies.

Laws that mandate the pursuit of unrealistic goals or unreasonable methods for social regulation are attractive candidates for revision. In the case of the basic statutory approach underlying the regulation of job safety, for example, regulatory reform is not only a matter of achieving greater economic efficiency. To achieve a major improvement, it is necessary to shift to a regulatory regime that is more likely to achieve the intended goal of a safer workplace. Several fundamental revisions in the OSHA statute have been suggested:

1. Change the basic role of OSHA from that of a legal adversary, making inspections and insisting on compliance with complex detailed standards, to that of a safety leader. Such an organization should investigate new techniques in safety engineering, publish and disseminate information, and assist the safety departments of individual firms in solving their specific problems.
2. Make explicit what is "reasonable" and "feasible" by allowing decisions to be made on the basis of a comparison of the benefits to workers to the compliance costs. Such analyses should include the explicit costs of safety equipment and the implicit but substantial costs of the paperwork burdens of compliance.
3. Shift the basic orientation of enforcement from punishing employers if workers do not comply to a shared system of incentives, to encouraging cooperation and flexibility in responding to specific job-safety problems.

Reducing Regulatory Involvement

The CAB experience has also generated increased attention to the general notion of using alternatives to regulation for achieving public objectives. In the case of other traditional, one-industry types of regulation of business (such as by the FCC), a greater role could also be given to competition and to market forces. "Unregulated" markets are subject to the antitrust laws, a form of government intervention designed to maintain a workably competitive marketplace. As discussed in chapter 7, antitrust enforcement is a form of government regulation—but, unlike other regulations, it can be designed to foster the conditions of a competitive market rather than attempting to offset its defects.

Improved Information

In the area of consumer safety, as we have seen in chapter 3, a greater provision of information on potential hazards can be more effective than banning specific products or setting standards requiring expensive alterations in existing products. The information approach takes account of the great variety of consumer desires and capabilities. More

Views on Regulation of Cancer-Causing Chemicals
(Excerpt from a National Survey)

We are surveying public reaction to four different kinds of chemicals that studies have shown to cause cancer in some people. Please tell us which one of the four approaches you think the federal government should take:

	Percent of Respondents			
Chemical	*Ban*	*Warning Label*	*Do Not Regulate*	*No Opinion*
Used to preserve food like bacon (nitrites)	33%	57%	5%	5%
Used as an ingredient in some hair dyes	31	60	3	6
Saccharin	16	66	12	7
Used to color food like hot dogs and soft drinks (red dye #2)	47	44	4	5

Source: From 1980 survey sponsored by Council for Environmental Quality and Environmental Protection Agency.

widespread dissemination of data on product-associated accidents, for example, might encourage firms to devote more attention to safety in the design of the goods they sell. (See the box "Views on Regulation of Cancer-Causing Chemicals" for an indication of consumer support for this approach.) A similar approach might be taken in the case of disseminating data on factory accident statistics in an effort to promote safer workplaces.

Although mandatory disclosure is a form of regulation, it may be viewed at least in part as a preferable alternative mechanism because it neither interferes with the production process nor restricts individual choice. The greater flow of information may also be seen as an effort to achieve a more competitive economy. However, as noted in earlier chapters, when the government sets the standards for information rather than relying on competitive forces, many inefficiencies can result, such as overloading the consumer with unusable details.

Market Incentives

Through its taxing authority, government can send strong signals to the market. Pollution-control taxation may provide a more effective and less costly mechanism than the existing standards approach in achieving desired ecological objectives. As noted in chapter 4, such taxes, by increasing the prices of highly polluting means of production and consumption, could encourage shifts to more ecologically sound production and consumption patterns. The basic approach, then, would be to reduce the incentive to pollute—on the assumption that people and companies alike pollute when it is easier or cheaper to do so. Price incentives tend to force the environmental agencies to explicitly consider the cost of cleaning up pollution, whereas direct controls make it very easy to adopt extremely expensive and unrealistic goals (such as zero pollution).

Fees for discharging effluents into bodies of water would encourage the most extensive efforts to improve pollution abatement by those who can do so at relatively low cost and who would thereby avoid paying the fees. Less antipollution effort would be made by those for whom the costs of reducing pollution would be greater than the required fees. Standards, in contrast, do not make such distinctions. By virtue of their uniformity, standards result in higher costs of attaining the same total environmental cleanup. Perhaps the greatest virtue of pollution taxation, in lieu of rigid standards, is the ability to provide incentives for behaving in a socially desirable fashion without freezing technology or eliminating individual choice. Incentives using the price system always reward additional reductions in pollution. The less the firm discharges, the lower its tax bill. This continuing incentive to find more effective ways to reduce pollution is absent once a company meets the detailed standards in the conventional approach. (See the box "Limits to the Use of Economic Incentives.")

Judicial Responses

Yet another alternative to detailed regulation is to rely on the courts more heavily for handling individual claims. In such cases as product hazards, job accidents, and environmental pollution (where risks may not be well known), scholars have suggested changes in tort law that would encourage the production of safer products or the greater use of pollution-free processes. The notion behind these proposals is to increase the risk of liability, and thus the cost, for those firms that can most readily reduce the risks of accidents or the level of pollution. However, in the case of some hazards, the costs of using the courts can be high, and the deterrent effect may not be sufficiently great to obviate the need for standards or other regulatory approaches.

Clearly, there are many ways of responding to the concerns that give rise to government regulation of business. Given the great variety of areas subject to regulation and the multiplicity of regulatory devices that are used, it is unlikely that any single set of reforms will eliminate the shortcomings of the status quo. There does, surely,

---

Limits to the Use of Economic Incentives

A town was once plagued by an alarming growth in the number of rats, which ate crops and bit people while they slept and generally made life unpleasant. The town council, in desperation, decided on strong measures to cut down the rat population. The town would pay a bounty of so many dollars for each dead rat brought in to the town pound. At first, this measure, though costly, seemed very successful. There was a gratifying decline in the rat population. After several months, however, the town treasurer noticed a striking increase in the disbursements for dead rats. He quietly started an investigation to determine where they were coming from. To his dismay, he discovered that some of the more enterprising citizens had taken to raising rats—and had found it most profitable.

Source: A mythical tale.

seem to be a useful role for more formal analysis of regulatory impacts to provide an ancillary guide to policy makers in this area. The next section presents an introduction to such economic analysis.

BENEFIT–COST ANALYSIS

The motive for incorporating benefit–cost analysis into public decision making is to lead to a more efficient allocation of government resources by subjecting the public sector to the same types of quantitative constraints as those in the private sector. In making an investment decision, for example, business executives compare the total costs to be incurred with the total revenues expected to accrue. If the expected costs exceed the revenues, the investment is usually not considered worthwhile. To be sure, capital constraints require a further sorting to determine the most financially attractive investments.

The government-agency decision maker, however, usually does not face such constraints. If the costs to society of an action by an agency exceed the benefits, that situation has no immediate adverse impact on the agency, as would be the case if the private business executive makes a bad investment decision. In fact, such analytical information rarely exists in the public sector, so that, more often than not, the government decision maker is not aware that he or she is approving a regulation that is economically inefficient. In requiring agencies to perform benefit–cost analysis, the aim is to make the government's decision-making process more effective, eliminating those regulatory actions for which net benefits are negative. This result is not ensured by benefit–cost analysis, as political and other important but nonquantifiable considerations may dominate, resulting in actions that are not economically efficient but that are desired on grounds of equity or income distribution. Yet benefit–cost analysis can provide valuable information for government decision makers.

Such a comprehensive analytical approach also helps counterbalance the strong attraction toward regulatory activity on the part of government agencies and their supporters, who can crow about the benefits and ignore the costs—because the costs are transmitted to the consumer, not by the government in the form of higher taxes but by businesses as prices rise to reflect the growing costs of complying with government mandates. In fact, regulatory activists can have some fun needling business about price increases even when they result from the costs of complying with the regulations proposed by those activists themselves.

The Economic Rationale

It may be useful to briefly consider the economic rationale for making benefit–cost analyses of government actions. Such analyses have been used for decades in examining government spending programs. Thus, benefit–cost reviews are neither a revolutionary idea nor an invention of the far right. Measurement of benefits and costs of government activities has been attacked by both ends of the political spectrum—by the far left because not every proposal for government intervention passes a benefit–cost test, and by the far right, who oppose it because this approach can be used to justify government intervention when the likely benefits exceed the expected costs. No analytical approach is totally value-free, but benefit–cost analysis has less ideological baggage than most alternatives.

Economists have long been interested in identifying policies that promote economic welfare, specifically by improving the efficiency with which a society uses its resources. This assumes, of course, that an increase in economic welfare will raise total welfare and that theoretical problems such as making interpersonal utility comparisons will be ignored.

Benefits are measured in terms of the increased production of goods and services. Costs are computed in terms of the foregone benefits that would have been obtained by using those resources in some other activity. The underlying aim of benefit–cost analysis, therefore, is to maximize the real value of the national output (GDP). For many years, benefit–cost analysis has been applied by federal spending agencies, such as the Corps of Engineers and the Bureau of Reclamation, to evaluate prospective projects.

Despite important operational difficulties, including choosing an appropriate discount rate that corresponds to a realistic estimate of the social cost of capital, over time these analyses have helped improve the allocation of government resources. They have served as a partial screening device to eliminate obviously uneconomical projects—those for which prospective gains are less than estimated costs. The analyses have also provided some basis for ranking and comparing projects and choosing among alternatives. Perhaps the overriding value has been in demonstrating the importance of making relatively objective evaluations of essentially political actions and narrowing the area in which political forces dominate. Thus, if economically inefficient programs are adopted, government decision makers at least know the price that is being paid for those actions.

Benefit–Cost Analysis of Regulation

Figure 9.1 shows the basic relationship between costs and benefits that tends to exist for most varieties of regulatory programs. Typically, the initial regulatory effort, such as cleaning up the worst of the pollution in a river, generates an excess of benefits over costs. But the resources required to achieve additional cleanup become disproportionately high, and at some point the added benefits are substantially less than the added costs. For example, a study of the impact of environmental controls on the fruit and vegetable processing industry revealed that it costs less to eliminate the first 85 percent of the pollution created than the next 10 percent.[5] Similarly, in sugar beet plants, it costs less than $1 a pound to reduce BOD (biochemical oxygen demand—a measure of the oxygen required to decompose organic wastes) up to 30 percent. But it costs an additional $20 for a one-pound reduction at the 65 percent control level and an added $60 for a one-pound reduction when more than 95 percent control is achieved.[6]

A more aggregate comparison is equally telling. The pulp and paper industry spent $3 billion complying with federal clean-water standards to achieve a 95 percent reduction in pollution. But to reach 98 percent would have cost a further $4.8 billion, a 160 percent increase in costs to achieve a 3 percent improvement in water quality. Thus, it is important to look beyond the relationship of the total costs and the total

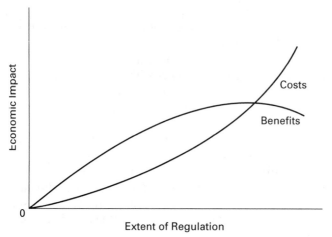

FIGURE 9.1 Benefit–Cost Analysis of Regulation

benefits of a proposed undertaking to the additional (marginal) benefits and costs that would result from each extension or addition to the activities in a given field.

Ultimately, if regulatory power goes unchecked, the result could tend to be an excess of total costs over total benefits. Thus, performing benefit–cost analysis can be helpful in identifying the optimum amount of regulation, rather than merely being a tool for debating the general pros and cons.

When there is more than one alternative for attaining a regulatory goal, benefit–cost analysis can also be used to compare the various methods and to help choose the most attractive one. Consider the following hypothetical example. Suppose a government agency wishes to control the amount of pollutants a factory is spilling into a river. Assume present technology allows for two possible means of reducing the pollution, system A and system B, of which system B is costlier (see Table 9.1).

System B, in this example, has greater benefits per dollar spent than system A. Despite the fact that system B has a larger total annual cost than system A, we see that system B will yield the larger annual net benefit to society (a larger benefit-to-cost ratio). Thus, the layperson's impression that economic analysis seeks the least expensive alternative is inaccurate. Rather, the purpose of these evaluations is to identify the most efficient ways of meeting regulatory goals.

TABLE 9.1 Applying Benefit–Cost Analysis

System	Total Annual Cost	Total Annual Benefit	Benefit–Cost Ratio
A	$14,000	$17,500	1.25
B	26,000	34,000	1.31

If a business decision in the private sector places an external burden, such as pollution, on its neighbors, the individual firm does not include such a cost in its accounting because it does not bear the burden. Public-sector decision makers, however, must, or least ought to, consider the effects of their decisions on the entire society. Unlike their private-sector counterparts, regulators should attempt to include all costs and benefits, including those external to the government itself.

The agencies should do so because any regulatory action will have indirect effects on the economy. Requiring safety belts in automobiles has direct impacts on the cost of automobiles and on the safety-belt industry. But it will also influence the number of accidents, have a ripple effect on the suppliers of the safety-belt industry and their suppliers, and so on. At some point in the benefit–cost analysis, good judgment must be relied upon in deciding which indirect effects are important and which are not.

Quantification

In general terms, the benefits and costs attributable to regulation are measured by the difference between the benefits and costs that occur in the presence of regulation and those that would prevail in its absence. Although the basic idea may seem quite straightforward, its application can be complex. Determining what would occur in the absence of regulation—which establishes a benchmark or reference point for the calculations—may involve a considerable amount of judgment.

Table 9.2 shows how the incremental costs (the expenses that would not have been made in the absence of regulation) were computed in one study of water pollution

TABLE 9.2 Calculation of Incremental Cost of Regulation

Steps	Example
Company identifies an action taken to comply with a specific regulation.	Installation of wastewater pretreatment system to remove 99 percent of pollution in compliance with the Clean Water Act
Would action have been taken otherwise?	Pretreatment system (without regulation) would have been designed to remove 95 percent of pollutants
What was the cost of the action?	$1.2 million (from fixed-asset ledger data)
How much would the action that would have been taken in the absence of regulation have cost?	$800,000 (the cost of installing a 95 percent system)
What was the incremental cost?	$1,200,000 − $800,000 = $400,000

Source: Arthur Andersen & Company.

control. It is interesting to note that the bulk of the costs apparently would have been undertaken voluntarily.

It is useful to examine an actual benefit–cost analysis of regulatory activity. Table 9.3 presents the highlights of such an analysis of the Coast Guard's enforcement of its oil-spill-prevention program. A few points stand out. The bulk of the costs are "off budget," in the form of business compliance with government regulation. The benefits are, in effect, costs avoided. The benefit–cost ratio is clearly positive: It cost society $5.1 million a year in regulatory actions designed to prevent oil spills; the cleanup costs averted are $6.0 million, approximately 20 percent higher.

Sometimes the indirect effects of regulation are as important as the direct. Consider, for example, the question of mandatory standards to ensure the production of less hazardous consumer products. Suggestions have been made from time to time to require more protection in helmets and other equipment used in playing football. Those players using the safer helmets would be expected to receive the benefits of fewer or less severe injuries. However, such a safety standard could impose substantial costs on lower-income young people. Perhaps of greater concern, the standards might even contribute to more injuries if the price increases resulted in more youngsters playing football without any protective equipment at all. This example illustrates another basic thrust of benefit–cost analysis: to view the proposed government action not from the viewpoint of the initial impact on the business firm but from the vantage point of the ultimate effects on the consumer.

When it is not appropriate or practical to put a dollar sign on the benefits, the analyst can use a cost-effectiveness approach rather than a cost–benefit analysis. This methodology estimates the dollar cost of a variety of alternative ways of accomplish-

TABLE 9.3 Benefit–Cost Analysis of Coast Guard Regulation of Oil Spills

Benefits	
Cleanup costs avoided	$1,510,000
Market price of oil saved	985,400
Reduced environmental damages	3,478,000
Total benefits	$5,973,400

Costs	
Coast Guard enforcement	$1,750,000
Industry prevention measures	2,558,000
Industry time spent on inspections	776,000
Total costs	$5,084,000

Ratio of benefits to costs	1.2

Note: Adapted from Mark A. Cohen, "The Costs and Benefits of Oil Spill Prevention and Enforcement," *Journal of Environmental Economics and Management,* June 1986, pp. 167–188.

ing a given objective. Cost-effectiveness analyses permit policy makers to identify least-cost solutions. In this more limited approach, the analyst takes the objective as something worth accomplishing in the first place. In the regulatory field, this approach may be most useful in dealing with programs to reduce personal hazards. Rather than dealing with such imponderables as the value of a human life, the emphasis shifts to identifying those regulatory approaches that will maximize the lives saved or pain avoided from a given dollar outlay. Rather than a "green eyeshade" approach, such attempts at objective analysis, it is contended, show true compassion for our fellow human beings by making the most effective use of the limited resources available to society.

Discounting

A regulatory action today has an impact not only in the present but also in the future. It is necessary, therefore, to value future costs and benefits less than costs and benefits immediately available — the basic notion being that a dollar today is worth more than a dollar tomorrow. For this reason, we discount the value of future benefits and costs. That is, we modify their monetary value so that they have less weight in our current decision making than immediately received benefits and costs.

This practice is important in evaluating regulatory actions. An example would be two alternatives, each showing total benefits equal to total costs. If the benefits in one case are achieved far off in the future and, in the other case, right away, the preferred alternative is the one in which benefits occur immediately. We value this action more because the value of a benefit occurring in the future is less than the value of the same benefit today. Discounting the future thus implies that the timing of any action's costs and benefits is crucial in its evaluation.

Assuming we are able to quantify all the costs and benefits in a given instance, it is then necessary to correctly discount the net benefits accruing in future periods. The correct discount rate (r) can be crucial, as is clear in the highly simplified, two-period example shown in Table 9.4.

If all costs accrue in period 1 and the discount rate is 10 percent, then clearly plan A is superior to plan B. However, if the correct discount rate is 5 percent, not 10 percent, then plan B is preferable. The appropriate discount rate is obviously very important in benefit–cost analysis. Such analyses can be biased if Congress or an agency designates an unrealistically low interest rate.

TABLE 9.4 The Role of Interest Rates

				Discounted Benefit in Period 1	
Plan	Benefit Period 1	Benefit Period 2	Cost Period 1	$r = 10\%$	$r = 5\%$
A	$200	0	$200	$200	$200
B	0	$215	$200	$195	$205

Benefit–Risk Analysis

In many cases, dollars are an inadequate or inappropriate measure of the impacts of government regulation. That does not necessarily mean there is no opportunity for analysis in the decision-making process. For example, the drug that cures Rocky Mountain spotted fever also causes fatal anemia in one out of every 10,000 people who use it. A simple-minded approach would prohibit the use of this "dangerous" drug. Yet the fever itself kills about 8 out of every 10 people who contract the disease. Thus, the benefits of the drug tend to greatly outweigh the risks.

A more forceful way of stating the matter is the plaintive statement by a prospective user of beta blockers developed for heart patients (at a time when they had not been approved for general use in the United States because tests on rodents revealed carcinogenicity): "I am over 50. I have had two coronary bypass operations. I have severe angina. I don't give a damn about what happens to the rats."[7]

A comparison of benefits and costs in these cases is not a matter of dollars and cents, but rather involves weighing the advantages of the cure versus the additional risk from the drug's side effects. In practice, this is an instance where the decision making is decentralized. No regulator in Washington rules on the matter. Rather, the individual patient and physician decide. (See the box "The Courts on Benefit–Risk Analysis" for a judicial opinion along these lines.)

Risk itself is not a uniform concept. People differ in their perception of risk and in their willingness to assume different types of risk. Many drivers and passengers do not put on their seat belts because the bother is greater than the risk of injury or death by accident that they voluntarily are willing to take. Some people place a higher personal evaluation on avoiding risks than do others. Thus, some consumers buy used cars or used lawn mowers because they are cheaper. Other consumers would rather do without the product or do without some other product in order to buy a new and safer version. Consciously or subconsciously, each of us makes a benefit–risk decision each time we cross a busy intersection. To cite the words of a federal court ruling on the Consumer Product Safety Act, "A sharp knife might pose a reasonable risk of injury, because dulling the blade to make it safe would also make it useless. A sharp knife in a child's silverware set, however, might be unreasonable."

To avoid the problems inherent in placing monetary values on human lives, benefit–cost analysis can be structured in terms of lives themselves. Sodium nitrite, which is used to preserve food, is a mild carcinogen. Its use creates the possibility that a limited number of people will incur cancer. On the other hand, a large number of people would die of botulism if nitrites were not used as a preservative in meat. A comparison of the costs and benefits of restricting the use of nitrites in meats indicates that more lives are saved by its continued use. This type of comparison was the basis for the federal government's decision not to ban nitrites in meat and, instead, merely to urge a lessening of their use.

A similar situation exists with asbestos, which can cause cancer in production workers but is also an important component in brake pads. If the standards for protecting workers were so severe as to stop asbestos production altogether, we might have a large increase in deaths due to inadequate brakes in automobiles. Therefore, the benefits from asbestos regulation in terms of workers' lives prolonged must be weighed against the number of individuals expected to die because of poor brakes.

The Courts on Benefit – Risk Analysis

In a decision on pharmaceutical products, the Appellate Division of the Superior Court of New Jersey upheld the notion of "unavoidably unsafe products." The pertinent language follows:

> There are some products which, in the present state of human knowledge, are quite incapable of being made safe for their intended and ordinary use. These are especially common in the field of drugs. An outstanding example is the vaccine for the Pasteur treatment of rabies, which not uncommonly leads to very serious and damaging consequences when it is injected. Since the disease itself invariably leads to a dreadful death, both the marketing and the use of the vaccine are fully justified, notwithstanding the avoidable high degree of risk which they involve. Such a product, properly prepared, and accompanied by proper directions and warning, is not defective, nor is it unreasonably dangerous. The same is true of many other drugs, vaccines, and the like, many of which for this very reason cannot legally be sold except to physicians, or under the prescriptions of a physician.

Source: Carol Ann Feldman et al v. *Lederle Laboratories and American Cyanamid Company,* Superior Court of New Jersey, Appellate Division, A-4428-79T1, May 10, 1983.

Public policy in both cases—nitrites and asbestos—would lead to attempts to reduce exposures to carcinogenic hazards, but within some rule of reason.

Moreover, we can compare the cost of saving lives through different mechanisms. It has been estimated that dialysis treatment costs $270,000 per life saved, whereas OSHA's coke-oven emissions standards cost about $5 million per life saved. It is institutional barriers that prevent an obvious reallocation of resources to the more cost-effective activity.[8] It is much easier to assess the coke-oven costs on business than to finance the dialysis treatment out of taxpayers' contributions to the Treasury. (See the box "What Is an Acceptable Risk?")

Uses and Limitations of Benefit-Cost Analysis

Reliable measures of costs and benefits are not easily specified. Quantification is not always possible. Should the loss of a forest be measured by the value of the timber eliminated? What of the beauty destroyed? What of the area's value as a wildlife habitat? Given such questions, agency decision makers are not faced with simple choices.

The quantification problem is further complicated by a lack of information. The adverse impact of some products on health is often uncertain. Dioxin, for instance, has only recently been found to be a cancer-causing agent, and—despite a great deal of publicity and public concern—the extent of any damage actually caused by the use of this material is at this time not discernible. It is often the case that both total costs and total benefits will contain some nonquantifiable variables, leaving much opportunity for political value judgments.

However, the difficulties involved in estimating the benefits or the costs of regulatory actions need not necessarily serve as a deterrent to pursuing the analysis.

What Is an Acceptable Risk?

According to Milton Russell, former Assistant Administrator of EPA, there are more toxins—natural, and synthetic—than we can ever hope to eliminate. He offers the following explanation:

In a world of limited resources, removing every toxic substance would lead to chasing ever smaller quantities of a pollutant at exponentially rising expenditures of labor, dollars, and scientific and engineering talent. A brute fact should be engraved on our consciousness: given finite resources, when we choose to reduce one toxin, we also choose to tolerate another. Even where we concentrate on one toxin—whether it be PCB or dioxin or whatever—we cannot expect to achieve perfection.

We need a stopping point, at which we will agree that we have cleaned up far enough in a given case, and it is time to turn to another. What is the basis for stopping? It has little to do with the specific toxin or its concentration and much to do with the risk it poses to people and the environment.

If our goal is not purity, or even neatness for its own sake, we must identify risk and reduce it to the point at which it becomes acceptable to our society—thus, the concept of *acceptable risk.* The difficulty of this question for a public policy maker is that it is not scientific, technical, or administrative in nature. To answer it, we must ask ourselves what kind of society we really want.

The American people want a safe and healthy environment, but they also want a strong national defense, first-rate transportation, better and cheaper medical care, good homes, labor-saving appliances, a varied diet, and entertainment. Those who uphold the environment as a primary value compete daily with the advocates of these other worthy objectives.

So what is acceptable risk? That question cannot be answered in any absolute sense. It is a relative thing. It is a function of private ethics and public choice. If that seems little enough to go on, it nevertheless seems to be the best we have.

Note: Adapted from a speech by Milton Russell, then Assistant Administrator of the EPA, to the Texas Water Pollution Control Association, February 14, 1986.

Merely identifying some of the important and often overlooked impacts can be useful. Examples on the cost side include the beneficial drugs that are not available because of regulatory obstacles, the investments in new factories that are not made owing to stringent environmental requirements for new sources, and the radio and television stations that are not broadcasting because they could not be licensed. On the benefit side, examples range from the more productive workforce that results from a lower rate of accidents on the job to savings in medical care as a result of the safer products and healthier environment achieved from compliance with regulatory efforts.

At times the imperfections of benefit–cost analysis seem substantial. Nevertheless, this type of analysis can add some objectivity to the government's decision-making process. Although benefit–cost analysis can represent only efficiency considerations, the subsequent decisions of elected officials and their appointees might be envisioned as representing society's evaluations of the equity effects of regulatory actions. Economists can provide these decision makers with information via benefit–cost studies and analysis of the distributional impact of regulations, leaving the final decision to society's representatives. With such information, these individuals are better able to make objective decisions on the impacts of the actions they contemplate.

Despite its shortcomings, benefit–cost analysis is a neutral concept, giving equal weight to a dollar of benefits and a dollar of costs. After all, showing that a regulatory activity generates an excess of benefits is a strong justification for embarking upon it. But the painful knowledge that resources available to safeguard human lives are limited causes economists concern when they see wasteful use of those resources because of inefficient regulation.

Conclusions

At the heart of the benefit–cost, cost-effectiveness, and benefit–risk analyses is the proposition that the existence of finite resources requires society to set priorities. Ultimately, the type and degree of regulation that the business community and citizens will face depend more on perceptual and political concerns than on economic reasoning. Statistics are rarely compelling in terms of public perception and reaction. Nevertheless, it is important to continue to attempt to evaluate the factual basis for public discourse on such controversial areas as government regulation of business.

Notes

1. For recent examples, see Paul MacAvoy, *Industry Regulation and the Performance of the American Economy* (New York: W.W. Norton & Co., 1992); and Thomas Hopkins, *Regulatory Costs in Profile* (St. Louis: Washington University, Center for the Study of American Business, 1996).

2. Executive Order 11821, November 27, 1974.

3. Executive Order 12044, March 24, 1978 (President Carter); Executive Order 12291, February 17, 1981 (President Reagan); and Executive Order 12866, September 30, 1993 (President Clinton).

4. Murray Weidenbaum, "Regulatory Process Reform: From Ford to Clinton," *Regulation,* Winter 1997, pp. 20–26.

5. U.S. Congress, Joint Economic Committee, *The Economic Impact of Environmental Regulations* (Washington, DC: U.S. Government Printing Office, 1974), p. 203.

6. *Environmental Quality, Second Annual Report of the Council on Environmental Quality* (Washington, DC: U.S. Government Printing Office, 1971), p. 118.

7. Quoted in Murray L. Weidenbaum, *The Future of Business Regulation* (New York: Amacon, 1980), p. 137.

8. Thomas G. Marx, "Life, Liberty, and Cost–Benefit Analysis," *Policy Review,* Summer 1983, p. 53.

PART THREE

The Global Marketplace

To state that the modern business operates in a global marketplace is merely to acknowledge a phenomenon that is increasingly obvious. Of course, the international economy has been a fact of life since ancient times. What is new and different is the scale and scope of cross-border business activity and especially the impact of technology.

It took Marco Polo years to go to China and back. Today's business executive or tourist can fly the round trip in a matter of days. Information can flow across the globe in a fraction of a second.

In this light, Part III presents a global perspective on the external environment facing the American business firm. The government policies that influence the flow of international trade and investment are examined, as are the variety of business responses.

CHAPTER 10

Business and Government in the World Economy

Transportation and communication barriers between nations have fallen as technology has dramatically reduced the expense and time required to move people, goods, and information across borders. The cost of ocean freight has fallen from $95 a short ton in 1920 to $29 in 1990 (both estimates are in 1990 dollars). During the same period, the cost of air travel has dropped from 68 cents a passenger mile to 11 cents. Simultaneously, the cost of a 3-minute phone call from New York to London declined from $245 to $3.32. As a result, international trade has expanded much faster than domestic production. Between 1960 and 1990, world exports (in real terms) grew at an annual rate of 6.1 percent a year, while world output increased only 3.8 percent annually.

Yet the key changes in international relations have not been economic, although the economic ramifications are powerful. The world has witnessed not just the breakup of the Soviet Union, but also the reunification of Germany, the expansion of the European Union, the emergence of East Asia as an engine of global growth, and a widespread embrace of liberal political and economic ideals that transcends boundaries of geography and culture.

The structure of international relations in the decades after World War II provided a framework for thinking about the world and the U.S. role in it that was uncomplicated and precise. In the classic sense of the term, it provided a paradigm for policymakers and others interested in international affairs. With the end of the Cold War, that paradigm has lost its potency as a way to plan, evaluate, and predict the behavior of the United States and the other major actors on the international scene. The world is no longer bipolar. Political-military power is not now the most important measure of state power. National power itself is not so central a concern—economic affairs and national well-being have increased in importance. Many of these changes, of course, occurred before the collapse of the Soviet Union, and in some cases U.S. policy makers turned a blind eye to world developments because of a single-minded focus on the Communist threat.[1]

The roles of business and government in the world economy are undergoing fundamental shifts.[2] Following the end of the Cold War, the political and military rivalry between the United States and the Soviet Union was replaced initially by a three-way economic competition involving the United States, Germany, and Japan. But the post-Cold War world is witnessing the unfolding of a more complicated global marketplace than that triad. If government was the pace-setting player during the

Cold War, the business enterprise is now becoming the dominant influence in the global marketplace.

The resulting impact on individual business executives is pervasive. That can be seen by examining the employment want ads in one issue of England's *Daily Telegraph* (September 5, 1996). The following internationally related jobs were advertised, among many others:

1. General manager of a Singapore-based oil and gas contracting company.

2. Engineer for an industrial consulting firm operating in the United Kingdom, the United States, and Australia.

3. Purchasing manager of a manufacturing company to buy material across Europe.

4. Divisional marketing director of an environmental engineering company; to pursue global opportunities with a knowledge of German an advantage.

5. Technical director of a capital goods machinery producer selling to worldwide markets.

6. Project manager of Toshiba-Europe, responsible for Europe-wide projects.

7. Business development manager of a railroad equipment producer; need to know another European language, preferably French.

8. Accounts payable specialist with an auditing firm serving Europe, Asia, and North America.

9. Sales representative for the Marine Department of Bridgestone, serving the United Kingdom, Europe, the Middle East, and Africa.

10. Sales executive for a fiber optics producer selling in the United States, Canada, and South America.

11. Sales manager for an industrial products design and manufacturing company. Should be fluent in French and German.

12. European sales manager for ready-to-wear retailer; must be able to communicate in other European languages.

13. Sales engineer for a telecommunications company. French required.

14. Product support manager for a joint venture of BMW and Rolls Royce; knowledge of German an advantage.

15. Environment manager for an energy company in Qatar.

16. Purchasing director of a manufacturing company to deal with suppliers in Europe and Japan.

17. Regulatory affairs manager for a telecommunications company. Needs knowledge of European regulation.

18. Chief accountant of a paper products manufacturer exporting 80 percent of output and with a worldwide network of distributors.

A TRI-POLAR WORLD

The role of the nation-state is changing in important ways. It is true that three nations—Japan, Germany, and the United States—have become, at least for the present, the dominant economic powers. But the reality is far more complicated than that because of the rise of three key regional blocs: the European Community, the North American trading area, and East Asia.

North America and the Western Hemisphere

In 1994, the United States, Canada, and Mexico entered into a North American Free Trade Agreement (NAFTA), which is reducing barriers to commerce and business in North America. In the process, considerable potential is being generated for shifting people and other resources within the entire continent. From the viewpoint of the United States, the neighbor to the North, Canada, has long been the number one trading partner. Now Mexico, the neighbor to the South, is becoming the third largest market for American-produced goods and services (just behind Japan, the second largest economy in the world). The trend to regionalization is clear in the Western Hemisphere and, as we will see, elsewhere on the globe.

The creation of a North American free trade area could, after an extended period of adjustment, generate considerable benefit for the economies of all three nations. In the short run, some painful adjustments are visible. As shown in Table 10.1, during a recent 38-month period, approximately 118,000 U.S. workers were certified for aid under the NAFTA Transition Adjustment Assistance program—less than one-tenth of one percent of the nation's total labor force (or equal to the number of new jobs created in the United States every two weeks). With some fanfare, certain low-skilled, low-cost work has been moving to Mexico while, more quietly, some higher-tech business activity in Mexico no longer protected by trade barriers has begun to move northward. Overall, the changes resulting from more open trade are turning out to be much less than forecast by either the supporters or opponents of NAFTA. Specific impacts include the following:

1. By the year 2000, approximately 65 percent of all U.S. exports to Mexico will be free of import duties. When NAFTA entered into force in 1994, Mexico's tariffs dropped by 20 percent or more. One-half of U.S. farm exports to Mexico are now allowed to enter duty-free.

TABLE 10.1 NAFTA Transition Adjustment Assistance Program February 3, 1994, through April 4, 1997

Reasons for Certification	Certified Workers	Percent of Total
Shift in production to Mexico	51,908	44.1
Shift in production to Canada	10,086	8.5
Increased customer imports from Mexico	10,935	9.3
Increased customer imports from Canada	7,292	6.2
Increased customer imports not identified Canada/Mexico	17,262	14.6
Increased company imports from Mexico	10,192	8.6
Increased company imports from Canada	6,364	5.4
Increased company imports not identified Canada/Mexico	1,537	1.3
Increased aggregate U.S. imports from Canada/Mexico	2,417	2.0
Total	117,993	100.0

Source: U.S. Department of Labor.

2. Mexico is gradually eliminating its import licenses for a great variety of goods, including pharmaceutical products, tractors, computers, and industrial machinery.

3. U.S. and Canadian banks are now allowed to acquire Mexican banks, accounting for as much as 8 percent of the industry's capital. All limits on bank ownership will be removed by the year 2000.

4. Corporate executives and some professionals from all three countries are able to live and work anywhere in North America with fewer bureaucratic formalities.

5. All three countries treat each other's service firms no less favorably than local services companies. With few exceptions, U.S. firms may provide services in Mexico and Canada from locations in the United States.

The United States can expect that the growth of the Mexican economy encouraged by NAFTA will translate into benefits for the American economy through rising demand for U.S. goods. On average, for every $1 of income growth, Mexicans spend 14 cents on products made in the United States. Mexico purchases 70 percent of its imports from the United States.[3]

But focusing on the United States, Canada, and Mexico is too limited. Many nations in Latin America—especially Argentina, Brazil, and Chile—have begun to experience sustained economic growth and to increase their volume of trade with North American countries. The Western Hemisphere may become, at least in part, one major trading area in the early years of the twenty-first century.

The European Union

Across the Atlantic, with a minimum of fanfare, the European Union (EU) expanded from 12 member-nations to 15 when it took in Austria, Finland, and Sweden in 1995 (see Figure 10.1). With the elimination of most internal barriers to trade and investment, the European Union has become the world's largest marketplace. From the viewpoint of the United States, Western Europe now presents a high-income market for a wide range of advanced products and services. A few examples illustrate the potential for business cooperation:

- Models of Boeing commercial jet transports use engines made by the United Kingdom's Rolls-Royce, especially for European airlines. For its 777, Boeing entered into partnerships with Italy's Alenia to produce the outboard wing flaps and General Electric of Britain for the primary flight computers.

- Otis' elevator, the Elevonic 411, uses electronics designed by its Germany subsidiary, door systems made by its French branch, and small-geared components made by its Spanish division.

- Unisys is simultaneously a customer of and a supplier to Switzerland's BASF, the Netherlands' Philips, and Germany's Siemens—and also competes with each of these European electronics giants.

- Digital Equipment Corporation and Italy's Olivetti & Co. jointly fund and share the results from Olivetti's research laboratory in Cambridge, England.

- Pacific Telesis (now a part of SBC, a giant regional telephone company) is a 26 percent participant in a joint venture led by Mannesmann to provide mobile telephone service in Germany.

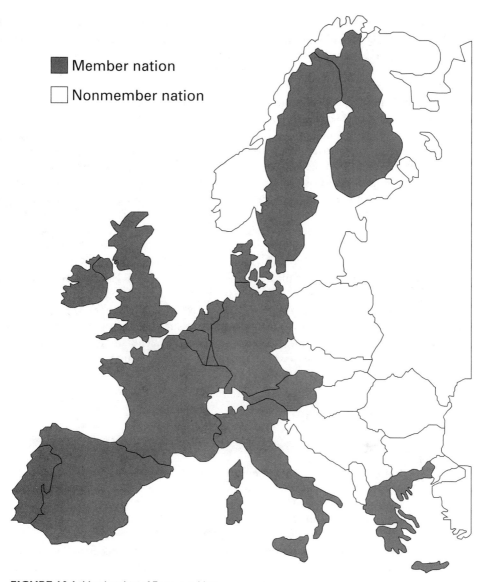

FIGURE 10.1 Membership of European Union

However, there is a substantial negative associated with the EU from the viewpoint of other nations. The trade wall around the EU is not coming down. Actually, its external barriers to commerce are becoming more prominent. In 1960, slightly more than one half (51 percent) of the foreign trade of the countries that are now members of the Union was outside of the EU. By 1996, only 35 percent of their trade was outside, and a substantial 65 percent of their foreign commerce consisted of exports to or imports from other EU countries.

The membership of the EU has not been static (see Table 10.2). It started off with only six countries: West Germany, France, Italy, and the Benelux Three (Belgium, Netherlands, and Luxembourg). Over the years, the size more than doubled, with the gradual addition of the United Kingdom, Denmark, Ireland, Spain, Portugal, Greece, Austria, Finland, and Sweden. Several countries in Eastern Europe—Hungary, Poland, and the Czech Republic—are active candidates for membership in the EU and may begin their relationship as associate members.

The impact of the Single Market on business is uneven, as is expected of any dynamic process, producing winners and losers on both sides of the Atlantic. The winners include the stronger European companies with high-skill and high-tech capabilities, enjoying the economies of scale and the benefits of expanding domestic markets. They also bring a special understanding of European needs, capabilities, and cultures. Many of them are emerging larger and stronger than ever. Hoechst, the giant German chemical firm, now employs more people in the Western Hemisphere than in Europe.

A final category of beneficiaries of the Single Market are the strong North American firms with an established presence in Western Europe. High-tech, well-capitalized North American companies are accustomed to competing on a continentwide basis. They use 1 EU country as a base to sell to the other 11. General Motors and Ford have more Europe-wide strength than such well-established European automakers as Volkswagen, Fiat, Peugeot and Renault. The same holds true for computer manufacturers such as IBM, Digital Equipment, Unisys, and Hewlett-Packard compared to their European counterparts.

TABLE 10.2   Milestones in the Economic Integration of Western Europe

1951	European Coal and Steel Community (ECSC) established. Members are Belgium, France, Italy, Luxembourg, The Netherlands, and West Germany.
1957	European Economic Community (EEC) created with same members as ECSC.
1959	EEC member tariff reduction.
1962	EEC members adopt Common Agricultural Policy.
1967	EEC renamed the European Community (EC), reflecting cooperation beyond economic sphere.
1968	EC eliminates internal tariffs and imposed common external tariff.
1973	Denmark, Ireland, and the United Kingdom join EC.
1979	First direct election of the European Parliament.
1981	Greece joins EC.
1986	Portugal and Spain join EC.
1987	Single European Act passed, providing qualified majority member approval of 282 measures needed to achieve single market.
1993	With signing of Treaty of Maastricht, EC becomes the European Union (EU), with closer focus on economic and monetary union and political unification.
1995	Austria, Finland, and Sweden join EU.
1999	Deadline for launch of the European Monetary Union.

Losers from the Single Market include the high-cost European companies that have been sheltered within their national markets. Some of these more tradition-bound firms are being hurt by continentwide competition. Not all barriers are down, however. Each member nation continues to possess individual values, needs, cultures, language—and tax systems. No matter what changes the EU makes, the French are not going to stampede for German wine, for instance, and the British will continue to want autos equipped to drive on the "wrong" side of the road.

Many North American firms are also losers as a result of the European economic unification. They find it more difficult to export to Europe. In addition, they face tougher competition in their domestic markets from the stronger EU businesses.

The Asian Rim

The Asian rim represents a far more complicated political and economic area than either Western Europe or North America. Formally, there is no counterpart to either the EU or NAFTA. The Asian governments have not embarked on a comprehensive effort to link their economies or to eliminate barriers to trade and investment. ASEAN, or the Association of Southeast Asian Nations (Malaysia, Indonesia, Philippines, Thailand, Singapore, Brunei, Vietnam, Laos, and Myanmar), is an embryonic effort to develop greater cooperation on the part of the nations in that part of the world.

The commercial and investment relationships across this region are substantial. For example, like the EU nations, a major share of the international trade and investment of the Asian rim countries stays in the area. The greater part of the capital flowing into China and Southeast Asia comes from Japan, Korea, and other East Asian nations. Likewise, most of the imports into and exports from Southeast Asia are to or from East Asian nations. This is a very different view than most Western observers hold of this region; this is a more inward-looking region than many people located outside of the Asian rim realize.

The role of Japan is extremely important. Citizens of developed nations in Europe and North America often are preoccupied with companies from other countries, notably Japan, buying some of their key economic assets. However, Japan is also a major provider of foreign investment for such Asian nations as Thailand, Malaysia, and Indonesia. East Asia is now a larger market for Japan than is the United States.

However, this is not an isolated situation. The other advanced economies in the Pacific rim—notably South Korea, Taiwan, and Hong Kong—are also large providers of investment capital and have become key trading partners for the less economically advanced nations in East Asia. "Greater China"—with the integration of mainland China, Hong Kong, and Macao—is becoming a fourth economic superpower.

The Chinese-based economy of Asia is rapidly emerging as a new epicenter for commerce and finance.[4] This strategic area contains substantial amounts of technology and manufacturing capability (Taiwan), outstanding marketing and services acumen (Hong Kong), a fine communications network (Singapore), a tremendous pool of financial capital (all three), and very large endowments of land, resources, and labor (mainland China). A talking doll, to take a modest example, may be designed in Hong Kong and assembled elsewhere in China, with a computer chip made in Taiwan. This "bamboo network," which transcends national boundaries, also includes other key locations where business executives, traders, and financiers of Chinese background make important economic contributions. According to some estimates, ethnic Chinese companies in Malaysia, Thailand, Indonesia, and the Philippines make up about 70 percent of the private sector in those countries.

The informal Chinese economy differs from the more official economies that usually are dominated by large multinational firms. The Chinese-based economy consists mainly of midsize family-run firms, rather than the huge corporations characteristic of Japan, Western Europe, and the United States. From Guangzhou to Singapore, from Kuala Lumpur to Manila, this influential network—often based on extension of traditional clans—is the backbone of the East Asian economy.

Despite their migration to other Asian countries, the individuals involved remain Chinese in a deep and significant sense—and are treated so. The Confucian tradition is remarkably persistent, especially the common core of values such as loyalty to a hierarchical structure of authority, a code of defined conduct between children and adults, and trust among relatives.

That code of conduct encourages a variety of cross-border ventures on the part of overseas Chinese enterprises. The Salim Group in Indonesia has teamed up with the Kuok family of Malaysia to build a cement factory in China. Stakeholders of the New China Hong Kong Group include Indonesia's Lippo Group, Hong Kong's Li Ka-shing's Group, Taiwan International Securities, Singapore's Trade Development Board, and 10 mainland Chinese companies and ministries.

Overseas Chinese firms have eschewed the sophisticated business structures of Western corporations in order to adapt to the weak system of contracting and law throughout Southeast Asia. When Taiwan had strict exchange controls, it was possible to deposit a large sum with a gold shop in Taipei and for a relative to withdraw the equivalent sum the next day from an affiliated gold dealer in Hong Kong. Core business groups obtain varying degrees of cross-ownership in dozens, and sometimes hundreds, of small to medium-size businesses.

This convoluted structure allows the family to maintain control, albeit circuitous, over a large array of business activities. Transactions of great size are often dealt with by common understanding. In the words of one analyst who has studied the phenomenon in depth, "ledgers are intended for the tax collector and true accounts are kept in the head."[5] That structure provides necessary secrecy in a region where the threat of expropriation is still pervasive. A widely held saying is "Keep your bags packed at all times."

China and Southeast Asia are currently the world leaders in terms of the rate of growth of economic activity, industrial production, and exports. That combined area contains an array of potential consumers that far exceeds the markets in Europe or the Western Hemisphere. Yet, not all of the vast Chinese mainland can be viewed realistically as a potential for early modernization. The major economic development is occurring along the East Coast—in the coastal provinces of Guangdong and Fujian, the special economic zones in Shenzhen and Xiamen, and the city of Shanghai. Although these areas are a modest fraction of the entire country, in the aggregate they constitute a very substantial economy.

Government is often heavily involved in the ownership if not the operation of many specific enterprises in China. These range from the central government's giant steel mills to local government factories. The trading companies, which engage in a variety of commercial, banking, and manufacturing activities, are owned by governmental units, ranging from the army to local counties.

Enterprises owned by the PRC government often engage in overseas business ventures. A prominent example is the China International Trust and Investment Corporation (Citic), which has subsidiaries in Mexico, Australia, Canada, the United States, and Europe. Citic's Hong Kong subsidiary—considered its crown jewel—owns substantial minority interests in Hong Kong telecommunications, Cathay Pacific airlines, and a Hong Kong chemical waste plant.

The close connection between the several parts of the greater China economy is illustrated by the operations of the Shanghai Far East Container Company. This joint venture between Shanghai, Hong Kong, and Taiwan involves enterprises in all three areas to produce steel containers in Shanghai.

Many Western firms have joined forces with ethnic Chinese business family enterprises in setting up activities in China and elsewhere in Southeast Asia. The CP Group of Bangkok has entered into joint ventures with NYNEX to install several million new phone lines in Bangkok. The Lippo Group has entered into extended arrangements, at different times, with such electronics giants as Japan's Mitsubishi and the Netherlands' Philips. Li Ka-shing's companies from time to time have joined forces with AT&T, Lockheed, and Britain's Cable & Wireless. The Salim Group has partnered with Amoco Oil and Radisson Hotels.

However, the Asian emphasis on personal relations can clash with the legalism so endemic in the United States. The head of the CP Group lamented that U.S. lawyers can destroy the chemistry needed between partners to make a deal work—soon after Wal-Mart terminated its joint venture with CP and instead decided to work with local companies in mainland China.

BUSINESS RESPONSES TO GOVERNMENT POLICY

While public attention focuses on the emerging intergovernmental regions or blocs, a great expansion of business enterprise is occurring across governmental borders. Already, one-third of all world trade occurs in the form of intracompany transactions, such as movements of goods and services from a parent in the United States to a subsidiary in Europe or Asia—or vice versa.

Many observers believe that the pressures for a more global orientation of business activities will overwhelm the trend toward governmental regionalization. Some of these forces include an equalization of earnings and a homogenization of tastes worldwide. Higher incomes have also given rise to international markets for national specialty products, such as Italian shoes, Swiss watches, and Japanese consumer electronics. In addition, a general reduction in trade barriers began in the 1980s and has continued to the present. Still, governments continue trying to restrict both imports and overseas investments to "protect" domestic jobs.

The spark that ignites global competition, however, is the need to find new markets for mass-produced goods when existing markets became saturated in the face of rising industrial productivity. In response, firms increase their presence worldwide by extending the scope of operations globally and by taking advantage of scale economies.

Governmental barriers to international business take many forms, ranging from tariffs to quotas on trade to restrictions on foreign ownership of domestic business — but the global enterprise increasingly is learning how to overcome them, albeit at a cost.[6] Indeed, technological progress makes possible, and economically feasible, a variety of business innovations that can overcome obstacles to international trade and investment imposed by countries and regional groupings of governments (see Table 10.3).

Although government policy continues to dominate public attention, the key decision-making power in the global marketplace is rapidly becoming the business firm. For example, while the United States and the European Union were deadlocked on international trade negotiations, British Telecom set up a joint venture with MCI. While Congress was debating NAFTA and considering ever more costly environmental statutes, U.S. mining firms expanded in South America. National policy keeps drilling rigs out of the Arctic National Wildlife Refuge — perhaps the United States' best prospect for new oil exploration — while at the same time, Chevron and Mobil are investing billions of dollars in far away Kazakhstan. U.S.-based oil and gas companies in total now invest more overseas than in domestic locations.

Likewise, U.S.-based pharmaceutical firms have introduced new drugs in Europe while waiting for the completion of the byzantine domestic regulatory procedures. Similarly frustrated by FDA hurdles, makers of innovative medical equipment have been moving their developmental work to the Netherlands and other Western European locations where standards are high but regulatory requirements are less burdensome. As shown in Table 10.4, substantial numbers of U.S.-headquarters companies have located a majority of their assets overseas.

TABLE 10.3   Business Responses to Governmental Barriers

Barrier	Business Response
Trade Barriers Tariffs and quotas Domestic content restrictions Reciprocity rules Government procurement restrictions	Establish manufacturing operations in target country Acquire local firm Subcontract or purchase locally Develop products jointly Shift to higher-priced exports (for quotas)
Investment Barriers Limits on foreign ownership of local enterprises	Enter into joint ventures with local firms Give away nominal majority ownership Franchise local firms Enter into licensing agreements Set up R&D cooperation or technology swaps
Restrictions on repatriation of earnings Fear of expropriation	Set up affiliate or correspondent relationships with local firms
Regulatory and Tax Barriers In home country In foreign nations Informal foreign barriers	Reinvest overseas Shift high value-added activities to low-tax, low-regulation nations Market through local distributors

Source: Center for the Study of American Business, Washington University.

TABLE 10.4 Companies with More than Half of Their Assets Overseas

Firm	Foreign Assets as % of Total	Firm	Foreign Assets as % of Total
Manpower, Inc.	72	Dow Chemical	56
NCR	71	McDonald's	55
Crown Cork	68	Hewlett-Packard	54
Mobil	67	AMP	53
Pharmacia & Upjohn	65	Bankers Trust	52
Gillette	62	IBM	52
CPC International	61	Xerox	51
Colgate-Palmolive	60	Digital Equipment	51
Citicorp	60	Sara Lee	51
Avon	59	JP Morgan	51
Exxon	58	Warner-Lambert	51
Sun Microsystems	57		

Note: Data computed from company financial reports.

Governmental barriers to international commerce and investment surely are not withering away. The reasons for the adoption of restrictionist trade policies are various. Usually, the motivation is to "protect" home industry owners, managers, and employees from international competition. The most frequently encountered barriers are tariffs, quotas, domestic content restrictions, and reciprocity rules. In one comprehensive survey, 45 percent of U.S. firms reported that trade barriers imposed by other countries presented the greatest impediment to selling abroad.[7]

Adjusting to government policies is both time-consuming and expensive. Nevertheless, companies are learning how to get around, under, or over those obstacles. The responses follow a variety of approaches. Exporters can absorb the added costs imposed by governments—at least to some extent. In the case of quotas—whether formally or informally adopted by the exporting country—imposed by the importing nations, companies frequently shift to higher-priced items on which unit profits are also greater.

In the early 1980s, American purchasers of Japanese-made automobiles often found they were required to buy all sorts of high-priced extras and that they were paying as much as $2,000 above the sticker price for the reduced supply of Toyotas, Nissans, and other Japanese automobiles. In that way, the Japanese producers actually benefited from the "voluntary" restrictions on their exports to the United States. They increased their profits substantially in the face of quantitative limits on their exports of cars to the United States. While the Japanese producers exported about 30 percent of their auto production to the United States during that period, they earned approximately one-half of their profits from sales in the United States.[8]

When faced with more onerous obstacles to international trade, businesses draw on a variety of alternatives to direct exporting. One approach is to set up new manufacturing facilities (so-called greenfield operations) in the host nation. When Monsanto's low-calorie sweetener NutraSweet was hit with a very high duty in response to a charge of dumping in the European Union (EU), the company entered into a joint venture with Ajinomoto, a Japanese food and pharmaceutical company, to build a plant in France to produce for the European market.

Many Japanese manufacturers moved the production of such products as textiles, watches, televisions, cameras, and calculators to facilities in Malaysia, Indonesia, Thailand, Singapore, and the Philippines in response to the restrictions against Japanese imports encountered in some of their major overseas markets (the lower costs of production were an augmenting factor).

Japanese automakers are also producing automobiles in other nations, especially in the United States, on a large scale. This approach provides the Japanese firms with direct access to the markets of the local economies in which they produce and minimizes their exposure to adverse policies by the host government. It also permits the Japanese companies to export to markets in other nations that maintain barriers against products made in their home territory. For instance, Honda sells cars to Taiwan, South Korea, and Israel from its manufacturing plant in Ohio. Those three countries have traditionally prohibited the importation of automobiles directly from Japan. (Honda notes that the cost of production in the United States is low enough to warrant some exports to its home market in Japan.)

Firms also respond by acquiring existing local companies. This has been a particularly important strategy for foreign businesses positioning themselves in response to the integration of the European market. Many American and Japanese companies fear that the removal of internal regulatory and economic barriers in Europe will result in an increase in reciprocity requirements and local content restrictions. Thus, acquisitions have been increasing steadily since the 1980s as firms seek to gain a foothold there.

Examples include Emerson Electric's purchase of the French firm Leroy-Somer, General Electric's acquisition of the United Kingdom's Burton Group Financial Services, American Brands' buyout of Scotland's Whyte & Mackay Distillers Ltd., and Scott Paper's purchase of Tungram Company of Germany. Other alternatives that business firms frequently rely upon to develop positions in the markets of other nations include subcontracting production, purchasing locally, and developing products jointly with local firms.

To overcome political objections to goods produced by workers in other countries, some multinational corporations set up so-called "screwdriver" operations: assembly plants using key components manufactured in the home country and performing no R&D locally. Thus, the economic contribution in the host country is minimized. Japanese companies frequently use this technique. One analyst has used the term "rainbow" to describe this tendency of large Japanese firms. "The U.S. plant is situated here, the mother plant is situated over in Japan and nothing touches in between . . . and the pot of gold is at the other end."[9]

Joint ventures, particularly those involving the operation of manufacturing facilities, are often necessary to overcome trade restrictions, especially in the case of the formation of protectionist trade blocs. This trend is evident in the aerospace and automobile industries, where every major company has formed alliances with foreign competitors. For instance, Ford Motor Company has formed a joint venture with a local producer in Taiwan to assemble Festivas for sale in that market. General Motors sells some of its automobiles in Japan through a three-way joint venture involving Suzuki and Nissho Isai Corporation.

In some circumstances, firms are able to export duty-free to countries possessing broad tariff policies in exchange for capital investments or for using local contractors or raw materials in the production process. A joint venture between General Motors and a state-owned automobile maker in Poland to manufacture cars domestically provides a significant inflow of capital, technology, and expertise to the beleaguered Polish carmaker. In return, General Motors is allowed to import into Poland a portion of its automobiles duty-free.

On other occasions, firms face sharp limits to foreign ownership of local enterprises. This type of governmentally imposed barrier has become more popular in a period when formal trade barriers have been reduced substantially. Investment barriers include formal restrictions on investment, or less formal but often equally powerful tax and regulatory advantages limited to local companies.

Cross-border mergers and acquisitions represented 79 percent of all foreign direct investment in 1996. Mergers and acquisitions are the dominant modes of penetrating Western European markets. In some Asian nations as well as in Eastern Europe, however, such foreign direct investment is greatly restricted. In Indonesia, no foreign company can buy a local firm or set up a new one (except in a very few designated areas). As a result, as elsewhere in the Asian rim, international enterprises, especially in high-technology industries, most often enter into joint ventures with local firms (see Figure 10.2).

Another strategy adopted by foreign governments is to demand a greater role in the production of public-sector products purchased from American companies. Faced with the prospect that several European governments might try to develop an indigenous military fighter aircraft to rival the F-16, the General Dynamics Corporation agreed to assign a major production role to domestic firms in prospective purchaser nations. This role included production of parts for aircraft sold to the U.S. Air Force.

Many countries with their own high-tech engineering and advanced manufacturing abilities are reluctant to import weapon systems produced elsewhere. Under these circumstances, U.S. aerospace companies, albeit reluctantly, have licensed their designs to local firms. Thus, McDonnell Douglas has received royalties for the version of its F-15 fighter aircraft produced in Japan by Mitsubishi Industries working with Kawasaki Heavy Industries. Korean firms, under license, have manufactured Northrop Grumman's F-5 aircraft while Textron's Bell division has licensed its Huey helicopter for production in Taiwan.

In some circumstances, a host government may be willing to accept the construction, expansion, or acquisition of a local branch by an American company on the condition that the firm meets a specified performance requirement or provides another concession. Before IBM was allowed to increase its operations in Mexico, the company agreed to set up a development center for semiconductors, to purchase high-technology components from Mexican companies, and to produce software for Latin America in Mexico. In the case of services, franchising to a domestic enterprise serves a similar purpose to licensing in adjusting to barriers to direct investment.

In other parts of the world, especially in less-developed nations, public-sector deterrents to business take different forms. Governments on occasion restrict repatriation of earnings, or foreign businesses fear future expropriation of their assets. Governments may also restrict location, financing, and technology inputs, and require local sourcing of raw materials and rigid technical specifications.

European Community

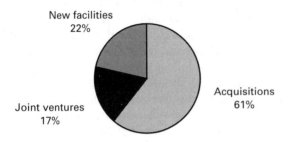

New facilities
22%

Joint ventures
17%

Acquisitions
61%

Asia

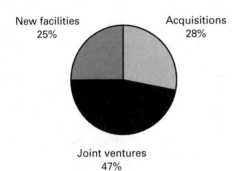

New facilities
25%

Acquisitions
28%

Joint ventures
47%

Source: Center for the Study of American Business, Washington University.

FIGURE 10.2 Variations in U.S. Business Responses to Global Markets in 1990

Some of the barriers to business enterprise are domestic, and the global economy provides opportunity to overcome them. Companies that have difficulty introducing products in the home country due to delayed approval or stricter governmental requirements can produce them in other countries in an effort to introduce them to markets more quickly. As noted earlier, this practice is common to some U.S. pharmaceutical firms.

In many other instances—especially in the more developed nations—companies face high business taxes and onerous regulatory costs. When these barriers to business occur in the home country, the enterprise can expand overseas. In more extreme cases, existing business operations are moved to a more favorable policy environment in another country. It is helpful under changing political circumstances to do business in several countries. In that event, when faced with rising government burdens in one nation, a firm can shift its high value-added activities to other nations in which it operates, specifically those with lower taxes and less burdensome regulation.

Traditional business reasons are also involved in the choice among the available methods of penetrating foreign markets. Indeed, those business concerns—such as cost and transportation advantages—may often be the dominating influence. Moreover, in the move toward globalization, individual firms may experience rough sledding and reverse some of their foreign commitments.

The alliance between General Motors and Daewoo of South Korea went sour when Daewoo's desire to expand in local markets conflicted with GM's global objectives. Great difficulties have arisen in the transitional economies of Eastern Europe and the republics of the former Soviet Union. Often, investors do not know if they have legal title to the items they purchase.

Metallgesellschaft AG, the large German metallurgy firm, pulled out of its 60 percent stake in a steel plant in Hungary in 1981. The German company said that the Hungarian government partners wanted it to foot a larger portion of the operating costs than its contract provided for. According to Peter Giesler, an official of Metallgesellschaft, "We learned that contracts which were made at the time were not enforceable at another time."[10]

Nevertheless, the total global stock of foreign direct investment doubled from 1993 to 1996, reaching $13.2 trillion.

THE FEEDBACK ON GOVERNMENT POLICY

The tension between business and government is nothing new. It has traditionally existed between large private enterprises and the rulers of developing countries (see Table 10.5). This tension between governments generally (both those with developing and those with more advanced economies) and the business firm is being exacerbated by the rapid rate of economic, social, and technological change.

TABLE 10.5 Tensions Between Developing-Country Goals and Business Activities

Developing Countries	*International Private Enterprises*
Promote local ownership	Maintain global standards and efficiency
Increase local control	Minimize cost and complexity of delivering technology and capital
Change payment characteristics and reduce duration of contracts	Receive just returns for risks
Minimize source firm's control over use of technology and capital in user nation	Gain assurance regarding property rights over use of private resources
Separate technology from normal private investments	Provide technology as part of long-term production and market development
Remove restrictive business clauses in investment and technology agreements	Maintain ability to affect the use of capital, technology, and associated products
Minimize proprietary rights of suppliers	Protect right to profit from private investments
Reduce contract security	Use contracts to create an environment of stability and trust
Encourage transfer of R&D to host country	Maintain control of R&D paid for by company
Develop products suitable for domestic markets	Gain global economies of scale to lower cost of products to consumers

Political scientists and economists have long understood that people vote with their feet. They leave localities, regions, and nations with limited opportunity in favor of those that offer a more attractive future. In the contemporary era of computers, telephones, and fax machines, enterprises are far more mobile than that. Information, that key resource, can be transferred in a matter of seconds, or less.

The mobility of enterprises—of their people, capital, and information—is reducing the effective power of government. Public-sector decision makers increasingly are being forced to understand that they have to become internationally competitive in the economic policies they devise. Governmental activities that impose costs without compensating benefits or that reduce wealth substantially in the process of redistributing income undermine the competitive positions of domestic enterprises. The result is either the loss of business to firms located in other nations or the movement of the domestic company's resources and operations to more hospitable locations. The fear of losing economic activity to other parts of the world can be expected to reshape future domestic political agendas in fundamental ways. Governments are learning that they, too, compete in the global marketplace that is developing for the 21st century.

An example of this enlightened attitude is a statement by Kurt Biedenkopf, Minister-President of the German province of Saxony:

> There is still a very difficult competition of systems . . . who can best allocate resources? Who finds the best . . . division of labor between government and the civic society? Who can trim government sufficiently and keep it flexible in order to respond to rapid change in the world at large? This will be a competitive process.[11]

Not all governmental involvement in international business is of a negative nature. On many occasions, public-sector policies actively encourage foreign companies to invest, to build new facilities, or otherwise to participate in the local economy. Such supportive actions include tax abatements, tariff waivers, liberal credit terms, and reduction in burdensome regulation.

Even as many public-sector barriers remain, the private sector is increasingly learning how to overcome them or even just to live with them. Of course, there are costs involved when businesses respond to governmental barriers to international business. However, in a global economy, these barriers become far from absolute.

The most striking examples of that mobility are the recent experiences of Chinese entrepreneurs. Even in the face of official hostility between Beijing and Taipei, thousands of Taiwanese firms have established their business presence in mainland China. The formal power of government is not to be discounted—and its destructive ability has been vividly demonstrated in innumerable wars. Nevertheless, the continuing ability of entrepreneurs to respond to the power of economic incentives and technological advance is impressive.

THE EMERGING TRANSNATIONAL ENTERPRISE

In the process of adjusting to government obstacles to international commerce, the traditional domestically oriented corporation often becomes transformed into an organization we can call the transnational enterprise (see Table 10.6). The internationalization of

TABLE 10.6 Levels of Globalization

Domestic	Regional Exporter	Exporter	International	International to Global	Global
Operate exclusively within a single country.	Operate within a geographically defined region that crosses national boundaries. Markets served are economically and culturally homogenous.	Run operations from a central office in the home region, exporting finished goods to a variety of countries. Some marketing outside the home region.	Regional operations are somewhat autonomous, but key decisions are coordinated from central office in the home region. Manufacturing and assembly, marketing and sales are decentralized beyond the home region.	Run independent and mainly self-sufficient subsidiaries in a range of countries. Some functions (R&D, sourcing, financing) are decentralized. The home region is still the primary base for many functions.	Highly decentralized organization operating across a broad range of countries. No geographic area is assumed to be the primary base for any functional area. Each function is performed in the most suitable location.

Source: Joseph Nemec, Jr., and Barbara A. Failer, *A Special Report on Globalization* (New York: Booz-Allen & Hamilton, 1991).

management is the clearest example of the transformation of the modern business enterprise. The top 400 people in Citicorp come from 42 countries; only 165 of them are natives of the United States. Of the bank's top 20 executives, only 11 are from the United States.[12]

The emerging transnational enterprise is not a monolithic organization that makes or even designs every aspect of the items it produces and markets. Rather, the largest, pace-setting firms are often taking on many of the characteristics of an open and interactive network, selectively sharing control, technology, and markets with different kinds of organizations in many parts of the world. As a result of rapid changes in technology and markets, the customary boundaries between formal enterprises and more informal business relationships are gradually blurring.

The traditional factory, such as Ford's Willow Run operation in Michigan, was fully integrated, with headquarters, design offices, production workers, and factories all located close to each other. In recent years, many of the production functions of large corporations have been farmed out to smaller, more specialized firms. Richard Rosecrance of UCLA refers to the "virtual corporation" as an entity with research, development, design, marketing, financial, and legal functions in its headquarters, but few or no manufacturing facilities, in his words, a company with a head and no body.[13]

Head corporations can design new products for a wide range of production facilities, often in different countries. Some analysts note that even the design of major components can be performed by suppliers who have special skills in that niche of the marketplace. Thus, the leading figures in the computer industry are no longer the integrated producers, but Intel, Microsoft, Oracle, and Hewlett-Packard—those that specialize in one key stage of the process or one vital component.[14]

For an increasing number of transnational companies, including Shell Oil, Exxon, Ford, Nestlé, and Procter & Gamble, profits and sales from abroad or on occasion from a single foreign country surpass that of the country of origin. In that sense, these businesses are losing their national identities.

An external observer of these enterprises sees large flows of resources, people, and information among relatively interdependent or autonomous units; the subsidiaries of Shell and Nestlé in the United States afford cogent examples. This type of arrangement means heavy reliance on a changing process of coordination, cooperation, and shared decision making.

Internal Organization

The traditional pyramidal organization facilitated the efficient division of labor in producing large quantities of fairly standardized products. With a more rapid rate of technological change, the life spans of individual products tend to shrink. Simultaneously, consumer incomes in many parts of the world are rising rapidly, permitting great variation in consumer tastes and in business responses.

Many firms are attempting to adjust to this new environment by shifting to a more nearly horizontal, decentralized organization. A mere flattening of the organizational pyramid does not, however, seem to suffice in the current information age. Many innovative forms are being suggested. In one intriguing concept, the business firm of the future consists of a central coordination center and several semi-independent internal organizations. Business activity, in this view, operates on the basis of fluid ties with the internal organizations of other companies and with informal enterprises. The concept of *networking,* popular in recent years, is traditional in several nonmanufacturing industries, notably construction and contract research, where so many of the key decisions on a product or structure are made by firms other than the prime or lead contractor.

Just as there are transaction costs in transfers between firms, there are internalization costs in intrafirm relationships, especially when they occur across national borders. The multinational enterprise relies more heavily on its own intellectual resources than did the old-fashioned exporter (particularly compared to the domestically oriented producer that sells overseas through a separate international trading company). The newer form of enterprise has to gain knowledge of foreign markets—including production possibilities, cost differences, relations with local suppliers—and deal with several levels of foreign governments. In contrast, a local firm may already have such information or can acquire it more cheaply. The establishment of a new subsidiary may also entail technical training costs similar to, or even higher than, those encountered in interfirm transactions.

Two very different strategies, which the multinational enterprise may follow, are emerging. In some industries, there is a trend toward globalization. With converging buyer preferences and uniform worldwide technical standards, it is possible to produce a narrow range of fairly standardized products from globally oriented factories. In such an environment, there is a premium on efficiency and a preference for internal control, unhampered by the divergent preferences of corporate partners.

In other industries, numerous factors—strong local customer preferences, varying technical standards in different countries, transportation and trade barriers, economic nationalism, and high technological risks—point to a more diverse strategy, including alliances with enterprises located in a variety of regions. Clearly, the emerging form of business organization encourages greater ease of entry—and exit!

Many of the larger and more sophisticated multinational companies with strong headquarters staff and substantial numbers of subsidiaries are now moving toward becoming transnational organizations with activities and responsibilities spread more evenly around the world. In the newer formulation, production for local markets is often regrouped into a few world supply centers. In the words of Wisse Dekker, then chairman of the supervisory board of Philips (the large Dutch electrical and electronics producer), they are becoming "global citizens."[15]

Notwithstanding the myriad of individual variations, it is helpful to try to generalize the nature of the corporate transition. Christopher Bartlett of the Harvard Business School sees corporations going through four distinct stages in responding to the rising pressures for globalization. The first and traditional step views overseas operations as mere appendages of a centrally directed domestic corporation. Although many assets and decisions are decentralized, the headquarters organization exercises strong financial and planning control.[16]

In a second stage, the enterprise adopts a multinational form of organization. Management comes to view overseas operations as a portfolio of relatively independently operated businesses. Many responsibilities are decentralized, with financial controls continuing to provide the key coordinating link.

In a third, more advanced stage, the company uses a global organizational structure. Overseas operations are treated as delivery pipelines to a unified global marketplace. Central control is maintained over decisions, resources, and information. But it is extremely difficult for such a worldwide operation run from Detroit, Tokyo, or Stockholm to maintain an adequate understanding of consumer expectations in distant markets—no matter how good its research or how many flight hours its executives log each month. Thus, companies increasingly are led to the fourth and most futuristic organizational model: the transnational organization. Large flows of resources, people, and information occur among relatively interdependent units. In the absence of traditional centralized controls, this structure relies on the goodwill of the many participants. It requires a complex process of coordination, cooperation, and shared decision making.

To an outsider, the performance of the transnational enterprise will likely be recognizable by two key characteristics: The first is the ability to attract employees, capital, and suppliers from global sources; the second is the appeal to customers all over the world—fostered by product designs that are constantly being revised. Building an organizational capability that allows corporate executives to manage diversity and change needs is of prime importance. The successful organization of the twenty-first century will need to adapt rapidly to changes in its markets and operating environment. It will be forced to engage in continuous experimentation.

Conclusions

The tension between business and government is not new. It is being exacerbated by the rapid rate of social, economic, and technological change around the globe. However, there is a third force that ultimately may carry the day: the citizen as consumer. Consumers vote every day of the week—in dollars, yen, Deutsche marks, pounds, francs, and lira (and soon the euro). The same protectionist-oriented voters, as consumers, purchase products made everywhere in the world. In spending their own money, most consumers give far greater weight to price and quality than country of origin. The real liberalization of international trade and investment in the years ahead will arise, not from changes in government policy, but from the competition among firms in the private sector of the various national and regional economies.

To the extent that human capital is increasingly seen as the key resource in that business and economic competition, the nations and companies that perform well will be those that can generate, attract, and keep educated, skilled, and experienced workers, managers, and entrepreneurs.

The shift in influence from the public sector to the private sector is underscored, especially in the United States, by the end of the Cold War. During the old rivalry between the two military superpowers, the national government by necessity played the dominant role. The position of the private sector was that of a supporting player. Business enterprises produced the weapons needed by the armed forces, but under detailed governmental supervision.

In the civilian-oriented economy, these responsibilities are reversed. It is the business firm that makes the key decisions that determine who is employed, what products they produce, and how competitive is the result. Government still has a vital part to play, but it is as a supporting player and facilitator.

The rapidly changing global marketplace of the early twenty-first century will provide both threat and opportunity for business firms, governments, and consumers. Invariably, this change will generate both winners and losers. The outcomes for spe-

TABLE 10.7   Alternative Business Responses to the Changing Global Marketplace

Alternatives	Characteristics	Advantages	Disadvantages
Direct strategies for marketing abroad	Exporting Turnkey operations	Expands markets Maintains control Maintains domestic production	Faces foreign barriers Sensitive to exchange rate fluctuations
Cooperative contractual agreements	Licensing Franchising Subcontracting	Requires small investments Concentrates on core activities	Minimizes control
Wholly owned affiliates	Greenfield operations Mergers and acquisitions	Maintains full control Localizes production	Requires large investment May be unpopular politically
Strategic nonequity alliances	R&D cooperatives Technology swaps Joint production/ marketing agreements Informal alliances	Accesses markets Provides global presence Flexible Co-opts potential competitors Reduces risk	Exhibits uncertain control Slows down decision making Potentially unstable May lose technology to competitors
Strategic equity alliances	Joint ventures Joint equity swaps Affiliates Other investment alliances	Accesses new markets/ fields Minimizes risks Results in lower costs than direct investment	Requires complex, detailed contracts Often difficult to manage

cific individuals, business organizations, and nations will depend in large part on their ability to understand and to respond promptly to changing economic and technological trends (see Table 10.7).

Notes

1. Brad Roberts, Stanton Burnett, and Murray Weidenbaum, "Think Tanks in a New World," *Washington Quarterly,* Winter 1993, p. 169.
2. Murray Weidenbaum, "Neoisolationism and Global Realities," *Business & the Contemporary World* 8, no. 314, 1997, pp. 104–118.
3. *U.S.-Mexico Relations* (Washington, DC: U.S. Department of State, Office of Public Communication, July 31, 1992), p. 1.
4. Murray Weidenbaum and Samuel Hughes, *The Bamboo Network* (New York: Free Press, 1996).
5. Robert S. Elegant, *The Dragon's Seed* (New York: St. Martin's Press, 1959), p. 8.
6. Harvey S. James, Jr., and Murray Weidenbaum, *When Businesses Cross International Borders* (Westport, CT: Praeger, 1993).
7. Dun & Bradstreet, *Comments on the Economy* 2, no. 4, August–September 1991, p. 2.

8. Robert W. Crandall, "Import Quotas and the Automobile Industry," *Brookings Review,* Summer 1984, pp. 8–16.

9. Cynthia Day Wallace, "Economic Overview," in *Japanese Investment in the U.S.* (Washington, DC: Nitze School of Advanced International Studies, 1990), p. 14.

10. Ken Kasriel, "Hungary's Troubled Business Ties," *Christian Science Monitor,* July 7, 1992, p. 2.

11. Quoted in *Washington International Business Report,* December 1995, p. 3.

12. John S. Reed, *Oh, the Modern World!,* CEO Series Issue no. 7 (St. Louis: Washington University, Center for the Study of American Business, 1996), p. 4.

13. Richard Rosecrance, "The Rise of the Virtual State," *Foreign Affairs* 75, no. 4, July–August 1996, pp. 45–61.

14. Everett M. Ehrlich, "Notes on a Borderless World," *Business Economics,* July 1997, pp. 32–36.

15. Wisse Dekker, "The Rise of the Stateless CEO," *CEO/International Strategies,* March–April 1991, p. 17.

16. Christopher Bartlett, "Managing Across Borders," *World Link,* July–August 1991, pp. 110–111.

CHAPTER 11

Government and International Commerce

Many discussions of international economic issues ignore the vital role of private enterprises. Thus, it is commonplace to say that Japan exports automobiles to the United States and that the United States exports jet airliners to Japan. But neither nations nor governments do more than record and perhaps tax those cross-border transactions. Typically, it is business firms that engage in international commerce.

When we examine foreign trade from that viewpoint, we gain new insights. For example, more than one-third of what governments call foreign trade actually involves cross-border transactions between different parts of the same company. That is, a major share of foreign trade consists of domestic firms shipping goods to or receiving items from their overseas subsidiaries—or foreign firms engaged in similar transactions with their divisions in other countries. In a geopolitical sense, all of this is foreign commerce. But, from a business viewpoint, these international flows of goods and services are internal transfers within the same firm. That is the global enterprise in full swing.

Often the products of those transnational firms cause great consternation to government officials. The estimation of domestic content has become a fine art as well as a cause of international disputes. An ironic incident along these lines occurred in the United States in connection with a charge by American producers that Japanese minivans were being dumped below cost in American markets. The U.S. International Trade Commission, the agency reviewing the dispute, raised the concern as to the cross-ownership of American and Japanese producers. It turned out that Chrysler, one of the U.S. companies that initiated the dumping charge, was also one of the importers of Japanese-made minivans.

Perhaps the most extreme case of transnational business was cited by former U.S. Secretary of State George Shultz. He tells of a shipping label on integrated circuits made by an American firm, which reads: "Made in one or more of the following countries: Korea, Hong Kong, Malaysia, Singapore, Taiwan, Mauritius, Thailand, Indonesia, Mexico, Philippines. The exact country of origin is unknown."

Government regulation of foreign trade and international investment reflects, in good measure, the globalization of domestic markets. Although many Americans view this nation as the epitome of free trade, in practice the U.S. government has established a variety of restrictions over imports and exports and over the flow of foreign

TABLE 11.1   International Trade in the U.S. Economy, 1960–1996 (dollars in billions)

Category of Trade	1970 Amount	1970 Percent of GDP	1980 Amount	1980 Percent of GDP	1990 Amount	1990 Percent of GDP	1996 Amount	1996 Percent of GDP
Exports of goods and services	$65.7	6.6%	$339.8	12.9%	$557.0	10.1%	$855.2	11.3%
Imports of goods and services	59	5.9	316.5	12.1	625.9	11.3	953.9	12.6
Balance of trade	$6.7	0.7%	$23.3	0.8%	$68.9	1.2%	$98.7	1.3%

Note: Data are on a national income and product accounts basis.
Source: U.S. Department of Commerce.

investment into the United States. As a result, some of the strongest defenders of protectionism wind up doing business overseas. In the words of retired Chrysler chairman Lee Iacocca, "If you don't go to the lowest-cost source, you're an idiot." In any event, all nations regulate, at least to some degree, the flow of goods, services, and capital across their borders.

Each year, the United States imports and exports vast arrays of goods and services in the world marketplace. Table 11.1 shows the rising importance of international trade to the U.S. economy. The total volume of foreign commerce (imports plus exports) grew almost twice as rapidly as the GDP between 1970 and 1996. The individual items involved range from automobiles, jet aircraft, textiles, and computer software to clothespins, baseball bats, and works of art.

THE CHALLENGE OF PROTECTIONISM

Domestic producers in nearly all of the industries involved with imports or exports feel the pressures of lower-priced competition from producers in other nations. Foreign penetration of U.S. markets ranges from overwhelming domination of color television sets and VCRs to less than 1 percent for folding paperboard boxes. Potentially, any sector of the American economy can be hurt by foreign competition—whether autos or clothespins are at stake. As a result, calls for protection from imports are legion. The rationale for such government intervention can vary. It often ranges from offsetting "unfair" dumping (selling in U.S. markets at prices below market prices abroad), to combating foreign barriers against our exports (*their* protectionism), to promoting our own perceived national security interests.

Numerous industries—notably automobiles, steel, textiles, shoes, and machine tools—have at times exerted pressure on the federal government to restrain the free flow of trade between the United States and the rest of the world. On occasion, the restrictionist impetus comes from the government itself, often as an adjunct to foreign policy—and these restraints usually aim at limiting exports rather than imports.

Key Industry Actions

In the 1980s, some of the most powerful calls for restraint of international trade and investment came from the American automotive industry and the United Auto Workers Union, which earlier had been bastions of free trade. This shift in sentiment was rooted in the fact that sales of imported cars, especially those made in Japan, had captured large shares of the domestic market. Beginning in 1981, Japan was cajoled to impose "voluntary" restraints on its exports of passenger motor vehicles to the United States. (See the box "How 'Voluntary' Export Restraints Work.")

How "Voluntary" Export Restraints Work:
The U.S.-Japanese Auto Agreement

The Japanese imposed restraints on automobile exports to the United States in 1981 to preempt more restrictive measures advocated by many, especially labor groups, within the United States. Earlier that year, Senators John Danforth and Lloyd Bentsen had introduced a bill to limit automobile imports from Japan to 1.6 million units annually during 1981–83, which is very close to the self-imposed "voluntary" export restraint of 1.68 million. (Other proposed legislation was more restrictive in providing for smaller import quotas and in specifying the minimum content of American parts and labor for automobiles sold in the United States.)

Protectionist pressures had been increasing since the late 1970s as automobile sales by U.S. producers declined and foreign producers captured larger shares of the American market.

With the restraints, the prices paid by U.S. consumers for Japanese automobiles rose. This reduced the competitive pressures on U.S. producers and non-Japanese exporters to the United States, increasing prices for these automobiles—but not as much as the rise in Japanese prices. The higher automobile prices reduced U.S. purchases. The effects on U.S. and non-Japanese producers, however, were mitigated by the relatively larger rise in the prices of Japanese automobiles and the resulting shift away from Japanese automobiles.

The restraints also induced quality changes as Japanese producers responded by shifting their mix of exports toward larger and more luxurious models that generated more profits per unit. In addition, more "optional" equipment was installed in each unit. Consequently, the average sales price of Japanese automobiles increased because of the price effect as well as the quality effects associated with the restraints.

For all new cars sold in 1984, prices rose an average of $1,649 (17 percent), which consisted of a pure price effect of $617 per car and a quality effect of $1,032 per car. The higher price led to an estimated reduction in 1984 purchases of approximately 1.5 million.

The price increase for domestically produced automobiles of 12 percent was less than the increase for imports from Japan of 22 percent. This relative price change allowed the U.S. producers to increase their market share by almost 7 percentage points. The number of domestically produced cars was unchanged from the previous year even though Americans bought fewer new cars in total. Thus, the U.S. reduction in 1984 purchases of 1.5 million cars was borne by foreign producers. These production changes were estimated to generate increased domestic automotive employment in a range from 40,000 to 75,000 jobs.

The higher automobile prices—over $6 billion for the year—represent one facet of the losses for consumers. In addition, U.S. consumers were worse off to the extent that quotas limited their range of automotive choices. The losses to consumers were in effect transfers to domestic and foreign producers. Of the foreign producers' gain from higher prices, Japanese producers received approximately $5 billion. This figure provides an obvious reason why the Japanese government continued the restraints beyond 1985 when the Reagan administration decided not to request an extension of the agreement. The formal restraints lapsed in 1988. Much of the Japanese imports have subsequently been replaced by domestic production by subsidiaries of Japanese-owned automobile firms (so-called "transplants").

Goaded by foreign competition, domestic automobile producers streamlined their operations, improving productivity and quality substantially. Although Japanese imports continue to win a substantial but minority share of the U.S. market, U.S.-headquarters companies have regained the initiative and have stabilized their market shares. Some of the imports have been replaced by production from subsidiaries of Japanese (and also German) firms that have been established in the United States. Some of these "transplants" use substantial proportions of U.S. labor and domestically produced parts. As noted in chapter 10, the "domestic content" provisions of the North American Free Trade Agreement have encouraged this trend.

The concern of the American steel industry over steel imports, primarily from the European Union (EU) and the Asian rim, predates Detroit's auto import concerns. The net steel trade balance of the United States shifted from positive to negative as early as 1959, and imports have been substantial since then.

This penetration of imports has, from time to time, prompted domestic steel producers to level charges that importers were *dumping,* or selling steel at lower prices than the producers charge in their home markets. United States law provides for antidumping duties to be levied on imports if the sale of dumped goods causes "material harm" to a domestic industry. Also, countervailing duties can be imposed to offset subsidies by foreign governments if subsidized imports cause harm to American producers.

In 1982, the International Trade Commission ruled that subsidized steel had injured the U.S. domestic steel industry. This action was a necessary step for the imposition of the protective duties. In order to halt the application of the new tariffs, European governments agreed to quotas that would keep their steel imports to about 5 percent of the U.S. market. The U.S. steel producers then withdrew their original complaints, which were the basis for the countervailing duties. The quotas that Western European producers established in response to U.S. pressures meant, in effect, that they had been forced to establish a cartel or market-sharing arrangement in order to head off large tariff increases in the United States. These quotas expired in 1992 and were not renewed. In 1993, the International Trade Commission dismissed most of the domestic steel industry's charges of dumping on the part of their major foreign competitors. The Commission only upheld special high tariffs on high-grade steel used for making automobiles.

"Voluntary" export quotas, also known as orderly marketing agreements (OMAs), were imposed on footwear imports to the United States in the 1970s. They were terminated in 1981 and the experience is quite illuminating. The OMAs hit low-priced shoes disproportionately hard, as foreign producers attempted to maximize their profits within the confines of the trade restraints. Indirectly, the quotas induced an increase in the supply of higher-quality footwear (which is higher in price), thereby resulting in smaller price increases for those shoes that are generally purchased by higher-income groups.

The implicit tax imposed by footwear quotas on the lowest-income group (individuals then earning less than $7,000 annually) was more than three times that imposed on higher-income groups (those with incomes greater than $25,000 a year).[1] Imports of shoes rose rapidly with the termination of the trade restrictions, and pressures for new quotas mounted in 1984. However, the International Trade Commission ruled that the domestic industry was not sufficiently injured to warrant action to restrict imports. Moreover, as shown in Figure 11.1, it became increasingly clear that restricting imports of footwear means that U.S. purchasers of shoes pay more.

Demands for Reciprocity

From time to time, American business and labor interests have voiced demands for a new type of "reciprocity": erecting import barriers to the goods of foreign nations that close or restrict their markets to specific exports from the United States. In its customary use, the term *reciprocity* has had a more positive connotation. It traditionally was viewed as a positive means of promoting equivalent trade opportunities in other countries, rather than as a threat to force trade concessions on a quid pro quo basis. In the older sense, the term was normally equated with unconditional "most-favored nation status," under which the reduction of tariffs for the products of one country must apply to all eligible countries.

The current sentiment for reciprocity is antithetical to this original concept, consisting of both protectionism and retaliation against countries with less open trading policies in the particular commodity under consideration. The main assumptions underlying the new concept are that many nations have not offered trade and investment opportunities as freely as the United States and that existing means of trade enforcement are not strong enough to correct the imbalance. Under the new approach, unilateral action and enforcement on the part of the United States would be stressed, rather than bilateral or multilateral agreements. Thus, the proposals for reciprocity legislation call for closing American markets to those nations that do not grant American firms adequate access to their markets—even though the United States may already have restricted the imports of other products from those same nations.

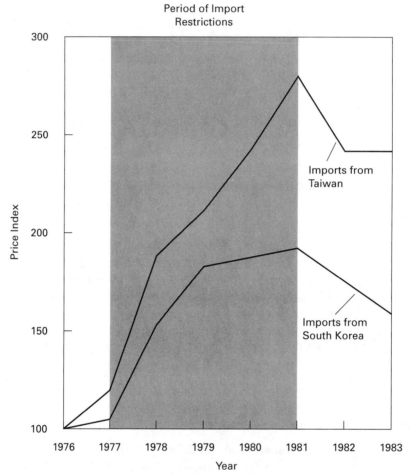

Note: Data from Footwear Industry Association and U.S. Department of Commerce.

FIGURE 11.1 Price of Imported Footwear, 1976–1983 (1976 = 100)

THE CASE FOR FREE TRADE

Given the widespread use of protectionist devices to inhibit the flow of trade among nations, it is useful to examine the key conceptual and historical justifications for an open trading system. The case for free trade is rooted in a basic economic law: the principle of comparative advantage, which holds that total economic welfare will be enhanced if each nation specializes in the production of items that it can produce relatively most efficiently. This is an important case of Adam Smith's more general point concerning the advantages of the specialization of labor. To cite Smith's immortal words:

> It is the maxim of every prudent . . . family, never to attempt to make at home what it will cost . . . more to make than to buy. The tailor does not attempt to make his own shoes, but buys them of the shoemaker . . . What is prudence in the conduct of every private family can scarcely be folly in that of a great kingdom.

Historical Experience

The arguments in favor of freer trade are supported by historical evidence. Through most of the twentieth century, the United States has played a leadership role in developing the world trading system. During the 1930s, however, the United States and many other countries followed "beggar-thy-neighbor" trade policies that contributed to the worldwide depression. The Smoot-Hawley protectionist tariff epitomized this approach in the United States. The results for many companies were extremely negative. Firms that had relied on foreign business were limited to the domestic market, which for some was inadequate for survival.

After World War II, the United States embarked on a program of reciprocal trade agreements. Initially arranged bilaterally, they evolved into the further improved multilateral trading system of the postwar years. This approach broke down many of the historical barriers to world trade. In the 1960s, the acceleration in world trade and economic growth followed a sharp and mutual reduction in tariff barriers. We continue today to reap benefits from the policies initiated in those years.

Our own economic history provides earlier examples of the benefits of an open economy. The United States began as a trading nation. If the concept of "gross domestic product" had existed in the eighteenth and nineteenth centuries, people would have pointed to this country as one of the more open economies, as measured by the share of GDP involved in foreign trade. The United States was then among the more trade-oriented economies in the world. We were major exporters of a wide variety of agricultural products and raw materials. In addition, America's service exports, such as shipping, were an important economic activity. In turn, we were a major importer of manufactured goods and a recipient of large amounts of foreign capital. These factors continued to play a critical role in the development of the U.S. economy during the nineteenth century.

Around the turn of the century, the dynamics of the American economy shifted. Exports and imports became smaller shares of GDP. United States investment abroad increased, gradually transforming us from an international debtor into a world creditor. Increasingly, we became a self-sufficient economy. Only in the last 20 years has the international sector once again begun to increase its relative importance in our economy.

Generalizing from historical experience, the advantages of freer trade are numerous:

- Open trade contributes to lowering inflationary pressures by increasing the supply of goods and services competing for the consumer's dollar. Thus, the question of free trade is basically a consumer issue.
- Open trade minimizes the role of government in influencing private-sector decisions, thus allowing individuals and business firms to respond to the needs and pressures of the international marketplace.
- Open trade improves the efficiency with which our own resources are allocated by permitting the operation of the principle of comparative advantage. Thereby, the society achieves more growth, higher levels of employment, and an improved living standard.

Aside from the direct and measurable aspects, trade stimulates competition, stirs creative energies, rewards individual initiative, and increases national productivity.

Among nations, it speeds the exchange of new ideas and technology. In the long run, international trade means the creation of new jobs and the reduction of inflation. In sum, it contributes to a healthier economy—one with more job opportunities and a wider variety of goods and services. Moreover, despite the many specific departures from free and open trade that exist in practice, a basic symmetry exists in world trading patterns. For example, in 1996, the United States was the world's largest exporter and importer, Germany was the second largest, and Japan was the third largest.

THE POLITICAL POWER OF PROTECTIONISM

It is helpful to understand why protectionism is popular. It is a means by which relatively small, well-organized groups use the political process to their advantage. The benefits are received by the protected industries, while some costs are shifted to other companies that buy from those industries. Ultimately, most of the costs are borne by consumers in the form of higher prices. Thus, protectionism can be viewed as a hidden tax on the consumer. (See Table 11.2 for some examples.) That "tax" was estimated in 1990 at $70 billion.[2]

The balance of political power is extremely uneven, given the limited knowledge that consumers have about these matters. Those who are harmed by the reduced supply of goods and services are generally not even aware of the process by which they are hurt. Although the total costs of protectionism far exceed the benefits, the higher prices to consumers are widely diffused among the 50 states and 250 million residents. Any single consumer's stake in the outcome is small. The individual almost surely is not aware of why the price of a given item is going up. Consequently, resistance at the grassroots level to protectionist measures is often considerably less than pressure for their adoption.

TABLE 11.2 Cost to Consumer of Protection, 1988

Item	Free Market Price	Price with Trade Restrictions	Cost of Protection per Item	Percentage of Free Market Price
Automobile	$7,500	$10,000	$2,500	33%
Blue jeans	14	18	4	29
Box of candy	2	3	1	50
Clock radio	30	32	2	7
Leather handbag	40	44	4	10
Man's sweater	20	25	5	25
Rubber boots	10	12	2	20
Teddy bear	8	10	2	25
Vinyl handbag	10	12	2	20
Woman's leather gloves	33	40	7	21

Note: Data from Institute for International Economics and U.S. Department of Commerce.

The nineteenth century reformer Henry George may be best known as the proponent of a single tax (on land), but he provided one of the most telling criticisms of protectionism:

> Protective tariffs are as much applications of force as are blockading squadrons. . . . The difference between the two is that blockading squadrons are a means whereby nations seek to prevent their enemies from trading; protective tariffs are a means whereby nations attempt to prevent their own people from trading. What protection teaches us is to do to ourselves in time of peace what enemies seek to do to us in time of war.

It is interesting to note that "protecting" the consumer against low prices is not limited to the United States. A letter to the editor of a Tokyo newspaper written by a Japanese housewife furnishes an interesting example. (See the box "A Tokyo Housewife Criticizes Japanese Protectionism.")

A Tokyo Housewife Criticizes Japanese Protectionism

To the Editor:

Many of us city wives are now fed up with having to pay as much as 500 yen to 700 yen for 100 grams of beef because the government keeps restrictions on its import. Husbands are asked to buy beef for *omiyage* (souvenirs) at American or Australian airports on their way home to bring back to their families because beef is much cheaper in those countries. Oranges and grapefruit can also be much cheaper if only our government liberalizes their imports.

The government says it cannot lift the restrictions because the Japanese farmers should be protected. But the Japanese farmers are now the most privileged people. They are paying much less tax than salaried people in the cities. Some of them are even paid for not growing rice in their paddy fields. The farmers are much better off in politics because rural *senkyo-ku* (constituencies) elect more Diet members than city *senkyo-ku* per population. Sometimes a city Diet member represents four times as many electors as a rural MP.

I cannot but suspect that politicians and officials are not so patriotic as they claim, and they seek their own good by spoiling our farmers. Politicians can retain their seats in the parliament and get political funds from the farmers' organizations. Bureaucrats can keep key posts in corporations and other bodies which control the import regulations for their own postretirement jobs. Why should we city people support these farmers (and politicians and bureaucrats) by paying much more for beef and oranges (and rice too) than in other countries?

Etsuko Kinoshita

Source: Mainichi Daily News, January 20, 1983.

Protectionism can also hit hard the domestic industries that use "protected" items in their own production. A striking case in point is the different impacts on steel-making companies and steel-using industries. The 1984 voluntary export restraints (VERs) on steel potentially "saved" about 14,000 jobs in American firms producing steel. However, the higher prices for domestic steel that resulted from the import restrictions made domestic automobile and other durable-goods products less competitive. Consequently, the VERs resulted in 50,000 fewer manufacturing jobs in steel-using industries than would have been the case without the restraints.[3]

With the increased globalization of business operations, many more domestic companies feel the effects of trade restraints than is generally suspected. Because so much of the imports and exports of the major trading nations are now in the form of transactions between domestic firms and their foreign affiliates or parents, the distinction between American- and foreign-made products is increasingly more difficult to determine.

This leads to a set of questions on which experts answer differently. Is Honda USA part of the U.S. economy? What about IBM's operations in Tokyo? What is clear is that the consequences of the internationalization of business are profound for many firms. Half of Xerox's 100,000 employees work on foreign soil. Less than one-half of Sony's workers are Japanese. Most of Nestlé's production occurs outside of Switzerland.

FOREIGN GOVERNMENT OBSTACLES TO U.S. EXPORTS

A perennial source of protectionist sentiment is generated by the numerous tariff and nontariff barriers that face the producers of products and services when they try to penetrate overseas markets. These obstacles to trade range from direct "transparent" tariffs to hidden and arcane licensing requirements.

Quotas on Imports

A major category of trade restraint is quotas, or restrictions on the quantity of foreign imports. Many nations have numerical restrictions on agricultural products. Japan maintains 27 separate restrictions covering farm and extractive industries. These comprise a long list: meat, milk and cream, processed cheese, shore fish and cod roe, scallops, squid, shellfish, edible seaweeds, citrus fruits, pineapples, fruit juices, tomato juice, ketchup, starch and insulin, grape sugar, wheat, rice, groats, flour, beans, peas, peanuts, coal, and leather products. Quotas on foreign films and television programs are also common. Other limits on imports range from manufactured goods to technical services.

Tariffs on Imports

Tariffs, depending especially on their level, also hamper international trade. Brazil at the end of 1992 levied a high average effective tariff of 17 percent, albeit down from 32 percent in 1990. Nominal tariffs in China range from 3 percent on goods whose import is being encouraged to 250 percent on automobiles; in practice, however, most transactions involve substantial reductions from these "listed prices," depending on very special circumstances (which provides opportunities for favoritism, bribery, etc.).

Tariffs have advantages over quotas for both consumers and foreign exporters. Provided the tariff rates applied are not prohibitively high, foreign producers can remain competitive by cutting costs or improving quality. Quotas do not provide incentives for better meeting consumer needs, since market shares are limited regardless of the improved efficiency of the potential exporter. However, the European Union protects its agriculture by means of variable tariffs that raise the prices of imported items above the prices prevailing in the EU.

Buy-Domestic Restrictions

Many foreign countries maintain *buy-domestic* practices. The criteria for award of a public works contract in Brazil may include "percentage of national ownership" of competing firms. Most U.S. international trading partners use their own airlines, place insurance for government projects exclusively with domestic firms, and use only domestic computer capacity for data processing needs, whether by law or "understanding."

Other Regulatory Barriers to Imports

Many if not most nations have adopted internal regulations that, inadvertently or not, serve as obstacles to international trade. (India, for example, operates a licensing system that bans the majority of foreign consumer goods entirely.) Laws protecting foreign franchises, patents, and copyrights are often indifferently enforced. Such irregularity makes international operation of a patented process or product line both very complicated and in danger of outright pirating. This is a growing problem in the protection of copyrights on telecommunications and computer software, products that are expensive for a U.S. firm to develop and very difficult to protect in another country.

Most countries maintain regulatory restrictions on franchising of foreign firms, whether it be technical, professional services, banking, or consumer services such as restaurants or retail stores. The fact that regulations are vague and are often subject to interpretation by local bureaucracy makes entry by foreign firms both expensive and time-consuming.

China often requires testing and certification of foreign products to ensure compliance with specifications and standards not even made available to exporters. In Korea, retailers of imported compact discs must submit 31 documents to three different regulatory authorities who each require six separate application forms for each recording—and to pay "administration fees" that amount to more than the price of the CD.

Barriers to Financial Services

Banking and other financial services are heavily restricted. Differential access to domestic rediscounting, discriminatory tax treatment and reserve requirements, outright prohibition of retail banking, and restrictions on foreign ownership often make it difficult for U.S. banks to compete with local financial institutions. Pakistan does not license new foreign insurance companies; foreign banks are generally limited to three branches, although one U.S. bank has received an exception. In Indonesia, any new foreign bank must be a joint venture between an Indonesian bank and a foreign bank from a country that offers reciprocity.

Another aspect of overseas trade barriers is internal marketing systems. In Southeast Asia, ethnic Chinese family-oriented firms are accustomed to informal business dealings with fellow members of the "bamboo network" who they trust and who have a similar linguistic and cultural background. Such practices make it difficult for other companies to penetrate those markets.[4]

Japan's *kieretsu* distribution system gives preference to local products. No practical way exists to bypass this highly traditional way of doing business. Informal vertical integration, in the form of long-term business "relationships" (often several generations old), tend to effectively deny U.S. firms access to retail markets. The most difficult characteristic of this type of barrier is the fact that change is almost impossible to negotiate. As far as Japan's government is concerned, no trade barrier exists, and entry is free.

Invisible Barriers

Many nations inhibit imports by means of administrative procedures that can be more difficult to deal with than formal trade barriers such as tariffs and quotas. China maintains a complex import approval process. Depending on the locality, as many as 15 "chops" (clearances) from various ministries or bureaus may be necessary. Permission to import is often required from both local and central government authorities. Vagueness and uncertainty also complicate foreign trade. China also maintains that in many cases it does not resort to quantitative restrictions on imports, but the government does not make public the criteria that do apply.

South Korea makes frequent, unannounced changes in its standards on labeling and documentation requirements for imports of consumer goods. Because import approvals often involve numerous ministries and the various entry procedures operate sequentially, delays of 30 to 90 days are frequently encountered. Combined with tariffs of 30 percent or higher, imports of food products are effectively inhibited by the Korean trade-regulation system.[5]

THE ROLE OF INTERNATIONAL AGENCIES

An often overlooked category of impediments to international trade is the array of codes and restrictions enacted by international agencies such as the European Union (EU) and the United Nations (UN) and its many specialized agencies (see Figure 11.2). Some of the international agencies' actions are broad; others are directed at specific business activities. Some of these regulatory efforts are in the form of advisory resolutions or voluntary guidelines; others are legally binding treaties.

UN Regulatory Activities

The International Labor Organization is the oldest of the UN agencies. More than 5,000 government ratifications of over 300 ILO policy declarations have been recorded. They cover standards dealing with employment, training, working conditions, and industrial relations.

UNITED NATIONS	Operations	Marketing	Finance	Technology	Services	Information
General Assembly	■	■				■
Conf. on Trade and Development (UNCTAD)		■				
Environmental Program (UNEP)	■					
Development Program (UNDP)	■			■		
Economic and Social Council (ECOSOC)	■	■	■			
Regional Commissions	■				■	■
Comm. on Transnational Corps. (CTC)	■	■	■	■		
Food and Agriculture Organization (FAO)		■				
International Maritime Organization (IMO)	■			■		
International Labor Organization (ILO)	■					
Int'l. Telecommunications Union (ITU)				■		■
Educational, Scientific, Cultural (UNESCO)		■				
Industrial Development Organization (UNIDO)				■		
World Health Organization (WHO)	■					
World Intellectual Property Org. (WIPO)				■		
European Union (EU)	■	■	■			
Org. for Econ. Coop. & Develop. (OECD)	■	■	■			

Source: Center for the Study of American Business, Washington University.

FIGURE 11.2 Regulatory Activities of International Organizations by Business Function

Companies involved in international marketing of products face a variety of regulatory measures by UN agencies. The best known of these is the Infant Formula Code, adopted by the UN's World Health Organization (WHO). This code calls for a wide variety of restrictions on the marketing and distribution of breast-milk substitutes, applying not only to advertising, distribution of samples, and labeling requirements, but to the activities and compensation of marketing personnel. The Infant Formula Code is not legally binding, but companies such as Nestlé, a major maker of infant formula, have encountered overwhelming public pressure to abide by it.[6]

The UN's General Assembly has adopted the Economic and Social Council's consumer protection code, which creates voluntary guidelines. The Food and Agricultural Organization has approved an International Code of Conduct in the Distribution and Use of Pesticides. The Code provides guidelines for marketing and using pesticides, especially in developing countries.

In contrast to these various regulatory activities—which tend to restrict trade—the recently established World Trade Organization (WTO) is dedicated to opening markets for international trade. In 1997, the United States and 68 other members of the WTO concluded a precedent-setting agreement to open markets for basic telecommunications services around the world to competition and foreign investors. By opening the $600 billion global telecommunications market to competition, the Federal Communications Commission estimates that the average cost of an international call could drop from one dollar a minute to 20 cents.

The European Union

Firms operating within the EU have become aware of costs of complying with a host of international regulations. For example, standards on the preparation of annual financial reports—covering accounting categories, asset valuation rules, capitalization of companies, inflation accounting, and auditing procedures—are mandated under the EU's Fourth Company Directive. The Seventh Company Directive requires corporations operating in the EU to make public financial reports on their subsidiary operations. The reporting requirements depend on the level of parent-company ownership and apply whether or not the headquarters of the controlling company is within the EU.

EU patent regulation has resulted in the establishment of protectionist trade barriers. Under one such law, products patented both outside and within the EU cannot be imported into member countries without permission of the EU patent holder. For example, a drug patented in both the United States and in Germany that the U.S. patent holder wishes to distribute in the Netherlands would be affected. Because the United States is not a member of the EU, the German patent holder is able to deny importation by the Netherlands of any products containing the patented drug that the German patent holder also markets abroad.

In 1996, the EU's European Works Council Directive came into force. It requires each multinational with one thousand or more employees in Western Europe and with at least 150 workers in two different member states to set up a European Works Council. The Council is a formal procedure for management to inform and consult with employees. The employer pays the costs involved, including employee time, travel expenses, interpreters, and so on. Depending on the labor relations policies of the individual nations, employers can set a council up on their own or negotiate with unions to do so. French law, for example, specifies that the unions will choose the representatives to the Works Council, while in Ireland the entire workforce participates in that decision. The United Kingdom, in contrast, has opted out of the whole process.[7]

The EU's new environmental regulations are often a source of contention for U.S. firms doing business in Western Europe. To qualify for the EU's new eco-labels, firms have to agree to cut chlorine and sulfur emissions and curtail energy consumption during the production process. In addition, paper products companies have to demonstrate that the pulp used comes from environmentally sound forestry practices that maintain biodiverse forests and reduce water effluent levels. United States producers claim that no American firm can currently meet these standards.[8]

It is useful to examine the liberating as well as the restrictive features of the European Union. Controls on the physical movement of goods across internal national borders within the EU have been removed. Customs checks have largely disappeared, and customs forms are no longer required at internal border crossings.

Many of the barriers to the movement of people have been eliminated. Citizens of one member nation can reside in any other member nation, although in practice workers are not as mobile as in the United States. The flow of money and credit has been enhanced by the decision that one country will supervise each banking or insurance institution—the country where the organization's head office is located. In addition, mutual recognition of licenses issued in the country of origin is provided. Thus, the authorization of only one member country is required to operate throughout the

EU. As a general proposition—exceptions are inevitable—all enterprises established inside the EU have equal rights irrespective of the location of their headquarters or source of capital.[9]

A major advance in the activities of the EU occurred in 1998 when, under the Maastricht Treaty, a single European currency was authorized and a European Central Bank set up. The formal decision on national membership of the European Economic and Monetary Union (EMU) is a difficult issue. Under the Maastricht treaty, member nations have to meet stringent criteria on monetary, fiscal, and economic parameters, (e.g., a limit on the size of the budget deficit in relation to the GDP).

A single currency will greatly change Europe's financial landscape. The elimination of much of the foreign exchange trading that now occurs among member nations will reduce the costs of most international transactions.

U.S. OBSTACLES TO INTERNATIONAL COMMERCE

Contrary to a widespread belief, the United States is not an island of free trade in a world of protectionism. The federal government imposes numerous obstacles to imports, restricts various types of exports, and also discourages or prevents certain types of foreign investment.

Five major types of trade obstacles inhibit imports into the United States:

1. Buy-American statutes, which give preference in government procurement to domestic producers.
2. The Jones Act, which prohibits foreign ships from engaging in waterborne commerce between U.S. ports.
3. Statutes that limit the import of specific agricultural and manufactured products.
4. Selective high tariffs on specific items.
5. Regulatory barriers aimed at protecting domestic producers.

"Buy-American" and Merchant Marine Statutes

Buy-American provisions have been enacted by many government units. The Buy American Act requires federal agencies that purchase commodities for use within the United States to pay up to a 6 percent differential for domestically produced goods. As much as a 50 percent differential is paid for military goods produced at home. In addition, the Surface Transportation Assistance Act requires that, for most purchases over $500,000, American materials and products be used. Also, American flag vessels must be used to transport at least 50 percent of the gross tonnage of all commodities financed with U.S. foreign aid funds.

The buy-American laws of the states are varied (see Table 11.3). New York requires state agencies to buy American steel. Arizona stipulates that all construction materials must be purchased in the state. The Missouri law also requires cities to adopt procurement guidelines that reflect the buy-American philosophy. In addition, numerous states and municipal authorities require use of American materials in privately owned as well as government-owned utilities.

TABLE 11.3 Buy-American Practices Imposed by the States

State	Buy-American Preference	In-State Preference
Alabama	Construction	
Alaska		All purchasing
Arizona		Construction materials
Arkansas		Commodities, printing, construction
California	Food	Vendors in distressed areas, enterprise zones
Florida	Meats	
Georgia	Beef, lumber	Forestry products
Hawaii		Commodities, printing
Idaho		Printing
Illinois	Steel	Coal
Indiana	Steel	Coal
Iowa	Motor vehicles	Coal
Kansas	General[a]	
Louisiana	Motor vehicles	Products
Maryland	Steel	
Massachusetts		Commodities
Michigan		Printing
Minnesota	General[b]	
Missouri	Products, commodities	
Montana		Commodities
New Jersey	Public works material	
New Mexico	General[c]	Commodities, services, construction
New York	Steel	Food
Ohio	General[b]	Commodities, services
Oklahoma	Beef	Commodities
Oregon		Printing
Pennsylvania	Steel, motor vehicles	
Rhode Island	Steel	
South Carolina	General[d]	Commodities
South Dakota	Beef	Grade A milk processors
Virginia		Coal
West Virginia	Aluminum, glass, steel	Construction, repair, public improvements
Wyoming	Beef	Construction, printing

[a]The purchasing director may reject a bid because a product is manufactured or assembled outside the United States.

[b]The Department of Administration may set a preference for American-made products.

[c]Requires only that goods must be assembled in North America, above the equator.

[d]Requires that first choice be for products made or grown in South Carolina, provided price is no more than 5 percent higher.

Source: National Institute of Governmental Purchasing.

The Merchant Marine Act (the Jones Act) requires that all oceangoing shipments from one point in the United States to another be transported in U.S. flag vessels. This law effectively bars foreign competition in U.S. domestic marine transport. The perverse effects are great. At times, Canadian lumber transported in Japanese flag vessels has undersold domestic timber from Oregon in the lucrative Southern

California market. Both the American merchant marine and the American timber industry suffer loss of business. The benefits of trying to help the American merchant
marine by restricting foreign trade are received by foreigners!

Import Restrictions

Numerous federal statutes and agreements restrict the import of specific products.
Section 22 of the Agricultural Adjustment Act of 1938 permits the president to regulate the imports of agricultural products if such imports "materially interfere" with
agricultural price-support programs. Section 22 quotas currently limit imports of
wheat, peanuts, cotton, and sugar.

Some of the annual limits on imports into the United States are very specific. Ja-
maica is restricted to exporting 621,149 gloves and mittens, the Philippines to
7,882,316 brassieres, and Pakistan to 4,391,160 pillowcases.

U.S. companies that believe they have been hurt by "unfair" trade policies or
practices overseas have a variety of opportunities to seek federal help (see Table 11.4). For example, the long-standing escape clause of the Trade Act of 1974 and
its predecessor statutes provide for temporary "relief" from low U.S. tariffs in the case
of industries that show serious injury, or threat of that condition, from imports. That

TABLE 11.4 U.S. Laws Dealing with Complaints about Imports

Nature of the Law	Agency's Responses	Action Complained About	Nature of Relief Granted
Section 301 of the Trade Act of 1974	USTR investigates and recommends to president retaliatory measures	Violations of a trade agreement or special foreign market barrier	Negotiations to stop foreign practice, with threat of retaliation
Countervailing Duty Law	DOC determines foreign subsidy; ITC determines injury	Foreign subsidies on imports; injuring or threatening to injure a U.S. industry	Countervailing duties equal to the computed subsidy
Antidumping Law	DOC determines dumping; ITC determines injury	Selling foreign goods in U.S. below cost; injuring or threatening to injure a U.S. industry	Antidumping duties equal to the amount by which the goods are sold below cost
Section 201 of the Trade Act of 1974	ITC determines injury and recommends relief; president determines relief	Increased imports that cause or threaten serious injury to a U.S. industry	Almost any form of protection and/or adjustment assistance

Note: DOC = Department of Commerce
ITC = International Trade Commission
USTR = U.S. Trade Representative

procedure was used in 1984 to increase the tariff on motorcycles tenfold and to restrict copper imports.

Also, the federal government can impose tariff increases in the form of antidumping and countervailing duties on what U.S. law considers to be unfair practices in international trade (see Table 11.5). In 1995 alone, action was taken against 13 nations in product categories ranging from fresh garlic to silicomanganese.

Dumping is defined as selling a product for export below its "fair value," generally the price prevailing in the home market or, if insufficient sales are made there, in third markets.[10] Two actions are required before antidumping duties can be imposed: (1) a finding by the Department of Commerce of sales at less than fair value and (2) a finding by the International Trade Commission of "material" injury to domestic producers (ignoring any benefits to American consumers). Countervailing duties are levied when it is shown that a foreign country is subsidizing an export to the United States. A finding of material injury is also required.

A domestic company hard hit by import competition can petition for a tariff increase under the "escape clause" of the Trade Act of 1974. (See the box "A History of the Escape Clause.") The basic requirement to "escape" from negotiated tariff reductions is to show that increased imports "cause or threaten serious injury to domestic producers."

TABLE 11.5 U.S. Findings Against Charges of Unfair Foreign Trade Practice Charges, 1995

Nation	Product	Finding
Argentina	Steel pipe, oilfield tubulars	Dumping
Brazil	Stainless steel bars, steel pipe	Dumping
China	Fresh garlic, paper clips, pencils, silicomanganese	Dumping
Germany	Steel pipe	Dumping
India	Stainless steel bars	Dumping
Italy	Steel pipe	Dumping, subsidy
Japan	Stainless steel bars, oilfield tubulars	Dumping
Mexico	Oilfield tubulars	Dumping
Russia	Ferrovanadium, nitrided vanadium	Dumping
South Africa	Furfuryl alcohol	Dumping
Spain	Stainless steel bars	Dumping
Thailand	Furfuryl alcohol, canned pineapple	Dumping
Ukraine	Silicomanganese	Dumping

Source: International Trade Commission.

A History of the "Escape Clause"

In 1930, to aid a faltering economy, the United States enacted the Smoot-Hawley tariff, which raised average tariff rates by nearly 50 percent. Instead of increasing domestic production, Smoot-Hawley led to retaliation by foreign governments and contributed to the severity of the depression. In 1934, the Congress empowered the president to negotiate bilateral tariff agreements that would reduce tariffs on specific commodities by up to 50 percent. These agreements paved the way for the adoption of the General Agreement on Tariffs and Trade (GATT) in 1947 and the establishment of the World Trade Organization in 1995. Under the auspices of GATT, successive rounds of tariff liberalization occurred, and the average tariff on imports into the United States is now 20 percent of the levels established by the Smoot-Hawley tariff in 1930.

While WTO's primary goal is to establish a more open international trade environment, it recognizes the right of a government to part from free and open trade in certain circumstances. In particular, WTO allows a country to "escape" from negotiated tariff reductions, if the increased imports can be shown to "cause or threaten serious injury to domestic producers" of competitive products. In those cases, the country can unilaterally elect to reinstate the trade barrier that was in effect before the concession. The provision was meant to give industries time to adjust to increased competition.

In the United States, requests for protection are made to the International Trade Commission (ITC), which has the responsibility for determining whether the industry has been seriously injured or threatened with serious injury by imports. If so, it recommends to the president the type of trade relief needed to alleviate the injury. The authority to adjust tariffs or impose quotas is reserved for the president. In addition, the ITC can recommend that employees and firms be given trade-adjustment assistance.

In determining appropriate relief, the president is required to consider its effectiveness in facilitating adjustment, as well as its costs on consumers and the economy. Often the president does not impose relief in cases where the ITC has recommended it. The president may also decide to seek import relief even though the ITC has found that imports were not the major factor behind the industry's injury, as President Reagan did for the automobile industry in 1982. There have also been several instances where trade protection has been awarded without a formal escape-clause proceeding.

Section 201 of the Trade Act of 1974 relaxed the requirements to qualify for escape clause relief. It severed the connection between trade liberalization and import protection, making the term "escape clause" somewhat of a misnomer. In addition, the importance of imports in causing the injury was reduced. Previously, it had to be shown that imports were a more important cause of injury than all other causes taken together. Under the revised standard, imports merely had to be the most important cause. Despite these liberalizations, securing trade relief via the escape-clause route remains a far-from-certain proposition. In 1995, the Commission instituted only one escape clause investigation, involving fresh winter tomatoes. In that less-than-earthshaking instance, the petition was withdrawn after the International Trade Commission determined that provisional relief should not be granted.

Source: Congressional Budget Office and International Trade Commission.

Selective High Tariffs

Despite low average duties (4.7 percent in 1996), some individual U.S. tariffs are quite high. Customs duties on certain kinds of fabrics range up to 36 percent—three times the rate in Western Europe. The rate on clothing averages 20 percent; the duty on tobacco is 11 percent (see Table 11.6). However, the proportion of imports entering the United States duty-free rose from a low of 27 percent in 1982 to a high of 51 percent in 1996. When it aggregates all the imports (dutiable and duty free), the International Trade Commission estimates that the average tariff collected in the United States came to 2.3 percent in 1996.

Internal Restrictions

Domestic regulation often acts to limit imports, whether that is the intent or not. In the United States, more than 2,700 state and local governments require particular safety certifications for products sold or installed within their jurisdictions. These requirements often are not uniform. Acquiring the necessary information and satisfying the established procedures is a major undertaking for a foreign enterprise.

A major import barrier is the array of state and local building codes. Government authorities typically enact the standards drawn up by private building associations. This procedure opens the way for imposing discriminatory rules favorable to the local industry. Ceramic tile provides a good example. After Japanese imports captured much of the U.S. market for floor tile in the 1960s, many building codes were revised to screen out imported wall tile by requiring a thickness of 1/4 inch. That rule disallowed tile produced in Japan and Europe, which had a standard 5/32 thickness.

The federal government restricts, and at times prohibits, foreign companies and citizens of other countries from investing in specific sectors of the economy. Foreign corporations are effectively barred from defense contracts and atomic energy facilities; they cannot hold more than 25 percent of the stock of domestic airlines or more than 20 percent in the case of TV and radio stations. The chief executives of fishing companies and dredging firms must be U.S. citizens.

TABLE 11.6 Selected U.S. High Tariffs

Product	Tariff
Clothing	20–34.6%
Soccer uniforms	35
Silk and wool-blend fabrics	38
Ceramic tiles	20
Tableware	26–35
Glassware	20–38
Footwear	35
Garlic and dried onions	35
Zinc alloys	19

Note: Data from Commission of European Union, 1993.

Barriers to U.S. Exports

The United States has adopted more restrictions on its own exports than any other capitalist nation. These barriers range from direct export controls to indirect regulatory barriers.

Export Controls   Despite the desire to promote exports, two types of U.S. statutes and regulations prevent or restrict the export of specific commodities, the first relating to national security and foreign policy matters and the second to domestic concerns. Different laws and bureaucracies administer the formal controls, ranging from limiting of specific weapons to enforcing embargoes on such nations as Cuba. In addition, the Trans-Alaska Pipeline Authorization Act effectively prohibits the export of oil from North Slope fields. A rider to an appropriation act for the Interior Department bans timber exports from federal lands west of the 100th meridian. In both of those cases, the supply restrictions were adopted in periods of temporary shortages, but the barriers are embedded in permanent legislation.

Three federal departments administer the export control laws: State handles the Arms Export Control Act, Commerce the Export Administration Act, and Treasury and Commerce jointly the Trading with the Enemy Act and the International Emergency Economic Powers Act. The result has been overlapping and confusing regulatory systems and duplicative licensing forms and review staffs.

All sorts of inconsistencies arise from the profusion of export restraints. U.S. commercial jet aircraft are routinely approved for export with all technology intact, while communications satellites with less technology content are excluded from export. Moreover, the satellites are launched into orbit and are not "delivered" to any foreign customer or country. Moreover, most economic sanctions are ineffective because other nations are usually willing and able to serve as alternative suppliers.[11]

Nevertheless, export controls are politically attractive because the costs they impose are "off budget," being borne by the employees, managers, and shareholders of the affected companies. Restricting exports as a matter of domestic or foreign policy does more than limit U.S. international trade for the time the restrictions are in force. They call into question the reliability of the United States as a supplier of products to other countries, which are likely to develop alternative sources. A clear example is soybeans. Although the intent was to prevent a short-term increase in domestic prices, the main effect of U.S. controls over soybean exports instituted in 1974 was to induce Japan to turn to other producing countries, particularly Brazil. Japan encouraged the development of alternative sources to U.S. production, thus effectively and permanently reducing the U.S. share of the world soybean market.

Regulatory Burdens   The United States conducts a great variety of domestic regulatory activities that raise the prices of U.S. goods. Foreign producers often are not subject to similar burdens in their home country. A comparison of U.S. and U.K. environmental regulatory policies concluded that the U.S. government's approach has been relatively insensitive to the goals, and unresponsive to the objections, of private enterprise. The study also showed that the U.S. regulatory regime is more coercive than those of other industrial democracies.[12]

The federal government also has imposed special burdens on companies involved in foreign trade. The Foreign Corrupt Practices Act requires strict recordkeeping standards to monitor the antibribery sections of the statute. Violators of the Act face severe penalties. A company may be fined up to $1 million, and its officers who participate in violations or "had reason to know" of them face up to five years in prison and $10,000 in fines.

Many business executives contend that the language of the Foreign Corrupt Practices Act is so sweeping and ambiguous that American firms turn down foreign business when they merely suspect they could be charged with bribery. Businesses are forced into marketing approaches that are unnaturally conservative. That view is supported by the fact that very few cases are prosecuted under the Corrupt Practices Act. Thus, one of the major criticisms of the Act is that it has cost American firms export opportunities without reducing the level of foreign corruption. By precluding American firms from taking part in questionable transactions, which may be perfectly legal and acceptable practices in many other nations, the law simply reduces the ability of U.S. firms to compete overseas. A 1996 study by the National Bureau of Economic Research supported the conclusion that, by acting unilaterally, the United States weakens the competitive position of American firms without significantly reducing the importance of bribery to foreign business transactions.[13]

Several environmental programs impose special requirements on exports. Under the Federal Insecticide, Fungicide, and Rodenticide Act, exporters of products deemed hazardous in the United States must notify the importing country 30 days in advance of shipment—even if the item is not viewed as hazardous under the laws of the importing country. The importing nation must notify the exporter that the notice was received. No other country has such a restriction.

U.S. Barriers to Foreign Investment

Most countries restrict or prohibit foreign investment to some degree. The United States is no exception. The most significant barrier is the Exon-Florio provisions of the Trade Act of 1988. Under this law, mergers and acquisitions by foreign companies deemed to affect national security are reviewed by an interagency committee chaired by the Treasury Department. If the Committee finds that the merger or acquisition will harm the national security, the president may order the foreign parties to divest themselves of those U.S. assets.

A 1993 amendment strengthened the review process by requiring the president to report to the Congress on the results of each review by the interagency committee. Moreover, that review must be broadened to cover the potential effect on the international technological leadership of the United States "in areas affecting the national security."

Although very few foreign investments have been formally vetoed through the Exon-Florio process, the prospect of going through an intensive public review has discouraged foreign acquisitions of high-tech American firms. Of approximately 918 filings of foreign acquisitions registered through the end of 1994, only 15 were subject to a full committee investigation. Five were terminated when the parties withdrew and 10 were sent to the president for a decision. In only one case did he formally block a transaction, ordering CATIC, an arm of the Chinese government, to divest its interest in MAMCO, a Seattle-based maker of airplane parts.[14]

INTERNATIONAL POLITICAL RISK ASSESSMENT

Because of the possibility of sudden and massive changes in the public policy environment facing multinational enterprises in their various overseas markets, political risk assessments often accompany, if not precede, more conventional evaluations of financial and economic risk.

Between 1960 and 1981, over 1,500 individual firms from 22 countries were expropriated in 511 separate actions by 76 nations. As a result, many large companies began to undertake more systematic means of assessing and managing the political risks of overseas business activities. Clearly, the risk of doing business abroad, especially in the case of the developing nations, extends to more than customary market uncertainties or even to traditional changes in monetary and fiscal policy. The possibility of fundamental changes in a nation's government policies and institutions cannot be safely ignored.

Major multinational corporations in the leading countries systematically monitor political risk and the possibility of economic policy changes in countries where they have or are contemplating foreign direct investments. Other companies usually undertake risk analysis prior to a specific investment decision.

The term *political risk* refers to the legal and social environment in which a firm has to operate. Some analysts rely mainly on written materials, such as newspapers

TABLE 11.7   Composite Analysis of Political Risk

Low-Risk Nations	Moderate-Risk Nations	High-Risk Nations
Austria	Argentina	China
Australia	Brazil	Columbia
Belgium	Chile	Egypt
Canada	Czech Republic	India
Denmark	Greece	Indonesia
Finland	Hungary	Jordan
France	Israel	Morocco
Germany	Korea	Nigeria
Ireland	Malaysia	Pakistan
Italy	Mexico	Peru
Japan	Philippines	Russia
The Netherlands	Poland	Sri Lanka
New Zealand	Portugal	Turkey
Norway	Singapore	Vietnam
Sweden	Spain	Zimbabwe
Switzerland	Taiwan	
United Kingdom	Thailand	
	Venezuela	

Note: The entries and categories are a composite of numerous individual analyses of political risk. Borderline cases exist in each category.

and reference works. Many establish and interview a paid panel of experts, including those with specialized knowledge of individual countries. Analysis groups also commission outside experts to write reports on specific topics. Early practitioners were influenced by think-tank and military research, relying heavily on quantitative analysis to evaluate the relative risk of investments in different countries. This approach has been broadened as more subjective factors, such as traditions and culture, have been incorporated into the analysis.

The evaluation of the overall degree of turmoil or even uncertainty expected in any nation in a 5- or 10-year time span is extremely subjective. Nevertheless, most analyses of political risk classify in the *low risk* category the advanced industrialized and democratic nations, such as France, the Netherlands, and New Zealand, each of which has a strong legal system. In contrast, most of the nations labeled *high risk* are the relatively undeveloped nations, especially in Africa, with limited economic or political infrastructure. The emerging economies in East Asia, South America, and Eastern Europe usually hold intermediate positions (see Table 11.7). There is, in general, a high and inverse correlation between the anticipated level of turmoil and the projected environment for exports and direct investment.

Notes

1. Joon H. Suh, *"Voluntary" Export Restraints and Their Effects on Exporters and Consumers: The Case of Footwear Quotas* (St. Louis: Washington University, Center for the Study of American Business, 1981).
2. Gary C. Hufbauer and Kimberly Elliott, *Measuring the Costs of Protection in the United States* (Washington, DC: Institute for International Economics, 1994).
3. Arthur T. Denzau, *How Import Restraints Reduce Employment* (St. Louis: Washington University, Center for the Study of American Business, 1987).
4. Murray Weidenbaum and Samuel Hughes, *The Bamboo Network* (New York: Free Press, 1996), pp. 121–151.
5. Office of the U.S. Trade Representative, *Foreign Trade Barriers* (Washington, DC: Government Printing Office, 1993).
6. S. Prakash Sethi, "A New Perspective on the International Social Regulation of Business," *Journal of Socio-Economics* 22, no. 2, pp. 141–158.
7. *European Works Council* (New York: Conference Board, 1997), pp. 1–23.
8. William H. Lash III, *Green Showdown at the WTO* (St. Louis: Washington University, Center for the Study of American Business, 1997), p. 6.
9. Michael Calingaert, "A Perspective for U.S. Business in an Integrated Europe," *Business Economics,* July 1995, pp. 39–43.
10. The calculation of "fair" price must include an 8 percent profit, compared to the average of 5 percent prevailing in U.S. manufacturing and trade industries in recent years.
11. Claude Barfield and Mark Groombridge, "U.S. Unilateral Sanctions Are Overused and Undereffective," *The American Enterprise,* September/October 1997, pp. 76–77.
12. David Vogel, *National Styles of Regulation* (Ithaca: Cornell University Press, 1986).
13. James Hines, *Forbidden Payment: Foreign Bribery and American Business After 1977* (Cambridge, MA: National Bureau of Economic Research, 1996).
14. *Foreign Investment: Implementation of Exon-Florio and Related Amendments* (Washington, DC: U.S. General Accounting Office, 1995), pp. 3–4.

CHAPTER 12

Promoting Global Competitiveness

Over the years, dissatisfaction with the performance of American industry—especially in relation to the global economy—has led to interest in various government efforts to influence the allocation of investment and the location of productive activity. Initially, the result was an awakening of interest in national economic planning. That was followed by more specific proposals for *industrial policy*. In the 1980s, *competitiveness* became the most popular label for this style of governmental intervention, and that notion has lingered on.

In the 1990s, policy advocates have been focusing on *technology policy,* in the belief that the applications of science and technology are the strategic factors in determining the international competitiveness of an advanced industrial nation. Although differences are substantial, all of these initiatives are variations on a similar theme of greater government involvement in business decision making to improve the overall performance of the economy.

BACKGROUND

Many of the specific proposals currently advanced to promote competitiveness and technology can be traced back to the wave of interest in the 1960s in the idea of national economic planning. In an economy characterized by *stagflation* (a painful combination of low growth and high inflation), many people became discouraged by the limits of macroeconomic tools such as monetary and fiscal policy.

The central idea of national economic planning was that the federal government should take the lead in exercising foresight over the future direction of economic activity. Although the specific powers involved were indicated only vaguely, considerable detail was supplied on organizational structure. In the typical national economic planning system, the president's office would include a central planning unit, which would work with states, localities, private business, unions, and various civic groups.

With the growing disillusionment of the public with governmental bureaucracy, interest in such a centralized approach waned. However, recessions in the 1970s and early 1980s spawned proposals for industrial policy to provide comprehensive governmental assistance to industries and regions of the country in economic distress.

Technically, industrial policy can be defined as any selective governmental measure that prevents or promotes changes in the structure of an economy. Industrial policy supporters argue that macroeconomic policies are not as evenhanded as they appear. Tight control of the money supply hits small and new businesses harder than large established firms. Even among established industries, monetary policy has differential effects on companies with varying capital intensities and whose sales respond differently to changes in interest rates. Tax cuts to promote economic growth mainly benefit those consumers with the highest taxable incomes.

Most industrial policy proposals involved a tripartite policy planning group and a financing agency. Typically, the tripartite group would contain high-level representatives of government, business, and labor. Such groups would focus on identifying specific actions to shore up lagging regions and industries. In some versions, this high-level agency would have direction or control over the financing agency, which, fundamentally, would use government money to bail out private enterprises that need assistance (chapter 14 analyzes the various effects of such governmental credit programs).

Like the early wave of interest in national planning, the pressure for industrial policy subsided during the recovery in the national economy in the mid 1980s. However, the rapid inroads of foreign firms and the continued high unemployment in some parts of the older industrialized "rust belt" of the Midwest led to growing support for improving American industry through *competitive policy*. This effort lost momentum as the traditional manufacturing sectors regained their market positions. The Clinton administration, when it assumed office in 1993, embarked on an effort to promote technology policy. Most of the specific policies advocated to promote technology turned out to be a subset of the proposals for strengthening the nation's industrial base.

The stated objectives of the proponents of industrial policy and technology policy are generally similar: to mitigate the impacts of industrial decline on unemployment and to ensure adequate new job opportunities in the private sector during a period of increasingly global competitiveness. To overcome the perceived failure of market forces and conventional economic policy tools to cope with these social needs, advocates propose a host of new government policy actions and, inevitably, expansions in government outlays. The Clinton administration, for example, enlarged the size and scope of the Commerce Department's technology promotion programs.[1]

This approach is not entirely new. In his *Report on Manufactures*, Alexander Hamilton argued for a strong government role in the encouragement of American industry. He noted in 1792 that other nations already offered subsidies and inducements to their manufacturers, thus inhibiting free competition. Yet, as will be shown later in this chapter, such special assistance ignores more fundamental and positive contributions that public policy can make to enhancing competitiveness by reducing the barriers to productivity.

COMPETITIVENESS

The expanded attention to competitiveness in the United States is a response to the high penetration of domestic markets by foreign producers. As noted in chapter 11, imports rose from 6 percent of GDP in 1970 to over 12 percent in 1996. Many advocates of new government policy initiatives see the imports' large share of U.S. markets for such key products as automobiles, steel, and electronics as the most visible symptoms of the deterioration of the domestic industrial economy. They also cite shortcomings in management performance and low labor productivity in many American firms as well as the decline in high-tech defense procurement following the end of the Cold War.

The United States, leaning heavily on foreign savings to finance huge budget deficits, has become the world's largest debtor nation. The historically high budget and trade deficits, in turn, have increased pressure for legislation that would retaliate against foreign countries that close their markets to U.S. goods. In contrast, a national competitiveness policy would be a far more positive response to the current weaknesses in the American economy than old-fashioned protectionism.

As economist Paul Krugman has noted, the concept of national competitiveness is elusive.[2] The Commission on Industrial Competitiveness has developed the most widely accepted definition of this amorphous term: "the degree to which a nation, under free and fair market conditions, produces goods and services that meet the test of international markets while simultaneously maintaining and expanding the real incomes of its citizens."

The underlying notion is that competitiveness is not simply the ability of a country to achieve balance in its foreign trade. Rather, it is the ability to do so while attaining an acceptable rate of improvement in its standard of living. After all, trade can be balanced through a steady decline in a country's real wages and standard of living—as in Britain in the years following World War II. And living standards can be increased through rising trade deficits—as in the United States in the 1980s.

The key to enhancing competitiveness is productivity, raising output per worker (or more specifically, per worker hour). Higher levels of productivity allow companies to produce goods and services at lower cost and hence sell their output at lower prices. Price reductions, in turn, generate a higher demand for the firm's output and ultimately greater employment and higher wages.

Numerous blue ribbon commissions and high-level study groups have urged efforts to improve productivity by expanding technology, speeding up the rate of innovation, financing more capital investment, and reforming regulation. What is perhaps most noteworthy about the recent proposals is the concentration on education. A variety of factors have led to that development.

Business firms have responded to the competitive challenge in a variety of ways: cutting costs, emphasizing quality, restructuring, and merging with other businesses in order to reduce overhead and consolidate facilities. These are important initial reactions, but they may not suffice for the long term. Productivity—how efficiently a firm uses its labor and capital to produce goods and services—is the key challenge, and that gets back to human resources (the tax system provides incentives for modernizing and expanding the capital stock; see chapter 13).

With the increasingly technical nature of industrial production, many firms are finding they have to provide time-consuming and costly in-house training for such basic skills as the ability to read instructions and to understand mathematics. At a time when the competitive strength of Asian companies has become a staple of business conversation, it is especially disconcerting for American executives to note the experiences of their overseas counterparts doing business in the United States. Tasks that are normally performed by high school graduates often require higher-paid college graduates in the United States. Moreover, in some instances, the U.S. college graduates need some sharpening of their mathematical skills to perform up to standard.

SPECIFIC PROPOSALS

When corporate management is asked to rank the key issues of public policy involved in improving U.S. competitiveness, they do not respond in terms of such obvious concerns as cutting taxes. Rather, as shown in Table 12.1, the focus primarily is on education and secondarily is on research and development. With few exceptions, business leaders rank the issues in the same order as government officials and university representatives. Education and human resources are seen as paramount in terms of the competitiveness of both the individual firm and the nation as a whole.[3]

Education and Human Resources

The task of improving American education so that the future workforce is adequately prepared has many dimensions, involving both the public and private sectors. Elementary and secondary education is basic. Here, the bulk of the effort is located at the local government level but with a substantial private component. Controversial issues abound, ranging from the adequacy of funding to enforcement of discipline to the degree of attention that should be devoted to such social concerns as busing and praying in schools.

A fundamental difference of opinion exists between the defenders of the existing educational system and the proponents of fundamental reform. The first category, which includes advocates of incremental change, focuses on the need to increase financial support for the nation's schools, primarily the public schools. The second group urges the introduction of competition in the educational system in a major way by permitting students (or their parents) to make a choice among alternative educational institutions in both the public sector and the private sector. Often this approach is called the voucher system.

TABLE 12.1   Key Issues Affecting the Ability of U.S. Businesses to Compete (as ranked by business executives)

Rank	Issue
1	Development of education and human resources
2	Promotion of research and development
3	Appropriate fiscal and monetary policy
4	International trade policy and practice
5	Federal regulation of business
6	Transfer of technology to business users

Source: Conference Board.

That is not a debate that is likely to be resolved quickly. However, some movement is noticeable in a few states, such as California and Minnesota, where at least some choice is allowed students among an array of public educational institutions. Meanwhile, business firms are making several contributions in the training of the nation's workforce. The first is to provide direct support to elementary and, especially, secondary schools via such measures as (1) taking the lead in supporting school tax increases and bond issues, (2) making available company personnel to "enrich" the teaching cadre, especially in scientific areas, and (3) providing direct on-the-job training to new hires as well as existing company workers who lack the skills required in the rapidly changing marketplace.

Another cluster of issues deals with the college and university level. At present, a large proportion of all those receiving doctoral degrees in science, engineering, and mathematics at U.S. universities is comprised of foreign students, many of whom return to their home countries to work. This situation does not exist in most other fields. In the social sciences, fewer than 20 percent of doctoral degrees are awarded to for- ents.

perennial shortage of high school science and math teachers can be ameliorated by means of a modest amount of regulatory reform—reducing the rigid requirements in terms of formal courses in education. Many experienced engineers, scientists, and mathematicians would like to teach at the high school level, especially those who are hit by plant closings or large-scale layoffs. However, such professionals have gone through the traditional two- to three-year sequence of courses in educational theory, practice, and administration. The supply of science and math teachers could be enhanced quickly by setting up a special one-year graduate program in education for people with substantial technical training and experience.

Private industry can play an important supporting role. In the past three decades, annual corporate support of colleges and universities has risen from $40 million to more than $1 billion. In addition, companies finance scholarships and fellowships, donate equipment, and make available staff members to serve as adjunct faculty. A great many large corporations also encourage employees to continue their education via tuition refunds and time off for advanced degrees. They also conduct substantial in-house programs of education and training. U.S. companies spend about $40 billion a year to make their workers more productive.[4]

Research and Development

The role of research and development (R&D) in enhancing productivity and thus national competitiveness transcends issues of the amount of annual funding. Rather, determining public policy toward R&D raises basic questions regarding the size and scope of the public and private sectors in a private enterprise economy. At the outset, we should recognize that both sides of the perennial debate can marshal impressive evidence.

Those who advocate larger government outlays for R&D can point to such clear successes as the development of nuclear energy, the initial design of supersonic aircraft, and the start of the Internet. Likewise, those who oppose direct federal R&D spending on a large scale can point to such abysmal failures as the synthetic fuel program, the Clinch River breeder reactor, and the aborted superconducting super collider.

Surely, the invention of the semiconductor shows the limits of government assistance. During World War II, the government sponsored a huge research program in the fundamental properties of germanium and silicon to respond to the limitations of silicon diodes used in radar. Over 30 research laboratories were involved. Nevertheless, the important early semiconductor device was invented at the civilian Bell Laboratory, which did not receive a research and development grant from the military for semiconductors—until after they had been invented.[5]

As a practical matter, public policy has constituted a changing combination of the two approaches, always avoiding either polar alternative. Thus, the federal government continues to be a large supplier of funds for R&D because many of its departments and agencies require a large input of science and engineering in order to achieve the objectives that Congress has assigned them. Despite the substantial cutbacks following the end of the Cold War, the Department of Defense is still the major financier of weapon system R&D, and that basic function is unlikely to change. To lesser but substantial degrees, several civilian departments have similar responsibilities (the Department of Health and Human Services in the field of health, for example).

Yet it is important to recognize that a basic change has occurred in the relative importance of the public and private sectors in R&D in the United States. Since 1980, the federal government has yielded to the private sector the primary role of sponsoring and financing science and technology. As shown in Figure 12.1, private industry

FIGURE 12.1 Financing of U.S. Research and Development, 1953–1996

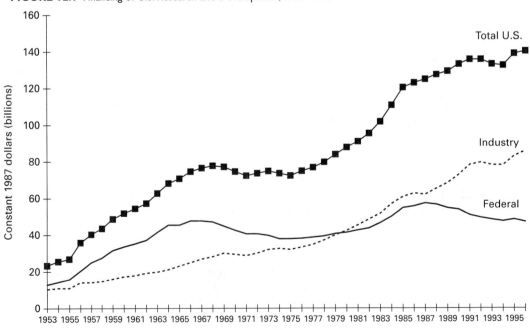

Year

Source: U.S. National Science Foundation.

has become the prime source of R&D funding, and the gap between government and business funding has steadily widened. It is interesting to note that the crossover between the federal and industry lines in the chart occurred during the height of the Cold War, when military R&D spending was rising substantially. Clearly, the rise of private R&D has not come at the expense of military R&D but has been an independent force.

Yet, the public and private sectors continue to be intertwined. Many of the actions the federal government takes, by design or inadvertently, can alter the incentive of private firms to risk investments in the relatively unknown, that is, to pay for research that may or may not culminate in new or improved products or production processes. These governmental actions include tax policy that affects the availability of funds to invest in the commercialization of R&D and regulatory policy that can inhibit the introduction of new goods and services.

But indirectly, government can also be a powerful or negative influence on the process of innovation. For example, financing large budget deficits pulls away from the private sector the funds needed for investments in new undertakings. Similarly, a tight monetary policy (which may be necessary to deal with serious inflation) can reduce the amount of private investment capital.

On the positive side, there is an important and relatively noncontroversial role for the federal government in financing one key type of R&D: basic research. That specific category of R&D generates new scientific information that can benefit competing firms as much as those that pay for the work. Under the circumstances, there is a tendency for the society to underinvest in basic research—unless the nation, through government or research universities, sponsors such undertakings.

In addition, there is a more modest but direct role for government in encouraging commercially oriented R&D. A simpler and more effective patent system would encourage the creation and diffusion of new technology. Such a change would ensure that smaller inventors are not overwhelmed by the cost of obtaining patents and defending them against legal challenges. Also, larger firms would be more likely to seek patents rather than protecting their new products and processes by maintaining secrecy.

EXISTING U.S. POLICIES

Promotion of Industry

Advocates of expanded and more generalized government aid to business claim that the United States already conducts a variety of activities promoting business competitiveness but does so in an uncoordinated manner. It is true that there is no shortage of government programs to aid specific sectors of the American economy. There is a long history of government intervention in individual industries. However, the typical federal action arose from a specific desire to enhance the performance of a particular part of the U.S. economy. Some aids to business reflect the concern over the adequacy of the defense production base; other measures respond to the desire to aid small business; still others are designed to strengthen the nation's maritime position. As shown in Table 12.2, federal support of business presently covers a wide variety of tax incentives, credit assistance, expenditure subsidies, and indirect aid, using the purchasing power of the federal government.

TABLE 12.2 Types of Federal Support of Business

Industry or Sector Benefited	Type of Federal Support
Tax Incentives	
Investment	Liberalized depreciation system
Small business	Lower rates on corporate income
New technology	Expensing of research and development
Energy companies	Percentage depletion of expenses of exploration
Pollution control	Issuance of tax-exempt bonds
Utilities	Tax-free reinvestment of dividends
Shipping companies	Deferral of income tax
Pharmaceutical companies	Tax credit for orphan drug research
Credit Subsidies	
Exports	Export–Import Bank loans
Railroads	Federal Railroad Administration loans
Small business	Small Business Administration loans
Companies in rural areas	Rural Electrification Administration loans
Housing	Credit via Government National Mortgage Association and FHA and VA loan guarantees
Defense contractors	Progress payments and foreign military sales credits
Direct Expenditure Subsidies	
Defense contractors	Conversion grants
Aerospace companies	Aeronautical research and technology
Waterborne companies	Coast Guard assistance
Energy companies	Research and development contracts
Mining companies	Stockpile purchases
Companies in urban areas	Community development grants
Savings and loan associations	Bailouts of many S&Ls
Indirect Procurement Subsidies	
Shipbuilders	Prohibition on building navy vessels in foreign shipyards
Ship operators	Bar military from using foreign-owned vessels
Construction companies	Preference for U.S. firms in building overseas diplomatic facilities
Clothing and fiber producers	Limiting Department of Defense to domestic sources
Twine producers	Limiting Forest Service to domestic sources
Companies in "labor-surplus areas"	Providing preference in federal procurement
Small business	Requiring a "fair" portion of government contracts to go to small business
U.S. manufacturers generally	Buy-American Act, provide preference to domestic sources in government purchases

Because each of these programs was enacted in isolation, many of them work at cross-purposes, and few would pass the most elementary benefit–cost test. Thus, water-resource subsidies increase the amount of land on which farm products are grown, while agricultural subsidies take much of that output off the market. Export financing promotes overseas business, while export controls inhibit the same activities. Many subsidy programs, notably to mining and other extractive industries, encourage the wasteful use of resources and otherwise degrade the environment, offsetting the hard-earned benefits of EPA regulation.[6]

Although government aid has at times enhanced the international competitiveness of individual American industries, much of it has been provided to achieve other objectives, mainly by responding to the needs of articulate pressure groups. The numerous buy-American statutes are barely disguised efforts to protect powerful economic interests that do little to enhance the competitiveness of the companies that benefit.

Retardation of Industry

Many government policies have contributed to the difficulties now being faced by American industry. These negative impacts are mainly unintended side effects of laws designed for other purposes. Examples include policies to provide a more equitable tax structure (by reducing investment incentives), to enhance the quality of life (by imposing a variety of social costs on business), and to improve the physical environment (by imposing a host of burdensome regulatory requirements).

Most of these policies ignore the needs and operations of the private enterprise system by focusing on noneconomic, social goals—rather than seeking a balance between economic and social priorities. As a result, these policies often have weakened the private sector of the economy. This can be seen in the numerous companies that have shifted portions of their workforce away from the creative and productive areas of business, such as product development, manufacturing, and marketing. This shift has resulted in an increase in the overhead functions: legal activities, accounting and finance, public affairs, and government relations. For the individual firm, this change has been an essential way of responding to pressures from government agencies and public interest groups with noneconomic orientations, but the cumulative effect is to increase costs and erode productivity.

If we overlook the burdens imposed by existing government policy, all we see are the pleas for subsidies and other special assistance. However, on reflection, the willingness of government to provide special help is not surprising. It is the price that Congress is willing to pay to avoid dealing with the underlying industrial problems that arise from the existing pattern of government intervention in the private economy.

Government policy toward industry has not always been negative. In the 1950s and 1960s, the United States did in fact, although not in name, carry out positive policies that helped promote American industry. Massive contracts from the Department of Defense, NASA, and the Atomic Energy Commission helped foster new high-growth companies in the aerospace, electronics, and nuclear fields as well as in many supporting industries. In a more general way, the institution of the investment tax credit (eliminated in 1986 and only restored for small business in 1993) was a part of that generally positive approach to foster economic growth in the private sector.

REVIEWING THE MAJOR ARGUMENTS

The recurring shortcomings in a private enterprise economy predictably give rise to proposals for expanded government intervention in business. Defenders of the free market approach, it must be acknowledged, are frequently derided for advocating a "do-nothing" policy.[7]

Because of this continued interest, it seems appropriate to review and critique the major arguments presented on both sides of the issue of expanding federal direction of the American economy by adopting industrial policy, competitiveness policy, or whatever is the current euphemism.

Arguments in Favor of a Larger Government Role

Five major arguments have been presented in favor of the adoption of a policy of more direct government involvement in business in the United States.

1. *We can improve on the status quo.* Repeated sequences of recession and inflation plus declining U.S. shares of world markets are cited as demonstrating the need for overall planning of the nation's economy. Advocates of this approach believe that the "invisible hand" that guides the economy is not very effective in the present environment. In their view, the pace of technology is too rapid for the society to accommodate unassisted to the often painful adjustments of the marketplace.

2. *We need to coordinate government activity.* A great deal of specialized long-range planning is currently carried out by government agencies but in an uncoordinated fashion. Figure 12.2 presents the array of existing federal government agencies

FIGURE 12.2 Federal Agencies with Planning Responsibilities

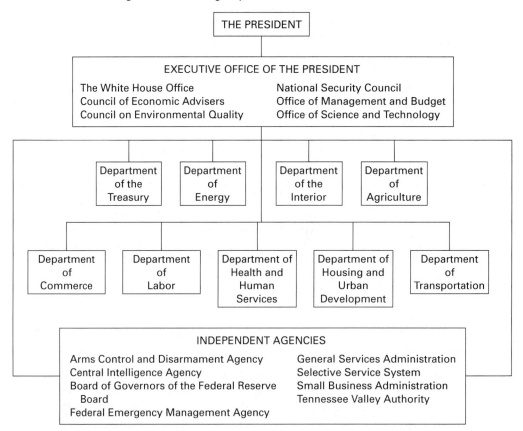

with some planning responsibility. To supplement that picture, Table 12.3 indicates the major types of planning activity now conducted by these various existing government bodies.

Nevertheless, the Department of the Interior invests large sums to develop the agricultural lands of the West, while the Department of Agriculture plans and conducts even more generous subsidy programs to deal with the resultant farm surpluses.

TABLE 12.3   The Variety of Current Government Planning Activities

Type of Planning and Agency	Key Activity
Macroeconomic Planning	
The White House	Overall executive branch responsibility
National Economic Council	Economic policies and trends
National Security Council	Foreign policy and military strength
Office of Management and Budget	Overall fiscal planning
Department of the Treasury	Overall financial planning
Federal Reserve System	Monetary policy
Economic Data Gathering	
Department of Agriculture	Economic and Statistics Service
Department of Commerce	Bureau of the Census
	Bureau of Economic Analysis
	Bureau of Industrial Economics
Department of Energy	Energy Information Administration
Department of Health and Human Services	National Center for Health Statistics
Department of Labor	Bureau of Labor Statistics
Central Intelligence Agency	Classified information
Sectoral Planning	
Council on Environmental Quality	Ecological trends and planning
Office of Science and Technology	Scientific trends and planning
Department of Agriculture	Small community and rural development
	Forest Service
Department of Commerce	International Trade Administration
	Economic Development Administration
	National Telecommunications and Information Administration
Department of Housing and Urban Development	Community planning
Department of the Interior	Bureau of Mines
Department of Labor	Employment and Training Administration
Department of Transportation	Federal Aviation Administration
	Federal Highway Administration
	Maritime Administration
Federal Emergency Management Agency	Planning for emergencies and disasters
General Services Administration	Stockpile of strategic and critical materials
National Capital Planning Commission	Regional planning
Selective Service System	Military manpower planning
Small Business Administration	Analyzing small business sector
Arms Control and Disarmament Agency	Planning for smaller military sector

The Departments of Education and Health and Human Services train teenagers for jobs, while the Department of Labor enforces the statutory minimum wage, which makes it less likely that inexperienced workers will find employment. Yet, on reflection, these inconsistencies in government policy do not result from a lack of planning. Rather, they reflect that government decision makers primarily respond to the political pressures from important interest groups, rather than making their decisions on the basis of objective analysis, economic or otherwise. For example, it is now generally acknowledged that about $3 billion were wasted on the abortive effort in the 1970s to develop a domestic synthetic fuels program. However, Congress was warned about the problems at the time the legislation was debated.[8]

3. *Price competition and profit maximization unduly emphasize short-run factors.* The preoccupation with short-term influences is at variance with the nation's long-term interests in such areas as employment, energy, and the environment. These long-term interests, according to proponents of national planning, require long-term investments in R&D, education, and infrastructure beyond the desires of the marketplace.

4. *Many other nations do national planning.* Coordinated long-term national planning is in common use in many industrial countries, notably France, Great Britain, Japan, and the Scandinavian nations. Comprehensive planning in the United States has been quite successful in specific large projects. The space program is an example in the public sector, and the Alaska pipeline is a comparable long-term investment in the private sector. Moreover, long-range planning is a staple of modern corporate practice.

5. *Planning in the United States would be democratic and voluntary.* Planning would be carried out on an open basis through an elaborate process of reviews at the federal and state levels of government. The existing U.S. system of checks and balances would be expected to prevent excesses. Also, compliance would be voluntary, although various government incentives would be used to induce the desired response. A recurring theme is that the new policy does not involve federal control over business, just some helpful government assistance. Retired Democratic Senator William Proxmire has responded that money will go where the political power is. He believes that anyone who thinks government funds will be allocated according to merit has not lived or served in Washington very long.

Arguments against a Larger Government Role

The major arguments against centralized economic planning in the United States also can be analyzed in five categories:

1. *Economic and political freedom would be threatened.* The most serious objection to a system of national economic planning for the United States is the threat to economic freedom, leading eventually to possible loss of political liberty. Opponents of the national government taking on the responsibility for economic activity believe that the new apparatus that would be required would gradually shift the levers of economic power from broad public markets where people "vote" with their dollars to a narrow group of technocrats in Washington.

The motive of many advocates of more activist government seems to be to re-shape national objectives and priorities to their ends, rather than simply to improve the process of attaining a given set of objectives.[9] Their counterargument is that the proponents of change are reading too much into their proposals.

2. *Control is inevitable in national planning.* Otherwise, say the critics, the national planning process would become a mere bureaucratic routine, and the plans themselves would become academic documents to be ignored by policy makers. As a practical matter, how can a government plan steel capacity without determining the production of automobiles, office buildings, and other end products—or without planning for sources of raw materials, skilled labor, and other inputs? In a more general way, economist Herbert Stein has noted that, if the government can make a private citizen an offer that he or she cannot refuse, it can thus exercise coercion.[10]

3. *National planning did not succeed in the Communist nations.* Even where the planning offices were buttressed by the full authority of the state, widespread inefficiencies were pervasive. The counterargument that can be offered is that it would be expected that the coercive powers of the totalitarian state are not available in a democratic society.

4. *Planning in non-Communist nations cannot be adopted in the United States.* Close government–business cooperation in Japan is associated with a paternalistic and protective government attitude toward various industries and also with a tradition of lifetime employment in the larger companies. Rather than a substitution of government action for private decision making, it is a continuing consultative process that develops "visions" or guidelines that private industry is free to ignore.

The parliamentary system in some countries provides for a unified executive and legislative majority, which greatly simplifies long-term planning and implementation. Critics contend that, in the United States, political interests in Congress would invariably lead to decisions that benefit the economic interests in the states or congressional districts of the most powerful committee heads and other legislative leaders. Moreover, the experience with government trying to call the shots in the economies of other capitalist nations has not received rave reviews. Indeed, the more recent trend is toward denationalization and greater reliance on private markets.

5. *The private enterprise system works better than government.* Contrary to the claims of the advocates of governmental leadership in the economy, the very complexity of the advanced economy of the United States would work against such efforts. Ultimately, a national planning agency in the United States either would completely replace market processes or would amount to still another federal office set on top of the existing bureaucratic structure. Many critics of greater government involvement in the economy believe that the efficiency of the existing economic system would be enhanced by reducing rather than expanding government intervention. According to economist Paul Samuelson:

> One of the small virtues of a market laissez-faire system is that when it makes a terrible mistake and produces mousetraps that people don't want or which don't work, somebody runs out of money and gets rapped on the knuckles. That's why the Lord created bankruptcy.[11]

Opponents of a greater government role in the economy also note the potential conflicts that are likely to develop between a centralized economic control agency and existing bureaus representing specific interest groups. They cite as examples the long-term links between the Department of Agriculture and farmers, between the Department of Labor and trade unions, between the Department of Commerce and business firms, between the Department of the Interior and the owners and users of natural resources, and between the Department of Defense and military suppliers. These traditional arguments, however, do not seem to satisfy the proponents of newer, more active public policy.

Historical Review

Interest in a more forceful government role in the economy of the United States has tended to come to the fore during periods of economic difficulty and to recede in times of prosperity. Interest in such planning was most widespread during the depression of the 1930s and again following the end of World War II, when there were worries about stagnation and the "inevitable" postwar depression. The energy crisis of the 1970s brought renewed pleas for such an interventionist undertaking by the national government, yet the oil "shortage" disappeared without the adoption of a national planning mechanism. The massive trade deficits of the 1980s, however, continue into the 1990s as depreciation in the foreign exchange value of the dollar (which tends to narrow the trade deficit) is followed by a major strengthening of the currency.

A POSITIVE APPROACH

There is a positive approach to the current concerns about the competitiveness of American business. It is geared to enhancing productivity by eliminating the numerous government obstacles to private capital formation and entrepreneurial activity. Along these lines, the prospects for investment can be enhanced by reducing the heavy tax burden on saving and investment. In addition, less uncertainty about future changes in regulation and about obtaining the approval of a host of regulatory authorities for any new project would encourage investment and new undertakings in general.

The policy approach described here runs counter to some of the recent changes in public policy described in other chapters of this book. Costly social regulation of business, especially in the environmental area, continues to be in a major growth trend. Expensive government social mandates on employers discourage domestic job creation. Tax changes justified to promote "fairness" increase the burden on saving and investment and hamper the growth of productivity, an essential ingredient in enhancing international competitiveness.

However, there is a fundamental shortcoming in the positive approach. In a truly dynamic, competitive economy, we do not know in advance where the new product breakthroughs will occur. The benefits, moreover, will not be evenly distributed. Specific regions and companies may be bypassed during periods of strong overall growth. But we do have reason to believe that society as a whole will be better off because it is likely that most—but not all—workers and employers will enjoy higher real incomes and living standards in a more productive economy.

A decent concern for the human costs imposed by economic change is a hallmark of a compassionate people, and society can try to reduce those costs in two very different ways. First, it can short-circuit market forces and try to slow the pace of change through trade restrictions, subsidies, and regulations designed to prop up declining firms. The alternative is to ease the transition by changing the economic condition of the individual employee through such measures as unemployment compensation and retraining programs. Although neither approach will work to perfection, the second alternative does hold the promise of not impairing the basic growth processes of the economy. It represents some sharing of the benefits of competition and economic expansion. The United States tolerates a higher rate of job terminations than do most other industrialized nations—but we also enjoy a far higher rate of job creation. Those two factors are hardly independent of each other.

All in all, some modest contribution to capital formulation, productivity, and innovation may result from the renewed interest in facing national economic problems—an interest that is represented by the continuing debate over U.S. competitiveness and the developing interest in technology policy. Yet, a truly dynamic economy implies that some sectors will grow while others will not. To respond to the political pressures of the declining industries often means foregoing opportunities for the growth sectors. In view of the difficulties experienced by some of the older manufacturing companies, it is comforting to note, in the words of David L. Birch, that "we have become successful at selling our wits at a time when our muscles offer little competitive advantage."[12] The United States now sells 20 percent of the world's services. This nation runs a steady surplus of exports over imports of high-technology products such as aircraft and scientific instruments. It is in the invention, design, and marketing of new and better products and services that the United States has been especially successful in the past and is likely to continue to be so in the future.

Outlook

The American economy is still the strongest in the world. In many important industries, American firms are the leaders. As shown in Table 12.4, U.S. firms rank number one (in terms of sales volume) in 16 major industries.[13]

Within some high-tech industries, the U.S. lead is overwhelming. Five of the world's six largest computer manufacturers are headquartered in the United States. One U.S. firm (Intel) leads the world's semiconductor business and another (Microsoft) the software market. The lead of the United States in the service industries is even greater. This country, especially New York City, has become the global marketplace for capital. No other nation's capital market can match the United States's ability to distribute massive new issues—or to provide sufficient liquidity so that large buyers can sell their holdings without precipitating huge declines in the prices of stocks and bonds.[14]

The prospects for American companies continuing to be in the lead are very bright. There is a special reason for optimism. All through the 1990s and beyond, the United States can be expected to benefit from the upsurge of industrial R&D during the 1980s and early 1990s.

There is a positive macroeconomic aspect to continued technological progress. When the persistent trade deficit of the United States is disaggregated, we find that

TABLE 12.4 Industries in which the United States Is the Sales Leader

Industry	Company
Aerospace	Boeing
Airlines	American Airlines
Beverages	Coca-Cola
Brokerage	Merrill Lynch
Chemicals	DuPont
Computers and office equipment	IBM
Electronics	General Electric
Entertainment	Walt Disney
Food services	Pepsico
Forest and paper products	International Paper
General merchandisers	Wal-Mart
Health care	Columbia/HCA
Motor vehicles	General Motors
Scientific, photo equipment	Kodak
Soap and cosmetics	Procter & Gamble
Tobacco	Philip Morris

exports of high-tech products steadily exceed high-tech imports. This country does indeed seem to enjoy a comparative advantage in the production and sales of goods and services that embody large proportions of new technology—notably advanced materials, aerospace, biotechnology, flexible manufacturing and robotics, life sciences, nuclear technology, and weapon systems.[15]

Perhaps the most striking indicators of continuing American competitiveness—and surely of our influence, if not power, in the world—are quite unconventional measures. Elites everywhere want to send their children to American universities; few want to go for an MBA to Moscow University. People risk death on the high seas to get into this country; farm laborers and Nobel prize winners alike want to move to the United States. All the movie studios of Europe and Asia combined cannot break the hold of Hollywood. And most of all, businesses want access to the American market.[16]

Notes

1. President William J. Clinton and Vice President Albert Gore, Jr., *Technology for America's Economic Growth, A New Direction to Build Economic Strength* (Washington, DC: The White House, February 22, 1993).

2. Paul Krugman, "Competitiveness: A Dangerous Obsession," *Foreign Affairs,* March–April 1994, p. 31.

3. John Yochelson, "Can the U.S. Compete?", *Chief Executive,* June 1997, p. 34.

4. Ben J. Wattenberg, "Dispelling America's Gloom," *The American Enterprise,* March–April 1990, p. 34.

5. Joseph Grunwald and Kenneth Flamm, *The Global Factory* (Washington, DC: Brookings Institution, 1985).

6. Murray Weidenbaum, Christopher Douglass, and Michael Orlando, "How to Achieve a Healthier Environment and a Stronger Economy," *Business Horizons,* January–February 1997, pp. 9–16.

7. The author frequently has urged congressional committees to "Don't stand there, undo something." This refers to the many government obstacles to economic progress, discussed elsewhere in this chapter.

8. Linda R. Cohen and Roger G. Noll, *The Technological Pork Barrel* (Washington, DC: Brookings Institution, 1991), p. 297.

9. See Lester R. Brown et al., *State of the World, 1996* (New York: W. W. Norton, 1996). The annual reports by the Worldwatch Institute invariably urge that the problems facing society be dealt with by more-focused government efforts.

10. Herbert Stein, *Economic Planning and the Improvement of Economic Policy* (Washington, DC: American Enterprise Institute, 1975), p. 25.

11. Paul A. Samuelson, "Some Dilemmas of Economic Policy," *Challenge,* March–April 1977, p. 35.

12. David L. Birch, *Job Creation in America* (New York: Free Press, 1987), p. 83.

13. See also "1997 Global 500," *Fortune,* August 4, 1996, pp. 119–125 et ff.

14. John Hennessy, "Slouching Toward A Global Economic Revolution," *Chief Executive* (November 1995), p. 19.

15. U.S. Bureau of the Census, *Statistical Abstract of the United States: 1996* (Washington, DC: U.S. Government Printing Office, 1996), p. 798.

16. Samuel P. Huntington, "The Erosion of American National Interests," *Foreign Affairs,* September–October 1997, p. 44; Josef Joffe, "How America Does It," ibid., p. 24.

PART FOUR

Government Promotion of Business

"I'm from the government and I'm here to help you," is a staple wise-crack at business meetings. Yet, many government actions—tax incentives, credit programs, and massive procurements—are designed to assist or at least influence some aspect of business operations.

Part IV takes on the task of analyzing the various ways in which government helps—and hinders—business performance.

CHAPTER 13

Business and Tax Policy

Business acts as the major tax collector for government, directly paying the taxes on business sales and earnings and withholding and transmitting the great bulk of the income and employment taxes. In the process, business also generates much of the data flow needed for the operation of social insurance systems such as social security and unemployment compensation.

Federal tax policy also encourages employers in powerful ways to provide pensions and health insurance to their employees. If they do so pursuant to law and regulation, their expenditures are tax deductible. Should the employees finance similar benefits on their own, however, they must do so out of their after-tax incomes. Moreover, employer payments of health insurance in behalf of their workers are not considered taxable income to the beneficiaries. As a result, companies have become major suppliers of medical and retirement insurance and benefits.

In recent years, federal tax and regulatory policies, unintentionally or otherwise, have encouraged companies to change the fundamental nature of the pension plans they provide their employees. As noted in chapter 6, traditionally most company retirement plans were of the "defined benefit" variety, where the employee was promised a specific schedule of payments after retirement. In order to subsidize underfunded pension plans, however, the Pension Benefit Guaranty Corporation—established under the Employee Retirement Income Security Act (ERISA)—has been raising the special tax it levies on covered pension plans. Thus, the financially healthy companies that fully fund their pension programs wind up subsidizing those in poor financial shape.[1]

Taxation influences business decision making in many other ways. To a substantial degree, governments act as a "partner," at least in sharing a significant fraction of corporate profits in the form of taxes. The indirect effects of the government's revenue collection are less measurable but are extensive, insofar as companies change their methods of operation so as to minimize their tax burdens or to take advantage of incentives in the Internal Revenue Code.

The collection of revenues by government generates a great variety of impacts on business and reactions by business firms. The cash flow between the public and private sectors is substantial. In the fiscal year ending September 30, 1996, corporations paid into the U.S. Treasury over $178 billion in income taxes. In addition, business firms paid $238 billion as the employer contribution to social security and related government-sponsored retirement programs and $28 billion to finance unemployment compensation benefits. In their further capacity as agents of the Internal Revenue Service, business firms also paid $73 billion in selective sales taxes (excises on such items as beer, cigarettes, and gasoline) and customs duties.

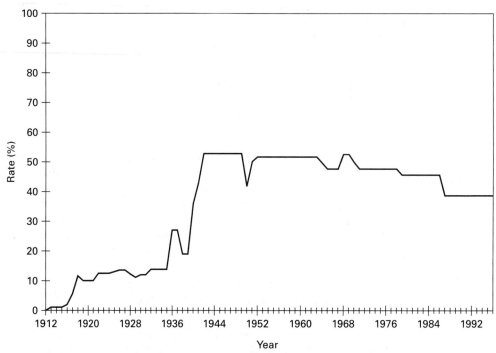

Source: U.S. Internal Revenue Service.

FIGURE 13.1 Maximum Marginal Income Tax Rates for Corporations

But it is not just a matter of financing a steady—or steadily rising—stream of business payments to government. Tax rates are changed frequently (see Figure 13.1), and business has to adjust to each of those shifts as well as the frequent changes in the structure of the revenue system.

Based on recent experiences, a cynic might conclude that the natural tendency of the Congress is to change the tax system frequently. During 1985–1986, when the two tax-writing committees of Congress (the Senate Finance Committee and the House Ways and Means Committee) were considering tax reform, the members of the committee received substantial campaign contributions from a variety of political action committees. It would be naive to expect such large-scale financial assistance to continue if Congress stopped enacting new tax legislation and other bills reported out by the Finance and Ways and Means Committees.

BUSINESS RESPONSES TO TAXATION

The revenue paid to government does not measure the full impacts of the tax system on business. Although official data are not available on the various indirect costs of business compliance with the tax system, there is good reason to believe they are substantial. The cost of complying with the federal corporate income tax can be viewed as the equivalent of a large surtax. Economist Arthur P. Hall of the Tax Foundation estimates that the average annual compliance cost rises from $7,400 for a corporation with assets of $1 million to $500,000 for a $500 million firm to $3 million for a company in the asset size of $10 billion. In relative terms, the proportional burden falls hardest on the smaller companies and eases as the size of the corporation increases. As is the case with regulation, there are economies of scale in complying with governmental directives. For all businesses—corporations, partnerships, and sole proprietorships—Hall estimates the cost of tax compliance came to a total of $123 billion in 1993.[2]

Changes in Business Practices

Companies often shift their ways of doing business in order to respond to various provisions of the Internal Revenue Code. As noted earlier, employer contributions to employee pension plans are tax deductible, providing they meet the requirements of the ERISA. Many firms devote considerable resources, including performing costly actuarial studies, to ensure their conformance with the variety of rules and regulations that have been issued under ERISA.

In order to receive special tax credits for the costs of hiring people with low skills, companies must employ members of designated "disadvantaged groups." To assure the tax deductibility of entertainment and other business deductions, many companies have had to change their accounting systems in order to provide adequate documentation to meet the standards of the Internal Revenue Service. Other companies have revised their overseas trading practices in order to avoid running afoul of the antiembargo provisions of the tax code.

To maximize their use of the tax credit for research and development (R&D) equipment, some firms have taken a new look at their existing classification systems for inventorying equipment. As a result, there has been considerable debate as to whether the tax credit has resulted in real growth in business R&D outlays. In the aggregate, the data do indicate that company outlays for science and technology are somewhat higher than they would have been in the absence of the credit, but only modestly. Part of the problem has been the unwillingness of Congress to extend the credit for more than a few years at a time. A permanent tax credit for R&D would be more cost-effective, with firms able to make long-term plans on the basis of availability of the credit. The estimated response to a temporary change in the tax credit is only about one-half of the reaction to a permanent change.[3]

The sums involved in tax-incentive provisions often warrant substantial business expense and change in order to qualify. Table 13.1 shows the tax savings arising from a variety of special federal tax provisions used by U.S. corporations. In the fiscal year 1997, those tax benefits are estimated to be worth $69 billion to the recipients. To some extent, however, that is an overstatement of their cost to the government.

Some of the special tax provisions, notably the investment incentives, encourage economic growth and result in a larger overall tax base, thus creating a positive feedback effect on Treasury receipts. In other cases, such as the tax benefits for scientific activities, the federal government's role is incremental—most of the costs are borne by the private companies doing the research and development. In the absence of the tax provisions, pressure would mount for Congress to enact larger appropriations to fund such scientific activities directly.

TABLE 13.1 Federal Tax Breaks for Business, Fiscal Year 1997 (value to companies, in billions of dollars)

Type of Benefit	Amount
Overseas operations:	
Exclusion of foreign sales income	$2.5
Special treatment of inventories	2.3
Subtotal	$4.8
Science and technology:	
Expensing of research and experimentation	0.2
Credit for increasing research	1.1
Subtotal	$1.3
Energy—various incentive provisions	$2.4
Natural resources and environment:	
Special treatment of mining costs and income	0.5
Special treatment of timber costs and income	0.4
Special treatment of reforestation expenditures	0.1
Subtotal	$1.0
Commerce and housing:	
Benefits to financial and insurance institutions	0.5
Rental housing investment incentives	9.0
Machinery and equipment investment incentives	27.3
Commercial structures and buildings investment incentives	5.8
Lower tax rate on smaller companies	6.3
Special treatment of income and costs	0.5
Special ESOP rules	1.0
Tax credit for business conducted in U.S. possessions	3.9
Miscellaneous investment incentives	1.1
Subtotal	$55.4
Exclusion of interest on industrial development bonds:	
for energy facilities	0.4
for pollution control and sewage and waste disposal facilities	0.9
for small issues	0.3
for airports, docks, and sports and convention facilities	2.6
Subtotal	$4.2
Total	$69.1

Source: U.S. Office of Management and Budget.

Political Responses

Yet another type of business response to taxation is more political than economic. That is, because of the large amounts of money involved in governmental revenue matters, many companies find it advisable to participate in the political arena in which tax legislation is developed. As will be shown in chapter 16, larger companies tend to establish their own offices in Washington, DC, to represent their interests. Other firms, large and small, work through their trade associations or hire law firms or other lobbying groups as the need arises. Because direct corporate support of federal candidates is illegal, a rising number of companies have established political action committees (PACs) to raise funds from their executives to support individual candidates.

These PACs provide political contributions to candidates who may be sympathetic to the firm's positions on public policy issues (see chapter 18 for detail on these activities).

As a general proposition, business is more effective in obtaining a special tax break for a firm or industry than in influencing the general course of federal fiscal policy.[4] There is no shortage in the federal tax code of "goodies" for individual companies and industries. Here is a sampler of the beneficiaries of special provisions. In accord with customary congressional etiquette, the names of the recipients are disguised in the statute by euphemisms:

- "A paint and glass project which was approved by the management committee of a company on September 11, 1985."
- "Rental property which was assigned FHA number 023-36602."
- A project which was "the subject of law suits filed on June 22, 1984 and November 21, 1985."
- "Any taxpayer incorporated in September 7, 1978, which is engaged in the trade or business of manufacturing dolls and accessories."
- "A corporation which was incorporated on December 29, 1969 in the State of Delaware. . . ."
- ". . . 10 warehouse buildings built between 1906 and 1910 and purchased under a contract dated February 17, 1926."
- A company that entered into a binding contract "on October 3, 1984, for the purchase of 6 semi-submersible units at a cost of $425,000,000."[5]

Business hardly presents a monolithic position on the typical revenue bill. In the case of the 1986 Tax Reform Act, a powerful coalition of firms initially lined up in opposition, including Alcoa, AT&T, Caterpillar, Dow Chemical, DuPont, Exxon, Ford, Rockwell International, Texas Instruments, and Weyerhaeuser. Simultaneously, an equally prestigious group of corporations favored the tax reform bill: Allied-Signal, Dart & Kraft, General Mills, General Motors, IBM, Levi Strauss, 3M, Pepsico, Philip Morris, Procter & Gamble, R. J. Reynolds, and Sara Lee.

However, by the time Congress was getting ready to enact the final version, most business groups that were vocal on the subject jumped on the tax-reform bandwagon. Their motives varied from not wanting to be seen as sore losers to trying to insert provisions in the bill to help their company or industry. The debate on tax increases in 1993 revealed a similar split in the business community. The wood products company Champion International favored the House of Representatives version because it would provide some relief to companies subject to the alternative minimum tax. Yet Weyerhaeuser, another wood products company, supported the Senate bill because it dropped the broad-based energy tax contained in the House version.[6]

FUTURE CHANGES IN THE U.S. TAX SYSTEM

The prospects for reform of the federal tax system ebb and flow. Specific proposals become hot issues and then recede, at least for a while. Looming on the horizon are proposed taxes on carbon emissions (users of fossil fuels) or on energy in general to deal with the issue of global climate change.

Shifting to Consumption as a Tax Base

The most basic change in the nation's revenue structure would be to introduce a new form of federal tax, one levied on consumption instead of income. For years, economists have debated the respective merits of income and consumption as the basis for taxation. The United States uses consumption tax to a far lesser degree than most other developed Western nations. In 1994, the 28 members of the Organization for Economic Cooperation and Development obtained an average of 30 percent of their revenue from taxes on consumption (see Table 13.2). For the United States, however, the ratio was only 16 percent, slightly more than half of the OECD average.

In recent years, the traditional preference for income-based taxation has eroded. In a recent poll of macro economists at 15 U.S. universities, *The Economist* reported that 63 percent favored "a fundamental reform of the American tax system towards a consumption tax," with only 37 percent opposed.[7] Tax experts have devised, and criticized, a variety of specific consumption-based taxes. No consensus, however, has been reached on the details. It is likely that two interrelated clusters of issues—the desirability of a tax on consumption and the specific form that it should take—will receive increased public attention in the late 1990s. The following sections of this chapter deal with these matters, which could have substantial impacts on private business firms.

Many analysts believe that it is fairer to tax people on what they take from society, rather than on what they contribute by working and investing. In the nineteenth century, classical economist John Stuart Mill made this point in advocating the exemption of saving as part of a "just" income tax system. In the 1940s, American economist Irving Fisher argued that the income tax involved double taxation of saving and distorted the choice of individuals in favor of consumption. Thus, not only is the income tax unjust, it encourages consumption and leisure at the expense of thrift and enterprise.

TABLE 13.2 Consumption Taxes as a Percentage of Total Taxation in Selected Countries, 1994

Country	Percentage	Country	Percentage
Australia	24	Japan	14
Austria	29	Luxembourg	27
Belgium	25	Mexico	47
Canada	24	Netherlands	23
Czech Republic	31	New Zealand	32
Denmark	30	Norway	37
Finland	30	Poland	35
France	26	Portugal	44
Germany	28	Spain	26
Greece	39	Sweden	25
Hungary	40	Switzerland	15
Iceland	46	Turkey	37
Ireland	37	United Kingdom	34
Italy	26	United States	16
		AVERAGE	30

Source: Organization for Economic Cooperation and Development.

The U.S. Treasury actually proposed a "spendings tax" in 1942 as a temporary wartime measure to curb inflation. The proposal was quickly rejected by Congress. A major argument against the expenditure tax—then and now—is that the exemption of saving would favor the rich since they are better able to save large portions of their incomes. Some believe this would lead to greater concentrations of wealth in the hands of a few. Proponents of an expenditure tax respond that it can be made as steeply progressive as desired. Moreover, the trend in income taxation in the United States since 1980 has been away from progressivity and toward a flatter, more proportional revenue structure. The 1981 and 1986 tax statutes are striking cases in point.

Another objection to the consumption base is that it would favor the miser over the spendthrift, even when both have similar spending power or ability to pay. The response offered to this argument is that consumption uses up the resources available to the nation, while saving adds to these resources. Moreover, the fundamental way for an individual to minimize consumption tax liabilities is to consume less; the incentives to work, save, and invest are unimpaired. By contrast, the basic way to minimize the income tax is to earn less, which dampens incentives to work, save, and invest—with deleterious effects on economic growth and living standards.

Taxes on Consumed Income or Expenditures (Top-Down Consumption Taxes)

In practice, much of the impact of shifting to a consumption tax base would depend on how the tax was structured. The two major categories of alternatives are (1) expenditure (or income) taxes levied on the portion of income not saved (which is conceptually the same as consumption) and (2) sales or value-added taxes collected on individual purchases. In essence, the first category is comprised of *top-down* taxes while the latter consists of *bottom-up* taxes. In theory, the base of the two types of taxes is the same—the value of goods and services purchased—and the yields could be very similar. Each of the revised tax systems could be *revenue neutral,* raising as much revenue as the current income tax.

The Flat Tax   In the top-down category, the two major alternatives are the *flat tax,* popularized by erstwhile presidential candidate Steve Forbes, and the *savings-exempt income tax,* often referred to as the USA tax (for Unlimited Savings Allowance). The key feature of the flat tax is that one rate would be levied on all income above a generous family deduction.

In effect, the flat tax would be a form of consumption tax because the returns on saving and investment would not be taxed. The tax would only be paid on wages, salaries, and retirement income. Interest, dividends, and capital gains would be exempt for individual taxpayers based on the justification that adequate taxes had been levied at the business level. Thus, *double taxation* would be avoided. No deductions would be allowed for interest payments, charitable contributions, or state and local taxes.

Companies (and also individuals) would be required to fill out a postcard return (see Figure 13.2). Thus, in its essence, the flat tax would be much simpler than the current income tax. A key reason for the comparative simplicity of the flat tax is the absence of "transition" rules. For example, with the substitution of a flat tax for the current income tax, the holders of municipal bonds (the interest on which is exempt from

Form 2	Business Return (Flat Tax)		1998
Business name		Employer Identification Number	
Street address		County	
City, state, and ZIP code		Principal product	

1	Gross revenue from sales	1	
2	Allowable costs		
	(a) Purchases of goods, services and materials	2a	
	(b) Wages, salaries, and retirement benefits	2b	
	(c) Purchases of capital equipment, structures, and land	2c	
3	Total allowable costs *(sum of lines 2(a), 2(b), and 2(c))*	3	
4	Taxable income *(line 1 less line 3)*	4	
5	Tax *(19% of line 4)*	5	
6	Carry-forward from 1997	6	
7	Interest on carry-forward *(6 percent of line 6)*	7	
8	Carry-forward into 1998 *(line 6 plus line 7)*	8	
9	Tax due *(line 5 less line 8, if positive)*	9	
10	Carry-forward to 1999 *(line 8 less line 5, if positive)*	10	

FIGURE 13.2 Business Return under Flat Tax

federal income tax) would experience a substantial reduction in the market value of their portfolios. That is likely because investors buy these low-yielding "munis" for their tax-exempt feature—and all bond interest would be tax-exempt on the individual return. Thus, the retroactive loss of this special characteristic would reduce the value of these bonds substantially.

Unlike the other variations of consumption taxation, the flat tax on business covers all domestic operations, including domestic sales *and* exports. Likewise, all purchases (including capital equipment) are deducted from taxable revenue *including* imports.[8]

The Savings-Exempt Income Tax   The proposed USA tax (or *consumed income,* as technicians often refer to the concept) would be collected much as income taxes now are. The annual taxpayer return would continue to comprise the heart of the collection system, and a rate table accompanying the return could insure as progressive a tax structure as Congress desires. However, one major change would be instituted: The portion of income that is saved would, in effect, be exempt from taxation—until it was spent.

Figure 13.3 is a hypothetical example of a *short-form* version of a savings-exempt income tax return for an individual taxpayer or family. It shows how the difficult bookkeeping requirement to tally all consumption outlays can be finessed. Basically, it carries out the notion that, if income equals consumption plus saving, consumption can be readily estimated, indirectly but accurately, merely by deducting saving from income (and taxpayers are used to developing estimates of their incomes).[9]

INCOME AND OTHER RECEIPTS	AMOUNTS
1. Wages, salaries, tips, etc.	_____
2. Dividends	_____
3. Interest	_____
4. Rents and royalties	_____
5. Pensions and annuities	_____
6. Net receipts of sole proprietorships	_____
7. Withdrawals from partnerships	_____
8. Receipts from:	_____
a. sales of financial assets	_____
b. gifts and bequests	_____
c. insurance	_____
9. Net decrease (if any) in bank accounts	_____
10. Total (add lines 1 through 9)	_____

Saving

11. Purchases of financial assets	_____
12. Capital contributed to partnerships	_____
13. Net increase (if any) in bank accounts	_____
14. Other investments	_____
15. Total (add lines 11 through 14)	_____
16. Gross consumption (subtract line 15 from line 10)	_____

Deductions

17. a. Itemized deductions	_____
or	
b. Standard deduction	_____
18. Exemptions	_____
19. Total (add lines 17 and 18)	_____

Tax Base

20. Taxable income (subtract line 19 from line 16)	_____
21. Tax from rate table	_____

FIGURE 13.3 A Consumption (or USA) Tax Return

A companion shift to the adoption of a top-down consumption tax would be the conversion of the corporate income tax to a cash-flow tax on business. A major change—and one that would encourage investment—would be to *expense* or write off all capital investments, such as purchases of production equipment and factories in the year in which they are acquired. At present, these outlays are deductible on the income tax over the useful life of the asset, which is a period of several years or even decades.

In many ways, such a business version of the consumption tax would be simpler than the existing corporate tax. For example, by focusing on cash flows, it would avoid the complicated transfer pricing arrangements under which domestic subsidiaries of foreign corporations minimize their U.S. tax payments (see Table 13.3).

Although these changes may sound quite technical, a top-down consumption tax would be a move toward simplification. Taxation based on income is by its nature

TABLE 13.3 Two Top-Down Reforms of Business Taxation

The Flat Tax	The USA Tax
Allows immediate write-off of all business purchases.	Allows immediate write-off of all business purchases.
Maintains deduction for employee compensation.	Eliminates deduction for employee compensation.
Eliminates deductions for employee benefits other than retirement benefits.	Eliminates deductions for all employee benefits.
Eliminates deduction for employer's share of payroll taxes.	Provides tax credit for employer's share of payroll taxes.
Interest and dividend income not taxed; interest and dividend expense not deductible.	Interest and dividend income not taxed; interest and dividend expense not deductible.
"Origin based": exempts imports, taxes exports.	"Destination based": exempts exports, taxes imports.

more complicated than extracting revenues from consumption. Income taxation is inherently complex for many reasons. Complicated timing rules are necessary, such as depreciation allowances, capitalization of expenses, and inventory accounting. Inflation distorts the tax base by eroding the value of depreciation allowances and overstating the real value of capital gains. Being based instead on cash flow, taxation of consumption automatically avoids these problems. Of course, simplicity is not inevitable in any tax system. A potentially simple consumption-based tax can be made complex, just as the present income tax is far more complicated than it needs to be.[10]

Although any consumption-based tax would replace rather than supplant the existing income tax, it could increase federal revenues over a period of time. This would come about from the higher rate of economic growth that could result from the encouragement given to saving and thus to investment. Bottom-up types of sales and value-added tax would likely generate similar feedback effects.

Sales and Value-Added Taxes (Bottom-Up Consumption Taxes)

An expenditure or consumption tax, as shown above, can be calculated via a top-down approach, building on the records that are already available to provide the data needed for enforcement of existing corporate and personal income taxes. In contrast, *sales* and *value-added taxes* (VAT) represent a very different way of collecting a general tax on consumption.

National Sales Tax   On the surface, a national retail sales tax seems like a very simple device for collecting revenues in place of the complicated income tax structure. However, because consumption tends to be a smaller share of income as we go up the income scale, many supporters of the sales tax recognize the need to soften the regressive impact on the poor. The required modifications inevitably introduce complication. The most widely used approach, at the state level, is to exempt categories of purchases on which the poor spend a larger fraction of their income than other citizens, such as food, housing, and medicine. Another proposal is to provide each taxpayer with a "smart card" with credit for sales taxes based on family size. Yet another alternative is to give every taxpayer an automatic standard refund, also based on family size.[11]

A national sales tax levied at the retail level may present special problems for small businesses. Unlike larger companies, which buy from wholesalers or directly from manufacturers, smaller enterprises often make their purchases from the same retailers as do consumers and, therefore, would have to pay the retail sales tax. Problems such as this led France and other Western European nations to move from relatively simple sales taxes to the more sophisticated but complicated VAT. In either case, a mechanism would still be required to collect social security and Medicare payroll taxes.

Because any sales tax (including the VAT) is included in the price of purchases, it registers in all of the price indexes and, hence, exerts an inflationary force on the economy. The counterargument is that this is only a one-time effect, occurring when the tax is enacted or increased and that inflationary impact could be offset by appropriate changes in monetary policy, albeit at times with an adverse effect on the levels of production and employment. A study of 35 countries that introduced a VAT revealed that in only six did the new tax contribute to a faster rate of inflation.[12]

Opponents also charge that either a national sales or a VAT would invade the area of sales taxation, traditionally reserved for state and local governments. However, states have come to rely on income taxes despite heavy use of the same tax base by the federal government.

Turning to administrative aspects, federal imposition of a sales or value-added tax would require establishing a new tax-collection system by the government and new recordkeeping on the part of taxpayers. However, much of the current tax collection system could be eliminated (except for the collection of payroll taxes for social security and Medicare).

Value-Added Taxes   The VAT is, in effect, a comprehensive sales tax that avoids the double counting otherwise inevitable when the same item moves from manufacturer to wholesaler to retailer.

In total, a VAT should be equivalent in yield to a single-stage sales tax levied at the retail level. Essentially, a firm's value added is the difference between its sales and its purchases from other firms. As shown in Table 13.4, value added can also be estimated by adding labor and capital inputs supplied by the firm itself—represented by wages and salaries, rent and interest payments, and profit. Although the top-down consumption tax notion remains a theoretical concept, the VAT is now an existing tax in many countries.

Proponents of the VAT contend that it is economically neutral because ideally it would be levied at a uniform rate on all items of consumption (unless exceptions are made to soften its regressive nature). The VAT does not distort choices among products or methods of production. Thus, shifting to a more capital-intensive and perhaps more profitable method of production does not influence the tax burden. Nor is the allocation of resources across product, market, and industry lines affected. In these regards, the VAT is far superior to the existing array of selective excise taxes.

TABLE 13.4 Two Methods of Computing Value Added in the Production Process

Item	Raw Materials Producer	Manufacturer	Wholesaler	Retailer	Cumulative
Purchases of inputs	—	$100	$500	$800	$1,400
Value added:					
Wages	$60	$275	$200	$100	$635
Rent	10	25	40	50	125
Interest	10	50	25	25	110
Profit	20	50	35	25	130
Total value added	$100	$400	$300	$200	$1,000
Sales of output	$100	$500	$800	$1,000	$2,400

Note: Value added can be estimated in two ways:

1. Deducting purchases from sales of output.
2. Adding inputs by the firm itself (excluding inputs supplied by others).
3. Thus $2,400 − $1,400 = $635 + $125 + $110 + $130 = $1,000.

Advocates of the value-added tax also point out that, in contrast to an income tax, there is no penalty for efficiency and no subsidy for waste. Moreover, the VAT is neutral between incorporated and unincorporated businesses and, theoretically, even between public and private enterprises. By focusing on consumption, it avoids a double tax burden on the returns from capital. This tax starts off with no exclusions or exemptions and thus, at least initially, provides a broader and fairer tax base, one that the underground economy will have more difficulty evading.

Another argument in favor of U.S. adoption of a value-added tax is that so many other nations have adopted this form of revenue. It fits in better than other taxes with the growing international character of production. The VAT has become one of the revenue workhorses of the world. Virtually every important country in Europe imposes the tax, and it has spread throughout the Third World. France has used VAT taxation since 1955, and other members of the European Union have done so since the late 1960s or early 1970s. Japan imposed a broad-based 3 percent sales tax in 1989, and Canada adopted a 7 percent VAT in 1991.

But, unlike the situation in the United States, the adoption of a tax on value added was true reform in those countries. That is, value-added taxes typically replaced an extremely inefficient form of consumption tax that was already in place: a cascading sales or turnover revenue system. Those latter taxes apply to the total amount of a firm's sales rather than only to its value added. Thus, sales taxes would be paid over and over again on the same items as they moved from firm to firm in various stages of the production process. Cascade-type taxes favor integrated firms (who can legally avoid one or more stages of the tax), but they severely discriminate against independent companies that operate at only one phase of the production process.

An added, widely cited reason for adopting a VAT is the anticipated foreign trade benefits. Unlike an income tax, a sales-based tax can be imposed on goods entering the country and rebated on items leaving—supposedly encouraging exports and discouraging imports. Thus, at first blush, a VAT would seem to help reduce this nation's presently large deficit. However, most economists believe that fluctuations in exchange rates would largely offset these initial effects and result in little change in the balance of trade.

Opponents of a value-added tax offer an extensive list of shortcomings. They contend that a VAT, as in the case of any consumption-based revenue source, is inherently regressive: Those least able to pay face the highest rates. That regressivity can be softened by exempting food and medicine or in refunds to low-income taxpayers, but such variations make the collection of the tax more complicated. They also provide opportunity for people in the underground economy to avoid paying taxes.[13]

A variety of approaches has been suggested for collecting the new tax. The simplest is the credit method (see Table 13.5). Under this approach, the tax is computed initially on a company's total sales, and the firm is given credit for the VAT paid by its suppliers. To a substantial degree, the VAT would be self-enforced. Each company would have a powerful incentive to ensure that its suppliers paid their full share of the tax because any underpayment would have to be made up by the next firm in the chain of production and distribution.

In practice, the collection of the VAT may not be as simple as shown here. That would be the case if certain transactions were exempted (such as food) and if nonprofit institutions and government enterprises were treated differently from business firms. Exemptions are no minor matter in terms of the administrative complexity they generate. In France, a long and extensive debate occurred over whether or not Head and Shoulders antidandruff shampoo was a tax-exempt medicine or a cosmetic subject to the full VAT. (The product is taxable.) Food eaten at a location away from the business at which it was purchased may be tax-exempt. What happens if a McDonald's sets up tables outside of the restaurant?[14]

Contrasting Bottom-Up Taxes   Table 13.6 shows the major differences as well as similarities between the two major bottom-up consumption taxes.

TABLE 13.5   Computing the VAT Using the Credit Method

Item	Raw Materials Producer	Manufacturer	Wholesaler	Retailer
Sales of output	$100	$500	$800	$1,000
Less purchases	0	100	500	800
Value added	$100	$400	$300	$200
Tax on total sales	$10	$50	$80	$100
Credit on purchases	—	10	50	80
Tax liability	$10	$40	$30	$20

Note: Assumes 10 percent VAT on a consumption basis.

TABLE 13.6 Characteristics of Bottom-Up Consumption Taxes

Characteristic	National Sales Tax	Value-Added Tax
Coverage	Retail sales	Sales at every level of business
Tax base	Retail sales price	Value added by each company
Taxpayer	Business	Business
Incidence of tax	Consumer	Consumer

Conclusions

The four approaches to tax reform analyzed in this chapter—the flat tax, the USA tax, the national sales tax, and the value-added tax—are all variations on the same theme. All would shift the base of federal taxation from income to consumption and in the process simplify the process of complying with federal tax law. From a macroeconomic viewpoint, the four alternatives, by expanding the pool of saving, would increase the rate of capital investment in the economy and thus enhance the prospects for economic growth. In turn, faster economic growth would raise employment opportunities and living standards and also increase the flow of revenues into the U.S. Treasury.

It may not be too surprising that many business leaders advocate a general shift to consumption as the primary tax base, and quite a few endorse one (or more) of the specific approaches to making that fundamental shift. Nevertheless, consumption taxes in general have their critics, especially those concerned about the "distributional" effects. Each of the four approaches would alter the distribution of the federal tax burden by income classes. As noted in this chapter, the bottom-up sales and VAT reforms would require substantial modifications in order to avoid the regressive results that many fear. Also, the allocation of the business tax burden would be different under each of the alternatives. As a general proposition, capital-intensive firms catering to industrial markets tend to favor consumption taxes. Labor-intensive companies and especially those serving consumer markets are far less enthusiastic, and many are quite hostile to the entire approach.

The flat tax is the simplest of the top-down reforms of the federal income tax. Its critics mainly are concerned with the potential capital losses to homeowners and investors in state and local bonds that would arise from the absence of transition rules. Also, the reduction in the tax burden on upper incomes (those earning over $100,000 a year) is troublesome to those who give greater weight to "fairness" than to economic performance.

The USA tax, in contrast, maintains the progressive nature of the current federal tax system while shifting the tax base from income to consumption. As a result, however, it is far more complicated than the flat tax. Because all saving is exempt, the top tax brackets on consumption are higher than the current rate table in order to maintain revenue neutrality.

The national sales tax is the simpler of the bottom-up tax reforms. For most individual taxpayers, it would eliminate the need for dealing with the Internal Revenue Service. Responding to the concerns about "regressivity," however, would introduce new complexity. Establishing a separate collection system for this tax raises administrative issues.

The value-added tax, well-known around the world, is the most sophisticated sales-based revenue approach. It would eliminate the worry that small business would be treated less favorably (as in the sales tax case). However, in common with the USA tax, it is a complex concept to explain to the average taxpayer. Like the sales tax, it raises difficult questions about fairness (e.g., regressivity) and would require a new method of collection.

It typically takes several years for Congress to consider and enact a comprehensive tax reform. In the process, numerous changes are usually made in the original proposal on which it holds hearings. Some tax analysts believe that some combination of the four approaches to consumption taxation is likely to emerge—in the form of a tax that is flatter than the current income tax (but not flat), that defers taxation on much saving (but not all), and that is somewhat simpler than the status quo (but still filled with all sorts of complexities).

Notes

1. Gregory Acs and Eugene Steurle, "The Corporation As a Dispenser of Welfare and Security," in Carl Kaysen, ed., *The American Corporation Today* (New York: Oxford University Press, 1996), p. 373.

2. Arthur P. Hall, "Accounting Costs, Another Tax," *Wall Street Journal,* December 9, 1993, p. A14.

3. Bronwyn Hall, *R and D Tax Policy During the Eighties: Success or Failure* (Cambridge, MA: National Bureau of Economic Research, 1992).

4. This may reflect a more general problem for the business community, the tendency for individual companies to free-ride "public goods" that benefit business in general and to concentrate their resources on "private goods" (gains limited to their company or industry).

5. Not all of the tax breaks go to business. Other beneficiaries include a "state which ratified the United States Constitution on March 29, 1790," and "a university established by charter granted by King George II of England on October 31, 1754."

6. Rick Wartzman, "Companies Try to Decide Which Version to Support," *Wall Street Journal,* June 28, 1993, p. A10.

7. "Economists for Clinton," *The Economist,* October 5, 1996, p. 27.

8. Robert Hall and Alvin Rabushka, *Flat Tax* (Stanford, CA: Hoover Institution Press, 1995).

9. David F. Bradford, "An Uncluttered Income Tax: The Next Reform Agenda?", in Gerhard Fels and George Von Furstenberg, eds., *A Supply-Side Agenda for Germany* (Berlin: Springer-Verlag, 1989), pp. 379–398.

10. Charles E. McLure, Jr. and George R. Zodrow, "A Hybrid Approach to the Direct Taxation of Consumption," in Michael J. Boskin, ed., *Frontiers of Tax Reform* (Stanford, CA: Hoover Institution Press, 1996, p. 71.

11. For more esoteric approaches, see Lawrence J. Kotlikoff, "Saving and Consumption Taxation," in Boskin, *Frontiers of Tax Reform*, p. 171.

12. Alan A. Tait, ed., *Value-Added Tax: Administrative and Policy Issues* (Washington, DC: International Monetary Fund, 1992).

13. Some economists contend that, although the ratio of consumption to income declines with respect to annual income, there is little decline in relation to long-term average income.

14. Gregory Ballentine, "The Administrability of a Value-Added Tax," in Charls E. Walker and Mark A. Bloomfield, eds., *The Consumption Tax* (Cambridge, MA: Ballinger Publishing Co., 1987) p. 297.

CHAPTER 14

Government Credits and Bailouts

One of the least understood components of the government's arsenal of power over the private sector is its ability to provide credit to various individuals, business firms, and other organizations. Over the years, many programs to extend credit have been established by the federal government, most at terms far more generous than are available in private, competitive markets. Because few of these government credit activities appear in the federal budget, they seem to be a painless way of achieving national objectives. In reality, these credit programs are a form of hidden subsidy and represent a key mechanism whereby government can influence the fortunes of individual companies.

THE NATURE OF CREDIT SUBSIDIES

The federal government subsidizes private economic activity in a great many ways and, as we will see, the typical credit program generates a specific benefit or subsidy to the recipients. The common characteristic of all subsidies—credit programs as well as other aids—is that they constitute a wedge between the cost to the seller of a product or service and the price paid by the buyer. A subsidy may go to producers or to consumers, or it may be shared. The general intent of a subsidy is to encourage some activity, usually to cause more to be produced or consumed than would result from the unaided operations of the competitive marketplace. A subsidy is not a purchase per se because the government does not directly acquire the good or service. Nor is it a transfer payment; there is a quid pro quo: The recipient of the subsidy does have to engage in a particular undertaking in order to receive it.

Some government subsidies are direct and visible; the public and Congress are readily aware of the magnitude of the federal aid being extended and the identities of the recipients. Examples include farm price supports and operating subsidies for shipping. In the first case, the U.S. Department of Agriculture pays farmers more than the competitive marketplace. In the second, the DOT offsets the difference between the high cost of U.S. flag operations and the lower cost of foreign competitors.

Indirect subsidies are more numerous, in part because they are far less visible. For example, at least half of all waterborne shipments by U.S. government agencies must be carried in U.S. flag vessels. Keeping out foreign competition keeps the price up. In the mining industry, restrictions against selling surplus items in the stockpile of strategic materials also keep prices high, benefiting producers (at the expense of the users).

In some cases, the creation of winners and losers is quite clear. As noted earlier, airport landing rights are provided below cost to general aviation (private planes other than scheduled airlines). Airline passengers do not realize that their fares include the cost of higher landing fees to make up the difference. This is an example of cross-subsidization, a process whereby one group pays more for a good or service in order to subsidize its use by others.

Federal credit programs constitute a large part of government subsidies. The benefit to the recipient is usually in the form of lower interest rates than would normally be paid, longer maturities, and less collateral. Thus the borrower is receiving a benefit from the involvement of the government in the credit market. By the nature of the operation, credit subsidies are indirect or hidden, which adds to their political attractiveness.

In the main, the federal government "merely" guarantees private borrowing or sponsors ostensibly private lending institutions, albeit with federal ties. Examples range from the Export-Import Bank to the Federal National Mortgage Association to the federal land banks.

Is the use of the federal government's credit power a variation of the proverbial free lunch? Surely, many of the recipients benefit from such hidden subsidies as lower interest rates, and at least initially, no federal money seems to be required. But, as will be demonstrated, upon closer inspection we find that the government's extension of credit results in substantial costs to the private sector—to business and consumers—as well as to taxpayers. Furthermore, it generates opportunities for the application of federal controls over private economic activity, credit serving as the sweetener for the acceptance by the recipient of the added regulation. Simultaneously, substantial social benefits accrue from these programs in terms of achieving various national priorities. More housing can be built. More farms and businesses can continue operating that otherwise would go bankrupt.

The advantages of using the government's credit power arise from its effectiveness in channeling more funds—and ultimately additional real resources—to specific groups of the society. In each case, Congress has passed a law stating in effect that it believes the national welfare requires that the designated groups receive larger shares of the available supply of credit than would result from the operation of market forces alone.

What are not apparent are the costs and other side effects that result from this expanded use of government credit. If the borrower defaults, the government is left holding the bag. In terms of their overall economic impact, these lending programs do nothing to increase the total pool of capital available to the economy. They result in a game of musical chairs. That is, by preempting a major portion of the annual flow of saving, the government-sponsored credit agencies reduce the amount of credit available to unprotected borrowers: mainly consumers, state and local governments, and new and small business firms.[1]

During periods of general credit stringency ("tight money"), it is difficult for some unassisted borrowers to attract the financing they require. They are forced to compete against the government-aided borrowers. It is an uneven contest. Federal loan guarantees reduce the riskiness of lending money to the insured borrowers. The result of that unequal competition is still higher interest rates, especially for unsubsidized borrowers.

Over the years, substantial numbers of credit programs have been created through the legislative process of the federal government. These programs emerged on an ad hoc basis, with each directed toward providing assistance in overcoming a specific problem at hand. As a result of this gradual but substantial accretion, federal credit subsidies are now provided to many sectors of the American economy—housing, agriculture, thrift institutions, energy, transportation, health, education, state and local government, small business—as well as to foreigners. Congress has authorized more than 200 separate direct loan programs. In addition, approximately 150 different types of loans can be made by private lending institutions, with interest costs and repayment of the principal guaranteed by a federal department or agency.

Table 14.1 shows the relative importance of the major uses of the federal government's credit power. In the fiscal year 1996, the federal government held outstand-

TABLE 14.1 Major Federal Credit Programs, Fiscal Year 1996 (outstanding amounts, dollars in billions)

Agency	Direct Loans	Guaranteed Loans	Government-Sponsored Enterprises	Total
Agency for International Development	$ 13	$ 9	$ —	$ 22
Agriculture	96	18	—	114
Defense	1	—	—	1
Education	12	102	—	114
Health and Human Services	1	3	—	4
Housing and Urban Development	11	957	—	968
International Security Assistance	8	6	—	14
Veteran Affairs	1	155	—	156
Export-Import Bank	8	18	—	26
Farm Credit Agencies	1	—	56	57
Federal Home Loan Banks	—	—	153	153
Federal Home Loan Mortgage Corporation	—	—	526	526
Federal National Mortgage Association	—	—	838	838
Overseas Private Investment Corporation	—	2	—	2
Small Business Administration	11	31	—	42
Student Loan Marketing	—	—	37	37
Transportation	—	3	—	3
All Other	3	—	—	3
TOTAL	$166	$1,304	$1,610	$3,080

Source: Budget of the United States Government, Fiscal Year 1998.

ing direct loans of $166 billion, had guaranteed outstanding private loans of $1,304 billion, and sponsored "quasi-government" enterprises that had extended another $1,610 billion in credit to private borrowers.

TYPES OF GOVERNMENT CREDIT PROGRAMS

Direct Loans by Federal Departments and Agencies

Direct loans, such as the credit supplied by the Department of Agriculture, involve significant subsidies because the funds usually are loaned at rates much below those available in the private sector. Also, the maturities are longer and the collateral requirements are lower. In many cases, the federal government also absorbs the administrative expenses and losses arising from loan defaults, further increasing the amount of the subsidy. In recent years, direct loans have become a less important form of federal credit aid, in part because they require unequivocal use of federal money in a period of general budget stringency.

Although not formally considered a federal credit program, the generous progress payments made by the DOD represent interest-free provision of working capital to government contractors on a very large scale. Moreover, the terms are much more generous than usually extended on their commercial business.

Loans Guaranteed by Federal Departments and Agencies

Loan guarantees account for a major share of the current array of federal credit subsidies. The primary attraction of loan guarantees to federal policy makers is that the loans are made by private lenders and thus are excluded from the federal budget. Technically, all the government does is assume a contingent liability to pay the private lender if the private borrower defaults. When there is little collateral in connection with the guarantee, the government may be assuming relatively high risks. This was the case when the Treasury guaranteed a portion of New York City's debt. If New York City had defaulted, how could the federal government have taken over its "collateral"? Could it have sold Central Park? Given the public outrage that would be precipitated, it is hard to think of a private individual or organization willing to bid on that property.

Loan guarantees, depending on the specific terms, transfer some of the risk of default from the lender to the government. The limiting case is where the government guarantees the timely payment of 100 percent of the loan principal and interest. Such action comes close to transforming a private loan into a government security. However, the private debt does not have all of the attributes of a government issue. For example, it is likely to be less liquid and not as readily transferable to other investors. Thus, guaranteed loans bear interest rates above the yields on otherwise comparable Treasury securities.

Loans by Federally Sponsored Enterprises

Credit extended by enterprises sponsored by the federal government includes a variety of off-budget entities whose outlays are not included in the reported budget totals. These ostensibly privately owned agencies have various tax advantages and are able to borrow funds in financial markets at relatively low interest rates because of the implicit government backing of their debentures and their potential to borrow directly from the Treasury when necessary. One expert contends that these enterprises function in a *terra incognita,* somewhere between the public and private sectors.[2]

Loans made by these sponsored agencies have increased sharply over the years. They now comprise the dominant form of federal credit assistance to the private sector. There are currently four major groups of federally sponsored, privately owned credit enterprises:

1. The Student Loan Marketing Association (Sally Mae), which purchases guaranteed student loans to create a secondary market.
2. The Farm Credit Banks, consisting of several hundred financial intermediaries providing credit for farmers, ranchers, agricultural firms, and agricultural cooperatives.
3. The Federal National Mortgage Association (Fannie Mae), which maintains a secondary market for home mortgages.
4. The Federal Home Loan Banks, which provide financial assistance to savings and loan associations (S&Ls).

Congress established Sally Mae to provide funds to college students, the farm credit banks to aid agriculture, and the other two groups to broaden the flow of credit to the housing market. Although the securities the government-sponsored enterprises issue are not guaranteed by the federal government, they are afforded many privileges not available to other financial institutions:

- They are exempted from having to register debt issues with the Securities and Exchange Commission.
- Their interest income is exempted from state and local taxes (except for Fannie Mae).
- Their debt issues may be used as collateral when commercial banks borrow from the Federal Reserve.
- The Federal Reserve can buy their bonds in its open-market transactions.
- Their bonds can be used by banks as collateral for public deposits.
- National banks may invest and deal in their securities without limit.

As a result of these benefits, the federally sponsored credit agencies can usually issue their securities at lower yields than the highest-rated corporate bonds of similar maturities (but at higher interest rates than Treasury issues).

During the 1980s, the farm credit banks and the home loan banks encountered substantial financial difficulties due to the widespread distress among farmers and savings and loan associations. In both cases, Congress enacted large programs of assistance. Thus, although the legal connection between these enterprises and the federal government may technically be remote, in practice the relationship can be quite close (see Table 14.2).

In the case of the farm credit banks, Congress established three specialized government-sponsored enterprises in 1988 to shore up the federal farm credit system. It created the Farm Credit System Financial Assistance Corporation to help the federal farm banks raise needed capital. Unlike those of the farm banks, the bonds issued by the new corporation are guaranteed by the federal government. Moreover, the Treasury paid the entire interest cost on the bonds during the first five years and half the interest cost during the next five years.

TABLE 14.2 Government Ties of Federally Sponsored Credit Agencies

Agency	Stockholders	Influence of Executive Branch	Line of Credit with Treasury	Federal Tax on Income[a]	State and Local Tax on Interest Income of Investors
Federal Home Loan Banks	Member thrifts	These banks are regulated by the Federal Housing Finance Board	$4.0 billion	No	No
Federal National Mortgage Association	Owned entirely by private stockholders	President selects 5 of 18 board members; subject to general supervision by HUD	$2.25 billion	Yes	No
Farm Credit Banks	Owned by farm cooperatives and credit associations	President selects 12 board members; Secretary of Agriculture	$112 million for Federal Credit Banks; $149 million for Banks for Cooperatives; $6 million for Federal Land Banks	No	No
Student Loan Marketing Association	Lenders under the Guaranteed Student Loan Program (individual investors hold nonvoting stock)	President selects 7 of 21 board members including the chairman	$1.0 billion[b]	Yes	Yes

[a]Interest on all debt of the sponsored agencies is subject to federal taxation.
[b]Sallie Mae also has the authority to sell to the Federal Financing Bank securities backed by student loans.

The Federal Agriculture Mortgage Corporation provides a secondary market for farm mortgages and rural housing loans. Its initial capital comes from sales of its stock to banks, insurance companies, and other financial institutions. The new mortgage corporation can borrow up to $1.5 billion from the Treasury. Finally, the Farm Credit System Insurance Corporation insures the bonds issued by the federal farm banks. Like the FDIC, this insurance corporation is financed by fees collected from the member banks who benefit from the insurance.

As part of the massive bailout of S&Ls (described later), Congress set up the Office of Thrift Supervision in the Department of the Treasury to replace the Federal Home Loan Bank Board as the regulator of the thrift industry. The Federal Home Loan Banks are now regulated by the Federal Housing Finance Board.

IMPACTS ON TOTAL SAVING AND INVESTMENT

The impacts of federal credit programs on the flow of saving and investment in the economy are clear. These programs do nothing to increase that total flow. They mainly change the share of investment funds going to a given industry or sector of the economy.

The Initial Impacts

Because these governmental borrowers have few worries about creditworthiness or meeting interest payments, they can preempt large portions of the nation's credit markets. As a result, federal credit programs have become a source of upward pressure on interest rates. (Overall levels of interest rates may not necessarily rise because of offsetting action by the Federal Reserve System.)

This phenomenon requires some explanation. The total supply of credit is broadly determined by household and business saving and the ability of banks to increase the money supply. In an open economy, the available credit also includes funds supplied by overseas investors. The normal response of financial markets to an increase in the demand for funds by a major borrower, such as a federal credit program, is upward pressure on interest rates. The resultant rise in rates helps to balance out the demand for funds with the supply of savings by discouraging some from borrowing while encouraging others to save more.

But the federal government's demand for funds is *interest inelastic.* That is, the Treasury will generally raise the money it requires regardless of the interest rate it has to pay. Also, the interest elasticity of saving is relatively modest; higher interest rates will not attract a great amount of additional saving. Thus, the rise in federally subsidized borrowing is not likely to be offset fully by added saving. Weak and marginal borrowers will be "rationed" out of financial markets in the process, while the Treasury as well as other borrowers pay higher rates of interest than they otherwise would.

Since federal credit activities primarily involve guarantees and implied guarantees by sponsored credit enterprises, the direct outlays included in the budget are modest. The federal government appears to be able to deliver something for nothing, or almost nothing. But as with all such sleight-of-hand feats, the truth is different. In practice, there are extra costs associated with the operations of government credit agencies in capital markets. These costs include selling issues that are smaller than the minimally efficient size and selling securities that only in varying degrees approximate the characteristics of direct Treasury debt in terms of perfection of guarantee, flexibility of timing and maturities, and "cleanness" of instrument. As a result of such considerations, the market charges a premium over the interest cost on direct government debt of comparable maturity. That premium has ranged from one-quarter of 1 percent on the financially strong Federal National Mortgage Association to more than 1 percent on the troubled federal farm credit banks when they were viewed by investors as "troubled."

If cost of financing were the only considerations, it would be most efficient to have the Treasury itself provide the money for direct loans by issuing government debt in the market. The Treasury's Federal Financing Bank (FFB) does just that. However, as is often the case with government undertakings, the FFB has expanded beyond the role initially planned for it. It now purchases private loans that have been guaranteed by a federal agency, thus providing a new form of "back-door" spending, bypassing the appropriations process and its controls.

Reduced efficiency occurs in the economy when a federal "umbrella" is provided over many credit activities without distinguishing among their differing credit risks. A basic function that financial institutions are supposed to perform is that of assigning appropriate risk premiums to borrowers of different financial strength. This is the essence of the resource-allocation function of credit markets. As an increasing proportion of all issues coming to the credit markets bears the guarantee of the federal government, the scope for the market to differentiate credit risks inevitably diminishes. Theoretically, the federal agencies issuing or guaranteeing debt could perform this role by charging programs varying insurance premiums for the federal guarantee. In practice, these agencies avoid the hard decisions involved in differential pricing of risks.

More Basic Impacts

The degree to which federal credit assistance, such as loan guarantees, affects the reallocation of resources depends in good measure on the degree of subsidy. At one extreme, the potential transaction being financed may be considered so risky that no financing would be available without federal participation. In this case, the subsidy will be large and will have a dramatic effect on the allocation of credit.

At the other extreme, the federal credit program may result in only a small subsidy and may not change the allocation of credit to any significant degree. Some beneficiaries of loan guarantees for new home mortgages, for example, would have been able to obtain funds without government support, albeit at a moderately higher cost. Table 14.3 shows the subsidy component of a variety of federal credit programs.[3] This information demonstrates the very large subsidies provided in some federal programs (such as almost one-half of the face value of the loan in the case of rural development) and the much smaller subsidies in other credit activities (such as 2 percent for Export-Import Bank loans).

In fiscal year 1998, the present value of the subsidies imbedded in new direct federal lending programs came to $2.0 billion, primarily for various aids to farmers. In the aggregate, subsidies imbedded in federal loan guarantee programs were approximately the same, totaling $1.9 billion. The recipients of the largest amounts of these credit subsidies were participants in the various education loan guarantee programs.[4]

Federal credit programs contain other forms of subsidies, such as deferral of interest, allowance of grace periods, and waiver or reduction of loan fees. Also, default clauses in government loans often offer the borrower greater protection from foreclosure actions by the government than would similar clauses in loans available from private lenders.

TABLE 14.3 Subsidy Component of Selected Federal Lending Programs	
Program	*Subsidy as Percent of Loan Disbursement*
Rural development loans	48%
Community development financial institutions	38
Bureau of Reclamation loans	32
Rural economic development loans	24
Rural housing insurance	18
FCC Spectrum auction loans	12
Small Business Administration — disaster loans	11
Small Business Administration — business loans	10
Minority business resource center program	10
Foreign military sales	9
Rural community advancement program	9
Transportation infrastructure	9
Agricultural credit insurance program	8
Veterans (general)	7
Disaster assistance	6
Direct student loans	4
Overseas Private Investment Corporation	3
Rural electrification and telephone	2
Rural telephone bank	2
Export-Import Bank	2
Veterans housing	1
Fisheries finance loans	1

Source: Budget of the United States Government, Fiscal Year 1998.

IMPACTS ON SECTORS OF THE ECONOMY

The very nature of federal credit assistance is to create advantages for some groups of borrowers and thus disadvantages for others. The proponents of credit assistance in Congress as well as in the private sector rarely ask who will tend to be rationed out in the process. It is unlikely to be the large, well-known corporations or the U.S. government. On the basis of past experience, it is more often state and local governments, small and medium-size businesses, home buyers not protected by the federal umbrella, consumers—marginal borrowers generally.

The competition for funds by federal credit programs also increases the cost to taxpayers by raising the interest rates at which the Treasury borrows its own funds. The size and relative importance of federal government credit demands have expanded over the past three decades and more. In the 1960s, the federal portion of funds raised in private capital markets (including Treasury borrowing and guaranteed and sponsored enterprise debt) averaged 17 percent. In the period 1991–1995, the government's share had risen to an average of 60 percent, an all-time high. This trend was described by one analyst as the largest and quietest takeover of the U.S. credit market in the country's financial history.[5]

Relation to Government Controls

Federal credit assistance is often accompanied by government controls or influence over the recipients of the credit. Federal guarantees for shipbuilders are part of a broader program whereby the federal government requires the builders to incorporate "national defense" features into the vessels.

The largest federal program for guaranteeing private credit, that administered by the Federal Housing Administration (FHA), contains numerous controls that accompany the credit assistance. The FHA conducts an inspection of each residence to determine whether the builder has abided by all of the agency's rules and regulations governing the construction of the homes that it insures. There are four separate "veto" points facing a builder applying for FHA insurance of mortgages for a new project: (1) affirmative marketing to minority groups, (2) environmental impact, (3) architectural review, and (4) underwriting.

Because responsibilities are divided among the various federal housing offices, considerable confusion and delay can arise. For example, after the underwriting has been approved, and assuming it yields an appraised value high enough to cover the builder's costs, additional requirements may be imposed by the environmental impact or architectural review offices. These actions can raise the cost of the project substantially. If this occurs, the builder must return to the first office and attempt to obtain a revised underwriting. In these cases, a portion of the implicit credit subsidy being extended by FHA in effect is being absorbed by the federal government's own social objectives.

Summary of Economic Effects

Contrary to the popular view, government credit programs are not costless, either to the Treasury or to citizens in general. Three distinct costs can be identified:

1. *The economic cost.* Since they do little to increase the total supply of investment funds in the economy, government credit programs take credit away from potential private borrowers. These unsubsidized borrowers might have produced more for society than the recipients of government-supported credit.

2. *The initial fiscal cost.* To the extent that government credit programs increase the total size of government-related credit, they cause an increase in the interest rates that are paid in order to channel these funds away from the private sector. Some increase, therefore, results in the interest rates paid on the public debt, which is a direct cost to the taxpayer.

3. *The ultimate fiscal cost.* When defaults occur on the part of the borrowers whose credit is guaranteed by the federal government, the Treasury winds up bearing the ultimate cost of the credit. In 1996, the federal government had to write off $1.1 billion of direct loans, mainly for credit extended to farmers. In addition, $11.2 billion of guaranteed loans defaulted that year, mainly Federal Housing Administration mortgages and student loans.

Boiled down to the essence, federal guarantees of bonds issued by business and other institutions do not create new investment funds for the economy. Rather, they move capital to the designated sectors of the economy by taking those funds away from other sectors, and often they lead to similar requests for aid by those unsubsidized sectors. Government guarantees also tend to raise the level of interest rates in the economy, both for private as well as for government borrowers. They thus increase an important element of business costs.

The rise in interest rates leads to pressure on the Federal Reserve System to increase the reserves on the banking system in order to supply adequate financing to the private sector. If the Federal Reserve accommodates these pressures, this action may contribute to the general inflationary condition of the economy. Federal credit programs therefore raise the private cost of production in two ways: (1) by causing an increase in interest rates and/or (2) by resulting in a higher general rate of inflation than would otherwise be the case.

Several approaches have been suggested to deal with the problems that arise from the expansion of federal credit programs. One is to require that all proposals to create new credit programs or to broaden existing ones be accompanied by an appraisal of the relation between the interest rate charged in the program, the rate that would be charged by competitive private lenders, and the rate necessary to cover the government's costs. The idea is to encourage Congress, when it approves new credit programs, to distinguish between their natural desire to do favors for constituents by providing funds to a particular sector of the economy and the separate and much tougher question of paying for those funds.

A more detailed method is to establish controls over the total volume of federally assisted credit. These programs would no longer be treated as a "free good." A rudimentary credit budget has been part of the annual budget preparation since 1980. However, binding ceilings are not established on the total use of federal credit. Another way of controlling lending programs is to impose a firm limit on the total borrowing of federal and federally sponsored credit agencies, both those "in" and those "out" of the budget. In addition, Congress could enact a ceiling on the overall volume of debt created under federal loan guarantees.

Congress has taken one important but only partial step. Since the enactment of the Federal Credit Reform Act of 1990, it must appropriate annually the subsidy component of the new federal loans and loan guarantees to be provided during the fiscal year. By incorporating federal loans and loan guarantees directly into the federal budget, the new law has made governmental decision makers more aware of the cost of this use of the federal credit power. As part of a determined effort to reduce federal budget deficits, the total volume of direct loans has stabilized since 1990. However, a sharply upward trend is still visible in total federal loan guarantees.

Most fundamentally, an economic climate more conducive to private saving and investment would reduce the need for private borrowers to seek federal credit assistance in the first place. The creation of that climate requires a tax system that tilts in favor of saving rather than consumption and a durable fiscal policy that avoids as a matter of policy the Treasury deficits whose financing competes with private borrowers. Until these fundamental changes are achieved, pressures for continued expansion of federal credit programs can be anticipated.

BUSINESS BAILOUTS: FEDERAL CREDIT ON A LARGE SCALE

When federal credit programs work as intended, they involve little cash drain on the Treasury. Fees paid by users typically cover administrative costs and modest amounts of defaults. In several dramatic cases, however, the federal government has provided credit to selected business firms on a massive scale, and at times the losses to the Treasury have been severe.

The Chrysler Bailout

Chrysler has become the favorite example of proponents of federal financial assistance to enterprises in "temporary" difficulties. On the surface, the government's bailout of the company was successful. Not only did Chrysler survive, it repaid the loans guaranteed by the government ahead of schedule.

A variety of arguments had been presented in support of Chrysler's request for federal loan guarantees. They boiled down to the claim that it was cheaper for society to provide the assistance than to have permitted the company to go bankrupt. This policy conclusion was based on six key points:

1. The impact on the federal budget of a Chrysler failure would have been greater than the cost of assistance. Projected increases in unemployment benefits, trade adjustment assistance payments, and other social programs, as well as reduced tax revenues, would have exceeded the total amount of assistance provided to Chrysler. Also, the federal aid was "only" a guarantee and not a direct loan by the federal government. (All this ignores the negative impacts on Ford and General Motors as a result of government subsidizing their competitor.)

2. The social upheaval attendant on a Chrysler failure would have imposed substantial, albeit unquantifiable, costs on society. (This is an argument for propping up every failing enterprise.)

3. Production and employment at Chrysler was more heavily concentrated in the Detroit metropolitan area than the other U.S. auto manufacturers. Consequently, the geographic impact of a Chrysler failure would have been felt disproportionately in a major city, one that already had substantial economic problems. (This approach argues against economic change.)

4. A Chrysler failure would have led to further concentration of the domestic automobile industry and greater monopoly power in the hands of the surviving corporations, which would in turn lead to higher prices. (This argument ignores the very substantial rise of foreign competition.)

5. The U.S. balance of payments, already severely in deficit, would have been pushed further into the red as foreign producers captured a share of Chrysler's domestic market. (What happened to the Chrysler arguments that the bailout was needed to prevent GM and Ford from assuming "greater monopoly power"?)

6. While Chrysler's ability to produce small cars in model years 1979 and 1980 was restricted to approximately 300,000 units, Chrysler was building up to a yearly output of almost one million small-car units, which promised to sell strongly in the marketplace.[6] (This is an odd argument for a government bailout. It sounds like the standard case for a bank loan.)

The Chrysler case is the most widely cited precedent for additional federal bailouts of individual companies. Yet, a careful analysis of this experience concluded that the decision to approve the loan program was made on an ad hoc basis, without regard for any articulated policy.[7]

The events that occurred after the congressional approval of the loan guarantee did not follow a simple pattern. The Chrysler Corporation avoided declaring bankruptcy, but it experienced many of the benefits of such action. Specifically, the Chrysler Corporation Loan Guarantee Act of 1979 required creditors to make "concessions" to the company. As a result, Chrysler was able to pay off more than $600 million in debts at 30 cents on the dollar.[8] It also laid off about 40 percent of its workers. That, in retrospect, is not a stellar precedent for a generalized program of government financial aid to industrial companies that are in difficulty.

Other Rescue Efforts of Individual Enterprises

The arguments offered for the Chrysler bailout are not unique, in the sense that they can be expressed in more general terms and made in connection with virtually any large corporate failure. Nevertheless, the federal government has not invariably bailed out every loser in the marketplace. Consider the many large firms that went bankrupt during the 1980s and reorganized to become leaner and lower-cost competitors. Examples of successful post-bankrupt firms range from giant retailer Federated Department Stores to Continental Airlines. Of course, the stockholders suffered during the process, but that is a characteristic—painful but necessary—of a healthy private enterprise system.

However, the federal government has provided special assistance to many corporations prior to the 1980s, when the federal government began to take a harder position in these matters. The Reconstruction Finance Corporation (RFC) operated in the depression and wartime period of the 1930s and 1940s to shore up companies that could not obtain adequate private financing. The activities of the RFC during the Great Depression and in wartime were generally applauded. However, a great show of favoritism during the post-World War II period led to widely publicized congressional investigations and to the agency's termination in 1952.[9]

More recently, Lockheed benefited from $250 million in federal loan guarantees from 1970 to 1977. Conrail, the rail freight system of the Northeast, was extended more than $3 billion in aid to help it stay in operation. Special tax relief was granted to American Motors, now a part of the Chrysler Corporation. All of these firms were similar in that they were highly leveraged and had high wage costs. Supporters of aid claimed in each case that it was cheaper to provide government assistance than to bear the costs of their collapse. And supporters of each bailout were able to marshal the political clout necessary to win the required votes.

In addition, the Federal Deposit Insurance Corporation (FDIC) has rescued numerous banks from going under. In each of these cases, the FDIC maintained that it was cheaper to provide the financial assistance to keep the bank going than it would have been to pay off the depositors whose accounts were insured up to $100,000 each. Frequently, the FDIC attempts to merge an ailing bank with a stronger financial institution, often providing some capital infusion to cover a portion of the bad loans assumed by the acquiring bank. Altogether, the FDIC has responded to several hundred bank failures since 1980.

In 1984, the FDIC rescued the Continental-Illinois Bank of Chicago in one of the largest bailouts of a private company in American history. To prevent the failure of the bank, whose assets totaled approximately $40 billion in 1983, the FDIC bought its loan portfolio for $3.5 billion and agreed to provide an additional $1.5 billion in direct funding. In this case, the FDIC acted not solely to avoid having to pay off the depositors whose savings it had insured but also out of concern over the repercussions throughout the banking industry had one of the nation's largest financial institutions been allowed to fail.[10]

The S&L Bailout

The largest and surely the most expensive bailout in American history occurred in the S&L industry in the late 1980s and early 1990s. A major portion of the entire industry was liquidated and the federal government wound up selling the remaining assets of the bankrupt thrift institutions, often under "fire sale" conditions. This case dramatically illustrated the potential cost of the federal government "merely" guaranteeing or insuring private credit and related financial transactions.

During the extended S&L bailout (1980–95), the federal government closed down over 300 S&Ls at a cost of over $30 billion. In addition, over 800 thrift institutions were sold to new owners, typically with the federal government picking up the accumulated losses (over $100 billion). In many cases, the S&Ls, greatly reduced in size from their previous operation, were merged into healthier and often larger financial institutions. As shown in Table 14.4, the cost of the S&L bailout was over $180 billion.[11]

Ironically, one of the ways of financing the S&L bailout increased the likelihood of more thrift institutions going under. In order to minimize the already heavy load on the general taxpayer, Congress required that a substantial part of the cost of rescuing the sick S&Ls be paid for by a levy on the healthy S&Ls. Aside from the questionable fairness of well-run financial institutions having to subsidize their poorly run competitors, the added cost may have pushed some of the marginally healthy S&Ls over the brink. In any event, raising the operating costs of thrift institutions made it more difficult for them to compete against commercial banks for the business of individual depositors and consumer borrowers.

TABLE 14.4 Cost of the S&L Bailout

Year	Number of Thrifts Resolved		In Millions	
	Yearly	Cumulative	Yearly	Cumulative
1980	11	11	$ 166	$ 166
1981	28	39	760	926
1982	63	102	806	1,732
1983	36	138	275	2,007
1984	22	160	743	2,750
1985	31	191	1,022	3,772
1986	46	237	3,066	6,838
1987	47	284	3,704	10,542
1988	205	489	35,790	46,332
1989	37	526	4,899	51,232
1990	316	842	38,383	89,614
1991	232	1,074	33,833	123,447
1992	68	1,142	7,172	130,619
1993–1995	300[a]	1,442	51,000	181,619

[a]Estimated.
Source: Congressional Budget Office.

Hindsight also reveals that the delays in the 1980s in closing down the failed thrifts increased the size of the bailout substantially. Many managers of insolvent S&Ls proceeded to make extremely risky investments in the hope that they could turn around the situation—knowing that the government was eventually going to pick up the tab if the deals went sour. The Congressional Budget Office estimated that the delay in closing failed institutions, often as much as two to four years, roughly doubled the ultimate cost of resolving them.[12]

The S&L bailout was no simple matter for the federal government. What does a federal agency do with the country club on which a failed thrift institution had foreclosed? Dealing with the many aspects of the situation involved more than just paying out large sums of money. Congress assigned responsibilities to a large and confusing array of federal agencies, old and new:

1. The new Office of Thrift Supervision replaced the Federal Home Loan Bank Board in chartering and supervising individual S&Ls.

2. The new Savings Association Insurance Fund (SAIF) replaced the Federal Savings and Loan Insurance Corporation (FSLIC) in insuring deposits at S&Ls.

3. The new Resolution Trust Corporation (RTC) resolved (closed down or sold off, usually at a substantial loss) the failed S&Ls. This responsibility was gradually shifted to the SAIF.

4. The RTC disposed of the assets of the failed thrifts.

5. The new FSLIC Resolution Fund, administered by the FDIC, took over the S&Ls that the defunct Federal Savings and Loan Insurance Corporation (FSLIC) had held in receivership. This agency was responsible for completing the resolution of the receiverships created by the Federal Home Loan Bank Board and FSLIC.

6. The new Federal Housing Finance Board replaced the Federal Home Loan Bank Board in regulating the quasi-governmental Federal Home Loan Banks.

7. The Federal Financing Bank lent working capital to the RTC, which repaid the interest and principal from the proceeds of asset sales.

8. The new Thrift Depositor Protection Oversight Board, chaired by the Secretary of the Treasury, oversaw the operation of the RTC.

9. The new Resolution Funding Corporation (REFCORP) is a mixed-ownership (public and private) enterprise that helped finance the RTC. Of the original $50 billion appropriated for the RTC, $30 billion came from the sale of private debt by REFCORP.

Perhaps the saddest lesson of the S&L bailout is that governmental decision makers learned little from this painful and expensive episode. Congress, with President Clinton's urging and support, established a new venture requiring at least initially "little" federal money and mainly federal guarantees.

The idea is to encourage the formation of specialized community development banks to provide credit in poor areas where existing private financial institutions are deemed not to provide adequate funds for consumer and small business borrowers. The Community Development and Regulatory Improvement Act of 1994 provides subsidies of about $400 million for the first four years. It is accompanied by the usual assurances that more money will not be needed—aside from some loan guarantees.

The use of the government's credit power remains an attractive mechanism because, on the surface at least, it seems to provide that proverbial free lunch, large benefits with little if any costs—at least during the early part of the program.

Notes

1. James L. Bothwell, *Government Sponsored Enterprises (GSEs)* (Washington, DC: U.S. General Accounting Office, 1997).

2. Harold Seidman, "The Quasi World of the Federal Government," *Brookings Review,* Summer 1988, p. 25.

3. The subsidy is calculated as the difference between the present value of the government's cash outflow for the loan and the present value of the expected payments of principal and interest. The discount rate used to estimate present value is the interest rate on marketable Treasury securities of like maturity at the time the loan was disbursed.

4. *The Budget of the United States Government, Fiscal Year 1998,* Analytical Perspectives (Washington, DC: U.S. Government Printing Office, 1997), pp. 145–192.

5. Francis X. Cavanaugh, *The Truth About the National Debt* (Boston, MA: Harvard Business School Press, 1997).

6. Brian M. Freeman and Allan I. Mendelowitz, "Program in Search of a Policy: The Chrysler Loan Guarantee," *Journal of Policy Analysis and Management* 11, no. 4, 1982, p. 448.

7. Freeman and Mendelowitz, p. 452.

8. James K. Hickel, *The Chrysler Bail-Out Bust* (Washington, DC: Heritage Foundation, 1983), p. 2.

9. Arthur T. Denzau and Clifford M. Hardin, *A National Development Bank: Ghost of the RFC Past* (St. Louis: Washington University, Center for the Study of American Business, 1984); U.S. Senate, Committee on Banking and Currency, *Study of Reconstruction Finance Corporation and Proposed Amendment of RFC Act* (Washington, DC: U.S. Government Printing Office, 1951).

10. Eric N. Compton, *The New World of Commercial Banking* (Lexington, MA: Lexington Books, 1987), p. 14.

11. Congressional Budget Office, *Resolving the Thrift Crisis* (Washington, DC: Government Printing Office, 1993), p. 6.

12. *Resolving the Thrift Crisis,* p. 17.

CHAPTER 15

Government as a Market

G overnments in the United States—federal, state, and local—constitute large and often very special customers for a wide variety of private businesses. As shown in Table 15.1, the aggregate purchases by government agencies are substantial—$660 billion in 1996. These procurements are divided between federal buyers (48 percent) and state and local agencies (52 percent).

But it is far more than a mere matter of size. The composition of government purchases differs greatly between the levels of government and from the typical private sector buyer, and so does the manner in which these purchases are made. A large share of federal procurement is heavily high tech for the military establishment. In contrast, states and localities buy variations of more traditional supplies and equipment available to the rest of the economy.

FEDERAL CIVILIAN PROCUREMENT

Federal civilian procurement typically relies on the selection of the offerer of the lowest price based on sealed bids submitted by "responsible" bidders (those meeting the government's stated standards). Except for purchases of high-tech civilian space equipment by NASA, which uses an acquisition system similar to that of the DOD, the composition of federal civilian purchases is comparable if not identical to standard commercial items.

The Federal Supply Service in the U.S. General Services Administration is the agency in charge of buying most of the civilian procurements of the federal government. Given the wide variety of missions assigned to the numerous departments and agencies established by Congress, it is not surprising that this market is very broad. As can be seen in Table 15.2, the civilian purchases of the federal government range from alarm systems to storage tanks, from cattle guards to lawn and garden equipment, and from tires to trophies.

For companies that do substantial amounts of business with the federal government (civilian as well as military agencies), the very act of signing a procurement contract forces them to agree to perform a wide variety of socially responsible actions. These range from favoring disadvantaged groups to showing concern for the quality of life and the environment.

The federal government requires that firms doing business with it maintain "fair" employment practices, provide "safe" and "healthful" working conditions, pay "prevailing" wages, refrain from polluting the air and water, give preference to

TABLE 15.1 Composition of the Government Market, 1996

Level of Government Purchases	Billions of Dollars	Percent
Federal	$315	48
State and local	345	52
Total	$660	100

Note: Compiled from U.S. Department of Commerce data.

American products in their purchases, and promote the rehabilitation of prisoners and the severely handicapped. Table 15.3 contains a sample listing of such ancillary duties required of government contractors.

Although aimed at important social objectives, those special provisions are not without expense to the government procurement process. They increase overhead of both private contractors and federal procurement offices. Some of the provisions also exert an upward pressure on the direct costs incurred by the government. Special provisions such as the Davis–Bacon Act increase the cost of public construction projects through government promulgation of wage rates higher than those that would result if the market were allowed to operate without impediment.

TABLE 15.2 Categories of Federal Civilian Procurements

Alarm systems	Office furniture and decorations
Athletic and recreational equipment	Office machines and supplies
Cattle guards	Paint
Chemicals and chemical products	Photography equipment and supplies
Cleaning supplies	Prefab storage buildings
Clothing and footwear	Publications
Construction and building materials	Record equipment
Conveyors and forklifts	Recreational equipment
Data processing equipment	Recycling equipment and containers
Dental equipment and supplies	Relocation services
Drugs and pharmaceutical products	Road maintenance
Fire-fighting and rescue equipment	Shipping packaging and supplies
Food services	Signs
Hand and power tools	Storage tanks
Industry machinery	Subsistence foods
Internet products	Telecommunication and media supplies
Laboratory instruments and equipment	Tires
Law enforcement equipment	Training aids and devices
Lawn and garden equipment	Transportation services
Maintenance and repair shop equipment	Trophies and awards
Marine equipment	Water purification and sewer equipment
Medical supplies and equipment	Wheel and track vehicles
Musical instruments	

Source: U.S. Federal Supply Service.

TABLE 15.3   Social and Economic Restrictions on Federal Government Contractors

Program	Purpose
Improve Working Conditions	
Walsh–Healey Act	Prescribes minimum wages, hours, and work conditions for supply contracts
Davis–Bacon Act	Prescribes minimum wages, benefits, and work conditions on construction contracts over $2,000
Service Contract Act	Extends the Walsh–Healey and Davis–Bacon acts to persons imprisoned at hard labor
Favor Disadvantaged Groups	
Equal Employment Opportunity	Requires affirmative action programs for government contractors
Employment openings	Requires contractors to list suitable employment openings with state employment systems
Prison-made supplies	Requires mandatory purchase of specific supplies from federal prison industries
Blind-made products	Requires mandatory purchase of products made by blind and other handicapped persons
Small Business Act	Requires "fair" portion of subcontracts to be placed with small businesses
Labor-surplus area concerns	Requires preference to subcontract in areas of concentrated unemployment or underemployment
Favor American Companies	
Buy American Act	Provides preference for domestic materials over foreign materials
Preference to U.S. vessels	Requires shipping at least half of government goods in U.S. vessels
Protect the Environment and Quality of Life	
Clean Air Act	Prohibits contracts to a company convicted of criminal violation of air-pollution standards
Care of laboratory animals	Requires humane treatment by contractors in use of experimental or laboratory animals
Humane Slaughter Act	Limits government purchases of meat to suppliers that conform to humane slaughter standards

THE STATE AND LOCAL GOVERNMENT MARKET

Purchases by state and local agencies generally follow a pattern basically similar to that of federal civilian agencies. However, because of the great variety of state, county, and municipal governments, the specific procurement procedures followed are far from uniform. Each governmental unit tends to adopt its own practices, especially as they relate to the nature of competition and the discretion to buy items without a formal bidding process. Schools and highway departments represent the biggest buyers in this portion of the public sector. The heavy preponderance of hard goods (durables and structures) can be seen in Table 15.4, showing the character of state and local purchases.

TABLE 15.4 The State and Local Government Market in 1996	
Category of Procurement	*Amount (in billions)*
Durable goods	$ 46
Nondurable goods	78
Structures	138
Services	83
Total	$345

Note: Compiled from U.S. Department of Commerce data.

Privatization

In recent years, privatization—shifting functions and responsibilities from the government to the private sector—has become increasingly common. This trend is exerting a far more complicated effect on the size and composition of the government market than is generally realized. Depending on the form it takes, privatization can expand or contract the amount of goods and services that government purchases from the private sector. Contracting out the performance of an activity that previously had been conducted in-house (for example, in a printing plant operated by civil servants) is the most common form of privatization. However, it is by no means the only way in which government can engage the private sector in its business activities.

There is indeed a range of privatization actions that governments take, and the effects on the private enterprise vary substantially. At one end of the policy spectrum—*service shedding*—the entire function is shifted to the private sector, its financing as well as its performance. When a government arsenal is sold outright to a private company, the aggregate size of private markets is likely to expand, while the total amount of government spending contracts. The decision as to how much, if any, of the service to produce is then made in the marketplace by private producers and consumers.

A closely related type of privatization is *asset sales,* where government sells the ownership of some asset. The item may be a financial asset (a government-guaranteed loan that it holds and is servicing) or a physical asset. A typical example of a physical asset is a government-owned and operated electric utility that policy makers decide should no longer be a public-sector activity. In both of these cases, government continues to exert substantial influence on the activity. In the former instance, the government guarantee is still in force. In the latter instance, government retains the power to regulate rates and service.

As noted earlier, *contracting out* (or outsourcing) is the most popular form of privatization. Here, government hires private firms, typically to provide a service that the government had been providing to citizens directly. Municipal collection of garbage is a popular example. Government continues to finance and sponsor the activity.

The most modest form of privatization is *managed* competition. Here, government opens a market—an example is cleaning government buildings—and private firms are invited to bid against government agencies. The government continues to determine the extent to which businesses can enter these government markets. The extent of privatization depends on a number of factors, including the cost and efficiency of the private enterprise conducting the activity and the political power of the government employees who may have lost their jobs. Frequently, the former government workers obtain employment with the private company now conducting the activity, but with a more modest compensation package.

A significant feedback effect can occur from bringing in competition from the private sector. In response to government employee concerns that they would lose the work to a low-bid private firm, the city of Indianapolis laid off most of the supervisors in its road maintenance crews. The result was to "save" some of the municipal employees' jobs as well as to reduce government spending.[1]

At times, states and localities have taken back activities that had been privatized. This is easiest done in contracting out. In 1997, the state of Missouri brought back prisoners it had housed in proprietary jails in Texas after learning of the brutal treatment they had received.

The various types of privatization efforts are generally too recent to draw hard-and-fast conclusions. Nevertheless, several researchers claim that the initial results are impressive in terms of savings to taxpayers. Specific examples are shown in Table 15.5.

TABLE 15.5 Examples of Privatization in the United States

Activity	Type of Privatization	Preliminary Results
Maintenance of state autos	Outsourcing	Savings estimated at $300,000 a year (Georgia)
Operations of veterans home	Outsourcing	Cleaner home and better food (Georgia)
Maintenance of highways	Managed competition	Reduced overtime costs (Massachusetts)
Provision of security at government installations	Outsourcing	Savings estimated at $1.2 million a year (Michigan)
Armories	Asset sale	Michigan gained $400,000 from sale of surplus facilities
Hotel	Asset sale	New York received $141 million
Wastewater treatment	Outsourcing	Indianapolis saved $16 million a year
Airport management	Outsourcing	16% reduction in cost per enplaned passenger (Indianapolis)
Collection of delinquent taxes	Outsourcing	Improved collection of previously uncollectable accounts (Virginia)

Source: Privatization: Lessons Learned by State and Local Governments (Washington, DC: U.S. General Accounting Office, 1997).

In many foreign nations, the most popular form of privatization is to sell off commercial-style activities previously owned and conducted by government agencies. Unlike the United States, where the arsenal approach is very limited, a great variety of other countries—developed as well as developing—have traditionally conducted a large portion of economic activity in the public sector. In view of the poor performance on the part of these nationalized industries, outright privatization in the form of sales of ownership to private enterprise has often enhanced the efficiency of the national economy while yielding one-time revenues for the national Treasury. In 1996, such worldwide privatizations amounted to an all-time high of $88 billion, of which $68 billion occurred in the advanced industrialized nations.[2]

THE SPECIALIZED MILITARY MARKET

The military market remains the largest single component of public sector procurement. The basic reason for the still high level of defense spending is that the United States continues to live in a dangerous world. The end of the Cold War with the former Soviet Union has not ushered in a millennium of peace. The Middle East and the Balkans are constant reminders of the dangers of armed hostilities. The heavily armed republics of the former Soviet Union—which still contain large military arsenals—conjure up other potential threats of military action. So do the terrorist groups that are active on every continent.

Thus, it can be expected that, for the foreseeable future, the United States will need a substantial military establishment and, in a world of advancing technology, a strong defense industry. Realistically, the defense industry of the early 21st century will be much smaller than in the 1980s and perhaps a little smaller than in the early 1990s. From the viewpoint of business–government relations, perhaps the most significant aspect of the military market is that the companies producing weapon systems and other equipment for the military establishment continue to constitute the most heavily regulated sector of the American economy.

Private production of government orders generates some of the closest day-to-day interactions between federal agencies and individual companies. The Pentagon was once described as the place where Franz Kafka meets Alice in Wonderland.[3] In practice, military and civilian procurement differ so substantially that they are almost worlds apart. Specific purchases are made by the Army, Navy, Air Force, and by a few interservice agencies. These outlays encompass a wide spectrum of items, ranging from standard office supplies to food and clothing to medical equipment. All defense agencies make their procurements through regulations and procedures established by the Armed Services Procurement Act and federal procurement regulations. In 1996, their purchases totaled $109 billion; three-fifths of the contracts awarded were devoted to weapon systems. Figure 15.1 shows that aerospace programs—aircraft, missiles, and space systems—dominate the purchases of weapon systems, accounting for 57 percent of the procurement dollars in 1996.

Although the defense sector is not called a regulated industry, it is very much controlled by government, far more than is the case in utilities, railroads, and other traditionally regulated companies. The government's influence and control over defense contractors occur through the detailed process by which the military establish-

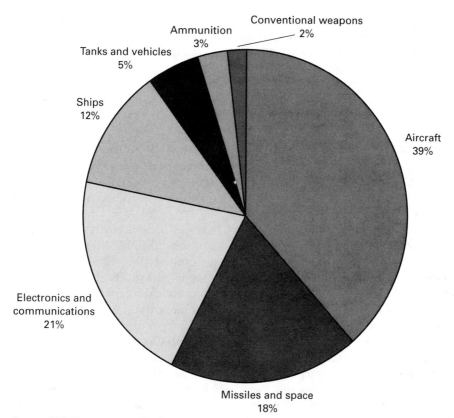

Source: U.S. Department of Defense.

FIGURE 15.1 Purchases of Weapon Systems in 1996

ment awards contracts to private firms and monitors the performance on those contracts. The military establishment purchases products that are not yet designed or for
which production experience is lacking and at prices for which there is little precedent. As a consequence, defense work has developed several distinguishing if not
unique characteristics.

The Military Market Is Monopsonistic

The DOD is the one customer for aircraft carriers, supersonic bombers, ICBMs, and
nuclear submarines. Because the market is so monopsonistic—completely subject to
the changing needs of this one customer—relationships between buyer and seller differ fundamentally from those in civilian sectors of the economy. By its selection of
contractors, the government customer controls entry into and exit from this market.
Thus, the government also determines the growth of the firms manufacturing military
equipment and imposes its ways of doing business on them. The regulations governing
military procurement take more than 2,000 pages, including numerous standard
clauses that must be inserted into defense contracts and a host of standard forms that
must be used. It is difficult to conjure up a civilian counterpart.[4]

This single-customer market makes for an extremely keen and novel type of either/or competition. For a specific product, a company generally is not competing for a share of the market but for all of it. Both Boeing and General Dynamics were rivals for the F-111 aircraft contract; General Dynamics won and produced all of this product. Similarly, McDonnell Douglas (now a part of Boeing) produces all of the F-15 aircraft as a result of a design competition it won against two other bidding companies.

The less efficient, commercially oriented firm may lose its market position, but at least for a time, it can count on making some sales of its product line, albeit at reduced prices. Rarely does it encounter the extreme peak-and-valley nature of military procurement characterized by intense initial government demand followed by the virtual disappearance of the market for the items as one generation of aircraft or missile is followed by the next.

Defense contractors commit their key scientists and engineers (who are their most strategic resource) to programs subject to unpredictable change or even cancellation—and to products where the ultimate profitability will not be known for a decade or more. This aspect of the business, coupled with its research-intensive nature, is much more similar to the risks of pharmaceutical companies, which are subject to substantial regulation, than to the larger and more traditional category of durable goods manufacturers with which the defense industry is often compared. Under these conditions of uncertainty, it is rarely feasible to predict the cost, schedule, performance, or quantity of the final product with enough precision to permit the buyer and seller to write a firm contract covering the entire process.

Thus, it is not surprising that the government as buyer assumes many of the risks that in more normal business activities are borne as a matter of course by the seller. Along with the assumption of risk, however, there is a corresponding involvement by the customer in the internal operations of its suppliers. The officials of the Department of Defense make many decisions that are normally part of the responsibility of business management.

Price Is Often Not the Determinant of Sales

Because of the nature of military requirements, the offer price frequently is a far less important factor than in commercial markets. In the case of major weapon systems, price is only one of several key factors considered by the customer. The major products purchased in this market provide examples par excellence of extreme product differentiation. Essentially, the military buyer is concerned with obtaining the product of superior quality—the second fastest fighter aircraft is no bargain. Since the significant competition occurs before the final product is completely designed, initial estimates of both total cost and final performance are tentative and of limited reliability and usefulness. The seller's previous cost experiences and demonstrated managerial capabilities are often given greater weight than the price estimates it offers.

Technical Capability Is the Major Asset

In the military market, the potential contractor's past record of technical achievement and the attractiveness of its design proposal are often the dominant factors in awarding a contract. Major suppliers of weapon systems are in large part product quality maximizers rather than cost minimizers. Their basic competence is invention and organization of huge teams of scientists and engineers. Cost overruns may arise from the great uncertainty that abounds in estimating the cost of designing and manufacturing items that have never been made before—and from the numerous changes in specifications that occur as technology advances.

Whether a particular program will reach the production stage depends in large part on the technical capability displayed during the research and development stage—as well as the budgetary pressures facing the military service sponsoring the weapon system. Competition among the prospective suppliers is keen, but it relates primarily to their technological capability. Nevertheless, elaborate procedures are used in determining price, including a variety of contract types designed to provide some of the incentives of a normal competitive market that otherwise would be absent.

Production Occurs after the Sale

The market for weapon systems is characterized by production undertaken after an order is received; production for inventory is rare. This differs from most areas of the private economy. Production of major military products—such as aircraft, missiles, space vehicles, ships, and tanks—normally begins after the receipt of the government order. Moreover, the government buyer frequently takes the initiative in developing new products by financing most of the research and development costs.

The Channels of Distribution Are Simple

The military market has deceptively simple channels of distribution. Basically, the manufacturer sells and delivers directly to the consumer. This results from the fact that the military establishment itself maintains an extensive internal distribution system. The flow of material from private-sector producers to central military warehouses to bases and to the final using command is analogous to the flow from manufacturer to wholesaler to retailer and to the final customer in the private sector. However, because the government customer handles most of the distribution, defense contractors have developed very limited and specialized marketing capabilities, which is a barrier to their attempts to use their technological capabilities in civilian areas.

The Industrial Distribution of Defense Work

Strictly speaking, there is no specific "defense" industry. A great many companies serve as prime contractors or subcontractors to the military services, yet most of them devote the greater portion of their resources to civilian markets. The composition of the major firms and industries supplying goods and services to the Department of Defense varies over time, it being largely a function of current defense needs. For example, during the Korean War, when military requirements were dominated by army ordnance equipment, General Motors (as a major producer of tanks and trucks) was the number-one military contractor. The shift to aircraft and missiles since then has brought aerospace and electronics companies into the forefront of military contractors, firms such as General Dynamics and Lockheed Martin (see Table 15.6).

A relatively few hard-goods-producing industries account for the great bulk of the dollar volume of military contracts: aircraft, electronics, motor vehicles, petroleum

TABLE 15.6 Major Defense Contractors, Fiscal Year 1996

Rank	Company	Military Awards (billions)	Key Products
1	Lockheed Martin	$12.0	Submarine missile systems; cargo and fighter aircraft.
2	McDonnell Douglas	9.9	Fighter and cargo aircraft; Tomahawk and Harpoon missiles.
3	General Motors (Hughes division)	3.2	AMRAAM, Maverick, TOW, RIM-66, RIM-67, Trident, Stinger, Peace and Shield missiles.
4	Raytheon	3.0	Patriot, AMRAAM, Trident, Hawk and Sea Sparrow missiles; fire control equipment; sonar.
5	General Dynamics	2.7	F-16 fighters; Abrams tanks; Stinger, Tomahawk, Trident and Atlas missiles; nuclear submarines.
6	Northrop Grumman	2.6	Fighter and bomber aircraft; radar and navigational equipment.
7	United Technologies	2.3	Aircraft engines; helicopters; advanced tactical fighter aircraft.
8	Boeing	1.7	SRAM and Minuteman missiles; ADP and telecommunication services; helicopters; cargo and tanker aircraft.
9	Litton Industries	1.7	Destroyers; amphibious assault ships; electronics and communications.
10	General Electric	1.5	Aircraft engines, Aegis and Trident missile system components.

Source: U.S. Department of Defense.

refining, chemicals, rubber, and construction. Most American industries, such as lumber, food, textiles, machinery, metal fabricators, services, and trade, do not loom large as prime defense contractors. Some firms in those industries, however, may participate in the military market as suppliers or subcontractors to the major producers.

Price Formation and Competition

The typical weapon-system contract is awarded to a company chosen as the result of a lengthy series of negotiations. This firm then enters into an extended contractual relationship with the military. As noted earlier, the typical civilian agency order is given at a fixed price to the company that has offered the lowest sealed bid.

When the military establishment enters into an arrangement with a firm to secure the production of a good or service, the final cost is dependent on the type of contract that the government negotiates. The DOD uses two basic types of contracts: cost reimbursement and fixed price.

The general category of cost-reimbursement contracts, at first blush, appears to be a simple concept, with the government paying the costs and the producer having little incentive to cut expenses. The actual amount that the government pays, however, is dependent on which costs are allowed. Many customary business expenses are not reimbursed by the DOD: technical displays, unapproved overtime, business conferences, bid and proposal expense, employee moving costs, operation of executive airplanes, personal property tax, interest payments, patents expense, and public relations. When the government disallows these items, that action arbitrarily reduces the company's profit.

Moreover, the government uses a variety of reimbursable contracts: cost-with-no-fee contract (typically for dealing with nonprofit organizations), cost-plus-fixed-fee (generally used on developmental contracts), and cost-reimbursable contracts (with an incentive provision to share the reduction in cost below the initial estimate).

Competitive and Negotiated Procurement

In the Competition in Contracting Act, Congress decreed that whenever possible the Pentagon should seek out at least two bidders on a project. In 1996, 82 percent of the military contracts awarded were made by means of competitive bidding (see Figure 15.2). However, only a minor share of that category is the result of sealed bids responding to formal advertising. Most "competitive" awards rely on negotiation between the government and its suppliers. The DOD maintains that procurement through negotiation does not signify lack of competition. The simple presentation of statistics tends to present a black-and-white contrast in procurement procedures that does not always reflect actual operations. On occasion, procedures under formal advertising and negotiation have tended to blend together. Often, there may be as many or more companies competing for a negotiated award as respond with sealed bids under formal advertising.

FIGURE 15.2 Distribution of Competitive and Noncompetitive Procurements, Fiscal Year 1996

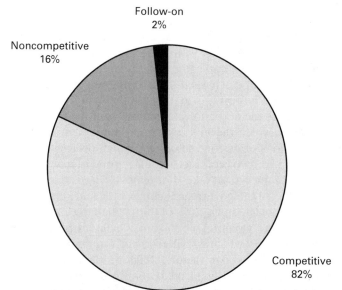

Source: U.S. Department of Defense.

LONG-TERM IMPACTS OF MILITARY PROCUREMENT

In its long-term dealings with those companies or divisions of companies that cater primarily to the military market, the federal government has directly or indirectly assumed many of the decision-making functions that are normally the prerogatives of business management.

This government assumption of, and active participation in, private business decision making takes three major forms: virtually determining the choice of products the defense firms produce; strongly influencing the source of capital funds that they use; and closely supervising much of their internal operations. The government involvement in private industry arises almost exclusively in the case of the unique and large-scale weapon systems. It does not characterize the procurement of desks, chairs, and other conventional items by government agencies (military or civilian) through fixed-price contracts awarded via sealed-bid competition.

By awarding billions of dollars of contracts for research and development (R&D) each year, the DOD influences strongly which new products its contractors design and produce. The government customer directly finances much of the supplier's R&D and thus assumes much of the risk of failure of new product development. In the commercial economy, in contrast, costs of scientific and technological advances are not borne by the buyer, but by the seller, who only recovers its investment if it results in the sale of profitable products.

Of course, defense contractors do sponsor and fund much of their own R&D. However, the bulk of their military-oriented scientific and technical effort is performed under government contract or charged as overhead on their government contracts. The DOD also uses its vast financial resources to supply much of the plant and equipment used by its major contractors for defense work. In addition, military contractors receive billions of dollars of outstanding "progress" payments (government payments made prior to competition and while the work is still underway).

Military procurement regulations provide specific disincentives for using private working capital. Progress payments equal to as much as 80 percent of the costs incurred on government contracts are provided without interest charge to the contractors. However, should these companies decide to rely on private sources for working capital, their interest payments cannot be charged to government contracts. The interest must come out of their profits. The result is to increase the extent to which public rather than private capital finances the operations of defense contractors.

The most pervasive way in which the military establishment assumes the management decision-making functions of its contractors is through procurement legislation and rules governing the awarding of contracts. Military procurement regulations require private suppliers to accept on a "take-it-or-leave-it" basis many standard clauses in their contracts, which give the government contracting and surveillance officers numerous powers over the internal operations of these companies.

The authority assumed by the government customer includes power to review and veto a host of company decisions: which activities to perform in-house and which to subcontract, which firms to use as subcontractors, which products to buy domestically rather than to import, what internal financial system to use, what minimum as well as average wage rates to pay, and how much overtime work to authorize.

Viewed as a totality, these restrictions represent substantial government regulation of industry. This regulation is not accomplished through the traditional independent regulatory agencies (such as the Federal Communications Commission or the Securities and Exchange Commission) but rather through the unilateral exercise of the government's dominant market position.

A few of the large aerospace companies—General Dynamics and McDonnell Douglas—are government-oriented enterprises, relying on the DOD for most of their income (see Table 15.7). Several others, such as Lockheed Martin, Litton Industries, and Northrop Grumman, obtain over 30 percent of their sales from the military market. In contrast, most defense contractors—Boeing, Raytheon, General Motors, and United Technologies, for example—look primarily to commercial markets for the bulk of their revenue. Because their contracts with the Pentagon are generally less profitable than commercial sales, some of these companies have responded to

TABLE 15.7	Dependence on the Military Market of the 25 Major Contractors, 1996	
Rank	*Company*	*Percentage*
	50–100% of sales to military	
5	General Dynamics	74
2	McDonnell Douglas	72
20	Tracor	54
	25–49% of sales to military	
9	Litton Industries	47
1	Lockheed Martin	45
14	Science Applications International	44
6	Northrop Grumman	32
	0–24% of sales to military	
4	Raytheon	24
25	Rolls-Royce (USA)	20
15	United Defense	18
17	Computer Sciences Corp	17
11	Westinghouse	15
13	Textron	13
7	United Technologies	10
21	Halliburton	8
18	ITT	8
16	TRW	8
8	Boeing	8
23	Texas Instruments	5
24	AlliedSignal	4
19	GTE	3
10	General Electric	2
3	General Motors	2
22	AT&T	1

Source: Center for the Study of American Business, from various sources.

shrinking military markets by leaving the defense business. Since the end of the Cold War, many commercially oriented companies have sold off one or more defense-oriented subsidiaries to companies specializing in military work.

General Motors sold its defense electronics activity to Raytheon. Ford, IBM, and Unisys each sold defense systems operations to Loral (which was subsequently acquired by Lockheed Martin). Northrop Grumman bought the defense division of Westinghouse. At the same time, several large defense contractors merged—Boeing and McDonnell Douglas, Lockheed and Martin, and Northrop and Grumman.

This trend has raised serious concerns about the adequacy of competition for key segments of the military market. For example, the number of U.S. makers of military aircraft has declined from eight in 1985 to three. The reality is that, for the foreseeable future, the military customer will be buying fewer weapon systems from a smaller group of companies than it was accustomed to during the Cold War era. Competition is likely to remain intense whether there are four, three, or two hungry competitors for each new program.[5]

The differences between military contractors and typical industrial firms are striking. Compared with commercially oriented companies, the major defense oriented firms have little commercial marketing capabilities and limited experience in producing at high volume and low unit cost. Moreover, their administrative structure is geared to the unique reporting and control requirements of the governmental customer. Those defense firms that do operate in civilian markets maintain operationally separated, insulated divisions that have little contact with each other, merely reporting to the same top management.

In a survey conducted by the Center for Strategic and International Studies (CSIS), 71 percent of the defense firms stated that the Pentagon's procurement policies make it difficult for them to enter or flourish in civilian markets. Bolstered by in-depth interviews, CSIS concluded that the DOD acquisition system is a major obstacle to civilian diversification and that military production has evolved into a business culture quite distinct and closed off from normal commercial culture. The view of one defense industry representative was typical: "With this high overhead, together with the facilities, manpower, and systems oriented toward that type of work, it is extremely difficult to find civilian markets where we can be cost-competitive."[6]

The lack of commercial marketing experience is another familiar refrain in defense industry circles. Grumman (which is now a part of Northrop Grumman) developed and tried to sell a minivan years before Chrysler popularized the vehicle. The project failed because of the lack of a distribution system. It is not hard to understand why defense company managements have become so reluctant to move from fields they have mastered into lines of business alien to them.

Their lack of knowledge of nondefense business is pervasive. It includes ignorance of products, production methods, advertising and distribution, financial arrangements, funding of research and development, contracting forms, and the very nature of the private customer's demands. These differentiating characteristics help to explain why most specialized defense contractors responded to the large cutbacks in military procurement during the past decade primarily by downsizing, consolidating, and merging. To a lesser degree, some of them have diversified into closely related high-tech markets, involving sales to governments or a relatively few large industrial customers.

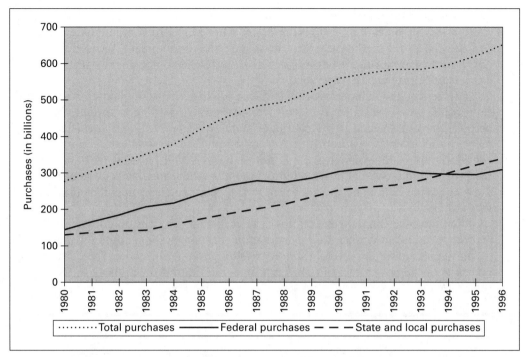

Note: Computed from U.S. Department of Commerce national income and product account data.
FIGURE 15.3 The Changing Government Market

Clearly, the type of company that can successfully design and build a new multi-billion dollar ICBM network or space exploration system has a very different capability from that of the soap, steel, toy or other typical cost-conscious but low-technology company operating in the commercial economy. The point made here was underscored when a former chief executive of Lockheed Martin, a large and successful defense contractor, was asked by the Russians how to convert a tank-producing facility into one producing refrigerators. His response was to tear down the tank plant and build a new refrigerator factory.[7]

With the end of the Cold War, a substantial shift has occurred in the composition of government purchases—away from the traditional dominance of federal procurement in favor of outlays by states and localities. Defense acquisitions have been declining, although they still represent a large share of federal procurement. In contrast, civilian buying at the state and local levels represents a rising share of the government market. To the extent that the "peace dividend" has been used by the public sector, little of the actual disbursements have occurred at the federal level (see Figure 15.3).

Summary and Conclusion

Just as commercial markets are far from uniform, the government market consists of a complex array of changing requirements. Much of this complexity, however, reflects a very special factor not present in other markets, at least not to the same degree: the important role of political decision making. Government purchasing is rarely motivated primarily by economic considerations. After all, there is no ultimate consumer that selects in the marketplace the items that are commercially successful. Rather, governmental authorities arbitrarily decide the size and composition of the goods and services to be provided to the public.

Moreover, the manner of production and distribution is not immune from political pressures. At least on occasion, major contracts are awarded to specific companies because they are located in the district or state of a powerful legislator. The employment generated by a government construction project likewise can be an important consideration in determining the amount of funds it will be provided—or whether the project is approved at all. In addition, public procurement activities, because they draw on taxpayer dollars, are subject to widespread scrutiny unparalleled in the private sector.

On the other hand, the activities of government agencies do not generally conform to the standards of accounting and audit that corporations routinely meet—nor do they generate similar economic incentives for good performance. Thus, the rewards and risks of the government market can be quite different from those in the private sector.

Notes

1. Elaine R. Davis, *Private Solutions for Public Service* (Seattle: Washington Institute Foundation, 1997), p. 14.
2. "Surge in Privatization Boon to Equity Markets," *OECD Letter,* May 1997, p. 5. See also *Bureaucrats in Business* (Washington, DC: The World Bank, 1995).
3. Philip Gold, "Tank Production and a Catch-22," *Insights,* May 14, 1990, p. 22.
4. The paperwork required in producing a comparable commercial product, such as a jet airliner, is insignificant by comparison (400 pages).
5. Murray Weidenbaum, "The U.S. Defense Industry After the Cold War," *Orbis,* Fall 1997, pp. 591–601.
6. Leo Reddy, *How U.S. Defense Industries View Diversification* (Washington, DC: Center for Strategic and International Studies, 1991), p. 27.
7. Norman R. Augustine, "The Real Dividend Is Peace," *World Link,* May–June 1990, p. 22.

PART FIVE

The Business Response

Because so much is at stake, private firms at times devote substantial amounts of resources to influencing the public policy environment as well as to complying with the many government policies and rules. Part V analyzes the major ways in which business can respond to government actions that affect it, ranging from making changes in internal organization to more actively participating in political campaigns.

CHAPTER 16

Business — Government Relations

V irtually every company has developed some capability to understand current and future developments in government and public policy as they relate to its activities—and to adjust and respond to these developments. Expansions in traditional staff functions, notably personnel and finance, often constitute the most direct company response to the rising role of government in business decision making. Many firms also have increased their resources devoted to other staff activities, especially public relations and government affairs. The latter includes establishing a Washington office and dealing with state, local, foreign, and international governments.

REVISED RESPONSIBILITIES
AND ORGANIZATIONAL STRUCTURES

Senior executives of the largest corporations are devoting substantial amounts of their time—often one-fourth or more—to problems stemming from external factors. Two or three decades ago, they could focus virtually all of their attention on the nuts and bolts of the business. The emphasis was mainly internal: how to improve efficiency to cut costs while improving quality in order to be more competitive. With a few exceptions, even the outward focus was mainly on the state of competition in the markets for the company's products. Today, these matters are still fundamental, but on occasion they are matched in terms of top management's time by a changing array of forces from outside the company and its markets.

Starting in the middle 1980s, however, somewhat of a backlash occurred, with company managements under pressure to restructure to meet takeover threats and foreign competitors. John Welch, the current chief executive officer (CEO) of General Electric, rejected the strong external-affairs focus that made Reginald Jones, his predecessor, the most admired and effective business leader in the country. Welch, in contrast, has achieved great benefits for his shareholders by concentrating on the more conventional market, product, and technological goals of the company. Nevertheless, General Electric as well as most other large corporations are substantial supporters of the various trade associations, think tanks, and other organizations that are heavily engaged in the public policy arena.

The senior managements of major companies now recognize that noneconomic factors can be as potent in fashioning corporate behavior as are economic forces. They generally accept the view that the worst possible strategy would be to be perceived by the public as unresponsive if not opposed to important interests of society. They believe that a strong and viable business system will not exist in a society where a majority of the public view the interests of the business corporation as being opposed to the social interests of the public.

Senior corporate executives often list four external areas as taking substantial shares of their time:

- Meeting with elected officials, say to discuss specific provisions of a tax bill scheduled for hearings and likely passage—or to oppose a pending reduction in the loans to business by the Export–Import Bank.
- Carrying on a dialogue with regulatory personnel—in EPA, FDA, OSHA, and so on, depending on the products the company produces and the markets in which it is active.
- Maintaining relations with the corporation's various constituencies—business associations, employees, suppliers, shareholders, unions, and a bewildering variety of public interest groups.
- Overseeing the company's communications with the public, including a substantial amount of speech making to business, civic, academic, and professional groups.

In general, the CEO tends to concentrate on external aspects, long-term planning, and basic policy, and the chief operating officer (COO)—usually the president—focuses on day-to-day managerial functions. But the typical pattern is not a clean split. The successful CEO is not divorced from the current management of the company, nor is the COO ignorant of broader corporate and national concerns.

To deal with the increasing array of government involvement, many companies have found it necessary or at least desirable to revamp their organizational structures. Initially, these changes have been modest, such as expanding the Washington office or establishing company interdepartmental committees on job safety, consumer affairs, or environmental compliance. The growth of public interest groups (often with an antibusiness orientation) is another factor that has encouraged business firms to expand their government liaison staffs (see Table 16.1).

In some cases, more substantial changes have been made. For example, a headquarters office on government relations is established, with direct ties to each of the operating departments. These offices may be involved in such company actions as introducing new products, making major price changes, and deciding the location of new facilities. The government affairs office frequently works with Washington law firms, public policy consultants, and trade associations.

TABLE 16.1 Functions of a Government Relations Department

- U.S. government legislative monitoring and analysis (federal, state, and local).
- Regulatory agency liaison and response.
- International legislative monitoring and analysis (other nations, UN, EU, World Bank).
- Domestic and international market development assistance.
- Trade association and coalition liaison.
- Government appointment assistance.
- Political analysis and response.
- Government information services.
- Relations with think tanks.

Traditionally, the strategy of most companies has been to maintain a low profile in public affairs and a predictably negative position against government initiatives affecting business. The rise of regulation and the simultaneous decline in public confidence in business have convinced a significant portion of corporate executives that such strategies are no longer appropriate. The prevailing approach is now the reverse. It is one of active involvement in the public policy process and of launching new initiatives to communicate with the various publics that business interacts with.

When he was chief executive of General Electric, Reginald Jones stated that the CEO, as designated leader of the corporation, must participate actively in the formation of public policy affecting business. His conclusion was that the time was well spent, not only in alerting the company to economic problems, but also in terms of positive customer, investor, and employee relations. As he put it, "These duties are part and parcel of the CEO's responsibilities for the strategic direction of the company."[1] In the words of John Hoving, a former senior vice president of Federated Department Stores, "Since this is a democracy becoming more participatory all the time, there is no hope at all that government will leave corporations alone. . . . There is no way in which a corporation can say to the political world: 'Stop! I want to get off!'"[2]

In practice, not every large corporation is active in public policy matters, nor is every smaller enterprise mute in this area of activity. In effect, companies and their heads take turns in serving in leadership positions in the key business associations, although not every CEO of a top corporation may necessarily get or want a turn. In addition, some companies still take an accommodating view toward the rising role of government in business decision making. They prefer to negotiate the best available deal, hoping to convey an image of "social responsibility."[3] The managements merely add compliance responsibilities to the functional jobs of general or line managers. Other firms take a composite position, whereby the senior management assumes a more active role in public policy and the operating managements concentrate on meeting government-imposed requirements.

REPRESENTATIVES TO GOVERNMENT

Many companies—foreign and domestic—find it useful to maintain a continuing presence in Washington, DC, as well as in other national capitals. One side effect of the global economy is that companies do business in many nations and thus are affected by the public policies in a great variety of governmental jurisdictions. These range from the United Nations to regional governments, such as the European Union, to individual countries to states (or provinces) and localities in many geographical areas.

In recent years, the specialized agencies of the United Nations (UN) have taken a substantial interest in economic issues and have attracted a substantial amount of lobbying by a variety of interest groups—representing consumers, labor, and business. Examples include the International Labor Organization issuing directives on working conditions, the World Health Organization developing a code on infant nursing formulas, the International Telecommunications Union generating rules governing cross-border communications, the International Maritime Organization dealing with shipping codes, and the World Intellectual Property Organization protecting patents and copyrights across borders.

At the UN agencies, the category of *nongovernmental organization* (NGO) is very specialized, and does not include every organization that is not a part of government. NGO is also a highly desirable designation because a certified NGO can attend many UN meetings and conferences. While it is relatively easy for environmental and consumer groups to become NGOs, few business associations qualify, and as a general rule individual business firms are unable to participate in the process.

In the United States, firms of substantial size generally have full-time Washington offices; smaller companies rely primarily on their trade associations as well as on Washington-based attorneys and consultants. The permanent Washington representative is no longer limited to the major government contractors (such as aerospace and electronics companies) or the closely regulated industries (such as chemicals and automotive manufacturing).

Most large corporations maintain full-time representation. Major government contractors traditionally have maintained representation in Washington, and many commercially oriented firms, including medium-size ones, have established a permanent presence in the capital. The expansion of government controls over business has led to "protective reaction" on the part of companies that historically have had little knowledge of or direct relationship with the federal government.

Over 500 companies currently have on-the-scene Washington representation compared with only about 100 in the 1970s. Their offices vary from one to two people plus a secretary (Sun Microsystems) to substantial operations with annual budgets of $1 million or more (BellSouth has a Washington office of 35 people). The typical corporate office in Washington employs 7 to 10 persons and is headed by an officer at the vice-presidential level. For a variety of reasons (including real estate costs and the locations of key government agencies), not all Washington offices are now located in Washington, DC, itself. Many have moved to the northern Virginia suburbs, and some have relocated to nearby Maryland.

Activities of Washington offices vary substantially according to the industry and markets served, the size of the firm, and tradition (see Table 16.2). One company compares its Washington office to an embassy in that it follows and interprets actions of the federal government that have significant impact on it, helps to formulate positions on those actions, and serves as the principal channel for communicating the company's views to the government. Most Washington government relations offices are in daily touch with the headquarters offices and other parts of their firms. The world of the larger government relations office goes beyond its own corporate clientele, often extending to suppliers, "grass roots" organizations, and opinion leaders. Its responsibilities often cover state governments and the international arena.[4]

In general, three primary functions are performed by company offices located in Washington, DC, and other national capitals:

1. Supplying information to the home office on actions taken or contemplated by government.
2. Assisting in obtaining government contracts.
3. Providing representation before legislative and regulatory bodies.

TABLE 16.2 Factors Affecting Size of Washington Offices

Size of firm (e.g., automobile manufacturers)
- Direct representation by most larger firms
- Economies of scale and variety of interests
- Greater public exposure

Importance of government markets (e.g., aerospace companies)
- Day-to-day contract administration function
- Market intelligence and forecasting
- Support base for sales efforts

Extent of regulation (e.g., chemical firms)
- Day-to-day dealings with regulatory agencies
- Desire to influence regulatory climate—through Congress and the media

Concern of management (e.g., petroleum corporations)
- Level of civic awareness or concern with national policy

Degree of public exposure (e.g., conglomerates)
- Defensive—to counteract adverse media and congressional attention
- Offensive—to obtain great public exposure for government marketing purposes and as institutional advertising

Supplying Information

Virtually all corporate offices in Washington and other national capitals provide a listening post for the home office. A constant flow of information is supplied to corporate officials on current government policies and on future plans and actions that might affect company operations. Although trade associations and industry publications are useful, at times a company's unique concerns can be met best by company personnel on the scene. Some companies refer to this intelligence function as an "early warning" system. It is the most time-consuming activity of the typical corporate office in the nation's capital.

Various communications channels are used. Representatives of some large companies prepare daily newsletters that are sent to senior executives in headquarters and operating divisions. Faxes and e-mail enable the Washington office to contact large portions of the company's managers very quickly when they want to bring an urgent matter to their attention. However, to a large extent information is still passed along by telephone, often to avoid a written record on sensitive matters. The typical Washington office also has day-to-day dealings with members of the government bureaucracy in order to follow up on questions or complaints by company personnel on specific regulatory actions.

A substantial amount of company information and views also are provided to federal agencies. Such a reciprocal relationship helps provide a more cordial welcome to company personnel making inquiries at a federal agency. It can also enhance the weight given to the company's expressed concerns. The more successful governmental representatives also have substantial impacts on company policies and operations. In contrast to the traditional company attitude on public affairs ("If they only saw our side of the story, they would understand"), the representative office can help adapt corporate actions to changing national policies.

Corporate staff members also interact regularly with government and private planning groups and with the numerous public policy analysis organizations that have been established in the capital cities of most industrialized nations. In the United States, these public policy research groups range over a wide ideological terrain. On the right, the American Enterprise Institute and the Heritage Foundation represent conservative, free market positions, while the Cato Institute upholds a free market and more libertarian viewpoint. At the center are the Brookings Institution (the granddaddy of Washington "think tanks"), the Center for Strategic and International Studies, and the Committee for Economic Development. On the left are new organizations, inspired by the successes of the earlier groups, such as the Economic Policy Institute and the Progressive Policy Institute. The Institute for Policy Studies occupies the far left end of the spectrum of DC policy research organizations. Some of these groups, as well as many more specialized units, blend research and advocacy.

The scope of the government relations function has broadened over the years to include a host of international issues. These range from U.S. government policies on international trade to the treatment of foreign investment by other nations. The change is personified by the experience of a very active Washington business policy analyst: "I remember that when I started out . . . in the 1970s and did corporate briefings on import policy, everyone in the room seemed to get up for a cup of coffee."[5] Today, in contrast, international trade and investment policies are among the key "bread-and-butter" issues of the Washington office.

Assisting the Marketing Function

For many company offices in national capitals, marketing is the basic bread-and-butter justification of their existence and accounts for the presence of the majority of the personnel assigned to the office. A variety of market research, selling, and contract administration activities are involved. The office often has the responsibility of keeping the company abreast of emerging government product requirements so that engineering and advance design departments can be prepared ahead of time for formal requests for proposals.

Moreover, through such on-the-scene representation, the company often can participate in developing the government specifications for the products that it wants to sell to government agencies. The basic objective is to ensure that the products of the company meet government requirements. Such representation also provides advance information on future sales possibilities as well as the opportunity to qualify company products. In the process, companies learn of and bid on exploratory research and development contracts that the government will be awarding prior to the actual production phase of a major project. On the more extensive and technical projects, the company will never make the deadline on its submission if it waits until the formal government request for proposal to begin preparing its response.

Although most actual selling is performed by company marketing and engineering personnel assigned to the home office, the capital-based staff will often be in a better position to open doors and to maintain day-to-day liaison with governmental research and development and procurement offices and to open doors for company specialists. In addition, by virtue of its location, this office can expedite the numerous and complicated steps involved in government contracting: obtaining the detailed bidding specifications, ensuring attention to company contract proposals, securing the necessary signatures, ensuring company compliance with federal procedural requirements, and expediting payments for work performed.

Some Washington offices also take advantage of their location in developing contacts with the embassies of foreign governments that provide market potential. In turn, those embassies try to open doors in the United States for representatives of business firms in their nations.

Representation ("Lobbying")

The effective Washington office is the focal point of a company's relations with the federal government, serving especially as the principal channel for communicating the company's views on matters of major importance to legislators and executive branch officials. Increasingly, the office keeps in touch with foreign embassies and with international organizations such as the World Bank and the Organization of American States. In good measure, the Washington office is a coordinator, drawing on specialized talents in the company, such as the legal, engineering, and public affairs staffs. Influencing Washington's largest industry—government—has become the city's second-largest industry. An experienced lobbyist, however, described his function in more negative terms—as "a damage-control operation."

Although many company representatives try to avoid using the term, *lobbying* usually is a primary part of their total function. One experienced company office director, who previously had served as legislative assistant to an influential senator, defines lobbying in very straightforward terms: "Lobbying is a communication with public officials to influence their decisions in a manner harmonious with the interests of the individual or group communicating. . . . A lobbyist's purpose is selfish in the sense that he [or she] seeks to persuade others that his [or her] position is meritorious."[6]

The total lobbying activity includes direct relations with legislative and executive branch officials and, in addition, dealing with the media that abound in national capitals and that influence national agendas. Thus, the Washington office of a large national corporation provides access to key reporters and influential columnists that cannot be readily obtained by senior management located in more remote areas. Similar relationships hold in other national capitals.

Although major issues of public policy may dominate the headlines, some of the most effective lobbying focuses on very specialized, relatively minor provisions of laws and regulations. Rather than trying to affect the passage of a major bill or the issuance of a new regulation, much effort is made to exempt a company or industry from a popular new tax or regulation—or to include it in an expenditure program working its way through the legislative process. Thus, ethanol producers wind up supporting (or at least not opposing) a new tax on energy if their industry is exempted from the impact of the statute. In a similar fashion, the Brussels office may try to modify a proposed ruling by the Commission of the European Union so as to provide the same treatment to European subsidiaries of U.S. firms as is received by European-owned firms.

The Changing Nature of Lobbying   One veteran journalist has remarked, "If all the lobbyists in Washington were crammed into Congress, the lid of the Capitol Dome would pop like a cork."[7] Although their numbers continue to be substantial, the nature of lobbying has changed dramatically from the flamboyant power-play-oriented stereotypes that many people still associate with the term. Today's lobbyist, whether working for a large corporation, a trade association, or a labor union, tends to be a dun-colored organization man or woman, who fades easily into the background—and likes it that way. As one highly regarded lobbyist stated, "Visibility is the last thing I need."

The public policy issues on which companies lobby are increasingly technical in nature and often require high-powered professional analysis in order to obtain serious considerations of their viewpoints. A proposal for reducing the tax rate on capital gains must be bolstered by an examination of the elasticity of federal revenues—to try to show that the revenue loss is minimal or even that total revenues will rise in the period ahead. This type of issue increasingly brings a new set of actors into the lobbying process: accountants, economists, and statisticians.

A company opposing a higher excise tax on beer or cigarettes will commission a report measuring the high degree of regressivity of such taxes—to demonstrate their unfairness. International trade issues invariably generate a demand for forecasting the macroeconomic impact of increasing (or decreasing) restrictions on foreign commerce—to estimate the effect on jobs and consumer prices.

Proposals for the award of government procurement contracts (for weapon systems, infrastructure, etc.) are bolstered by estimates of the impacts on specific regions—the areas winning the contracts as well as the losers. As we have seen, airline mergers have been defended by esoteric theories of antitrust (e.g., by contending that the airline industry consists of "contestable" markets). In the field of regulation, scientists present estimates of the risks inherent in the environment and the workplace while economists counter with ranges of the costs of proposals to deal with these matters.

As a result, staff-to-staff encounters are far more frequent. It is the rare Senator or cabinet secretary that can deal with these technical issues. Typically, the lobbyist's expert will present the findings to the staff expert at the Department or Congressional Committee.

A further complication in analyzing business–government relations is the fact that business is not monolithic in its dealings with the public sector. Some of the roughest battles in government occur between competing industries. Examples in dealing with regulation of financial institutions include investment and brokerage houses versus banks and, within the banking sector, large multistate banks versus small or "country" banks. Similarly, on proposals for federal subsidies, the interests of truckers diverge from those of railroads or companies using the inland waterways. Mutually owned life insurance companies often express very different views on tax legislation than do stockholder-owned life insurance carriers. (See the box "Business Versus Business on the Environment" for a more complicated example.)

On the positive side, business groups often cooperate with nonprofit associations on public policy matters of mutual interest. For example, high-tech companies join with universities in urging more federal money for research and development. Suppliers of environmental cleanup equipment team up with environmental advocacy groups in supporting stricter clean air and clean water statutes. Nonprofit hospitals and pharmaceutical companies share opposition to proposals to enact price controls on health care.

Business versus Business on the Environment

In 1991, two telecommunications companies, Sprint and MCI, began separate promotional efforts to encourage support of environmental activities. They pledged to devote five percent of a new customer's bill to an environmental group of the customer's choice, and for existing users who want such donations, one to four percent of the current billing. On the surface, it seemed that the two companies were on the side of the angels.

The timber industry, however, did not think it was fair that environmental advocacy groups, many of which differ vehemently with timber companies on clear-cutting and harvesting restrictions, should get subsidies from other business firms. Timber associations around the country banded together to express their disapproval through letters and phone calls to Sprint and MCI. Some canceled their services provided by the two carriers.

Sprint gave the timber groups a brush-off. MCI, however, donated an undisclosed but "significant" amount of money to the American Forestry Foundation's Project Learning Tree, a program to teach youngsters the principles of multiple-use forestry management. MCI's representative admitted that the company did not expect the range of reactions to its effort to be an environmental "good guy."

Variations on the Lobbying Function   Business liaison with the legislative branch can serve both "offensive" and "defensive" functions. The former is designed to get the company's views on pending legislation of special interest across to senators, representatives, their aides, and committee staff members. These efforts often are geared to opposing or amending the flow of government legislation that results in great public-sector control over business decision making. The defensive function, less widely known, is geared to avoiding embarrassing investigations of and attacks on the company and its executives. This is accomplished by providing additional information, and the "other side of the story," at an early stage of a committee's operations. Moreover, continuing liaison, although perhaps involving nothing more than an occasional luncheon or cocktail party, helps to soften or even avoid unpleasant encounters by introducing into the situation the natural reluctance to confront one's friends.

When the legislature is actively considering a proposed law vital to the company, the firm's representative office can arrange for a corporate officer to be invited to testify, then draft the actual testimony and prepare the officer for hostile questions and public interviews. Much influence on legislative deliberations, however, comes from informal telephone or face-to-face contact in a senator's or representative's office (often with staff members), rather than at a formal committee hearing. "Access" is the most important qualification for a lobbyist—the ability to make contact quickly with key people in government.

Regulation of Lobbying   Lobbying activities are subject to a modest amount of statutory control in the United States. The basic legal authorization for, and thus protection of, lobbying is found in the First Amendment of the Constitution: "Congress shall make no law . . . abridging . . . the right of the people . . . to petition the Government for a redress of grievances." A minimum of restrictive legislation has been enacted since.

Federal regulation of lobbying does not directly restrict the activities of lobbyists but relies primarily on making information on their lobbying activities open to the public. Organizations that solicit or receive money for the principal purpose of lobbying Congress do not have to register. However, they must file quarterly spending reports detailing how much they devote to influencing legislation. The purposes of lobbying organizations vary from closely focused, such as the groups opposing gun controls, to more general, such as those representing senior citizens favoring higher social security and health benefits.

The law requires those hired by someone else for the principal purpose of lobbying Congress to register and to report so that there is public knowledge of their activities. The Lobbying Disclosure Act of 1995 defines a lobbyist very broadly: anyone who is compensated for services that include more than one lobbying contact. Under that law, such individuals are required to register with Congress within 45 days after making a "lobbying contact" with any of a host of federal government officials, including the president, the vice president, heads of departments and agencies, and members of Congress and their staffs.

The 1995 law also requires registered lobbyists to disclose semiannually their income, assets, and liabilities and to tell who pays them, how much they are paid, how much they spend on lobbying, and what issues they work on. Inevitably, exceptions are made. In *United States* v. *Harris* (347 U.S. 612, 1954), the Supreme Court held that grass-roots lobbying is not subject to federal law. Only direct contact with designated federal officials is covered.

Congress has tried to minimize if not eliminate the paperwork burden on people who do very minor amounts of lobbying. Those who spend no more than 20 percent of their time meeting with senior executive branch officials, members of Congress, or their staffs, will not have to disclose the names of their clients and other details on their lobbying activities. Exempt from even having to register as lobbyists are people who are paid $5,000 or less and organizations that use their own employees to lobby and spend no more than $20,000 in those efforts.

Tax-exempt religious organizations also are not subject to the disclosure rules. On the other hand, representatives of U.S. subsidiaries of foreign-owned companies have to register as lobbyists, as do lawyer-lobbyists for foreign entities.[8]

Advising Government   Many companies find it advantageous to provide personnel to serve on governmental advisory committees, although many of these groups are technical rather than policy oriented. Approximately 10,000 business representatives serve on federal advisory committees, far more than any other interest group. Service on these bodies often permits company officials to obtain access to government decision makers.

Representing the corporation to the executive branch of government may involve both attempts to influence future policy and efforts to learn of current developments and how the company might successfully adjust to them. Viewed in this light, membership on government advisory committees is a desirable form of unpaid public service in that the government becomes aware of a broad array of views prior to taking action.

Advisory committees vary from those dealing with major matters of policy to bodies charged with providing advice on engineering and other technical matters. Virtually all federal agencies have set up one or more public advisory committees. These range from the Department of Defense's prestigious Industry Advisory Council (IAC) to the Business Research Advisory Council (BRAC) of the Bureau of Labor Statistics. The IAC, composed of senior management members of the major defense contractors, advises on Pentagon procurement policy; the BRAC consists of economists, statisticians, and other company specialists who comment on price indexes and such technical matters. Comparable apparatus exists in other nations and in international agencies. The Paris-based Organisation for Economic Cooperation and Development, for example, meets regularly with business and labor advisory groups.

Another function of advisory committees is to provide a sounding board or at least a mechanism for the exchange of views by various private interest groups. At the Department of Labor, the Bureau of Labor Statistics has for many years organized two parallel but completely separate groups of advisers: the Business Research Advisory Council and the Labor Research Advisory Council, also consisting of economists, statisticians, and other labor union officials. The two groups never meet jointly.

Much depends on the level of representation. In contrast to the staff people who serve on the BLS committees, the Department of Defense has appointed senior management members of major defense contractors and other large industrial corporations to its Industry Advisory Council. That committee provides a major vehicle for the defense industry to present its views to key officials in the Pentagon on such vital questions as changes in departmental regulations and procedures affecting defense contractors.

Lobbying in the Global Marketplace   In lobbying foreign governments, cultural differences can be profound. This was brought home when the author attended an international conference in Tokyo sponsored by the Ministry of Foreign Affairs. Suddenly, all of the Japanese officials at the meeting stood at attention. What could cause that? The Prime Minister was out of the country and the Emperor certainly would not make an appearance. It turns out that the head of the Keidenren, the leading business association, had entered the room! In the United States, the situation tends to be the reverse. Business executives stand when a cabinet officer arrives.

In the case of the European Union (EU), a new type of lobbyist has developed: the EU specialist. More than three thousand lawyers and other consultants, many of them former EU officials, offer to guide business firms through the maze of the Union's bureaus, primarily in Brussels. Social codes differ sharply from those familiar in the United States. Although Americans tend to mix business and pleasure, it is bad form for a European lobbyist to put forward a client's position in a social situation.

There is another side to the lobbying coin. Many foreign companies lobby government officials in the United States. Several restrictions are clear. Foreign nationals generally are prohibited from making campaign contributions. However, the domestic political action committees of U.S. subsidiaries of foreign firms can raise funds from U.S. citizens (and from foreign nationals who are permanent residents of the United States) and donate them to political causes. Registered lobbyists for foreign interests cannot serve on U.S. government advisory committees.

Although many foreign business and government interests continue to be represented in Washington, DC, their formal lobbying efforts have been declining in recent years. The number of foreign interests with registered "representatives" dropped from 2,079 in 1991 to 1,117 in 1996. In part, this represented a reaction to widespread public criticism of the magnitude of foreign lobbying. But also, as the staffs of foreign embassies become better trained in American customs and procedures, they find less need to retain expensive intermediaries. However, in 1996 the business interests in each of four nations—Canada, Japan, Mexico, and the United States—devoted over $1 million to lobbying on public policy issues in the United States.[9]

TRADE ASSOCIATIONS

Companies use trade associations to assist them in dealing with government. These associations traditionally have performed services in data collection, education, and other standard and relatively low-profile areas. They also take an active role in public affairs, particularly in the fields of health and safety, consumer affairs, the environment, energy, and foreign trade. (See Table 16.3 for the array of activities carried on.) These business associations range from the 125,000-member National Association of Home Builders to the 10-member Bow Tie Manufacturers Association.

TABLE 16.3   Key Activities of Associations

Activity

Performed by Most Associations

Inform members of legislative developments.
Help members express views to elected officials.
Inform members of government agency actions.
Testify before legislative committees.
Make recommendations on legislation.
Provide data to governments.
Analyze legislation at conventions.
Draft legislation.
Lobby and inform government of industry views.

Performed by Some Associations

Report court decisions.
Train members to become active in politics.
Collect and distribute funds to candidates.
Arrange plant tours for foreign visitors.
Sponsor courses on political participation.
Assist members with tariffs and trade agreements.
Represent industry in tariff negotiations.
Assist government in foreign trade fair participation.

Source: American Society of Association Executives.

Most U.S. business firms, large or small, belong to one or more trade associations, a majority of which are located in the Washington, DC area. (Like company Washington offices, there has been some movement to the Virginia and Maryland suburbs.) Small firms, especially, rely heavily on their associations for a Washington presence even in heavily regulated industries. The National Association of Broadcasters has a Washington office of 165. An airline executive was quoted as saying, "If we didn't have the Air Transport Association, I'd need four more people on my staff."[10]

Trade associations perform a variety of functions. They keep their members informed of new government regulations and pending legislation. On important issues affecting their industry, the associations develop positions and express them to the government, Congress, and the media. In addition, the trade groups sponsor conferences and other meetings, initiate litigation when necessary, undertake studies and analyses, issue a variety of reports and publications, and conduct many educational programs for the public and industry.

Business associations also provide a way to deal jointly with matters of common concern to an industry without sacrificing independence or violating the antitrust laws. At times, a trade association can act on behalf of individual companies in delicate areas of public policy. The American Electronics Association maintains an office in Japan to help assure "equivalent market access" for U.S. electronics firms. The association office helps firms deal with tariff and nontariff barriers, including complicated requirements for meeting local standards.

The broader the range of products and services a company provides, the more associations it is likely to belong to. The Air Products and Chemical Company, for example, holds memberships in the American Iron and Steel Institute, the American Petroleum Institute, the Chamber of Commerce of the United States, the Chemical Manufacturers Association, the Environmental Industry Council, the Fertilizer Institute, the Machinery and Allied Products Institute, the Manufacturers of Emission Controls Association, the National Paints and Coatings Association, the National Petroleum Refiners Association, and the Society of the Plastics Industry.

A single organization—such as the Polyisocynurate Insulation Manufacturers Association—may serve such a narrow membership that it cannot cover all the varied interests of a diversified national corporation. Also, the position of a specific association on a given issue may be at variance with a company's. Thus, membership in a variety of trade groups provides management with considerable flexibility on public policy issues.

Government Relations

Trade associations interpret government actions and attitudes toward business, and vice versa. Some ways in which they accomplish this mission are through testifying at hearings on legislation affecting the industry, appearing in proceedings before government agencies and regulatory bodies, and contributing to precedent-making cases before the courts. They also make available information that the government desires to get into the hands of business executives. As collectors of statistics for their industries, many trade groups provide government agencies and the public with information not otherwise available.

As government agencies promulgate new regulations, member companies more commonly look to their associations to explain the new rules to them as well as to take public stands they may not want to take individually. The public sector often fosters this relationship by encouraging companies in a given industry to present their views through a single association rather than scheduling separate sessions with individual companies.

The Umbrella Organizations

In addition to joining specific industry or trade associations, many companies support broader "umbrella" organizations. Of these, the Chamber of Commerce of the United States—with an annual budget of over $70 million—is the largest and most broadly representative business association in Washington. It is composed of approximately 200,000 members who represent virtually every kind of business, plus 3,000 state and local chambers and 78 foreign chapters. The Chamber has about 30 standing committees that initiate policy positions in such diverse areas as taxation, antitrust, environmental matters, labor relations, agribusiness, education, and community affairs. The committee members are officials of the companies that belong to the Chamber, and they work with staff experts.

The Chamber attempts to influence the legislative process through congressional testimony, its lobbyists who often work with the Washington representatives of its member companies, and through the grassroots contacts of its members.

The National Association of Manufacturers covers a more specialized but fundamentally important grouping of American businesses. Organized in 1895, its membership of 13,500 industrial firms makes it one of the major voices of private enterprise in the United States. Its policy committees develop stands on such key issues as labor relations, taxation, regulatory reform, and international trade.

Of the broad-based organizations, one of the smallest but most influential is the Business Roundtable. It is composed of 200 chief executives of the nation's largest and most prestigious companies, such as Alcoa, AT&T, Citicorp, DuPont, Exxon, GE, GM, IBM, Procter & Gamble, Sears, and USX. The association is a vehicle for getting members of top management personally involved in presenting business views to Congress and to senior officials in the departments and agencies. Committees are active in areas ranging from accounting principles and antitrust laws to taxation, budget policy, and labor–management relations.

The National Federation of Independent Business is the largest and most influential group representing small business. Its huge membership, in excess of 500,000 business proprietors, gives its representatives access to high places in both the executive and legislative branches. A newer organization representing firms of intermediate size is the American Business Conference (ABC), established in 1980 to represent the interest of growth companies. The ABC is limited to 100 CEOs of companies whose size ranges between $25 million and $1 billion in revenues and whose sales or earnings have been growing at least 15 percent annually. The organization concentrates on a few key issues, notably capital formation, tax policy, regulatory reform, and international trade. It rarely lobbies for special benefits for member companies, focusing instead on reducing obstacles to business expansion.

The trend toward the formation of more business umbrella organizations in Washington is continuing. Many specialized trade associations find it advantageous to work together on specific items of common interest. In responding to regulation of food production at the state level, for example, the Grocery Manufacturers of America has coordinated efforts with the Food Marketing Institute, the American Frozen Food Institute, and the Potato Chip/Snack Food Association.

A shifting array of trade associations and other organized interest groups bands together on specific issues. These temporary groups range from the Multilateral Trade Negotiation Coalition to the Energy Tax Coalition. Euphemisms are frequently used to describe the effort in lofty terms. Thus, the Fiber, Fabric and Apparel Coalition for Trade is the official name of the textile lobby against imports. Citizens for Sensible Control of Acid Rain is the business coalition urging less stringent air pollution regulations.

These one-issue efforts are not limited to the business community. The National Committee to Preserve Social Security and Medicare represents a narrow group of senior citizens who constantly advocate more federal benefits for themselves with no interest in how to pay for the increased governmental expenditures.

On occasion, the business community succeeds in reaching out to other important interest groups. For example, the various organizations opposing limits on Medicaid spending for prescription drugs have formed the Coalition for Equal Access to Medicines. In addition to the Pharmaceutical Research and Manufacturers of America, this umbrella group includes the National Medical Association, the National Multiple Sclerosis Society, the National Black Nurses Association, and the California Hispanic-American Medical Association. The common link among all the groups is the concern that poor people get the same access to pharmaceuticals as do other patients.

Trade Associations and the Consumer

Trade associations help deal with consumer complaints against member business firms and reduce the pressure for greater government involvement in business. An effective system for dealing with consumer complaints is the Major Appliance Consumer Action Panel, a joint effort of the Association of Home Appliance Manufacturers, the Gas Appliance Manufacturers Association, and the Retail Merchants Association. This panel, composed of private citizens not associated with the industry, hears complaints that have not been settled by a retailer or manufacturer and makes recommendations that generally result in action.

The advertising industry maintains an ambitious self-regulatory mechanism. The National Advertising Division (NAD) of the Council of Better Business Bureaus acts as the investigatory arm, initiating inquiries, responding to consumer and competitor complaints, and making an initial decision about whether it agrees with the substantiation of the advertising claims being challenged. If it does not, it negotiates with the advertiser to modify or discontinue the advertising. If the NAD cannot resolve the controversy, it appeals to the National Advertising Review Board, a joint creation of the American Advertising Federation, the American Association of Advertising Agencies, and the Association of National Advertisers. It selects an impartial panel to hear each appeal.

Relations with Foreign Governments

Relatively few American companies have the resources or need to maintain direct representation in foreign countries. With the array of international regulations facing private enterprise, however, companies and their associations maintain liaison with the European Union headquartered in Brussels, the Organization for Economic Co-operation and Development in Paris, and the United Nations and its hundreds of specialized agencies and programs in locations ranging from New York to Rome and Geneva. Memberships in organizations such as the U.S. Council for International Business supplement more domestically oriented associations. The Council interacts with a host of European-based trade groups, ranging from the European Association of Pump Manufacturers to the International Confederation of European Beet Growers.

A variation on this approach is the formation of the Business Council for Sustainable Development (BCSD), a group of about 40 heads of multinational companies. The group is trying to move private industry to take a more active stance in environmental policy at both the national and international levels. Unlike most other business associations, BCSD acts like a lobby for an outside interest—environmentalism—within the business community.

INTERACTION WITH STATE GOVERNMENTS

Many developments emphasize the role of state governments as regulators of private business. The Clean Air Act delegates the preparation of implementation plans to the individual states. Reduced federal regulation in other areas, such as transportation, has made the state role more conspicuous. Also, substantial reductions in the amount of federal grants-in-aid to states and localities have meant shifting a significant proportion of public-sector responsibility away from the federal government.

The revitalization of state governments often makes a representative in Sacramento or Albany almost as important as the one in Washington. State legislatures operate in a variety of areas of concern to business (see Table 16.4). In addition to the traditional areas of taxes and labor, state governments have established new departments and agencies in a variety of areas: hazardous waste, drug abuse, energy conservation, consumer protection, subsidized housing, bilingual education, and mental health. This phenomenon, referred to as "50 little Washingtons," has led many business firms and trade associations to set up formal liaison activities with state legislatures and executive agencies. In some cases, similar offices have been established to work with county and municipal governments.

With most of the nation's governors possessing an item veto on appropriations bills, the executive branch is not to be overlooked either. The well-prepared company representative, with established access to executive offices, is able to offer advice on appointments to advisory commissions, to influence approval or veto of legislation, and to contribute to a more favorable political climate for business.

Although state laws on lobbying differ substantially, several common threads pervade many of them. Every state and the District of Columbia require lobbyists to register, although the precise definition of *lobbying* varies among the states, as do the specific reporting requirements. Twenty-two of the states cover grassroots lobbying as

TABLE 16.4 Major Business Issues at the State Level

General Category	Specific Examples
Tax issues affecting business generally	Corporate income taxes
	Unitary taxes
Other issues affecting business generally	Plant-closing laws
	Corporate officer liability statutes
	Right-to-know legislation
Tax issues affecting selected industries	Gasoline, tobacco, or alcoholic beverage excises
Other issues affecting selected industries	Hazardous waste disposal requirements
	One-way container restrictions
	Clean air and clean water rules
	Food labeling laws
Infrastructure issues	Roads and sewage appropriations
	Power and zoning regulation
Issues affecting business indirectly	Economic development programs
	Regional councils
	Legislative redistricting
Social issues	Education and health
	Housing
	Youth programs

Source: The Conference Board.

well as direct, conventional lobbying activity. The other 28 states and the District of Columbia only regulate direct lobbying. Grassroots efforts may have important effects on voters, but they involve modest amounts of overt funding. In 1996, over $1.3 million of direct lobbying outlays were reported to the State of Illinois—and just a little over $3,000 in grassroots outlays.[11]

Many states also require the employers of lobbyists to register. In California, Massachusetts, Texas, and Washington, lobbyists before executive branch agencies of state government must also file in addition to those who lobby members of the legislature. All states—except Tennessee, Utah, Wisconsin, and Wyoming—require lobbyists and/or their employers to provide financial reports.

Notes

1. Quoted in George Steiner, *The New CEO* (New York: Macmillan, 1983), p. 29.

2. Quoted in Steiner, p. 36.

3. James Q. Wilson, "The Corporation as a Political Actor," in Carl Kaysen, ed., *The American Corporation Today* (New York: Oxford University, 1996), p. 425.

4. Selveig B. Spielmann, *Evolution of the Business–Government Relations Function* (Washington, DC: International Business-Government Counsellors, Inc., 1993), p. 3.

5. Spielmann, p. 5.

6. Richard W. Murphy, "Lobbies as Information Sources for Congress," *Bulletin of the American Society for Information Science,* April 1975, p. 22.

7. Marilyn Wilson, "The New Look at NAM," *Dun's Business Month,* April 1984, p. 44.

8. Jonathan D. Salant, "Bill Would Open Windows on Lobbying Efforts," *Congressional Quarterly,* December 2, 1995, pp. 3631–3633.

9. Julian E. Barnes, "The Canadian Menace," *U.S. News and World Report,* September 8, 1997, pp. 29–30.

10. Quoted in Seymour Lusterman, *Managing Federal Government Relations* (New York: Conference Board, 1988), p. 16.

11. *Information on States' Lobbying Disclosure Requirements, B-129874* (Washington, DC: U.S. General Accounting Office, 1997), p. 5.

CHAPTER 17

Issues Management

The widely used term *issues management* is a misnomer. It does not imply the ability of a firm to "manage" the course of a national policy issue. Rather, the general usage refers to a far more modest and relevant undertaking: managing the company's responses to key public policy issues affecting its markets, sales, profitability, and internal operations. As shown in earlier chapters, business firms often have a great deal at stake in the enactment—or on occasion the defeat—of pending legislation.

The development of public policy often goes through a readily identifiable cycle: development of the issue due to public dissatisfaction; politicization of the issue (frequently as a result of a dramatizing event); enactment of legislation and issuance of regulations; and implementation, often including substantial litigation. Many larger corporations have set up formal procedures to identify, monitor, and respond to issues of public policy that have a substantial impact on their operations.

Great variations occur in the manner in which individual companies set up and operate issues-management systems. Often, the identification of issues and trends is decentralized, while the establishment of company positions is assigned to a high-level management committee. Corporate responses to public policy issues range from passive to anticipatory to active, depending on the nature of the issue and the circumstances of the firm.

THE PUBLIC POLICY PROCESS

The first step in issues management is to develop an understanding of the process by which items become public policy issues. Although each policy concern is distinctive, specialists in this area tend to agree that it is useful to consider four stages as constituting the life cycle of a public policy (see Figure 17.1).[1] As a general proposition, the earlier an organization identifies a significant trend, the greater its opportunity to influence the outcome and, surely, the larger the number of possible responses.

Developmental Stage

The first stage of the public policy process is the latent or developmental phase. Issues do not usually erupt full-blown. They evolve over time from persistent frictions between important sectors of society or from strong and continuing dissatisfaction on the part of a significant interest group. The individual bits and pieces of a developing issue often come from relatively small numbers of people at the grass roots. However,

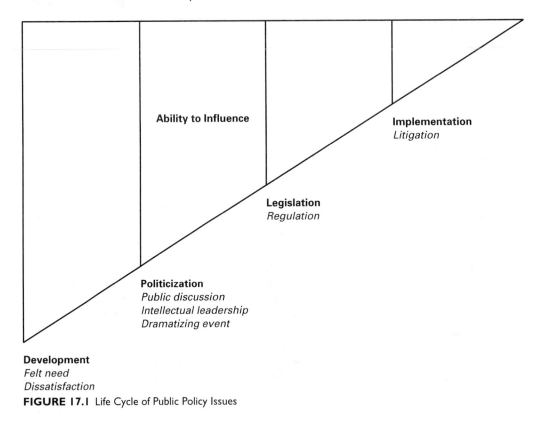

Development
Felt need
Dissatisfaction

FIGURE 17.1 Life Cycle of Public Policy Issues

potential issues that lack broad appeal or effective developmental strategies may never attract widespread public support.

The trigger for developing national attention can come from a dramatic event, such as a major disaster, or something far more basic, such as a change in public expectations or values. For example, the enactment in 1997 of fundamental welfare reform followed several decades of growing public dissatisfaction with the steadily rising outlays for public assistance. Repeated cycles of poverty within the same family group (often without the formation of a traditional two-parent household) led to a growing disenchantment with the status quo. The formation of a Republican majority in both houses of Congress was the triggering mechanism along with the advent of a presidential election campaign.

Politicization Stage

The opinion-formation or politicization phase is the second state of the public policy process. As a given problem commands more public attention, experts and advocates begin to comment. Organizations may adopt the issue. Such institutionalizing of the cause provides many public interest groups with a sustained base for advocating changes in public policy.

The issue is now likely to acquire a label: fair housing, truth-in-lending, clean air, welfare reform, and so on. It is discussed in speeches and on television specials, and written up in books, limited-circulation magazines, and professional journals. At this stage, these materials are heard or read by "influentials": academics, writers, clergy, think-tank analysts, columnists, and other idea brokers. With repetition, the message ultimately makes its way into the mass media, where it is popularized. Examples include Rachel Carson's *Silent Spring,* which spurred the environmental movement, Ralph Nader's *Unsafe at Any Speed,* which led to automobile safety regulation, and Charles Murray's *Losing Ground,* which generated support for moving away from the traditional "transfer payment" approach to alleviating poverty.

Sometimes a dramatizing event occurs, such as Earth Day, a staged media "happening." On other occasions, a disaster may occur, such as the explosion at the Union Carbide chemical plant in Bhopal, India, that led to tougher plant-safety regulation. In both cases, attention was suddenly focused on the matter, and it moved quickly into the national spotlight. Politicians latched onto a promising issue and pursued it with legislative hearings and further publicity.

The *Valdez* oil spill in 1989 gave the entire environmental movement a shot in the arm. The immediate result was the renewal and expansion of the Clean Air Act in 1990, an issue that had been pending since 1981. The spill had very little to do with air pollution, but the accident made the public more environmentally conscious.

It is within the developmental and politicization stages that the basic dimensions of a public policy issue are established. The influence on actions in the next two stages of the policy process may already be decisive. (See Table 17.1 for examples of the historical sequence of issue development.)[2]

Legislative Stage

The third stage of the public policy process is the institutional action phase, when statutes are enacted and regulations are promulgated. As issues generate widespread interest, pressures develop to resolve the problems. This may take the form of voluntary agreement. The debate on corporate governance in the 1970s mainly resulted in individual corporations voluntarily opening up business decision making by electing more outside directors and establishing public policy committees of company boards of directors in the 1980s and corporate governance committees in the 1990s. More often, however, the result is legislation and then detailed regulations.

It usually takes several years for Congress to write and approve major new laws. Although federal regulation of employee pensions originated in congressional hearings during the 1950s, the first significant bill was not introduced until 1967, and the Employee Retirement Income Security Act was not passed until 1974. In the case of the 1986 explosion in Bhopal, India, job-safety legislation was already on the books in the United States, and the issue moved directly to a period of tougher enforcement.

Sometimes numerous bills are introduced on a given issue. However, many legislators introduce or cosponsor a bill merely to pacify one or more influential constituents, with no expectation of passage or even hearings. Yet sometimes events overtake these passive intentions. For example, in the 1981–1982 congressional sessions, 17 energy-conservation bills were presented and only one passed. By the end of that decade, the issue had become moot—for a while. However, in 1993, President Bill

TABLE 17.1 Issue Development Phases

Issue	Triggering Event	Politicalization	Legislation	Implementation
Environmental protection	*Silent Spring,* 1963	Included in McCarthy political platform, 1968	EPA established, 1971	Clean air, clean water, toxic substance, and many other regulations
Automobile safety	*Unsafe at Any Speed,* 1966	Congressional hearings on auto safety, 1966	NHTSA established, 1966	Mandatory safety features
Discrimination	*Brown* v. *Board of Education,* 1964	Included in Johnson political platform, 1964	Civil Rights Act of 1964	EEOC and affirmative action regulations
Workplace safety	Federal study released in 1970	Congressional hearings, 1970	OSHA established, 1970	Regulations on job safety and health
Energy controls	OPEC embargo, 1973	Congressional hearings, 1973–1975	Energy Policy and Conservation Act, 1975	Energy allocation and price controls terminated in 1981
Growing role of imports in U.S. domestic markets	Rising trade deficit, 1980–1987	Congressional hearings and bills introduced, 1980–1988	Comprehensive trade law passed in 1988	Actions taken or threatened against unfair treatment of U.S. products

Clinton renewed public interest in the issue by proposing an excise tax on energy. The Congress responded by raising a narrower tax on gasoline. A vigorous debate is now underway on the seriousness of global warming. The most widely suggested policy response is a "carbon" tax to reduce the use of fossil fuel forms of energy, and the entire subject of energy conservation has been revived.

Implementation Stage

The final phase of the public policy process begins after the enabling legislation has been passed and the rules and procedures have been formulated by the appropriate executive-branch agency. The government agency assigned the new programs begins to organize to carry out its responsibilities. That is when compliance begins. After a while, entrenched interest groups develop, each hoping to receive specific benefits from the program.

Public-interest law firms regularly challenge the execution of the law, either advocating more speed in carrying it out or objecting to some aspect of the regulations. Most of these nonprofit legal organizations are activists, but quite a few are more oriented toward the free market. These actions are encouraged by some environmental statutes that provide for the plaintiff's attorneys to be paid by the government whether they win or lose!

Many companies enter the public policy process at this stage. The classic case is the enactment of the Occupational Safety and Health Administration Act in 1970. Most companies ignored the movement of the bill through the legislative process. After all, they reasoned, this was just some technical union matter. But small businesses reacted especially vehemently when they saw the avalanche of onerous, often nitpicking, regulations that was forthcoming. However, as shown in Figure 17.1, the potential for influencing the result is greatest during the early phases of the public issue development process, before the issue has been framed and attitudes have become entrenched. As an issue moves along the continuum from societal dissatisfaction to public policy, there is less and less opportunity for a business firm to affect the outcome significantly. Although, in its early years, OSHA evoked an unprecedented flow of complaints from business after the enactment of the basic statute, it was too late to make any fundamental changes in the program.

The gestation period for an idea to become public policy can vary substantially. In 1981, William Norris, former CEO of Control Data Corporation, conceived the notion of legislation to authorize cooperative research and development ventures. He held the first conference to discuss the idea with other CEOs in 1982. The initial bill to exempt such ventures from the antitrust laws was introduced late that year. A statute was enacted in 1984, three years after the effort began.

There is nothing inevitable in the process described here. For example, considerable pressure from consumer groups developed in the late 1970s for congressional enactment of a Consumer Advocacy Agency (also referred to as an Agency for Consumer Protection). The new government unit would intervene in regulatory deliberations on behalf of what it considered the consumer's interest. Many business associations objected to this additional layer of bureaucracy, citing the existing array of regulatory agencies. As the public became increasingly disenchanted with the ability of any group of government officials to determine what is "good for" the public, support for the proposal waned. Ultimately, the legislation was defeated. That is one among many examples of the effectiveness of well-organized and carefully thought through business involvement in the public policy arena. The earlier a company gets involved in the public policy process, the more leverage it can develop. Also, however, the more false starts it will make.

International Perspective

Viewed in an international context, the United States often has been a follower rather than a leader in public policy development, especially in the initiation of new governmental programs. For company planners, this relationship provides a useful side effect. Tracking the movement and response to public issues in other nations can provide a forecasting device. A fundamental shortcoming, however, is that no measurable lead or lag pattern emerges from an examination of history. Modern communications does seem to be shortening the lag in more recent time periods, and the United States has taken the lead in such areas as deregulation of transportation and communication.

- The United States abolished slavery in 1862, 68 years after France.
- The United States passed a pure food and drug law in 1906, 46 years after the United Kingdom.
- The United States voted old-age assistance in 1889, 46 years after Germany.
- The United States enacted workers compensation in 1935, 37 years after Germany.
- The United States began unemployment insurance in 1935, 30 years after France.
- The United States gave women suffrage in 1920, 27 years after New Zealand.

However, the United States deregulated airline transportation in 1978 and most nations have not yet followed suit.

ELEMENTS OF AN ISSUES-MANAGEMENT SYSTEM

Over the years, American companies have been developing increasingly more comprehensive responses to the various policy issues facing private business. Although the position of issues management director in a given company may come and go, the responsibility for the activity increasingly is lodged in senior management. There is growing recognition that the company's response to major public policy issues must be a shared responsibility of a constantly changing cast of corporate executives, depending on the issue involved. The accountability for a tax issue, for example, may lodge with the director of the tax department, with the public affairs department functioning as the secretariat or facilitator.[3]

Five basic elements provide the framework for the typical corporate issues-management program:

1. Identifying public policy issues and trends.
2. Evaluating their impact and ranking them by priority to the company.
3. Establishing a company position on the high-priority issues.
4. Designing company actions and responses to help achieve the desired outcome.
5. Carrying out the planned actions.

Identification

Many companies operate early warning systems, employing specialists to deal with trends and emerging issues in which traditional employees lack familiarity. A formal but simple structure can be established for this purpose. Many company employees, often volunteers, scan a variety of forward-looking magazines and other sources that reveal early changes in public attitudes, especially in bellwether regions. A smaller and more formal group will sort out these issues, focusing on those that are likely to generate the most direct impact on the firm. Relatively senior managers then develop proposed responses to the new trends.

Some corporations retain professional futurists and public-opinion analysts under contract to supplement in-house activities by monitoring social and political change. Two of the most common tools for identifying emerging public policy issues are literature scans and opinion polling. Many firms subscribe to one of several consulting organizations that survey local newspapers for data on social, political, and economic trends. Others assign executives to monitor selected publications systematically.

Most large corporations have been dealing with legislative concerns for many years. To identify and monitor current issues, they often rely on outside sources, such as trade associations and specialized newsletters, to supplement in-house policy analysts. Some businesses maintain formal inventories of corporate issues to keep management informed and to help organize their responses.

Evaluation

A number of companies use a formal methodology to evaluate emerging public policy trends that may affect the company's current planning and future operations. For example, a Delphi panel of experts may be commissioned so that a synthesis of disparate individual views is available to corporate decision makers. The most frequently used approach is an interdepartmental public affairs or issues committee that combines the expertise of key executives in many parts of the organization. Invariably, senior management makes the decisions that involve moving from staff analysis to corporate action.

Table 17.2 is an example of the survey approach, based on a composite of the views of several hundred corporate public affairs officers.[4] The key issues that emerge from the analysis are taxation, product liability reform, health care costs, environmental cleanup, deregulation, and competitiveness.

At some companies, an issue becomes active simply when a key line manager considers it important enough to bring it to the attention of the public affairs staff. The director of government affairs may then convene a steering group to develop specific actions and to adjust the company's strategies. As the Public Affairs Council has warned, the biggest problem that companies face in this area is not developing information but deciding which issues to tackle and what action to take.

Response

In practice, there is great variety in the ways in which companies respond to specific issues of public policy. Table 17.3 presents an analysis of the key issues facing large U.S. industrial companies and the nature of the firm's responses. It is a distillation of internal reports of a variety of corporations.

A company's issues-management action plan—after it has been approved by senior management—typically will involve the headquarters' public affairs department, the Washington office, and the managements of one or more operating divisions. James Post and his colleagues, in their pioneering research on the corporate public affairs function, ascertained the key techniques used to achieve company objectives in this area. The responses can be described, in descending order of frequency, as follows:

1. Monitoring emerging issues.
2. Lobbying for legislation within trade associations.
3. Scanning to detect new issues.

TABLE 17.2 Levels of Corporate Involvement in Public Policy Issues

Issue	Percentage of Firms Actively Involved	Percentage of Firms Closely Monitoring	Percentage of Firms Reporting General Interest
1. Tax reform	70	24	6
2. Product liability reform	47	31	20
3. Health care cost containment	40	34	22
4. Environmental cleanup			
Clean air	32	26	23
Toxic wastes	33	31	21
Other	30	25	27
5. Deregulation	42	25	28
6. Technology and economic competitiveness			
Research support	19	22	45
Copyrights and patents	18	22	42
Science and engineering education	14	20	46
7. Financial disclosure	15	48	30
8. Reregulation	25	33	35
9. Protectionism	26	30	25
10. Employment discrimination	12	45	51
11. Campaign financing reform	13	44	35
12. Budget deficit	16	38	44
13. Employment-at-will	6	42	48
14. Antitrust	10	27	49
15. Family issues	6	29	53
16. Privacy	5	28	59
17. Job creation and retraining	5	26	51
18. Education and business	10	10	50
19. Middle East	4	15	36
20. Farm prices	6	10	30

Source: Conference Board.

4. Updating managers on company positions.

5. Lobbying for legislation at the federal level.

6. Lobbying with state and local governments.

7. Expressing company positions to government agencies.

8. Communicating company positions to employees.

9. Using issues managers.

10. Expanding company information systems.

11. Changing company policies.

12. Setting up public-affairs-issues research committees.

13. Communicating company positions to the general public.

14. Revising company or divisional objectives.

15. Informing stockholders of company positions.

16. Strengthening company reward and penalty systems.[5]

TABLE 17.3 Responses to High-Priority Issues by Major U.S. Industrial Companies

Identification of the Issue	Nature of the Response
1. Fundamental changes in global market competition.	Emphasize growth markets in which competitors are weak.
2. Management of technology. Public misgivings about technology.	Information program to explain company research to public; formation of expert advisory committee.
3. Growing employee demands for changes in quality of life.	Deemphasize systems and rules; eliminate levels of supervision; expand involvement in decision making.
4. Growth of state and local government influence. Increased regulation of manufacturing and marketing.	Track developments in all 50 states; state government relations department given principal responsibility for coordinating state lobbying.
5. Excess manufacturing capacity, forcing layoffs and plant closings.	Consider community impact in determining when and how to close plants.
6. Impact of inflation on company, especially international operations.	More active management of foreign exchange operations.
7. Resource management to avoid shortages of materials.	Adopt sustainability approach to planning and operations.
8. Increasing requests for information about workplace safety and individual health histories.	Emphasize preventive health and safety measures; encourage complete, well-grounded disclosures.
9. Conflicting demands of employee groups. Conflicts among special interest groups at times of layoffs.	Offer alternatives to layoffs, such as redeployment; offer advance notice, severance pay, and job counseling when layoffs occur.
10. Management of multinational business.	Expand use of foreign nationals, minimizing American overseas employment; involve overseas managers more in decision making.

Experienced practitioners warn that an issues-response management system cannot be boilerplated but must be tailored to the needs and resources of the specific company. Table 17.4 illustrates some of the benefits as well as the inherent limitations of such a system. Generally, issues management systems help businesses become more aware of the political, social, and economic environment within which they operate. This is especially useful when aspects of that external environment change rapidly.

However, public policy monitoring programs fail when they overdramatize as immediate threats to company survival such esoteric issues as social responsibility. "I am not suggesting," states one public affairs official, "that these issues are irrelevant to corporate success over time, but they are seldom jugular concerns to a competently managed corporation."[6]

It is important to know when not to react. Some firms new to the public policy process are inclined to get involved every time any legislator introduces a bill that could affect the company if it passed. As previously mentioned, most bills do not even get to the stage where a committee hearing is held on it. However, when a large corporation focuses attention on what had been an obscure bill, it can find that the

TABLE 17.4 Benefits and Limitations of an Issues-Management System

Benefits	Limitations
A managed process by which issues are actively dealt with.	Cannot predict every issue that will affect the company.
An enhanced ability to react rapidly to unexpected or quickly breaking issues.	Cannot accurately forecast the environment many years in the future.
Greatly increased intelligence about the external environment.	Cannot assume that every issue will be resolved according to the corporation's wishes.
Involvement of management and enhanced sensitivity to effects of public issues on business.	Cannot work as an isolated staff function while the rest of the company continues its traditional routine.
Assurance to shareholders, employees, and activist groups that the company's responses are serious and thoughtful.	

proposal is no longer obscure. Under such circumstances, its early intervention can be counterproductive.

Reflections on Business and Public Policy

Contrary to a widely held notion that the business community maintains a monolithic approach to public policy, most scholars who have analyzed the question quickly conclude that the typical business viewpoint is anything but homogeneous. Some of the differences clearly reflect competitive positions: importers versus domestic producers (on trade policy), thrift institutions versus commercial banks versus investment bankers (on deregulation of financial institutions), proprietary drug manufacturers versus prescription drug companies (on drug regulation).

Other differences arise because of variations in the impact of government policies: manufacturing versus services (in the case of investment tax incentives), capital-intensive versus labor-intensive firms (for personnel regulation as well as environmental rule making), and high-profit versus low-profit corporations (on reducing tax rates versus maintaining special business incentives).

As pointed out in earlier chapters, business firms are usually far more effective in the public policy arena when they focus their efforts on specific programs that benefit them (import quotas or tax breaks) than when they attempt to do battle on broad issues of national concern, such as environmental policy.

There is substantial conceptual support for that disparity. In a decentralized political system, general interests shared by large numbers of people tend to fare poorly. In contrast, narrow interests usually do better. The reason is that a broad interest is comparable to a public good, which is available widely, whether the recipient pays for it or not. In such circumstances, it is expected that many individuals (or companies) "free-ride," that is, leave the costs of financing the public good to others. However, if that is a widely held response, an insufficient supply of the public good will be available. In contrast, there are compelling incentives for relatively small groups to organize for their mutual benefit.

An obvious example is the federal budget. Virtually every business firm and trade association pays lip service to the notion of a balanced budget. But, in most cases, their most ambitious public policy efforts are devoted to advocating increased spending for a specific item benefiting them—or opening (or expanding) a tax loophole with a similar effect. In the case of the overall budget, any single company or industry would receive extremely small shares of the benefits resulting from lower amounts of deficit financing. However, they obtain very large proportions of tax breaks or expenditure subsidies directed to their sector of the economy.

This conceptual approach cannot be carried too far. As noted in the previous chapter, many companies support such umbrella organizations as the Chamber of Commerce, the National Association of Manufacturers, and the National Federation of Independent Business. At times, these broad-based organizations have obtained the enactment of public policy of general benefit to business. A recent example is the substantial reduction in the capital gains tax rate, down to 20 percent for most taxpayers (included in a 1997 package of tax changes).

ORGANIZING FOR ISSUES MANAGEMENT

In a great many companies, formalized programs of issues management were originally assigned to the public affairs department, which, in turn, was an expansion and strengthening of the traditional public relations staff. Frequently, the formal function remains in the public affairs area, although the policy decisions are made by executives in the substantive areas. In some cases, the issues-management approach has evolved out of an embryonic social responsibility program. Viewed in that light, issues management is a response to bring company actions into closer alignment with society's expectation of business and—to a far more modest degree—vice versa.

Early Developmental Stage

Prior to the establishment of formal issues-management efforts, companies reacted to key public policy initiatives as they occurred. Civil rights legislation and accompanying regulations quickly led to the establishment of equal-employment-opportunity sections of personnel departments (often renamed *human resources*) and to new affirmative-action programs. Similarly, legislation and regulation in the ecology area soon led to environmental policy staffs and specific pollution control programs.

In an effort to do more than react to government policy initiatives, companies began establishing formal programs of issues management. Initially, these efforts involved little more than cataloging the pressure points from the public arena so that the company could respond a bit more rapidly. Corporate responses tended to highlight the near-term focus, as would be expected from the public relations departments that housed many of these efforts.

Some of these early efforts were avowedly straight advocacy programs, helping the company decide which issues to get involved in and then to speak out on them. The initial issues-management programs tended to be short-term, reactive, and traditional examinations of an outside world defined in traditional ways, thus yielding immediate reactions focusing on narrowly defined problems.

Acceptance and Use by Management

Issues management now also encompasses forecasts and evaluations of long-term societal trends, domestic and international. When the responsibility for the function is transferred from the public affairs department to the corporate planning department, the opportunity arises to integrate public policy analysis into the regular planning and decision systems of the company. That enables managers to give more attention to strategic assumptions about external factors in their long-range planning. Probably the most important result of the evolution of issues management and its formal integration into company operations has been the increased sensitivity of the individual manager to nontraditional forces that can affect the bottom line.

Naturally, corporations take varying approaches to issues management. A few companies have full-time staffs of issues managers. Their wide-ranging backgrounds include professionals trained as scientists, engineers, lawyers, marketing specialists, journalists, and social scientists. One corporate issues-management unit identifies between 15 and 20 issues that have potentially significant impact on the company and transmits its analysis to a higher-level public affairs committee that sets policy and strategy for dealing with them. The issues range from local matters (for instance, intergovernmental cooperation in the company's headquarters city) to international concerns such as proposed workplace standards in the European Union.

Most companies emphasize legislative and other governmental issues. Some firms, however, uses issues managers to spot emerging concerns for its community and philanthropic programs. Many companies do not have formal issues-management programs as such but rely on traditional staff to perform such functions, including planning, public affairs, and government-relations departments. A 1992 survey of 160 companies by the Foundation for Public Affairs revealed considerable support for the function. Forty percent of the respondents said the function was more important than previously, and only 6 percent said it was less important. The remainder characterized the status as "about the same."[7]

Further Expansion

Issues management efforts can also have applications to a company's marketing efforts. The insurance and financial-service company, Alexander and Alexander, for example, devoted the first 19 pages of a recent annual report to an analysis of public policy issues affecting business. The graphics dramatized the financial risks and implications for the firm's clients. For example, the report indicated the growing potential for litigation and subsequent losses arising from environmental impairment liability. Key industries likely to be affected were identified, notably food processors, chemical and pharmaceutical firms, and petroleum companies. (See the box "Issues-Management Successes" for examples of positive contributions to company operations.)

Issues-Management Successes

A staff activity such as issues management can easily deteriorate into a paper-shuffling operation. Although that danger may always be present, it is useful to note some of the genuine successes that have been reported.

- Through its issues-management process, American Express anticipated—well ahead of the event—the pending expiration of a federal law prohibiting merchants from imposing surcharges on consumer use of credit cards. The company realized that as soon as the ban expired retailers would quickly add surcharges, a practice that would discourage the use of credit cards. Such an eventuality never occurred. American Express headed it off by working with consumer groups and legislators to enact laws in many states barring such surcharges.

- ARCO credits its issues-management process for identifying—before other petrochemical and chemical companies—the cleanup of hazardous wastes as an issue that would bedevil the industry. Departing from the customary business opposition to new environmental legislation, the company supported the concept of Superfund and worked to modify the legislation. ARCO maintains that the entire industry adopted this approach subsequently.

- Allstate identified incipient public pressure for insurance companies to provide more affordable homeowner coverage in poorer, more densely populated urban areas in transition. The company formed an Insuring Urban America task force and tailored a new insurance policy to the urban market. Allstate believes that without such action many state governments would have mandated much more severe action.

- Monsanto credits its issue-identification committee with a key role in altering the basic strategy of the company. As part of its environmental scanning process, the Committee reported to management that the profit outlook for bulk or commodity chemicals was dim. That advance warning prompted the company to leave the petrochemical and oil businesses and concentrate instead on agricultural chemicals, biotechnology, and pharmaceuticals. In 1997, Monsanto spun off its traditional chemical units so that it could concentrate on the newer fields of business.

ALTERNATIVE STRATEGIES

Individual companies react to changing public policy in a great variety of ways. But four basic patterns of response to threats of government intervention are evident: passive, anticipatory, accommodative, and active. Often a company will use a blend of these four approaches.

Passive

Some corporate managements simply *react* to each new or expanded government initiative. The passive approach is the oldest and still the most popular. Before the passage of the Clean Air Act, many capital-intensive firms merely stonewalled when criticized by citizen groups for the large amounts of air pollution they were generating.

Those managements criticized the development of a public-sector response and attempted to postpone its effects through litigation and administrative appeals. But ultimately they were forced to gear their operations to meet the new government requirements. Companies in the passive mode typically respond to government regulation by digging in their heels and griping and then going along at the minimum acceptable rate. Inevitably, they are constantly complaining about the government trying to run their businesses.

Anticipatory

The expanding government role in business decision making has encouraged corporate managements to use their planning capability to forecast likely further changes in government policies that affect business. Such action enables them to adjust their own operations to minimize or obviate the impacts of those external changes. Thus, before congressional enactment of tightened air- or water-pollution controls, some firms incorporate more stringent ecological standards in their own capital projects. The intent is to minimize the likelihood of subsequently running afoul of new federal regulations.

Some companies also take socially responsible actions on a voluntary basis in an effort to reduce the likelihood of more stringent controls being enacted by government. An example is the extent to which companies and business associations have adopted standards for advance notification of plant closings, together with private programs to reduce adverse impacts on employees and on the surrounding community. Nonetheless, in 1988 Congress did pass legislation mandating advance notice. Some companies supported the statutory requirement as a way of imposing costs on competitors that did not have voluntary programs.

As corporate executives become more sensitive to evolving social demands, they begin to respond to some of the public's expectations as a normal aspect of conducting business. To the extent that this positive development occurs voluntarily, businesses themselves provide some constraint on the degree of political pressure that social activists can effectively exert against them. Why go to Ralph Nader if someone in the company can handle your complaint? The consumer movement today may seem to lack the dynamism of the 1970s, possibly because business firms have been better able to anticipate consumers' wishes and respond to them. (See the box "Trends in Consumer Activism.") Nevertheless, the consumer movement is far from dead, and on specific issues it can be a formidable force.

Accommodative

There is one approach to government intervention that companies are reluctant to admit they practice. Many firms try to appease their critics by making generous contributions to them.[8] Thus, some energy companies support the very environmental organizations that regularly attack their industry. Contributions from business firms are reported by such activist organizations as the Council on Economic Priorities, the Environmental Defense Fund, Greenpeace, INFORM, the National Wildlife Federation, the National Resources Defense Council, Operation Push, and the Wilderness Society. The individual businesses hope that the critics will pick on other businesses or at least that they will appear to be more socially minded.

Trends in Consumer Activism

Citizen groups involved in public policy range from the handful of residents who are temporarily aroused by an ephemeral local issue to Citizen Action, a broad-based federation of groups with approximately two million members. With affiliates in 26 states, Citizen Action is one of the most ambitious efforts to date to consolidate the resources of labor, environmentalists, poor people, and other activist groups. With its state affiliates, Citizen Action boasts a combined staff of 1,500 plus thousands of volunteers.

An activist training center in Chicago was the seedbed for the movement. In the 1970s, the Midwest Academy began to teach members of citizens' organizations the skills required to manage direct-action operations. Groups that had been sending their people to the Academy started to do the "macro" organizing. In many states, church leaders formed the initial sponsoring committees.

The Citizen Action platform, *Citizen Action Program for a Working America,* is based on the radical premise that "Corporate power has abandoned the well-being of America." The platform advocates a variety of new or expanded government powers over the economy. Specifics include limiting the movement of capital overseas, enacting a special tax on corporate profits, prohibiting agricultural corporations, establishing price controls, and setting up an elaborate system of government planning and direction of the economy.

State affiliates join with outside organizations on specific issues. Examples include the Citizen's Labor Energy Coalition, which delayed natural gas deregulation for several years, and the National Campaign Against Toxic Hazards, which helped pass federal and state Superfund legislation.

Citizen Action has encountered substantial criticism for its direct participation in political activities. The Federal Elections Commission fined the tax-exempt Illinois arm of the organization $5,000 for making illegal contributions to congressional candidates in 1984. In 1997, Citizen Action figured prominently in the investigations of campaign financing. It was accused of illegally funneling money from the Teamsters Union and the AFL-CIO to the campaign coffers of the Teamsters' president.

An older, more conventional activist association is the Consumer Federation of America (CFA), a coalition of some 200 national, state, and regional consumer, labor, cooperative, and other citizens' groups. CFA promotes industry responsibility for product liability and the provision of lifeline services by a number of key industries, such as utilities. In comparing CFA to a business lobby, its executive director was quoted as saying, "[W]e do have much better access to the press."

Simultaneously, more narrowly focused citizen or activist groups are continually involved in specific areas, such as environmental and pharmaceutical regulation. Thus, the Environmental Defense Fund (EDF) urges concerned citizens to press for testing local freshwater fish for dioxin levels and to join EDF's "incinerator network" to act as watchdog to warn of any proposed resource-recovery/solid-waste incinerators.

The Sierra Club Legal Defense Fund promotes citizen action to prevent paper companies from clear-cutting timber in old-growth rain forests. It also sponsors action to halt placer mining in portions of the National Wild and Scenic River System. The Fund provides postcards for concerned citizens to send to the Department of the Interior.

Public Citizen's Health Research Group (a Ralph Nader affiliate) urges the Food and Drug Administration to ban or limit the use of some pharmaceutical products and has been active in the effort to have nicotine classified as a drug. The National Resources Defense Council frequently enters environmental disputes, often taking positions opposite to those of business firms.

To some degree, taxpayers directly subsidize activists groups. Under the Superfund Amendments and Reauthorization Act of 1986, the federal government makes funds available to community organizations on a roughly two-for-one basis (65 percent federal money, 35 percent private). The grants are available to groups that can show that they are threatened by sites from a "health, economic, or environmental standpoint." In addition, several environmental statutes provide for the federal government reimbursing activist groups for their legal costs when they institute suits under those laws, even if they lose the cases.

Another trend in consumer activism is the tendency for national groups to form international networks. The International Organization of Consumers Unions (IOCU) is composed of 160 consumer groups in 52 countries. IOCU has official status in many of the UN specialized agencies. It fosters a variety of issue-oriented networks, such as Health Action International and Pesticide Action Network International, to lobby governments and pressure individual companies. In turn, the Pesticide Action Network consists of 350 consumer, labor, farmer, health care, and other organizations pushing for restrictions on the production and sale of pesticides.

Labor unions do not play this dangerous game because it strengthens the people who are attacking the contributor's own interests. The passive, anticipatory, and accommodative approaches to public policy issues all share a common shortcoming: The companies are always on the defensive in dealing with government and interest groups.

Active

Still other business executives attempt to head off or shape the character of government intervention by playing a more active role in the development and enactment of public policies. Thus, some companies have strengthened their Washington offices to deal with pending legislation and new regulation or have set up such operations if they did not exist. They join and strongly support trade associations that are active on Capitol Hill. Despite the restrictions on political contributions and practices, many businessmen and businesswomen, as individuals, attempt to exercise leverage on government decision making by participating more actively in the political process.

Business firms now make extensive use of in-house publications, communications to shareholders, and other media to raise the public awareness of political issues that affect the future of the business community. Businesspeople increasingly participate in public hearings. It is intriguing to note that, of the CEOs who attempt to influence the government, a majority believe their efforts have been successful.

Some firms have developed an outreach effort to open up communications with adversarial groups. Usually that is done after some serious confrontation has occurred. In the case of Nestlé, a variety of such efforts was undertaken after a sustained boycott of its infant formula on the part of a combination of church and activist groups.[9]

An improved knowledge of the public policy process enables business and its representatives to affect, in entirely legal and legitimate fashion, the formulation of new and revised government policies toward the private sector. Often the most effective form of influence is making available to government decision makers prompt, knowledgeable, and detailed analyses of the various impacts of the proposed legislation. In contrast to the traditional methods of exerting "political" pressure, the information approach may help to reconcile public desires and business reality.

PUBLIC RELATIONS EFFORTS

The public affairs function of the modern corporation has become an important part of the response to the expanding role of government in business decision making. The shift in emphasis to guiding the whole range of management responses to public policy challenges has been gradual but substantial. The expansion of the role of public affairs professionals has reflected in good measure the steady and rapid growth in government intervention in traditional business functions. It is also a corporate response to the rise of an array of external pressures and interest groups that can have powerful effects, often quite harmful, on the performance of the business firm.

Companies have moved beyond the initial and largely negative response to this external environment: merely opposing or at least trying to postpone the expanding array of restraints imposed on the discretion of corporate management. Increasingly, business has attempted to respond positively to the concerns that generate government and private pressures for changes in business practices. The entire social responsibility movement is a case in point, although in recent years the charitable aspect has been reduced substantially.

A more entrepreneurial approach is to rely on an expansion of traditional planning and analysis functions in order to understand the urgencies that are arising and to respond to them early enough to reduce the pressures for public intervention. As a result, most businesses—but far from all—have shed the Neanderthal image that much of the public has associated with the corporate sector. Management is learning firsthand that responding promptly to a Senate inquiry can be more timely than calling on a potential new customer. The effective public affairs function can improve and make less onerous that external environment that impinges on the internal operations of the business firm.

Increasingly, business is turning to the public to exert pressure on government for reforms it believes desirable. Numerous existing channels of communication are available to companies to express their views on public policy. They range from employee newspapers to customer magazines to annual reports to shareholders. In the past, such house organs have tended to be dominated by routine announcements, pictures of employees receiving 10-year pins, and bowling-league scores. Many companies are now including more substantial editorial content in these publications.

Companies can make noncoercive statements to their employees, including soliciting political contributions, expressing political support and corporate philosophy, and urging political and legislative activity. Regulations of the Internal Revenue Service permit deductions for advertising that presents views on economic, social, or other questions of a general nature. But the distinction between tax-deductible, "informational" messages and nondeductible, "persuasional" communications is at best arbitrary.

An important U.S. Supreme Court decision in 1978 (*First National Bank of Boston* v. *Bellotti*) held that corporations have a constitutional right of free speech to propagate their political and social views. The *Bellotti* case struck down a Massachusetts law that prohibited corporations from making expenditures for the purpose of "influencing or affecting the vote on any question submitted to the voters, other than one materially affecting any of the property, business or assets of the corporation." The First National Bank of Boston had opposed a proposed state graduated individual income tax. The decision held that corporations have a right of free speech.

Rulings by the Internal Revenue Service, however, set limits on tax-deductible grassroots lobbying and related activities. Internal Revenue Ruling 78-111, for example, states that the cost of printing and distributing the text of remarks of a company president on a pending state environmental bill are not deductible, even though the shareholders are not actually requested to contact their representatives. That activity, according to the IRS, is an attempt to influence shareholders to oppose that legislation. In Internal Revenue Ruling 789-112, the IRS holds that the costs of advertisements stating that company's objection to certain proposed land-use legislation and suggesting an alternative program also violates the prohibition on "grassroots lobbying" even if there is no specific request that the reader contact a representative in the legislature.

Business and the Media

One of the areas of greatest contention between business and the rest of society is in media coverage. Newspapers, magazines, radio, and television are the principal sources through which the public forms its opinions on issues of public policy. Editors and broadcast executives are the gatekeepers who determine which issues get public attention and hence strongly influence the setting of the public policy agenda.

There is great variation in media coverage of business. Some journalists have become veritable experts in reporting and analyzing current developments. Their work is relied upon as source information by scholars and government officials alike. Yet many writers on business topics lack a basic comprehension of the activities they are reporting on. No sports desk would assign a reporter to cover a baseball game who is not familiar with the rules of the sport. Yet a comparable level of competence is not a general requirement for covering an annual meeting of a major corporation or for reporting on a critique of business by an important interest group.

In recent years, a variety of efforts has been made to enhance the economic and business knowledge of practicing journalists. Several universities sponsor short courses in this area. The Foundation for American Communications (FACS) brings the classroom closer to reporters by holding short courses in many different locations, drawing print- and electronic-media journalists from the surrounding area. FACS courses range from the basics of economics to analyses of key policy areas such as foreign trade and environmental regulation.

The enlightened business executive also learns to accept the fact that much news reporting on business (as well as of other sectors of the economy) does not consist of praise. The late Theodore White, a noted journalist and author, described this problem in fairly colorful language:

> You don't make your reputation as a reporter and I did not make my reputation as a reporter, by praising anybody. You make your reputation as a reporter . . . by gouging a chunk of raw and bleeding flesh from this system . . . You gotta be able to prove you can snap your jaws for the kill.[10]

A certain degree of sensationalism, regardless of inaccuracy, does help to get an item into a publication or on the evening news. Fostering the production of such items is the keen competition that exists among reporters on a given newspaper, magazine, or TV or radio station.

On the other hand, experienced journalists present a fairly standard litany of the shortcomings of senior business management in their dealings with the press: They stonewall the media; they live a sheltered life in the corporate cocoon; and they are not used to the same give-and-take as the government official or politician; they are defensive and antagonistic—when they answer press calls at all. In any event, a retired managing editor of the *Washington Post* reminds the business community that the First Amendment does not guarantee a competent, fair, and accurate press—but "a free press, which often means a cantankerous, suspicious and inaccurate press."[11]

Conclusion

Identifying and responding to specific public policy issues that strongly affect private business is a difficult and challenging assignment. Given the increasing globalization of business and the continuing expansion of the range of governmental interests, the likelihood that those challenges will continue, if not accelerate, is very high. As one government affairs executive stated, "Our workload has increased through several presidencies. The next presidency will prove no different."[12]

Notes

1. See W. Howard Chase, *Issue Management* (Stamford, CT: IAP, 1984).
2. See Thomas G. Marx, "Integrating Public Affairs and Strategic Planning," *California Management Review,* Fall 1986, p. 145.
3. Raymond L. Hoewing, *Issues Management Yesterday and Today* (Washington, DC: Public Affairs Council, 1993), p. 7.

4. Catherine Morrison, *Forecasting Public Affairs Priorities* (New York: Conference Board, 1987), pp. 1–15.

5. James E. Post, et al., "Public Affairs Officers and Their Functions," *Public Affairs Review,* II (1981), p. 97.

6. Robert H. Moore, *Monitoring Governmental Regulation,* presentation to the 1983 Strategic Planning Conference, Conference Board, New York City, 1983, p. 5.

7. Hoewing, *Issues Management,* p. 6.

8. See Marvin Olasky et al., *Patterns of Corporate Philanthropy* (Washington, DC: Capital Research Center, 1992).

9. James E. Post, "Assessing the Nestlé Boycott," *California Management Review,* Winter 1985, pp. 113–131.

10. Quoted in John L. Poluszek, *Will the Corporation Survive?* (Reston, VA: Reston, 1977), p. 225.

11. Howard Simons, "The Media and Business," in *Dateline: Washington* (Washington, DC: LTV, Inc., 1979), p. 10.

12. Quoted in Seymour Lusterman, *Managing Federal Government Relations* (New York: Conference Board, 1988), p. 25.

CHAPTER 18

Business Participation in Politics

The substantial impact of government on business decision making has resulted in expanded interest by business executives in participating directly in the political process. The significant political role of other interest groups, such as labor, environmentalists, and senior citizens, and the antibusiness orientation of many political activists working under the banner of the public interest has encouraged executives in private enterprises to take a more active role in the political arena.

Industry leaders often attempt to use the political process to slow or shape government intervention in the private sector. However, they tend to be more circumspect in their efforts than are representatives of other interest groups. The glare of national publicity at times can be intimidating to people who, on a day-to-day basis, operate in a very different environment. Legislation enacted in the 1970s to prevent illegal political contributions by business has been an important factor in changing the nature of business participation in politics. Since then, many corporate executives have become far more knowledgeable of the legal limits to political participation and have developed innovative, permissible techniques.

PERMISSIBLE POLITICAL ACTIVITIES

Corporations can participate legally in a wide variety of political activities. Federal law governs only political activities involving candidates for president, vice president, and Congress. (See the box "Limits on Contributions to Federal Election Campaigns.") Involvement in state and local campaigns is covered by varying state statutes and local ordinances.

A corporation may encourage its employees and stockholders to register and vote, but it may not recommend to employees how they should vote. Candidates may tour a company plant or office to meet employees or may stand at an entrance to greet them, but the company must grant all candidates that right. However, it need not specifically invite every candidate. A corporation may not contribute funds to a candidate or an election campaign at the federal level, but it can sponsor a fund-raising effort on the part of its employees. (The role of such political action committees is discussed in the next section of this chapter.) The federal prohibition against corporations making monetary contributions for campaign financing, which goes back to the

---

Limits on Contributions to Federal Election Campaigns

Corporations and Labor Unions

- May sponsor Political Action Committees (PACs).
- May not contribute to candidates for federal offices.
- May contribute "soft dollars" for voter drives, party building (broadly defined), and state and local campaigns (subject to state law).

Political Action Committees

- May contribute $5,000 per candidate for federal office per election.
- May make unlimited "independent expenditures" that do not go directly to a candidate but are intended to benefit or hurt a specific campaign.
- May donate up to $15,000 a year to a party for its campaigns for national offices.
- May make unlimited "soft money" contributions to a party for voter drives, party building, and state and local campaigns (subject to state law).

Individuals

- May give $1,000 per candidate for federal office per election.
- May give no more than $5,000 a year to any one PAC.
- May contribute up to $20,000 a year to a national party for campaigns for federal office.
- May give directly to state and local party organizations, depending on state laws.
- May contribute up to $20,000 a year to a national party for state and local campaigns, party building, and voter drives.
- May donate up to $25,000 a year to presidential and congressional campaigns.

General Limitations

- No contributions may be accepted from individuals who are not U.S. citizens or lawful permanent residents.
- Contributions in the name of another person or entity are forbidden.
- Contributions of more than $100 must be by check, not in cash.
- Contributions from children under 18 are forbidden, unless the child controls both the money and the decision to donate. Contributions may not be made from the proceeds of a gift.

Tillman Act of 1907, was extended to labor unions in 1943. In some states, it is entirely legal for companies to contribute directly to election campaigns. However, 35 states have enacted ceilings on campaign donations, many similar to the federal rules. In the case of California, contributions are limited to $5,000 a year for political action committees (described below) and $1,000 a year for individuals.

The management of a company has a right to state its position on public issues affecting the company's well-being, including legislative proposals before Congress. It also may communicate to its employees and stockholders information on members of Congress and candidates for office, such as voting records. Company-sponsored programs explaining how to be effective in politics are another allowable form of political activity. Moreover, a corporation can provide political education programs for employees, and it can actively promote, on a nonpartisan basis, its employees' voluntary involvement in direct political action on their own time. An employee also may be granted a leave of absence without pay to work on a political campaign.

SUPPORTING POLITICAL CANDIDATES VIA PACS

For many years, it was illegal for corporations or unions to solicit political funds from employees or members. At first, unions circumvented the law by forming "educational" groups, such as the AFL-CIO's Committee on Political Education (COPE), as funnels for political contributions. But initially, businesses and trade groups had no such outlet and were restricted to individual voluntary contributions by executives. Before the reforms in campaign financing laws were enacted in the 1970s, these personal contributions, however, could be made in virtually unlimited amounts.

The Rules on PACs

Corporations and associations are prohibited by law from making political contributions or using the organization's resources for federal election campaigns. Since 1971, however, they can use company funds to set up and administer political action committees (PACs), comparable to labor's COPE. Contrary to its name, a PAC does not operate a political campaign; rather, it is a financing mechanism for political activity. PAC managers report that company-financed administrative costs—such as the expense of collecting and disbursing the funds—are 25 to 50 percent of the funds solicited, and often more, which constitute substantial indirect support.[1]

Specific statutory provisions contained in the 1971 Federal Election Campaign Act and spelled out in greater detail in later amendments allow business- and union-sponsored PACs to support candidates actively. As separate legal entities organized to solicit and accept voluntary contributions from shareholders and "executive or administrative personnel" and their families, business PACs in turn can make political contributions to candidates for federal office. Twice a year, they can solicit other company employees.

Despite the complex rules governing their operation—a PAC must have at least 50 members and give to at least five candidates—the number of business PACs has increased rapidly, from fewer than 100 in 1974 to nearly 1,700 at the close of 1995. Many PACs are small-scale, local operations that contribute to state or regional candidates and represent small businesses, local labor unions, and political clubs. Only one out of four PACs gave more than $20,000 to federal candidates in 1994.[2] Table 18.1 lists the 10 firms with the largest PAC expenditures in 1995–1996.

Individual contributors to PACs are limited to $1,000 a calendar year. Each PAC is allowed to contribute a maximum of $5,000 per election to each candidate, $20,000

TABLE 18.1	Ten Largest Business Political Action Committees, 1995–1996
Sponsoring Company	*Contributions*
United Parcel Service	$1,791,147
AT&T	1,311,232
Lockheed Martin	1,126,750
Federal Express	948,000
Ernst & Young	886,365
Philip Morris	883,619
BellSouth	870,867
Union Pacific	800,357
RJR Nabisco	763,150
Northrop Grumman	694,675

Source: U.S. Federal Election Commission.

a calendar year to national political parties, and $5,000 a year to other political committees. But there is no limit on total contributions by a PAC, nor on so-called independent expenditures (e.g., outlays on behalf of candidates without their cooperation or advance knowledge). Frequently, such outlays are used to attack candidates opposing the ones the PAC is directly supporting.

Some companies permit a PAC contributor to designate which party is to receive the money. More frequently, the PAC is allowed to use the money at its discretion. Decisions about which candidates will obtain PAC funds are usually made by special committees of the corporate PAC. In some cases, the PAC may not establish a formal committee. Instead, it will adopt the recommendations of a special adviser, such as the head of the Washington office or the director of government affairs.

Besides making cash payments directly to candidates, political action groups can provide support in other, often very important, ways. For example, a PAC may pay the salary and expenses of a consultant who goes into a congressional district to counsel a candidate or otherwise work on his or her behalf. It may conduct a target mailing to employees, shareholders, or others in a given congressional district, urging the election or defeat of a candidate. Such in-kind assistance can provide an opportunity for greater interaction with a candidate and staff than do ordinary cash contributions. Also, in-kind contributions can give the PAC greater control over how its help is used.

Soft Money

By the mid-1990s, a major loophole had developed by which corporations (and unions) could make virtually unlimited contributions to election campaigns. So-called "soft money" payments made directly to a political party are exempt from the size limitation because ostensibly the money is not going into the campaign of a specific candidate. In practice, the funds go to attack the candidate's opponent. The result is both to increase the money devoted to political campaigns and to accentuate the negative style of campaigning that increasingly characterizes political contests in the United States.

Party committees can accept unlimited amounts of soft money for "party-building" activities, and both major parties raise substantial amounts. In the 1995–1996 election cycle, Democrats reported contributions of $124 million in soft money while the Republicans raised $138 million.

Soft money has its origins in a 1979 campaign finance law (P.L. 96-187) allowing political parties to raise unlimited amounts of money for voter registration drives and get-out-the-vote efforts among their members. Over time, soft money has been used for airing commercials supporting or opposing a particular candidate or issue. The U.S. Supreme Court, in a series of decisions, has ruled that advertisements that did not specifically urge a vote for or against a candidate were not subject to the restrictions imposed by federal election laws.

Corporations and unions are required to disclose the amount of soft money spent only in regard to their express advocacy communications with members, but only when they exceed $2,000 per candidate, per election, and excluding communications devoted to other subjects.

The Development of PACs

In view of the public attention that has been devoted to business-sponsored PACs, it is intriguing to note how relatively few companies have set up such organizations. Not included on the list of corporate sponsors of PACs are such giants of American industry as Exxon, IBM, Ford, American Express, Monsanto, and Texaco. Indeed, many corporations consider direct political activity as inappropriate for a business firm. One business equipment manufacturer bluntly stated, "We do not feel we have the right to make political decisions with the money of our employees."[3] Other firms fear that the activity will be misunderstood and that they will be accused of exercising their financial influence in ways that are contrary to the public interest.

On the basis of Federal Election Commission data, it seems that business in general usually follows a predictable, low-risk pattern in its contributions. The bulk of the money in 1995–1996, for example, went to incumbents rather than challengers, in a ratio of more than 9 to 1 (in the case of union support, the ratio was 2 to 1). Business prefers to contribute to general elections rather than primaries or runoffs and helps less frequently in open-seat elections. Business groups are most apt to contribute to the highest ranking members of congressional committees who have jurisdiction over legislation of concern to the industry or company, regardless of the candidate's political philosophy or need for funds. Thus, many business political donations have the effect of maintaining access to current policy makers rather than of attempting to change the actual composition of government decision-making bodies.

Traditionally, Republican candidates have been supported more generously than Democrats, although the pattern has varied in recent years, as a result of the rising financial power of groups other than business. During the 1995–1996 political cycle, however, PACs contributed $118 million to Republican candidates and only $98 million to Democrats. Of the 10 senators who received the largest PAC contributions in 1995–1996, two were Democrats and eight were Republicans. The exact opposite occurred in the House of Representatives: the top 10 PAC recipients consisted of two Republicans and eight Democrats.

Indirect Political Contributions

Businesses can legally make indirect contributions to political parties. For example, corporate officers and directors may take positions in political parties, often in connection with fund-raising. Although these officials function in an individual capacity, their corporate affiliations usually are known, and their activities can result in political goodwill for the firm, at least in the case of winning candidates. However, corporations are rarely monolithic in the political sympathies of their individual executives, and frequently some members of a firm's management will actively support one candidate while others back the opponent.

There are many ways in which corporations can legally finance political involvement. They can advertise in convention and anniversary publications issued by political parties and even in national presidential convention programs—if that cost is deemed reasonable in light of the business the advertiser expects to gain. However, the Federal Election Commission currently prohibits political parties from accepting services, such as free automobiles or buses, that business firms had, at one time, customarily donated for use at national political conventions.

Members of Congress and state and local legislators, as well as candidates, may be invited to speak before trade associations, company management clubs, Chamber of Commerce groups, and similar business-oriented organizations. Until recently, their remuneration could range from merely having a convenient platform to present their views to generous honoraria. However, beginning in 1991, honoraria for members of Congress were prohibited as a result of special reforms enacted by Congress itself.

Any newspaper reader in recent years can readily recall numerous instances of flagrant abuse involving business and political campaigns—and attention to the less savory aspects of the subject is surely warranted. Nevertheless, it is useful to note that, even in politically active years, only a small portion of the officers and directors of the very largest industrial firms, including government contractors, contribute to political parties. Moreover, many experienced, political analysts contend that elected officials pay far more attention to the level of group influence within their state or district—and the potential for reprisals if they vote "wrong" in the eyes of a key constituency—than they do to financial contributions. Thus, although much attention is devoted to the support given by major defense contractors, the major concern of the congressional delegation from centers of defense production is the pleas of the large number of employees and their families who are voters in the district (or state).

Presidential election campaigns are financed primarily by the $3 checkoff on the federal individual income tax return. To be eligible to receive the Treasury funds, the candidates must agree to limit their spending to the amount of the grant and not to accept private contributions for their campaigns. However, political parties and independent groups—at the national, state, and local levels—may accept contributions for the various campaigns. This is where soft money plays such a key role.

Views on Business in Politics

Corporate political participation can be viewed as a continuum along which individual companies can be placed with regard to both the scope and the magnitude of their operations. Businesses in practice vary in their political efforts from no conscious participation by company executives to an occasional letter or phone call to a member of

Congress or a hundred-dollar campaign contribution to continuous and comprehensive government and electoral activity by political specialists on the company payroll.

Although most corporations engage in some form of participation in the political process, this activity varies substantially with a number of factors. These influences include the size of the firm, the degree of regulation of the enterprise by the government, and the extent to which company business and well-being depend on government decisions. The greater the importance of government to a firm's operations, the greater the likely scope and magnitude of its involvement in political activity. The larger the corporation, the more likely it is to attract the attention of government officials on such issues as taxation, pollution, and antitrust. The larger firm is also likely to have more resources to devote to political participation.

Smaller firms tend to work through the PACs of trade associations; larger companies are more likely to set up their own. Government involvement in business generates the basic pressure for business involvement in politics. Government contractors are more likely to sponsor PACs than companies selling mainly to private markets. Highly regulated firms tend to set up PACs at faster rates than entities less subject to government control. Recipients of special tax benefits and government subsidies are special candidates for political financing. Moreover, companies that face few competitors and operate in highly concentrated markets are more likely to see the benefits of political participation on behalf of their industry than firms in highly competitive markets with greater opportunity for the other firms in the industry to be "free riders."

Critics of the large amount of funds spent on election campaigns tend to focus on political action committees, especially those sponsored by business interests. While it is assumed that private donors are interested in a candidate's general philosophy and views on a range of issues, PACs are often seen as preoccupied with obtaining specific advantages. In the words of former Senator Robert Dole, "When PACs give money, they expect something in return other than good government."[4] At the very least, substantial PAC contributions bring the organization access to the elected official. Members of Congress rarely refuse to meet with the representatives of a group that supported their campaigns, although they may not necessarily follow the group's urging in voting. In the words of the late Justin Dart, former chairman of Dart & Kraft, "Talking to politicians is fine, but with a little money they hear you better."[5] A similar sentiment was expressed by a member of Congress to contributors, "My door is always open, but for you folks, it will be open just a little wider."[6]

But some perspective is useful on the comparative magnitude of PAC and other electioneering spending. The total of American political spending in the 1995–1996 election cycle—for presidential and congressional candidates, hard and soft money combined ($1,702 million)—did not quite equal the combined advertising budgets of six companies for a three-month period ($1,780 million). (See Table 18.2.) Moreover, even with huge advertising budgets, some products fail, as do some congressional candidates who outspend their opposition.

Attitudes toward PACs and other forms of financial contributions to election campaigns fall into two conflicting categories. One view is that these payments constitute a powerful potential for favoritism and corruption. Candidates are seen as changing their positions on public issues in order to attract the huge amounts of financing needed in current campaigns. As they have become larger, political contributions have come under substantial attack. According to one veteran representative, the way to get a member of

TABLE 18.2 Federal Campaign Spending Versus Six Companies with Highest Advertising Budgets (in millions)

1995–1996 Election Cycle Spending		1996 1st Quarter Advertising Expenses	
Category	*Amount*	*Company*	*Amount*
Presidential campaign[1]	$ 153	General Motors	$ 408
Congressional campaigns	790	Procter & Gamble	355
Democratic party	166	Philip Morris	330
Democratic party soft money	124	Chrysler	250
Republican party	331	Ford Motor	241
Republican party soft money	138	Pepsi Co.	196
Total	$1,702	Total	$1,780

[1]This figure represents public dollars earmarked for the presidential campaign and distributed to the major political parties. Ross Perot also received $29 million in public funds for the 1996 election cycle.

Source: U.S. Federal Election Commission and company reports.

the House interested in a particular issue is to "let him know you represent a political action committee that is going to be active in the next election." A key industry CEO made a similar point, "Politics is becoming a cash-and-carry game."[7]

The contrasting view sees private financing of election campaigns as a much more benign instrument, bringing more persons into the political process and thereby making government more representative. For example, then-Senator David Durenberger (Republican of Minnesota) was able to hold off wealthy challenger Mark Dayton, who had contributed nearly $7 million to his own campaign, largely by raising more than $1 million in PAC contributions. A different rationale for political contributions has been advanced by Representative Barney Frank (Democrat of Massachusetts): "I don't think that votes follow money. I think that money follows votes."[8] Moreover, PACs are no longer the dominant contributors to presidential campaigns. Government financing (via the voluntary checkoff on the federal personal income tax return) has replaced private funding in the general election period, aside from the soft-money loophole.

In 1997, Senators John McCain (Republican of Arizona) and Russell Feingold (Democrat of Wisconsin) joined forces in pushing for an outright ban on soft-money donations to political parties. The opponents of such a restriction emphasized the need to encourage political speech and thus the financing required.

Criticism of the role of money in politics should be tempered by the fact that they are not monolithic but represent varied and frequently contending interests. Thus, there is competition between business and labor, between liberals and conservatives, and between businesses in competing industries. (See the box "The Variety of Business PACs.")

The diverging business positions on matters of public policy was summed up by Don Cogman of MAPCO's PAC: "We don't agree with Mobil Oil, which is in our same business, much less International Paper, which ain't." He notes that their agendas differed and that they often take opposite sides on specific policy issues.[9]

The Variety of Business PACs

The PACs established by industries and individual companies constitute a fascinating variety:

- Bread-PAC by the American Bakers Association
- EggPAC by the United Egg Producers
- Fish-PAC by the National Fisheries Institute
- Food PAC by the Food Marketing Institute
- Bank PAC by the American Bankers Association
- Whata-PAC by Whataburger, Inc.
- NUTPAC by the Peanut Butter and Nut Processors Association
- Six-PAC by the beer distributors
- Phil-PAC by Philip Morris
- NEPAC by Northrop Grumman
- T-PAC by Travelers Corporation
- FEPAC by Federal Express
- Penney PAC by J. C. Penney Co.
- Torch-PAC by Torchmark Corporation
- AF-PAC by American Family Insurance
- LEPAC by Litton Industries
- CIPAC by Cooper Industries

Source: U.S. Federal Election Commission.

POLITICAL CONTRIBUTIONS BY OTHER GROUPS

Because of the amount of public attention given to the financial support of politics by business, the public tends to overlook the large efforts by other interest groups. Table 18.3 shows the 20 largest PACs in 1995–1996. It is intriguing to note that 12 unions made the list and only one company and one business association. Many individual companies have established sizable PACs. Yet the largest concentrations of financial power are represented by other interests, such as real estate and insurance agents, senior citizens, doctors and dentists, farmers, builders, unions, and gun owners.

The aggregate amount of financial contributions by business firms to political candidates should not be underestimated, however. Although the funds raised by individual business PACs are, on the average, smaller than those raised by unions, the aggregate amounts raised are larger. For example, in 1995–1996, the contributions of the corporate PACs totaled $78 million and those of the labor unions came to $46 million.

Much of labor's election effort does not show up in official reports and hence is not subject to legal limitations. Examples include the virtual full-time assignment of

TABLE 18.3 Twenty Largest PACs in 1995–1996

Rank	Organization	Category	Contribution
1.	Teamsters Union	Union	$2,647,165
2.	Government Employees Union	Union	2,513,821
3.	United Auto Workers	Union	2,475,819
4.	American Medical Association	Professions	2,442,576
5.	National Education Association	Union	2,356,006
6.	National Auto Dealers Association	Business	2,346,925
7.	Association of Trial Lawyers of America	Professions	2,341,938
8.	Laborers Union	Union	2,172,450
9.	International Brotherhood of Electric Workers	Union	2,171,262
10.	National Association of Realtors	Professions	2,099,683
11.	Food and Commercial Workers Union	Union	2,030,795
12.	Machinists/Aerospace Workers Union	Union	2,021,175
13.	United Parcel Service	Business	1,791,147
14.	National Association of Letter Carriers	Union	1,723,228
15.	American Institute of CPAs	Professions	1,690,925
16.	American Federation of Teachers	Union	1,619,635
17.	Marine Engineers Union	Union	1,591,365
18.	Carpenters Union	Union	1,571,466
19.	National Rifle Association	Gun Owners	1,560,871
20.	United Steelworkers	Union	1,524,650

Source: U.S. Federal Election Commission.

union organizers and clerks to get-out-the-vote duty. The AFL-CIO reports that its state campaign coordinator is usually the principal officer of the AFL-CIO in the state. The details are not left to chance, as shown by the organization's formal seven-step plan for election campaigning.[10]

Step 1. The campaign coordinator meets with the regional director of the AFL-CIO's Committee on Political Action and other union officials to plan the campaign (120 to 180 days before the election).

Step 2. They recruit helpers and volunteers, including phone bank supervisors, and arrange installations of phones (80 to 90 days before the election).

Step 3. They train and assign phone operations and begin mailings to undecided voters (60 to 70 days before the election).

Step 4. Volunteers begin distributing flyers for candidates and sign up supporters (30 to 40 days before the election).

Step 5. Volunteers call back the undecided voters; more mailings are sent, and handbills are prepared (12 to 20 days before the election).

Step 6. Door-to-door canvassing is conducted using handbills, and more calls are made (4 days before the election).

Step 7. Direct efforts are made to get out the vote of potential supporters of union-endorsed candidates (election day).

Although most of the campaign workers are volunteers, the union effort is quite professional. Volunteers are trained in how to call union members and record their responses on scanner cards. The undecided voters are asked what issues are most important to them and are sent "persuasion mailings" based on their responses. As an incentive to volunteers, incentives are provided by the local unions in the form of tickets to a ball game, a play, or a musical event.[11]

In contrast, it is difficult to find companies or trade associations that assign their executives to full-time campaigning as part of their paid work or that devote their reports to shareholders and executives to the campaigning in which union publications openly engage. There is nothing illegal in these union activities per se. But their widespread existence provides further encouragement for business to rely on financial contributions as a counterweight.

In response to the public concern over improper corporate political activities, some companies have adopted more open and at times rather severe policies on the subject of campaign contributions. DuPont discloses all U.S. political contributions by its top executives. In addition, all solicitations for more than $1,000 and responses to those requests are made public for inspection by reporters, shareholders, and employees. Exxon prohibits all corporate contributions to political candidates or to political parties. This policy extended to state, local, and foreign elections, where such political support by business is often legal.

A more radical approach, recommended by some observers who are unhappy at all interest group political contributions, is to rely almost entirely on governmental financing of election campaigns.[12] Such proposals ignore the tendency of government financing, sooner or later, to become accompanied by government strings on private discretion.

STATE AND LOCAL ELECTION CAMPAIGNS

The role of business (and of other interest groups) in state and local election campaigns is governed by those units of government, and the policies they follow differ substantially. Most of them are more lenient than the federal government. Altogether, 31 states allow direct contributions by corporations in their state and local elections, although specific restrictions vary. For example, all but eight of the states limit the size of corporate gifts, but there is no uniformity on the dollar amount of the legal limits.

The states that allow unlimited company contributions to their political campaigns are Colorado, Idaho, Illinois, Missouri, New Mexico, Oregon, Utah, and Virginia. Except for Oregon, each of these states also permits unions to make unlimited political gifts, as do Alabama and Mississippi.

At the other extreme, 10 states maintain restrictions as tough as those of the federal government. The following states prohibit either candidates or parties from accepting financial support from corporations or unions: Arizona, Connecticut, New Hampshire, North Carolina, North Dakota, Ohio, Pennsylvania, Rhode Island, Wisconsin, and Wyoming.

INTERNATIONAL COMPARISONS

On the surface, it would seem that the U.S. government is at least as generous in providing financing of national elections as are many of the other industrialized nations. For example, presidential candidates who meet statutory requirements for obtaining sufficient financial support from a variety of voters then qualify for generous federal financing. In an effort to provide a level playing field, the law provides that recipients of the federal money not raise any private funds. Such government support is limited to the race for president.

In contrast, Japan and the United Kingdom do not provide direct public financing. In the case of Germany, France, and Italy, the government reimburses candidates according to the number of votes received. Denmark provides an allowance to the political parties, based on their strength in the previous election. Some of these countries—the United Kingdom, France, and Japan—also limit the amount of fundraising or the amount of spending allowed on political campaigns.

However, indirectly each of those nations provides very important assistance to political candidates in a way that the United States does not: free time on television (which is the single most expensive election campaign item). Some countries provide that each party gets free and equal time; that is the procedure in France and on public stations in Italy and Denmark. In Britain, the TV time is allocated according to the party's strength in the previous election. Germany also provides free time to candidates on public stations, while Japan gives some free time for speeches by candidates and bars negative advertising.

Conclusions

Business executives, as well as the public, might bear in mind Peter Drucker's thoughts on the subject of business in politics: "If I were to have a criticism of the American businessman, it is that he has made no attempt to understand the political process. He attempts to influence it without understanding it."[13]

Some business organizations are attempting to meet Drucker's challenge. Many trade associations regularly sponsor political campaign-management seminars. Designed to be nonpartisan in nature, the seminars typically are aimed at business executives who become involved in campaigns for public office at various levels—federal, state, and local. The sessions are aimed at potential candidates, campaign managers, and finance directors, as well as rank-and-file volunteers. Staffed by professional campaign consultants, the seminars show the various steps in developing a campaign, including administrative and financial aspects. Table 18.4 reproduces the program outline of a political campaign management seminar of the U.S. Chamber of Commerce. The sessions are devoted to techniques of political campaigning and avoid advocating positions on specific issues or supporting individual candidates or political parties.

In viewing the entire subject of participation in politics, a word of caution is in order. An unwary management can get into trouble by naively participating in the funding of election campaigns. Contributions to political action groups are required to be voluntary, without pressure on employees in solicitation. Heavy-handed solicitation on the part of some firms could cause a backlash, both within the company and in the public arena.

Some analysts have pointed to the fundamental pressures for continuing and increasing financial contributions to election campaigns by business and other interest groups: the desire to obtain more of the largesse available from government treasuries and to avoid the restrictions that may result from new government regulations. As the size and power of public-sector departments and agencies continue to increase,

TABLE 18.4	Seminar on Political Campaign Management

Program Outline

Research and surveys
Planning strategy
Fund-raising, advertising, and publicity
Direct mail
Campaign organization
Volunteer activities
Graphics and photography
Campaign law
Computers and automated devices
Profile of a successful campaign
Reaching special classifications
    Absentee ballots
    Campus votes
    Rural votes
    Votes in high-rise apartments
Print and electronic advertising

Source: U.S. Chamber of Commerce.

it can be expected that more of the private sector's resources will be devoted to influencing the political process. To remind the reader of the obvious, every dollar spent by the federal government ends up in somebody's pocket as a salary, subsidy, purchase, loan, or transfer payment. Of obvious economic benefit also are tax provisions that induce customers to purchase a specific product, regulations that favor the "ins" against the "outs," and governmental credit programs that channel funds to favored groups.

Surely, the interactions between campaign financing and politics have been controversial for centuries. In 1750, when George Washington easily won his seat in the Virginia House of Burgesses, opponents criticized the amount disbursed during the campaign. Some attention was paid to the 150 gallons of liquor that Washington distributed among the district's 391 voters in his effort to gain office.[14] Perhaps Will Rogers deserves the last word on the subject: "Politics has got so expensive, it takes lots of money to even get beat with nowadays."

Notes

1. Catherine Morrison, *Managing Corporate Political Action Committees* (New York: Conference Board, 1986), pp. v–vi.
2. Computed from Federal Election Commission data.
3. Quoted in Morrison, *Managing Corporate PACs,* p. 3.
4. Quoted in Irwin Ross, "Why PACs Spell Trouble," *Reader's Digest,* July 1983, p. 108.
5. Quoted in Tom Richman, "Picking a PAC," *Inc.,* August 1982, p. 30.
6. Quoted in Morrison, *Managing Corporate PACs,* p. 23.
7. Randy Huwa, "Political Action Committees," *Business Forum,* Winter 1984, p. 13.

8. Quoted in Morrison, *Managing Corporate PACs,* p. 25.

9. Larry J. Sabato, "PAC-Man Goes to Washington," *Across the Board,* October 1984, p. 25.

10. Michael Byrne, "Getting Out the Vote," *AFL-CIO News,* June 25, 1992, p. 6.

11. Byrne, p. 7.

12. *Democratically Financed Congressional Elections* (Deerfield, MA: Working Group on Electoral Democracy, 1993).

13. "Inside Peter Drucker," *Nation's Business,* March 1974, p. 63.

14. Andrea Segedy, "Why We Have PACs," *Business Forum,* Winter 1984, p. 8.

PART SIX

The Future of the Corporation

Business and government both exist in a society in which a variety of interest groups attempt to impose their ideas on others. To the extent that business voluntarily responds to these other viewpoints, it may reduce the likelihood of additional governmental action. As shown in Part Six, in changing itself by adjusting to and complying with external pressures and desires, the corporation assures its continuance as a vital institution in modern society.

CHAPTER 19

Corporate Activists and Corporate Governance

Over the years, many special groups of shareholders—especially state and municipal pension funds, churches, unions, and other institutional investors—have taken an increasingly active interest in the decisions of major corporations in the United States. Using their stock ownership, they have used the corporation's voting procedures to raise a variety of questions, ranging from broad social and political concerns to specific matters of business performance.

Shareholder activism has gone through several stages, starting with matters of relevance to smaller investors in the 1930s and 1940s and moving to the violent social activism of the 1960s and 1970s. In the 1980s and 1990s, a maturation has been occurring, in which dissident shareholder groups raise issues of corporate governance and respond to concerns of employees and other corporate stakeholders.

Government is not the only vehicle that citizens can use to control or influence the actions of private business. Many citizen groups have learned that, at least to some extent, they can participate in a business's internal decision-making process. Some radical activists would use government's authority to charter corporations to alter the basic function and organization of the modern business firm and, in the process, increase their access to the centers of economic power. Specific suggestions range from restructuring company boards of directors to mandating business to conduct various activities deemed to constitute "social responsibility."

The governance of corporations in the United States is regulated primarily by the requirements contained in state corporation statutes. While these laws generally provide broad discretion to directors and officers in the normal running of business operations, they vary in the degree of power given to minority shareholders and in the types of company action requiring shareholder approval. Delaware, the state in which most large firms are incorporated, minimizes restrictions on company managements. Some other states, notably California, maintain a policy favoring shareholders at the expense of management discretion.[1]

In addition, the U.S. Securities and Exchange Commission regulates many aspects of corporate reporting as well as the issuance of company stock for interstate sale and, as discussed later, the voting process and related procedures at corporate annual meetings.

THE CRITICS OF THE CORPORATION

To many critics of business, the management of large corporations are oligarchies, responsible to no one but themselves. Shareholders are seen as largely at the mercy of the management, their only power being to sell their stock in a company when they do not approve of its activities. The typical stockholder is viewed as neither capable of understanding nor interested in the actual business of the company in which he or she owns stock.

Corporate boards of directors are thus characterized as self-perpetuating groups, accountable to themselves or to the chief executives who select them. Because the critics see corporations as private governments operating under legal constraints that are for the most part irrelevant, they advocate a variety of changes in the way corporations are governed. Although there is considerable factual basis for some of these views, this approach ignores the very active "market" for corporate control in which dissident shareholder groups attempt, often successfully, to wrest control of major corporations from their managements. Moreover, with top management compensation increasingly geared to the market price of the company's stock, large institutional holders as well as influential stock analysts have ready access to management attention.

Ralph Nader's Proposals

Ralph Nader and his colleagues have developed ambitious and far-reaching proposals to restructure the American corporation.[2] To achieve what he terms the "popularization" of the corporation, Nader advocates rewriting the rules governing corporation chartering. Under his proposed Corporate Democracy Act, the federal government would assume the chartering power now residing in the individual states. Nader wants to install full-time outside directors who would take an active role in the governance of the corporation.

Along these lines, the charter of the Equitable Life Insurance Company requires the Chief Justice of New Jersey to appoint several outside directors. Over the years, these appointees have included women civic leaders and physicians, who are far from typical corporate directors. Under the Nader approach, individual directors would be assigned responsibility for specific areas of concern, such as the environment or employee relations. In his concept, federal chartering would develop a "constitutionalism" for corporate employees and provide various protections for whistle blowers who object to specific company activities. He also urges a mandatory mail plebiscite of shareholders on all "fundamental" transactions.

The sum of his reforms, according to Nader, is a concept of *social bankruptcy* whereby a company would be thrown into receivership if it failed to meet its "social" obligations.

The Geneen-Williams Proposals

More modest—yet quite substantial—suggestions for change in the structure of the American corporation have come from several outspoken former corporate CEOs. The two that have received most attention are Harold Geneen, retired CEO of ITT, and Harold Williams, former chairman of the Securities and Exchange Commission and former CEO of Norton Simon. Williams contends that the ideal board of directors would include only one company officer, the chief executive. All other board members, including the chairman, would be chosen from outside the company. Williams's concept of outside directors excludes bankers, lawyers, or anyone else having business dealings with the company. In his view, outside-dominated boards could do a better job of representing the stockholders' long-term interests than executives who are responsible for day-to-day management.

There is considerable precedent for an outside director chairing the board meetings. That is the standard procedure at nonprofit institutions such as hospitals, museums, and universities, quite a few of which rival in size and complexity all but the largest for-profit corporations. Also, many Western European companies normally follow this practice, as do many American companies with concentrated ownership on the part of venture capitalists and other outside investors.

Williams, unlike Nader, would not allocate individual directorships to representatives of employees, consumers, minorities, or other groups. "It would be disastrous. . . . Constituency representation . . . makes the board a political body," according to Williams. Does his proposal infringe on private property rights? The former SEC chairman states that corporations are more than economic institutions owned by shareholders: "Corporate America is too important, and perceived as too powerful, to fail to address the kinds of issues that are noneconomic."[3]

Geneen would go further than Williams, barring all members of management from serving on the board of the corporation for which they work. The CEO and other members of management would continue to attend board meetings, but they would be there to report to the board and to explain their actions.[4]

In a variation of this approach, Walter J. Salmon, of the Harvard Business School and a veteran board member, suggests that the boards of larger corporations be limited to three inside directors: the chief executive (CEO), the chief operating officer (COO), and the chief financial officer (CFO). As the current leaders of the corporation, the CEO and COO are there to communicate, explain, and justify strategic direction to the outside directors. Because CFOs share fiduciary responsibility with the directors for the financial conduct of the corporation, they should also have a seat on the board.[5]

In 1997, the influential California Public Employees' Retirement System (Calpers) developed a set of proposals to restructure corporate boards that went into greater detail than most earlier suggestions. With $113 billion in assets at stake, Calpers urged strengthening the role of the outside directors in many ways:

- *Adopt a more stringent definition of independent director.* Such a board member would not be allowed to serve more than 10 years, hold a personal services contract with the company, or be affiliated with a nonprofit group that gets "significant" contributions from the company.

- *The chairman should be an outside director.* Alternatively, the board should select an independent "lead" director to deal with the chairman. Independent directors should meet alone at least once a year.

- *No director should serve on more than three boards.* Term limits should also be set as well as minimum experience guidelines. Pensions for directors should be eliminated, and no more than 10 percent of a board's directors should be older than 70.

- *A formal program, in addition to the annual meeting, should be set for shareholders to communicate with directors.*[6]

It does not seem likely that any of these sets of detailed proposals for the reform of corporate governance will be adopted on a compulsory basis. Nevertheless, voluntarily, many boards have been adopting reforms. In the United Kingdom, the influential Cadbury Committee on Financial Aspects of Corporate Governance has urged a variety of reforms, including limiting nonmanagement (outside) directors to service on one board (see Table 19.1).

TABLE 19.1 The Code of Best Practice for Corporate Governance

Highlights of the United Kingdom's "Cadbury Report"

Boards of Directors	*Outside Directors*	*Inside Directors*	*Reporting and Controls*
The board should meet regularly, retain full and effective control over the company, and monitor the executive management. Where the chairman is also the CEO, there should be a strong and independent element on the board, with a recognized senior member. The board should include outside directors of sufficient caliber and number for their views to carry significant weight in the board's decisions. The board should have a formal schedule of matters specifically reserved to it for decision to ensure that the direction and control of the company is firmly in its hands.	Outside directors should bring an independent judgment to bear on issues of strategy, performance, resources, key appointments, and standards of conduct. The majority of the board should be independent of management and free from any business relationship that could materially interfere with the exercise of their independent judgment. Outside directors should be appointed for specified terms. Reappointment should not be automatic. Outside directors should be selected through a formal process. Their appointment should be a matter for the board as a whole.	There should be full and clear disclosure of total compensation of the chairman and highest-paid inside director, including pension contributions and stock options, salary, and performance-related elements. The basis on which performance is measured should be explained. Their pay should be subject to the recommendations of a compensation committee made up wholly or mainly of outside directors. Inside directors' employment contracts should not exceed three years without shareholders' approval.	It is the board's duty to present a balanced and understandable assessment of the company's position. The board should ensure that an objective and professional relationship is maintained with the auditors. The board should establish an audit committee of at least three outside directors with written terms of reference that deal clearly with its authority and duties. The directors should report on the effectiveness of the company's system of internal control. The directors should report that the business is a going concern, with supporting assumptions or qualifications as necessary.

Source: Report of the Committee on the Financial Aspects of Corporate Governance (The "Cadbury Report").

Responses by the Corporation

Most changes in corporate governance take place voluntarily, in part to avoid overt action by government. A significant voluntary shift has occurred in the composition of the boards of directors of American companies. Outside directors—those who are not members of management—have become a large majority of most boards of large companies in the United States. By 1992, three-fourths of the average corporate board consisted of outside directors.

The larger the firm, the more likely the predominance of outside directors. In fact, the biggest companies were the first to name a majority of outside directors. Simultaneously, the prevalence of "dependent" outside directors (those who also provide services to the company) has diminished. In the 1970s, the average board included a commercial banker, an attorney, or both. That is true in only a small minority of instances in the 1990s.

Some movement is also being made voluntarily toward the Calpers view on board governance. By 1996, 36 percent of the largest corporations had appointed lead directors, up from 21 percent in 1995.[7] A broader diversity of backgrounds is also evident in the types of persons currently serving on corporate boards. Increased numbers of directors have public service, academic, and scientific experience. Boards now also include significant percentages of women, minorities, and academics—as well as directors from other countries (mainly Canada and Western Europe).

In 1996, 84 percent of the Fortune 500 companies had at least one woman on their board. Thirty-six percent of the companies—181 corporations—had two or more female directors. Only one had a majority of women on its board—Golden West Financial Corporation of Oakland, California.[8]

The rise of powerful board committees is also continuing, mainly on a voluntary basis. As recently as 1973, only one-half of large U.S. corporations had auditing committees. Auditing committees of boards of directors now have become a universal phenomenon. These financial-oversight bodies are usually composed entirely of outside directors. That is an absolute requirement for firms listed on the New York Stock Exchange. Audit committees have direct access to both the outside auditing firm that reviews the company's financial records and procedures and the firm's own internal audit staff. This information enables these committees to review the financial aspects of corporate operations in great detail and to probe into suspicious situations.

The boards of directors of most of the larger corporations have set up nominating committees to propose both candidates for the board and senior officers. These committees generally have a strong majority of outside directors, typically four out of five. However, these statistics do little to illuminate the continuing powerful role of the CEO in initiating or approving committee selections. In practice, most outside directors are selected by the chairman/CEO and in virtually all cases, he or she must be agreeable to their appointment.

In most large companies, compensation committees of the board evaluate the performance of top executives and determine the terms and conditions of their employment. These committees are composed largely or entirely of outside directors. However, most "comp" committees rely extensively on outside consultants hired by the management. Their surveys of the pay and perks of comparable positions in other companies and industries set the framework for committee deliberations.

On average, about one out of five of the larger companies has established public policy committees of their boards. These units give board-level attention to company policies and performance on subjects of special public concern. Topics with which public policy committees often deal include affirmative action and equal employment opportunity, employee health and safety, company impact on the environment, corporate political activities, consumer affairs, and business ethics. Some critics contend that this new activity may be mainly a sop to the proponents of greater corporate social responsibility rather than a substantive change in business decision making. Nevertheless, the potential for broadening the horizons of corporate policy deliberation is now present.

Despite the rising number of outside directors and special committees of corporate boards, in most cases the center of power remains with the management. CEOs serve as chairman of the board in 80 percent of the larger corporations, and they set the agenda and conduct the board meetings. Many of the directors they choose are CEOs of other companies who tend to be inherently sympathetic in their response to their colleagues' proposals.

Simultaneous with the expansion of the role of outside directors, a related development has been taking place: the rise of the corporate activist. As we will see, the role of the activist has undergone fundamental metamorphoses over the years, and an important feedback effect is evident in the governance of some of the larger companies.

THE RISE OF CORPORATE ACTIVISM

Raising Investor Issues (the Business Activists of the 1930s and 1940s)

In the 1930s, two individual shareholders, Lewis and John Gilbert, began attending corporate annual meetings and exercising the dormant right of stockholders to question management. They focused on issues of corporate policy of interest to investors, such as financial disclosure, stock reinvestment plans, and cumulative voting for directors (which would enable minority shareholders to concentrate their votes on one candidate). The Gilberts introduced motions on the floor and otherwise highlighted the power of the stockholders.[9]

In 1942, the Securities and Exchange Commission adopted a regulation that promoted the role of the small holder. SEC Rule 14a-8 requires companies to include shareholder resolutions in proxy statements routinely sent to each holder of common stock if the proposals are proper subjects for consideration by all shareholders. Thus, corporate activists were given access to all other shareholders at the company's expense. They also were assured some minimum amount of time at company annual meetings to discuss these issues.

As originally formulated, SEC Rule 14a-8 gave management three principal grounds for excluding proxy proposals from minority shareholders.

1. Those that, under the law of the state in which the corporation is chartered, are "not a proper subject for action by security holders."

2. Those relating to "the conduct of the ordinary business operations" of the corporation.

3. Those that "clearly appear [to be] submitted . . . primarily for the purpose of promoting general economic, political, racial, religious, social or similar causes."

Many corporate practices now considered traditional were pioneered by the Gilberts in the 1930s and 1940s. These include holding annual meetings at sites convenient to large numbers of shareholders, issuing reports on actions taken at the annual meeting, and disclosing substantial amounts of financial data. Because the Gilberts were persistent questioners of the amounts of executive salaries and bonuses, they came to be known as corporate gadflies. Nevertheless, the actions taken by the Gilberts were virtually all designed to promote the interests of stockholders as stockholders. Subsequently, however, the enhanced powers of individual shareholders were transformed into mechanisms for achieving very different objectives.

Raising Social Issues (the Social Activists of the 1960s and 1970s)

One of the first efforts to mobilize stockholders to achieve a social objective was launched in 1966 by activist Saul Alinsky. His aim was to convince Eastman Kodak to adopt a preferential hiring plan, whereby the company would train 600 unskilled, unemployed African-Americans over an 18-month period, to qualify for entry-level positions. When negotiations with Kodak broke down, Alinsky brought the battle to the company's 1967 annual meeting.

Buses of demonstrators were met by state troopers and Kodak guards. Several hundred picketed outside the meeting. Most of the session was devoted to the controversy. Kodak's board chairman recognized "that we have a continuing responsibility to you, the shareowners, and to our employees and customers, as well as to the community at large." Two months later, Kodak agreed to a settlement, although much less than Alinsky's demands.[10]

In retrospect, the Kodak episode marked an important turn in stockholder activism. The issue raised was irrelevant to traditional shareholders' concerns and was activated by purchasing just 10 shares of Kodak stock in order to gain admission to the annual meeting. But subsequently, the effort gained the support of church groups that owned more than 34,000 shares of the company's stock.

In 1968, the Medical Committee for Human Rights (which had received a gift of several Dow Company shares) requested that, as Dow shareholders, they be allowed to ask the board of directors to prohibit sales of napalm for military purposes. The SEC upheld Dow's refusal to include the matter in its proxy statement. But in 1970, a U.S. Circuit Court of Appeals reversed the agency's decision. Thus, the corporate proxy statement was opened up to social responsibility resolutions by minority shareholders.

The high point, or perhaps the low point, of Vietnam War activism aimed at corporate governance occurred at the 1970 annual meeting of Honeywell, a military supplier. More than a thousand demonstrators congregated outside the company's headquarters, and many tried to storm the entrance. About three hundred of the protestors, some stripped to the waist and daubed in red and white grease paint, managed to get inside. Such mob scenes were repeated elsewhere but with few positive results in terms of company responses.

Campaign GM   In contrast, Campaign GM represented a more carefully prepared effort, orchestrated by a nonprofit organization called the Project on Corporate Responsibility. It was a watershed for shareholder activism, for the first time successfully employing the proxy machinery to confront management on social issues. By virtue of its ownership of 12 shares of the company's stock, the campaign succeeded in getting two proposals included in the company's 1970 proxy statement:

1. To add three public-interest representatives to the GM board of directors. The campaign headquarters also named its likely nominees: a consumer advocate, an environmental specialist, and an African American.

2. To establish a shareholder committee on corporate responsibility, to be composed of 15 to 25 representatives of environmental, civil rights, labor, academic, and other groups. They would be chosen by a group consisting of a member of GM's board and representatives of the United Auto Workers Union and Campaign GM. The shareholder committee would report on the company's efforts to reduce pollution, develop safer products, encourage opportunities for minorities, and facilitate low-cost mass-transit.

In contrast to its stand in the Dow case, the SEC upheld the position of Campaign GM. This development opened up corporate proxy machinery to public-interest proposals. The SEC in effect determined that proposals with a clear social purpose did not automatically violate its Rule 14a-8. Campaign GM dominated the 1970 annual meeting of General Motors although both of its proposals were overwhelmingly defeated. Neither received the then minimum 3 percent vote that would have made it eligible for resubmission the next year. In the months that followed, the company took several steps toward meeting Campaign GM's demands, although indirectly.

The company created the first public policy committee of the board of directors of a major U.S. corporation. The committee's charter is very broad, covering instituting inquiries into every phase of the corporation's business activities that relate to matters of public policy and making recommendations on changes it deems appropriate to management or the full board of directors. Many other companies have since created board committees with such titles as "public policy," "corporate responsibility," and "public issues."

From the viewpoint of corporate governance, one of the more lasting impacts of Campaign GM was to motivate churches and other nonprofit and charitable institutions to use their corporate holdings to raise social policy questions at corporate annual meetings, especially via the proxy statement. In retrospect, the so-called "Wall Street rule"—that institutional investors register their disagreement with a company's policies and management by selling their stock—was badly breached.

Other Social Issues   The volume of public-interest resolutions appearing on corporate proxies has become substantial, and the issues covered have varied. In the 1970s, the social concerns raised at corporate annual meetings included terminating military production, improving consumer and environmental protection, increasing minority employment, and enhancing corporate accountability. By the early 1980s, the subjects covered an even wider terrain, ranging from environmental impacts to minority employment and purchasing practices to conversion of defense production to civilian uses.

Most shareholders ignore the agenda of the activists. In fact, they often get impatient at annual meetings when dissident shareholders raise questions that most owners of the company's stock do not deem relevant to the welfare of the company and especially of its stockholders. Corporate activists usually are pleased if they get 6 percent of the vote—the minimum amount needed to be able to resubmit the proposal the following year. However, as seen more recently, when issues directly involving corporate governance are raised, they receive much more shareholder support than do social questions.

The continuing importance of social issues was demonstrated in 1993 when a major customer of Baxter International, a large hospital supply company, reduced its purchases because of its unhappiness with Baxter's "ethics and business practices." The triggering event was the company's violation of the law against cooperating with the Arab boycott of Israel. The customer, Premier Hospitals Alliance, makes purchases in behalf of 150 hospitals.

Shifting to Economic Concerns (the Economic Activists of the 1980s and 1990s)

In recent years, the focus of many minority shareholders at annual meetings has shifted to cover ways of improving the economic performance of the business. With layoffs and plant closings becoming key issues, labor unions have become more involved in questions of corporate governance.

In 1983, the Securities and Exchange Commission tightened the rules for minority shareholders proposing proxy resolutions. Anyone advancing such a proposal must own, for one year or more, at least $1,000 of the company's stock or 1 percent of the stock outstanding, whichever is smaller. In addition, the minimum vote needed to resubmit a defeated proposal was raised from 3 percent to 6 percent in the second year and 10 percent in remaining years. The new rules also prevent any group from submitting more than one proposal to a company each year; the previous limit had been two. The revised SEC rules permit the exclusion of proposals that relate to operations that account for less than 5 percent of a company's assets, earnings, and sales and that are not otherwise significantly related to a company's business. Also, the corporate management can reject any proposal that deals with "substantially the same subject matter" as an earlier proposal that failed to gain enough votes to qualify for a place on the proxy in the coming year.

Nevertheless, individual shareholders continue to offer proposals for consideration at annual meetings, often as a way of getting public attention to their views. (See the box "Example of Shareholder Proposal.")

The new rules were adopted by the SEC in an effort to reduce frivolous proposals that do not have significant support among shareholders and to limit the use of the proxy machinery to people who have a genuine economic stake in the performance of the corporation. Previously, a person or group could buy free access to a company's proxy statement and its shareholders in order to publicize a social policy or other cause merely by acquiring a share of stock the day before a proposal was submitted. Despite these changes, corporate annual meetings and proxy statements are not likely to return to the relative quiet of the 1950s.

The SEC's changes have tended to weed out "cranks" who buy a few shares of stock just to pester the management about their pet peeves. Also, the circus atmosphere of the 1970s has disappeared at corporate annual meetings. However, church and other nonprofit groups with large investments have not been affected by the new SEC rules. They continue to be active users of corporate proxies to raise serious issues of public concern.

Example of Shareholder Proposal:
Nuclear Power

Proposal

Whereas:

The last viable U.S. nuclear power plant order was placed in October 1973; all subsequent orders were canceled because nuclear power is acknowledged to be dirty, dangerous and expensive;

General Electric is actively seeking foreign markets for nuclear reactors;

Nuclear fuel sales and reactor operation abroad provide material for possible diversion to weapons programs, and in spite of customer countries possibly being signatories of the Non-Proliferation Treaty, there is no enforceable way to prevent this diversion;

There is still no resolution for the safe isolation of radioactive wastes that must be sequestered from the environment for thousands of years;

The inordinate expense of nuclear power plants can threaten the fiscal equilibrium of customer countries, and jeopardize payment to GE; and

A serious accident at a GE reactor abroad could cause severe adverse economic, legal and health repercussions that would adversely affect the company;

Therefore be it resolved that the shareholders request the Board of Directors determine that GE will no longer seek new nuclear reactor and nuclear fuel sales abroad, and instead, promote the sale of safer, lower-risk, energy-efficient alternate generating systems to foreign markets.

Supporting Statement: The Nuclear Regulatory Commission has no technical specifications governing design or siting and no oversight on construction or operations of reactors for export. Compared to the United States, most customer countries have less stringent regulations, fewer trained personnel and less operating experience. The technology is sufficiently complex and hazardous that it is difficult to maintain an adequate level of safety even by our own experienced technicians. The potential for serious accidents is very clear.

Nuclear power is in great financial distress domestically in spite of continuing heavy government subsidies. Expansion of nuclear power to additional foreign markets, particularly developing countries, enlarges the pool of possible economic distress. Even government subsidies now in place for the export of reactors may not be maintained.

Nuclear power's bomb proliferation potential, the mounting evidence of adverse biological effects of radiation, the unresolved problem of nuclear waste disposal, and strong public opposition are additional reasons for the Company to cease the promotion of this technology abroad.

Exporting nuclear power, with its possible catastrophic consequences either as power plants or weapons, could threaten the financial integrity of the Company and is socially irresponsible.

Management Response

Nuclear power makes a significant contribution to meeting the world's demand for electricity. In 1996, approximately 17% of the world's electrical generating capacity came from nuclear plants. The Nuclear Regulatory Commission in the United States, and similar regulatory bodies in other countries, have the ongoing responsibility to ensure that nuclear facilities operate safely.

The major focus of GE's profitable nuclear business today is to provide nuclear fuel and plant support services with the aim of enhancing safe and efficient utility operations. These products and services should be available to utility customers throughout the world who need and want them. Your Board believes it is also appropriate for GE to participate in the development of advanced designs for nuclear generating plants for sale to utility customers in areas of the world where a mix of technologies will be necessary to supply a growing need for electrical generating capacity. Therefore, your Board recommends a vote against this proposal.

Source: Notice of 1997 Annual Meeting and Proxy Statement (Fairfield, CT: General Electric, 1997), pp. 42–43.

In the 1990s, shareholder proposals have been split about evenly between social and corporate matters. A significant change that has been occurring recently is the joining of a variety of institutional investors in sponsoring resolutions:

- Eliminate "poison pills," which make it very difficult to achieve a hostile takeover.
- Separate CEO and board chairs.
- Limit directors' terms to one year at a time.
- Create restrictions on executive pay.
- Provide for confidential proxy votes.
- Create shareholder advisory committees.

Overseas Developments

A counterpart effort to reform corporate governance is also becoming visible in Western Europe. The most comprehensive response in recent years is a voluntary one, the creation in the United Kingdom of a blue-ribbon panel under the joint auspices of the Financial Reporting Council, the London Stock Exchange, and the accounting profession. In 1992, the group—the Committee on the Financial Aspects of Corporate Governance—issued a highly esteemed report popularly known as the Cadbury report, after the name of the Committee's chairman, Sir Adrian Cadbury. The most important part of this private sector initiative is a proposed Code of Best Practice (see Table 19.1 for highlights), which instructs companies on how to choose, inform, organize, and empower a board of directors.[11]

Led by U.S. investors, the beginnings of shareholder activism are also faintly visible overseas. The lever available to the activists is the $120 billion in foreign equities held by American pension funds. The Caterpillar Overseas Company, the pension fund for the Swiss employees of Caterpillar, created somewhat of a stir in Switzerland in 1993. At the annual meeting of Nestlé, the country's largest company, the head of the Caterpillar Swiss pension fund criticized the company's dividends as being too low. He also questioned the tendency of the company to diversify away from its core food and beverage businesses.

At about the same time, the State of Wisconsin Investment Board objected to a secondary stock offering at Tubos de Acero de Mexico, a steel manufacturer. The Wisconsin fund, the largest foreign stockholder of the company, was unsuccessful in opposing what it claimed was favoritism to one large shareholder. A more effective action was the criticism of the United Mine Workers pension fund of a proposal to give the chairman of the industrial conglomerate Hanson PLC more power at annual meetings and in corporate governance. The chairman subsequently withdrew the proposal. A major London newspaper, *The Guardian,* called the pension funds' action "one of the most successful public demonstrations of shareholder power ever seen in British corporate affairs."[12]

Local shareholder rights groups have been set up in Great Britain, Germany, Australia, and the Netherlands. Interest in the Cadbury report has been reported elsewhere in Western Europe.

Institutional Investors

A more recent development in the United States is the changed role of a large segment of institutional investors, especially the managers of the pension funds of state and local governments and other large nonprofit organizations. The justification for their departure from the older "Wall Street" rule (if you do not approve of the company's management, sell your stock) is that those large investors are locked in to the companies whose shares they own. That is, they own such large blocks of stock that the price of the security would fall sharply if they tried to dispose of their holdings. Under such circumstances, some institutions believe it is more realistic to try to improve the operations of the poorly performing companies in which they have become large owners.

In 1993, Fidelity Investment, the largest for-profit institutional investor, informally joined the ranks of the corporate activists by participating in the ouster of the CEO of Eastman Kodak. Most of this new type of institutional activism focuses on traditional shareholder concerns. However, some of the state pension funds favor "economically targeted" investments. That is, they try to "do good" with the pensioners' money, rather than investing solely on the basis of conventional factors such as safety and earnings.

STRENGTHENING THE ROLE OF THE SHAREHOLDER

Numerous suggestions have been made to strengthen the ability of shareholders to influence the policy and operations of the company they own. Proposals for change range from revisions in the mechanics of shareholder voting to restrictions on the ability of management and the board of directors to act in specific circumstances. An example is the proposal for an independent tabulation of corporate proxies. Some critics contend that management often interferes in the voting process by urging managers of pension plans and mutual funds to change their votes. If the balloting were secret, there would be less opportunity for such pressure tactics.

Growing numbers of institutional investors have opposed management proxy proposals intended to deter takeover threats. Support has been rising for proposed prohibitions on boards of directors paying "greenmail" in an effort to buy off "raiders" or voting "poison pills" that make hostile takeovers extremely difficult. Another category of proposed changes is for large shareholder groups directly to nominate members of the corporation's board of directors. Suggested examples of nominees are candidates of state pension funds, teacher retirement funds, and similar important nonprofit shareholders. Most corporate boards of directors bridle at the notion of these outside groups attempting to dictate their decision making, and such proposals are usually turned down.

Meanwhile, the SEC took action in 1992 to make it easier for dissident shareholders to communicate with each other. Previously, no more than 10 shareholders could discuss an issue without triggering the proxy filings under the securities laws. Currently, only large shareholders (those who own more than $5 million of the company's stock) have to meet some filing requirement if they send out written materials or if they use prepared scripts for telephone contacts. Investors engaged in outright proxy fights with management have to meet the full panoply of filing rules. All other shareholders can communicate with each other without telling the government about it.

Alternatively, suggestions have been made to encourage existing board members to be more concerned about the welfare of the stockholders. One way of doing that would be to pay them in shares of the stock of the company rather than in cash. A related proposal is to require each director to own a minimum and substantial amount of the company's stock. Negative incentives are also evident, in terms of frequent suits brought by minority shareholders who contend that corporate boards have acted against the interest of the owners they are elected to represent. Surely, outside directors have become more aware of the desires of the shareholders who formally elect them.

Perhaps the real challenge is how to make the corporate directors independent of the corporate management without creating antagonism between these two vital groups. Anyone who has served on corporate boards knows of the special chemistry of the boardroom. It is bad form to rock the boat. In many cases, if directors question the management in more than a perfunctory manner, other board members will criticize them for not being loyal.

The penalty for being viewed as an obstreperous director may be severe. You may not be reappointed. Few board nominating committees will propose the election or reelection of a director if the CEO strongly objects. In practice, the CEO may be the key person in the selection process. Surveys of top corporate management reveal that, although lip service is paid to other characteristics, "supportiveness" is the most desired virtue on the part of outside directors. Moreover, a person who earns the reputation of being an obstreperous director finds that inquiries to join other corporate boards quickly disappear.

Nevertheless, virtually every study of corporate governance concludes that, in times of crises or severe stress, the board does take the lead in strategic decision making—and that its decisions are usually constructive. However, the board is usually late in making those tough choices.[13] In any event, the 1990s are a period of ferment in corporate governance.

The Governance Committee

One innovative and voluntary response to the concerns over the management of the American corporation is the establishment of new Governance Committees of corporate boards.[14]

The Governance Committees are designed to prevent crisis situations, such as the sudden firing of the CEO of a poorly performing company. Each committee almost universally is comprised entirely of outside directors (those who are not officers of the company). The Committee is usually charged with reviewing on a continuing basis the effectiveness of the CEO as well as the board itself. That review of performance may also extend to the committees of the board and even individual members. Typically, the governance committee also takes on the duties of the traditional nominating committee that selects a new CEO as well as new board members, subject, of course, to approval by the full board.

Thus, the Governance Committee is viewed as an effort at preventive medicine. Its formation is a way of trying to provide improved communication between the top management of the corporation and its board of directors as well as within the board itself. Questions can be raised and answered before they become serious criticisms of performance. Such a committee has its limitations. It is not a vehicle for managing the affairs of the company and should avoid acting in a way that causes the CEO to become concerned about infringements on his or her prerogatives.

At its best, the Governance Committee is designed to be merely a vehicle for improving the interaction between the board and the CEO, and within the board. The committee's annual review of performance does put the CEO—and others—on notice that their performance will be reviewed. The governance has the potential of enhancing the internal operations of the board itself, especially the functioning of the key committees (audit, compensation, finance, etc.), and of dealing with poorly performing directors. The conduct of successful new committees of this type is likely to follow a process of trial and error. Its effectiveness will depend in large measure on the continued confidence of the board as a whole.

At this early stage of its development, however, the Governance Committee is basically an experiment and has yet to demonstrate its value. By enhancing the ability of a company's board of directors to respond to shortcomings in the management of the enterprise, it does seem to be an attractive alternative to the continuing proposals for further governmental intervention into the workings of the business firm.

Top Management Compensation

In response to growing public criticism of top management compensating (fueled by accounts of annual compensation of $10 million or more), the SEC has required much more disclosure of the details. Under new rules issued in 1992, the company's annual proxy statement must list such data as the compensation of its chief executive and, if they earn over $100,000, of its four other highest-paid executive officers. An accompanying graph must compare the firm's total investment return over the past five years to a broad-based stock index and an industry index or peer group. A narrative report from the board's compensation committee must describe the rationale for executive pay decisions made during the year. (See Table 19.2 for details.)

However, it is too early to judge what impact such informational requirement will have on corporate, board, or shareholder decisions. It is useful, nevertheless, to distinguish between outstanding compensation for unusual achievement and generous compensation for poor performance. It is hard to justify such egregious (albeit unusual) examples as Texas Air increasing its CEO's compensation from $809,000 in 1987 to $1.2 million in 1988, while the company's net loss rose from $466 million to $719 million during the same time period. Subsequently, the company went bankrupt and ceased operations.

Labor Unions and Corporate Governance

As a result of the financial difficulties many companies encountered during the 1980s and early 1990s, some labor unions agreed to designate one or more members of the firm's board of directors as part of an overall package that contained reductions from customary wage increases and often outright cuts in labor compensation.

TABLE 19.2   Required Disclosure on Top Management Compensation to Be Included in Annual Proxy Statements

Report of the board's compensation committee

1. A statement of the company's compensation philosophy.
2. A description of each major component of executive pay, including base salary, annual incentive, long-term incentives, perquisites, and benefits.
3. A summary of all actions taken by the committee during the year, including those relating to plan design, changes, grants and incentive payouts, and how such actions relate to stated objectives.

Tabular compensation displays

1. A summary table to show all forms of compensation provided over the preceding three years to the CEO and, if they earn over $100,000, four other top paid executives. This includes deferred and noncash compensation, life insurance premiums, and severance payments.
2. A table on stock options and stock appreciation rights (SARs). This table must describe the terms and conditions of each grant received by the five executives during the past year. The present value on the potential gain must be shown.
3. A table showing grants under long-term incentive plans other than stock options, SARs, and restricted stock. The future payout must be estimated.

Performance graph

A chart comparing company performance over five years or more, as measured by stock price appreciation and dividends. A comparison must be made with returns for a broad-based stock index and an industry index or a peer group of companies.

Source: U.S. Securities and Exchange Commission

In 1993, several steel companies—Bethlehem, Wheeling-Pittsburgh, and LTV—agreed to having a representative of the United Steelworkers Union serve on their boards. At about the same time, Northwest Airlines and TWA both agreed to give their employees a major share of the corporation's ownership. As part of a move out of bankruptcy, TWA gave its employees a 45 percent ownership of the company plus four board seats. Northwest provided three boards seats plus 37.5 percent of the company's stock. Both airlines received several hundred million dollars of concessions in labor costs.

Union memberships on corporate boards are still isolated examples, and the entire subject remains extremely controversial. Although the concept of employee representation on the board is common in Western Europe, it is not a generally accepted notion in the United States. In Germany, codetermination laws have required worker representation on the boards of larger companies since 1951. However, that nation has a long tradition of labor–management cooperation. The fact that German worker compensation averages considerably higher than other industrialized nations is not an inducement to U.S. firms to copy the example.

Perhaps the most important change in the practice of corporate governance in the United States occurred during 1992–93 in the case of a few very large and poorly performing corporations: General Motors, Sears Roebuck, IBM, Eastman Kodak, and American Express. In each instance, the board responded to the concerns of major institutional investors and took decisive if not belated action. In most cases, the board replaced the CEO. The directors of GM selected an outside director (the recently retired CEO of Procter and Gamble) to be board chairman during a difficult transition period. IBM also created a new board committee of outside directors to nominate new directors, handle proposals from shareholders, and oversee the board's performance.

Such actions, even though few, provide a powerful signal to top management that inadequate performance can result in their replacement by a hitherto supportive board of directors. What was especially noteworthy is that these changes in management did not require formal takeovers ("changes of control") with their ancillary legions of expensive investment bankers, attorneys, and accountants and the widespread disruption of company operations that often occurs.

Notes

1. Ira M. Millstein and Salem M. Katsch, *The Limits of Corporate Power* (New York: Macmillan, 1981), pp. 3–4.
2. Ralph Nader, "Democratic Revolution in an Age of Autocracy," *Boston Review*, March–April 1993, pp. 3–6.
3. Harold M. Williams, *Corporate Accountability,* address to the Fifth Annual Securities Regulation Institute, San Diego, CA, January 18, 1978.
4. Harold S. Geneen, "Why Directors Can't Protect the Shareholders," *Fortune,* September 17, 1984, p. 31.
5. Walter J. Salmon, "Crisis Prevention? How to Gear Up Your Board," *Harvard Business Review,* January–February 1993, p. 69.

6. For a somewhat similar array of proposals, see National Association of Corporate Directors, *Report of the NACD Blue Ribbon Commission on Director Professionalism* (Washington, DC: NACD, 1996).

7. Joann S. Lublin, "Calpers to Back Corporate Governance Standards," *Wall Street Journal,* June 16, 1997, p. A2.

8. Adam Bryant, "Women Hold 10.6% of Fortune 500 Board Seats," *New York Times,* October 1, 1997, p. C11.

9. Lauren Talner, *The Origins of Shareholder Activism* (Washington, DC: Investor Responsibility Research Center, 1983), pp. 1–4.

10. David Vogel, *Lobbying the Corporation* (New York: Basic Books, 1978), p. 35.

11. Jeremy Bacon, *Corporate Boards and Corporate Governance* (New York: Conference Board, 1993), pp. 33–35.

12. Leslie Wayne, "Exporting Shareholder Activism," *New York Times,* July 16, 1993, pp. C1–C2.

13. Courtney Brown, *Putting the Corporate Board to Work* (New York: Macmillan, 1976).

14. Robert Lear, "Fire Power," *Chief Executive,* July 1997, p. 16.

CHAPTER 20

The Outlook for Private Enterprise

The demonstrated ability of the business corporation to gradually change in the face of shifting political, social, and economic forces is the key to its continuing strength and resilience. In responding to public policy demands and interest group influences in that practical and nondogmatic manner, the corporation is likely to continue to be the dominant way of organizing economic activity in the developed world through the twenty-first century.

Responding to a variety of new influences, the business corporation has gone through three stages of development: from the simple, competitive classical model of the nineteenth century to the managerial model of the first half of the twentieth century to the social environment model characteristic of the second half of the century. The changes relate especially to the increased attention on the part of management to forces external to the corporation, both domestic and international.

In this vein, we may speculate about the future of the private enterprise system in the United States. What will be its relationships with governments at all levels? And with various private forces? We may obtain some useful insights by contemplating how American business has adjusted to past threats and opportunities. If any common theme emerges from examining the transition of seventeenth-century colonial business to late twentieth-century global American enterprise, it is the gradual nature of the changes. This characteristic is borne out by an old cliché of historical analysis, "Every period is an age of transition."

Thus, it is altogether likely that the quintessential colonial businessman Benjamin Franklin, after the briefest period of adjustment, would feel rather comfortable at board meetings of a large modern multinational enterprise. Of course, not all of today's management has the widespread interest and notable resilience of Dr. Franklin.

The United States is in the midst of several important transitions that affect business–government relations in powerful ways. The most obvious is away from the Cold War competition with the former Soviet Union (and the emphasis on awesome nuclear armaments) to what can be called *cool peace,* a period where threats to national well-being are less intense but arise from far more diverse sources.

Simultaneously, we are witnessing a shift from less government involvement in business during the 1980s to more regulation of the private sector in the 1990s but not a simple return to the earlier policy framework. Similarly, the emphasis in government finance has moved from general tax rate reductions and simplification in order to promote growth back to a more complicated Internal Revenue Code that fosters a wide variety of special concerns.

Within the private sector, Americans have been witnessing a transition from heavy reliance on *junk bonds* (high-yield, high-risk securities) back to a greater use of venture capital for entrepreneurship. A related change is from debt-induced leverage to a reemphasis on equity ownership to strengthen business balance sheets. To the extent that these positive changes in the private sector occur voluntarily, the pressure for further government intervention to deal with business shortcomings is lessened. In any event, the role of government in financing business activity has been diminished.

Nevertheless, some observers of the large American corporation have produced extremely negative evaluations of its future prospects. They see the large company as too muscle bound to compete successfully against newer and smaller enterprises. Also, because of its high visibility, the large corporation is an especially attractive target for the continued encroachment of government on private initiative. The critics also cite the gradual erosion over the years of the right of managers to use corporate assets in the interest of shareholders—a development they attribute to the joining of forces of politicians and all sorts of special interest groups. As shown in many earlier chapters, these concerns are bolstered by a substantial factual foundation.

Yet this negative view likely has excessively discounted the powerful adaptive capability of private enterprise. Viewed from a positive standpoint, we can state with considerable confidence that the corporation, albeit with substantial modifications, is likely to continue to be the dominant institution in the economy of the United States well into the twenty-first century. Such optimism has a firm basis, for the modern corporation never has been a static or inflexible entity, and there is no reason to expect that it will become one.

The typical American corporation has become more aware and, in many ways, more responsive to the social needs of the society of which it is inescapably a part. This is an important aspect of its protective feedback mechanism. Here is a pertinent example. In 1988, when Richard J. Mahoney, then the chief executive of Monsanto, saw the large numbers on the emissions of pollution by the various factories of his company, he unilaterally and voluntarily ordered the company to reduce its total air emissions of toxic chemicals by 90 percent by the end of 1992. The company achieved this ambitious objective on schedule. Moreover, his successor, Robert Shapiro, has gone beyond voluntary compliance with existing government priorities to orient the company to the achievement of sustainable development, an advanced concept of the proper role of human endeavor viewed in global terms.[1]

Even a strong critic of American capitalism like Robert Heilbroner concedes that history has shown capitalism to be an "extraordinarily resilient, persisting and tenacious system." He cites as a key reason the fact that the driving force is so widely dispersed rather than being concentrated in a governing elite. Heilbroner also notes that the propelling force of profits has yielded a capacity for change that Karl Marx did not anticipate.[2]

TOWARD GREATER SOCIAL RESPONSIVENESS

We can develop some useful conceptualizations of the successive shifts toward greater business responsiveness to its external environment—a responsiveness that is basic to the public's continued acceptance and support of the private enterprise system.

In reality, of course, corporations—especially the larger and publicly owned ones—have always departed somewhat from the narrow confines of the profit-maximizing model of classical economics. Essentially, the departures have been a matter of degree, and in the past half century, those departures have been increasingly large. Thus, we can define three basic points on the continuum of change: the classical market model, the modern managerial model, and the contemporary social environmental model.[3]

Three Models of Organization

The *classical market model,* in large measure the original concept of business organization, was based primarily on the British economy of the nineteenth century.[4] That was a period characterized by many small companies producing fairly standard products. Competition was effective and centered mainly on price. The modest scale of most industrial enterprises forced businesses to focus on short-run profit maximization. The owner-manager style of business operation, which fits the classical model, continues to characterize many of the smaller and newer entrepreneurial firms of the present.

The *managerial model* was the next major development in terms of the fundamental approach to the organization and functioning of the business firm. It was the dominant business mode in the first half of the twentieth century. Its basic identifying characteristic is the acknowledgment of the effective separation of ownership from management.[5] The key goals of the enterprise are modified in the process, reflecting the importance of satisfying the desires of professional managers. The latter tend to emphasize growth in size and market share and the security of their position in the community and in society generally. As a consequence, market concentration becomes common, resulting from heavy investments in technology, product differentiation, and expanded advertising efforts.

A late variation on the managerial model focuses on the manager as trustee for various groups, including shareholders, employees, the community, customers, and other interests. This alternate view, it will be recognized, is a transition phase to the third approach. Yet both variations of the managerial model share a key assumption, that the behavior of the business firm is determined in large part by the discretionary power of management. The conduct of the corporation continues to be constrained by competition, but the constraints allow management considerable discretion within broad limits.

The *social environment model* is the most recent of the three approaches to business behavior. Under this concept, the enterprise reacts to the total socioeconomic environment, not merely to markets.[6] Corporate behavior responds to political forces, public opinion, and government pressures, regardless of whether those factors are welcome. It is widely understood that both market and nonmarket forces can affect the firm's costs, sales, and profits. At times, those two forces can become intertwined. For example, consumer or civil rights groups can launch a boycott of a company's products in order to force changes in its internal policies. On the positive side, private interest groups can sponsor "affinity" credit cards encouraging their members to make various purchases.

Thus, the modern enterprise does not behave either like the simple profit-maximizing firm or the traditional monopolist. It innovates, but its profit rates are average. For it, competition has expanded in new dimensions and involves many non-price variables. Management is very much concerned about shareholders—as a group. To underscore that relationship, a large portion of the compensation of senior executives is frequently tied to the firm's profitability or increasingly to the performance of its shares in the stock market.

Although the role of the individual investor remains quite nominal, the power of the shareholders as a group is enhanced by the activities of institutional investors (banks, life insurance companies, mutual funds, and pension funds) that hold large blocks of stock in individual firms and whose actions to buy or sell their substantial holdings can severely affect the compensation if not the future of a company's management. The many corporate takeovers that have occurred via stock purchases in the open market during the 1980s and 1990s underscore the point that the power of stockholders, albeit often latent, is not trivial.

Also, at times Congress and the White House have been interested in one important byproduct of business operations: the large array of capital represented by employee pension funds. These aggregations of finance receive special tax treatment and hence are vulnerable to government regulation. There is always a great temptation for politicians to try to do good with other people's money. In this case, it is to "encourage" pension fund managers to invest a portion of their resources in activities that the government considers "socially desirable"—whether or not the investment generates a good return for the pension recipients. So far, most of those proposals have not been converted into public policy. The few exceptions to date involve states and localities influencing the investment patterns of the government employee pension funds under their direct control.

The Variety of Corporate Concerns

According to many analysts, the contemporary giant corporation cannot be sensibly thought of as merely a private entity owned by its shareholders. Nor is it an agency of the state. Instead, in this alternative view, the large private firm is seen as a servant of multiple interests.

Most of those interests have both some plausible social claim to the attention of the corporation and some power to pursue that claim—through stockholder initiatives, collective bargaining, taxation, regulation, private litigation, and marketplace influence.[7] How can the large corporation be governed so as to allow appropriate consideration of multiple interests without becoming a political body in which governance becomes an end to itself? That is a difficult question to answer, and no specific response is likely to be adopted universally or to hold for long periods of time.

As noted in chapter 19, the most active critics of the private corporation advocate federal chartering, changes in the membership and role of boards of directors, and expensive new reporting requirements. Government aid to Lockheed, Chrysler, and other large corporations does confirm that, for whatever reasons, there are types of business enterprises that are generally believed to be serving important national interests beyond those of the shareholders. Some banks have been viewed as "too large to fail"—the government comes to their rescue to avoid the possibility of a "domino" effect on the rest of the banking system. On the other end of the policy spectrum, government regulations and court decisions have already gone a long way toward limiting the scope of business decision making and toward recognizing new rights for persons and interests that may be negatively affected by business behavior.

Under these circumstances, no company can afford to ignore public attitudes and expectations for long. In the current environment, to do so would result directly in loss of sales and customer goodwill or indirectly in increased costs—to the extent that public pressures lead to further government intervention in business. The knowledge that they can elicit such voluntary business responses, firmly motivated by enlightened self-interest, is a factor that some interest groups and government decision makers take into account before proposing or implementing additional government involvement in the activities of the private sector of the economy. The point is not that business should yield to every demand of every interest group but that such external forces are important enough to warrant considered and significant responses.

There are many forces at work in American society; few if any have achieved all of their objectives. Moreover, neither consumer groups nor labor unions nor corporations have monolithic views on all issues. As we have seen in earlier chapters, changing alliances among them make for great variation in the development of public policy in the United States.

THE CONTINUING DEBATE OVER GOVERNMENT AUTHORITY AND PRIVATE POWER

In the broad sweep of American history, the transcendent ideological debate has been between the Jeffersonian and Hamiltonian approaches to democracy: centralizing or decentralizing the government's power in society. To update that debate, the more pertinent and frequent question now is how to allocate power between, on the one hand, individuals and voluntary institutions in the private sector and, on the other, the sovereign authority of government at all levels in the public sector.

This dichotomy between centralization and decentralization of political and economic power is oversimplified, of course. Nevertheless, such a construction is useful in examining the ebbs and flows of public policy changes affecting the business system. Over the years, the public policy pendulum has continued to swing from one extreme position to another.

In the United States, national administrations from Franklin D. Roosevelt to Lyndon B. Johnson engaged in extremely ambitious efforts to expand the role of the federal government. Yet, every president since has made some attempt to reduce the power of Washington, although their levels of enthusiasm and effectiveness have varied.

Because so many of the government's policies are carried out through the business firm and thus are hidden from general view, the public is not always aware of how far down the path of government involvement the American economy has gone. As a point of reference, we can note that, in 1965, Adolph Berle (coauthor of the seminal work *The Modern Corporation and Private Property*) described the extent to which government had at that time limited the ability of business to use its "productive property." But, he added, the state "has not attempted (aside from policy limitations) to tell a man what or how he should consume—that would constitute an intolerable invasion of his private life."[8] Obviously, Berle wrote before the compulsory installation of seat belts in private automobiles or efforts to ban cyclamates and saccharin or attempts by regulatory agencies to get the public to reduce the amount of sugar or salt in its diet.

Yet some swings of the pendulum toward lesser involvement of government also have been visible. In recent years, the disenchantment with large-scale government in general has grown. At times it has taken the practical form of limits on state government spending and taxing voted by aroused taxpayers or simply the rejection of proposed tax and bond issues. The continuing support for an amendment to the Constitution mandating a balanced federal budget is another indication of public desire to constrain government power and activity. To some extent, this attitude is being translated into a slowdown in the growth of federal expenditures and the reluctance to embark on new government programs financed by general taxation. Also, as we have seen, government has attempted to be responsive to the numerous pleas to reform regulation of private activity or at least to reduce the avoidably burdensome aspects.

In late 1997, a move toward more market-oriented policies seemed quite strong in the United States. Cutbacks of traditional welfare benefits have occurred simultaneously with greater reliance on competition in the provision of electricity and telecommunications. However, some countermoves are also visible, ranging from requiring workers going off welfare to be paid the statutory minimum wage as well as the resurgence of the labor union movement.

In Western Europe, the recent defeats of the dominant conservative parties in favor of moderate labor and socialist regimes are cogent examples of continued change. The reluctance to rely fully on market-oriented policies can be seen in a report, *The Company in the 21st Century,* issued by a progressive group of 2,300 young French business executives. Stating that "The greatest misery in our society is social and spiritual rather than material," the report urged that companies be judged on their contribution to the well-being of society and their employees. In their rather advanced view, enterprises that harm society, ecologically or otherwise, should be closed down.[9]

However, for the most part, today's left-of-center governments have made their peace with the world of business. They rarely think of themselves as defenders of unions or champions of large, public-sector initiatives. Words such as *enterprise* and *opportunity* have become part of their everyday vocabulary.[10]

In part, a more limited or perhaps more positive approach to public policy toward business is encouraged by a growing understanding of the international dimensions of business. The typical worker is learning, often from sad personal experience, that domestic companies compete with increasingly powerful foreign enterprises in both domestic and foreign markets. Many of those overseas corporations, rather than being restricted by their governments, are often subsidized by, if not actually a part of, the governmental apparatus.

In any event, virtually every broad-based analysis of public opinion in the United States reports continuing and virtually overwhelming support for the private enterprise system. One such survey shows that two-thirds of the sample surveyed agree that capitalism provides people with the highest living standard in the world; it also affords all individuals the opportunity to develop their own special abilities; moreover, capitalists are entitled to the reward of profits because they assume the risk of loss.[11] Nevertheless, these and other surveys show substantial dissatisfaction with specific aspects of business performance, including the quality of products (too low) and the prices charged (too high)—and thus endorsement of a continuing large role for government in the private economy.

Viewed in that light, we can gain some insight into the changing nature of the large multinational firm by examining an increasingly common example. Unisys, a producer of computer and electronic equipment, has annual sales of approximately $10 billion. More than half of its revenues are from overseas sources. The company's information systems and services are sold in over one hundred nations, including Western Europe, Japan, Canada, and the major developing countries.

Unisys uses components that are produced in the United States as well as in Brazil, India, Ireland, Israel, Japan, Singapore, the United Kingdom, and sometimes elsewhere. Its financing is worldwide. In one instance, the corporation was able to assemble overnight a consortium of 50 international banks to raise $5 billion. Factors of production, in addition to financial capital, are also extremely mobile. In 90 days, Unisys shifted a complex production operation of a critical component from California halfway around the world to Singapore.

Intellectual capital and property rights are now also highly moveable. Unisys is both a customer of and a supplier to BASF, Philips, and Siemens in Europe; Fujitsu and Hitachi in Asia; and Honeywell and IBM in the United States. Together, these companies have engaged in joint ventures, coproduced, served as sources for each other, shared output, and competed. Finished products are dramatically more mobile today. All of Unisys's products are delivered by jet. Equipment leaving the factory reaches the customer anywhere in the world within 36 hours.[12]

The Unisys experience highlights how advances in technology have fundamentally altered—and basically strengthened—the way contemporary corporations now do business. These technological and organizational changes also have exerted an important feedback effect on the government's ability and desire to influence company decision making. In an increasing competitive global marketplace, at times government becomes an observer on the sidelines.

Undoubtedly, the corporation will continue to be a central institution of American society in the 21st century. As the late Neil Jacoby stated, "There is simply no promising alternative way of organizing and carrying out most of the tasks of production."[13] How well U.S.-based corporations perform those tasks will depend, of course, on myriad future decisions in both the public and private sectors. Thus, as an astute observer has noted, "One of the requirements of an effective business manager is the ability to live with ambiguity."[14]

A NEW POLICY CLIMATE

On the basis of the public reaction to developments in government during the 1980s, a new policy climate for business has taken shape in the 1990s. It is an external environment less hospitable than that existing during the administrations of Ronald Reagan or George Bush. However, this changed business climate is not a return to the 1970s, when business was almost uniformly portrayed as the villain and subjected to a host of new government restrictions and regulations. But we are seeing a step away from the relatively uncritically pro-business environment of the 1980s to a somewhat more ambivalent position.

This equivocal attitude reflects the dual views that many Americans hold about the private enterprise system. On the one hand, they view it positively, as the most important and effective way of providing jobs and income as well as goods and services. But on the other hand, they see all sorts of shortcomings, ranging from selfish or shortsighted actions on the part of profit-maximizing organizations to the truly venal and illegal acts on the part of a small but conspicuous number of executives.

In an attempt to please conservative and liberal critics simultaneously, government leaders have been seeking more effective and less burdensome ways of carrying out the government's desires. Thus, environmental statutes have been revised to reduce the adverse impacts of acid rain while simultaneously minimizing the economic costs by creating a market in which air pollution credits can be traded.

What the new external environment makes possible is another and perhaps different wave of government and public involvement in internal business decision making. Potential areas for deeper government involvement are numerous:

- Renewed emphasis on environmental protection and fairness in the treatment of employees. The newer issues range from global warming and species diversity to concerns over diversity in the workplace. Each of these potentially involves substantial private action along lines determined or reviewed by government officials.

- Reducing the sale of illegal drugs and dealing with the adverse impacts of widespread use of various "chemical substances" (including alcohol, etc.). This includes wider testing of employees. A related area is the effort to reduce very substantially the purchase of cigarettes and other tobacco products, especially by teenagers.

- Reducing the federal deficit, with special emphasis on cutting back outlays for the military establishment, particularly for the design, development, and procurement of expensive new weapon systems.

- Better education of the workforce so that American business can compete more effectively in an increasingly global market. This often gets translated into the odd position of business leading drives for higher school taxes and bond issues and supporting other extensions of government involvement in an effort to promote productivity and competitiveness. Perhaps not too surprisingly, some of the public interest groups that earlier saw strong business opposition to most extensions of government regulation are suspicious of the current efforts to become "good guys." This is apparent in the less than universal acceptance by environmental groups of company offers to participate in and finance annual Earth Day celebrations.

- An acceleration in the tendency of government to minimize its own expenditures—and hence make it easier to balance the budget—by imposing social costs on business. These range from higher minimum wages to broader requirements for employee leave for a variety of family and personal purposes.

- Rising attention to new forms of governmental revenue such as a national sales tax or a value-added tax to replace the traditional income taxes in an effort to reduce the economic burden of raising an increasing amount of government revenues.

- Renewed enforcement of antitrust laws, especially in the case of mergers of large corporations that are expected to result in increases in the cost of goods to consumers.

Political and economic change in the United States has been a gradual, evolving process. Dramatic departures have been few and infrequent. It is reasonable to predict, therefore, that the future of business–government relationships in the United States will be a continuing reconciliation of conflicting forces rather than an inevitable movement to a polar alternative.

Contemporary business has come a long way from the pristine world of small traders and craftsmen in which buyers and sellers could meet and satisfy their needs with scarcely little more coordination than that provided by the "invisible hand" of the free market. The corporation has become the fundamental organizing unit of the capitalist economy. Its most important attribute is its unique capacity for managing large-scale processes required for converting labor, raw materials, and energy into mass-produced and widely distributed goods and services.

With the demise of the communist regimes of Eastern Europe, it has become more apparent than ever that the American model of capitalism is just one variety—albeit a very important and unusual one—in a continuum of types of private enterprise systems. In countries such as Germany, France, Italy, Japan, Brazil, Korea, and China, much greater emphasis is placed on the relationship of business to the welfare of the nation. Simultaneously and reciprocally, these other countries manifest less of the adversarial nature of business–government relations so characteristic of the United States.[15]

In many other countries, government plays a measurably larger role than it does in the United States, and business institutions have adjusted to that reality. As shown in Table 20.1, in several Western European nations government spending (a useful but incomplete proxy for the total government role) equals more than one-half of the gross domestic product.

TABLE 20.1 Variations in the Importance of Government Spending in 1996

Nation	Percent of GDP
Sweden	65
France	54
Belgium	54
Italy	53
Austria	52
The Netherlands	50
Germany	49
New Zealand	47
Norway	46
Canada	45
Spain	43
Great Britain	42
Ireland	38
Switzerland	38
Australia	37
Japan	36
The United States	33

Source: International Monetary Fund.

Cogent examples of the fundamental difference in governmental influence in the economies of industrialized nations range from Sweden (65 percent) and France (55 percent) to the United States (33 percent) and Japan (36 percent). However, these relationships can change substantially over time. As recently as 1960, in none of the countries shown in Table 20.1 did government spending equal as much as 35 percent of GDP.

As in the past, the business system of the future will continue to be a developing institution characterized by dynamic responses to a constantly developing external environment, especially the powerful role of government.

Notes

1. *Environmental Annual Review, 1996* (St. Louis: Monsanto Company, 1997); Joan Magretta, "Growth Through Global Sustainability," *Harvard Business Review,* January–February 1997, pp. 79–88.

2. Robert L. Heilbroner, *Beyond Boom and Crash* (New York: W. W. Norton, 1978), p. 89.

3. Neil H. Jacoby, *Corporate Power and Social Responsibility* (New York: Macmillan Co., 1973), pp. 192–195.

4. See Alfred Marshall, *Principles of Economies,* 8th ed. (New York: Macmillan, 1949), pp. 240–313.

5. The classical work in this area is Adolph A. Berle and Gardner C. Means, *The Modern Corporation and Private Property* (New Brunswick, NJ: Transaction Publishers, 1991).

6. See Committee for Economic Development, *Social Responsibilities of Business Corporations* (New York: Committee for Economic Development, 1971).

7. Lee E. Preston, *Social Issues and Public Policy in Business and Management* (College Park: University of Maryland, Center for Business and Public Policy, 1986), pp. 25–26.

8. Adolph A. Berle, "Property, Production and Revolution," *Columbia Law Review,* January 1965, p. 12.

9. Barry James, "Executives' Warning on Raw Capitalism," *International Herald Tribune,* October 5, 1996, p. 23.

10. "The Future of the State," *The Economist,* September 20, 1997, p. S–7.

11. Robert A. Peterson et al., "The Public's Attitude Toward Capitalism," *Business Horizons,* September/October 1991, pp. 59–63.

12. Michael Blumenthal, "Macroeconomic Policy," in Martin Feldstein, ed., *International Economic Cooperation* (Cambridge, MA: National Bureau of Economic Research, 1987), p. 16.

13. Jacoby, *Corporate Power,* p. 269.

14. William E. Schlender, "Counter-Vailing Values in Business Decision-Making," in Donald G. Jones, ed., *Business, Religion, and Ethics* (Cambridge, MA: Gelgeschlager, Gunn & Hain, 1982), p. 183.

15. George David Smith and Davis Dyer, "The Rise and Transformation of the American Corporation," in Carl Kaysen, ed., *The American Corporation Today* (New York: Oxford University Press, 1996), pp. 28, 65.

Index